P O C

SCIENCE ENCY C L O PEDIA

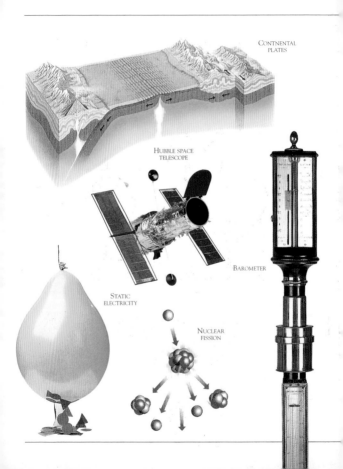

CONTINENTAL PLATES

HUBBLE SPACE
TELESCOPE

BAROMETER

STATIC
ELECTRICITY

NUCLEAR
FISSION

P O C K E T S

SCIENCE
ENCY
CLO
PEDIA

SEAHORSES

CARBON
ATOM

ASTRONAUT

DK PUBLISHING

LONDON, NEW YORK,
MELBOURNE, MUNICH, and DELHI

Writers and consultants David Burnie, Jack Challoner,
Philip Eden, Dr William A. Gutch, Cally Hall, Jeffery Kaufmann,
Scarlett O'Hara, Steve Setford, Carole Stott, Clint Twist, Dr Warren Yasso
US Editors Jill Hamilton, Constance M. Robinson

Produced for Dorling Kindersley by
PAGE*One*, Cairn House, Elgiva Lane, Chesham,
Buckinghamshire, HP5 2JD

REVISED EDITION

Project editor Steve Setford
Designer Sarah Crouch
Managing editor Linda Esposito
Managing art editor Jane Thomas
DTP designer Siu Yin Ho
Consultants David Glover, Ian Ridpath, Richard Walker
Production Erica Rosen
US editors Margaret Parrish, Christine Heilman

Second American Edition, 2003
Published in the United States by
DK Publishing, Inc., 375 Hudson Street,
New York, New York 10014

04 05 06 07 08 10 9 8 7 6 5 4 3 2

The material in this book originally appeared in the following *DK Pocket* titles:
Earth Facts, Essential Facts, Nature Facts, Science Facts, Space Facts, Weather Facts.

Copyright © 2003 Dorling Kindersley Limited

A Cataloging-in-Publication record for the First American Edition of this book
is available from the Library of Congress.

ISBN 0-7894-9602-X

Color reproduction by Colourscan, Singapore
Printed and bound in Italy by L.E.G.O.

See our complete product line at
www.dk.com

CONTENTS

COMPOUND
MICROSCOPE

EMERALD

INSIDE A
VOLCANO

MILKY WAY

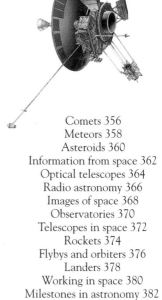

PIONEER 10
SPACE PROBE

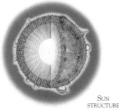

SUN
STRUCTURE

FOX CUB

HOW TO USE THIS BOOK

These pages show you how to use the *DK Pockets Science Encyclopedia*. The book is divided into four sections that provide information about chemical and physical science, the Earth around us, the universe, and the natural world. At the back of the book, conversion tables are followed by a comprehensive index.

HEADING AND INTRODUCTION
Every spread has a subject heading. This is followed by the introduction, which outlines the subject and gives a clear idea of what these pages are about.

CHARTS
Many pages contain charts. These supply facts and figures. The chart below compares the density of materials.

Chart

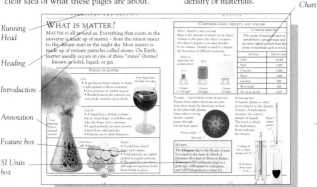

Running Head

Heading

Introduction

Annotation

Feature box

SI Units box

FEATURE BOXES
The feature boxes that appear on some pages contain detailed information and illustrations to explain a topic that is related to the main subject of the page.

SI UNITS BOXES
On some spreads SI units boxes explain a measurement relevant to the subject. SI units are an international set of standard units of measurement.

DATA BOX
Some pages have data boxes, which contain detailed numerical information. This box gives data about the Sun.

RUNNING HEADS
Across the top of the pages there are running heads. The lefthand page gives the section, the righthand the subject.

LABELS
For clarity, some pictures have labels. These give extra information about the picture, or provide clearer identification.

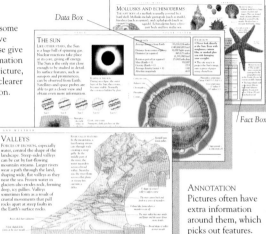

Data Box

Fact Box

VALLEYS
FORCES OF EROSION, especially water, control the shape of the landscape. Steep-sided valleys can be cut by fast-flowing mountain streams. Larger rivers wear a path through the land, shaping wide, flat valleys as they near the sea. Frozen water in glaciers also erodes rock, forming deep, icy gullies. Valleys sometimes form as a result of crustal movements that pull rocks apart at steep faults in the Earth's surface rocks.

ANNOTATION
Pictures often have extra information around them, which picks out features. This text appears in *italics* and uses leader lines to point to details.

Caption

FACT BOXES
Many pages have fact boxes. The information in these is related to the main topic on the page.

CAPTIONS
Each illustration in the book is accompanied by a detailed, explanatory caption.

INDEX
There is an index at the back of the book that alphabetically lists every subject. By referring to the index, information on particular topics can be found quickly.

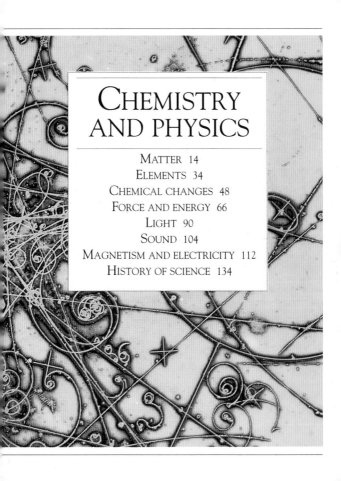

CHEMISTRY AND PHYSICS

WHAT IS MATTER?

MATTER IS all around us. Everything that exists in the universe is made up of matter – from the tiniest insect to the distant stars in the night sky. Most matter is made up of minute particles called atoms. On Earth, matter usually occurs in one of three "states" (forms) known as solid, liquid, or gas.

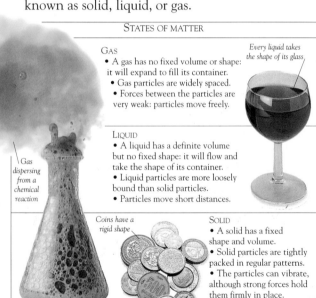

STATES OF MATTER

GAS
- A gas has no fixed volume or shape: it will expand to fill its container.
- Gas particles are widely spaced.
- Forces between the particles are very weak: particles move freely.

Every liquid takes the shape of its glass

Gas dispersing from a chemical reaction

LIQUID
- A liquid has a definite volume but no fixed shape: it will flow and take the shape of its container.
- Liquid particles are more loosely bound than solid particles.
- Particles move short distances.

Coins have a rigid shape

SOLID
- A solid has a fixed shape and volume.
- Solid particles are tightly packed in regular patterns.
- The particles can vibrate, although strong forces hold them firmly in place.

COMPARING MASS, DENSITY, AND VOLUME

MASS, DENSITY, AND VOLUME

Mass is the amount of matter in an object.
Volume is the space the object occupies.
An object's density is its mass divided
by its volume. Density is used to compare
the heaviness of different materials.

Blocks of
equal mass but
unequal density

BALSA

WAX

LEAD

Density
11,300 kg/m³

Density
900 kg/m³

Density
200 kg/m³

COMMON DENSITIES

The atoms of materials such as
metals have a greater mass and
are more tightly packed than the
atoms of materials such as wood.

MATERIAL	DENSITY KG/M³
Gold	19,300
Steel	7,900
Concrete	2,400
Water	1,000
Gasoline	800
Wood (oak)	650
Air (at sea level)	1.025

PLASMA – THE FOURTH STATE OF MATTER

Plasma forms when electrons are torn
from their atoms by electricity or heat.
In this glass ball, plasma
forms when a strong
electric current
passes through
low-pressure gases.

Plasma streaks

Electrode

SI UNITS

The **kilogram** (kg) is the SI unit of mass.
It is equal to the mass of a block of
platinum alloy kept at Sèvres in France.
There are 1,000 milligrams (mg) in a
gram (g), 1,000 grams in a kilogram,
and 1,000 kilograms in a tonne (t).

HYDROMETERS

A liquid's density is often
given relative to the density
of water. A hydrometer
measures the relative
density of liquids.
The level at which
the hydrometer
floats indicates
the density.

Water's
relative
density
is 1

Cooking oil
has a relative
density of 0.91

Hydrometer
floats lower
in oil

Changing state

The state of a substance is determined by its temperature. When heated, solids change to liquids, and liquids to gases because their particles vibrate faster, breaking the bonds that hold the particles together. When cooled, gases change to liquids (condense), and liquids to solids. Their particles slow down and the bonds between them re-form.

ICE

Ice forms when water is cooled sufficiently

Solid ice cubes have a definite shape and volume

LIQUID WATER

Liquid water takes on the shape of the flask

THE THREE STATES OF WATER
When its temperature falls below 32°F (0°C), water takes the form of ice. If its temperature rises above 212°F (100°C), water turns to steam. Between these temperatures water is in its liquid state.

When ice is heated it melts to form liquid water

Steam rises and escapes from the flask

STEAM

Safety valve lets out excess steam

PRESSURE COOKING
The increased pressure inside a pressure cooker raises the boiling point of water because the water molecules need more heat energy to escape as a gas. The higher temperature cooks the food more quickly.

Bubbles of steam form when the liquid is heated to boiling point

GAS CHANGES

• A gas usually condenses to form a liquid. Some gases can condense into a solid without first becoming a liquid.

• Condensation takes place at or below the boiling point.

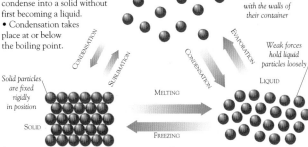

Gas particles collide with each other and with the walls of their container

Weak forces hold liquid particles loosely

Solid particles are fixed rigidly in position

SOLID CHANGES

• Above a temperature called the melting point, most solids become liquids.

• Some solids can change directly into a gas without first becoming a liquid. This is sublimation.

LIQUID CHANGES

• A liquid evaporates to form a gas. Above a temperature called its boiling point, all of the liquid becomes a gas.

• A liquid freezes to a solid below a temperature called its freezing point.

Ripples develop on glassware over centuries

GLASS

Some liquids can be "supercooled" below their freezing point. They may stiffen and become glass. Particles in glass are arranged more randomly than those in normal solids.

MELTING/FREEZING POINTS		
SUBSTANCE	MELTING POINT	
Alcohol (ethanol)	−272°F	169°C
Water	32°F	0°C
Wax	137°F	57°C
PVC	387°F	197°C
Nylon	417°F	212°C
Salt (sodium chloride)	1,474°F	801°C
Gold	1,947°F	1,064°C
Steel (stainless)	2,781°F	1,527°C
Diamond	6,422°F	3,550°C

KINETIC THEORY

ACCORDING TO KINETIC THEORY, particles of matter are constantly in motion. The energy of the "kinetic" (moving) particles determines the temperature and behavior of matter. The "gas laws" use kinetic theory to explain how gases behave.

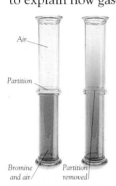

Air

Partition

Bromine and air

Partition removed

Diffusion of bromine gas in air

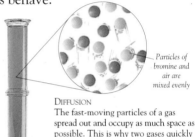

Particles of bromine and air are mixed evenly

DIFFUSION

The fast-moving particles of a gas spread out and occupy as much space as possible. This is why two gases quickly intermingle (diffuse) when they meet. Solids and liquids form solutions by diffusion, although they diffuse more slowly than gases.

MOVING MATTER FACTS

• Austrian physicist Ludwig Boltzmann developed kinetic theory in the 1860s.

• Scottish botanist Robert Brown observed Brownian motion in 1827. (Albert Einstein explained it in 1905.)

Pollen suspended in water

BROWNIAN MOTION

Seen under a microscope, pollen grains in water bounce about randomly. This phenomenon is called Brownian motion. It is caused by tiny, unseen water molecules that bombard the pollen grains.

CHARLES' LAW IN ACTION

1 COOLING GAS
When a gas-filled balloon is placed in liquid nitrogen at −321°F (−196°C), the gas inside cools down.

Balloon collapses

2 SHRINKING VOLUME
Gas molecules slow down as the gas cools. The molecules collide less with the balloon walls, so the balloon shrinks.

Liquid nitrogen

Balloon expands

3 REFLATION
Removing the balloon from the liquid nitrogen lets the gas warm in the air. The gas molecules speed up and the balloon expands again.

THERMAL EXPANSION OF SELECTED MATERIALS

Heating a solid gives its atoms more kinetic energy. The atoms vibrate faster and take up more space, causing the solid to expand.

SUBSTANCE	EXPANSION OF HEATED 1-M BAR AT 212°F (100°C)
Invar (steel/nickel alloy)	0.1 mm
Pyrex	0.3 mm
Platinum alloy	0.9 mm
Steel	1.1 mm
Aluminum	2.6 mm

GAS LAWS

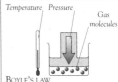

Temperature   Pressure   *Gas molecules*

BOYLE'S LAW
At constant temperature (T), the volume of a gas (V) is inversely proportional to the pressure (P) (the gas contracts if the pressure rises): PV=constant.

PRESSURE LAW
At constant volume, the pressure of a gas is proportional to the temperature (increasing the temperature raises the gas's pressure): P/T=constant.

CHARLES' LAW
At constant pressure, the volume of a gas is proportional to the temperature (the gas expands if the temperature rises): V/T=constant.

DESCRIBING MATTER

A MATERIAL CAN be described by its physical
properties as well as by its chemical makeup. Color,
shape, texture, and smell are the simplest properties.
Others include hardness, solubility,
and viscosity, and the way
a material behaves
when forces act on it.

VISCOSITY
A viscous liquid such as
honey does not flow
easily because of
friction between
its molecules. Free-
flowing liquids such
as water have a low viscosity.

HONEYCOMB

*The viscous honey
spreads out very slowly*

MOHS' SCALE OF HARDNESS		
HARDNESS	MINERAL	SCRATCHED BY
10	Diamond	Diamond only
9	Corundum	Silicon carbide
8	Topaz	Tungsten carbide
7	Quartz	Hard steel file
6	Feldspar	Sand
5	Apatite	Nickel
4	Fluorite	Glass
3	Calcite	Iron nail
2	Gypsum	Fingernail
1	Talc	Tin

HARDNESS
The ability to resist scratching is called
hardness. It is measured on Mohs' scale,
which compares the hardness of ten
minerals. A material will scratch any
other with a lower Mohs' rating.

DUCTILITY AND MALLEABILITY
Ductile solids such as copper
can be stretched out into
a wire. Malleable solids
can be shaped while cold
by hammering or rolling.
Gold is the most
malleable metal.

COPPER
WIRE

ELASTICITY

MOLECULE IN
UNSTRETCHED RUBBER

MOLECULE IN
STRETCHED RUBBER

RUBBER MOLECULE AFTER
FURTHER STRETCHING

*Strip is 15 cm
long when no
force acts upon it*

*1-kg mass
stretches rubber
to 17 cm*

*2-kg mass
stretches rubber
to 19 cm*

1 ELASTICITY
Elastic solids such
as this rubber strip get
larger (extend) when
stretched, get smaller
when squeezed, and
return to their normal
size and shape when no
force acts upon them.

2 STRETCHING
When a 1-kg
mass is hung from the
strip, the force of
tension stretches the
strip by 2 cm. The long
rubber molecules, which
are normally ramdomly
coiled, begin to uncoil.

**3 DOUBLE
STRETCHING**
Doubling the
force of tension
will also double the
stretching, so when a
2-kg mass is hung from
the strip, the rubber
stretches by 4 cm.

BRITTLENESS
Brittle materials break suddenly when
stretched or squeezed, and shatter if
given a sharp knock. But even fragile
materials such as glass and pottery have
some elasticity before they break.

*Glass shatters
into tiny pieces*

*A wine glass breaks
easily if dropped
on the floor*

SOLUBILITY IN WATER

The following masses
of each substance
dissolve in 100 g of
water at 77°F (25°C):

• Alcohol (ethanol):
almost limitless

• Sugar: 211 g

• Salt: 36 g

• Carbon dioxide: 0.14 g

• Oxygen: 0.004 g

• Sand: insoluble

ATOMS

SOLIDS, LIQUIDS, AND GASES are made of tiny particles called atoms. Atoms are the building blocks for all the familiar materials around us, including our bodies. There are just over a hundred different types of atom, which are themselves made up of even smaller "subatomic" particles.

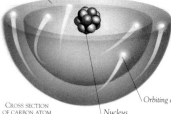

Electron shell

CROSS SECTION
OF CARBON ATOM

Orbiting electron

Nucleus

ATOMIC STRUCTURE
The center, or nucleus, of all but the hydrogen atom contains protons (positively charged) and neutrons (with no charge). Negatively charged particles called electrons orbit the nucleus in layers, or "shells."

NUCLEON NUMBER
The total number of protons and neutrons in the nucleus is the atom's nucleon number. The most common form of carbon has 6 protons and 6 neutrons, so it is called carbon–12.

CARBON–12 ATOM

Proton

Neutron

Nucleus contains 6 protons and 6 neutrons

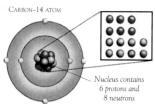

CARBON–14 ATOM

Nucleus contains 6 protons and 8 neutrons

ISOTOPES
All atoms of the same element contain the same number of protons, but some forms of the element may have different numbers of neutrons. These are isotopes. The isotope carbon–14 has two more neutrons than the isotope carbon–12.

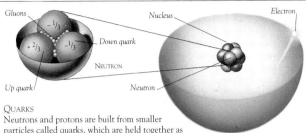

Gluons

Nucleus

Electron

$-\frac{1}{3}$

$+\frac{2}{3}$ — Down quark

$-\frac{1}{3}$

NEUTRON

Up quark

Neutron

QUARKS
Neutrons and protons are built from smaller particles called quarks, which are held together as they constantly exchange particles called gluons. "Down" quarks have one-third of a negative charge, and "up" quarks two-thirds of a positive charge.

PARTICLE COLLISIONS
Scientists discover new particles by smashing together subatomic particles at high speed. The collision briefly creates new particles, whose movements are recorded by computers.

DESCRIBING ATOMS

• The **relative atomic mass (RAM)** of an element compares the average mass of its atoms to the mass of a carbon–12 atom.

• An element's **atomic number** tells you the number of protons in the nuclei of its atoms.

RELATIVE ATOMIC MASS (RAM)		
ELEMENT	SYMBOL	RAM
Hydrogen	H	1.008
Carbon	C	12.01
Sodium	Na	22.99
Iron	Fe	55.85
Bromine	Br	79.90
Tungsten	W	183.9
Mercury	Hg	200.6

ATOM FACTS

• An electron is 1,836 times lighter than a proton, and 1,839 times lighter than a neutron.

• Over 200 different types of subatomic particle are known.

• Specks of dust contain a trillion atoms.

RADIOACTIVITY

THE NUCLEI OF some atoms are radioactive. This means they are unstable and will decay (break up) over time. Most elements have unstable forms called radioisotopes. As they decay, they give out three types of radiation: alpha, beta, and gamma rays. Radiation can be very dangerous.

Alpha particle

Beta particle

Gamma ray

Paper blocks alpha particles

Aluminum blocks beta particles

Lead blocks gamma rays

RADIATION
Alpha rays are streams of positively charged particles made up of two neutrons and two protons. Beta rays are streams of electrons. Gamma rays, the most penetrating type of radiation, are electromagnetic waves.

SI UNITS:
The **becquerel** (Bq) is the unit of radioactivity. The radioactivity of a substance measured in becquerels is the number of its nuclei that decay each second.

Geiger counter

Dial shows amount of radioactivity

GEIGER COUNTER
When a radioactive particle enters a Geiger counter, it causes a brief pulse of electric current to flow. The radioactivity of a sample is calculated by the number of these pulses.

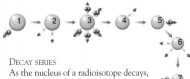

DECAY SERIES
As the nucleus of a radioisotope decays, the numbers of protons and neutrons it contains change, and it becomes a different element. The process continues until it becomes a stable nucleus. Such a sequence is called a decay series.

RADIOACTIVE HALF-LIVES
The time taken for half of the nuclei in a radioactive substance to decay is called the substance's half-life. Over each half-life period, radioactivity falls first to a half, then to a quarter, and so on. The half-life of each radioisotope is different.

HALF-LIVES OF RADIOISOTOPES		
ISOTOPE	HALF-LIFE	TYPE OF DECAY
Uranium–238	4,500 million years	Alpha
Carbon–14	5,570 years	Beta
Cobalt–60	5.3 years	Gamma
Radon–222	4 days	Beta
Unnilquadium–105	32 seconds	Gamma

RADIOACTIVITY FACTS
• Though radiation can be dangerous, it has many uses in medicine, including sterilizing equipment and killing cancer cells.

• Radioactivity was discovered by the French physicist Antoine Henri Becquerel in 1896.

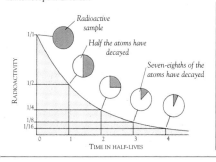

Radioactive sample

Half the atoms have decayed

Seven-eighths of the atoms have decayed

RADIOACTIVITY

TIME IN HALF-LIVES

BONDS AND MOLECULES

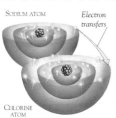

SODIUM ATOM

Electron transfers

CHLORINE ATOM

ATOMS MAY STICK together to form molecules by a process called "bonding." The bonds between atoms are electrical forces made by the movement of electrons. They form when atoms try to gain a full outer shell of electrons.

IONIC BONDS

In ionic bonding, electrons transfer between atoms, leaving the atoms as charged particles called ions. The atom losing the electron becomes a positive ion, or cation, and the atom gaining the electron becomes a negative ion, or anion. The force of attraction between the opposite charges forms a strong ionic bond.

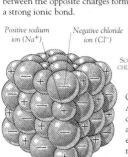

POSITIVELY CHARGED SODIUM ION

Both ions now have eight electrons in outer shell

Ionic bond

NEGATIVELY CHARGED CHLORIDE ION

Positive sodium ion (Na^+)

Negative chloride ion (Cl^-)

SODIUM CHLORIDE

GIANT IONIC STRUCTURE

A crystal of salt (sodium chloride) contains sodium and chloride ions arranged in a regular network that extends throughout the crystal. This network is called a giant ionic lattice.

COVALENT BONDS

In covalent bonding, atoms share electrons. Two atoms each "donate" an electron, and the electrons form a pair that orbits both nuclei, holding the atoms together as a molecule. In a double bond, each atom donates two electrons.

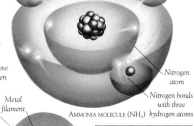

Hydrogen atom

Shared electrons form single bond

Nitrogen atom

Nitrogen bonds with three hydrogen atoms

AMMONIA MOLECULE (NH_3)

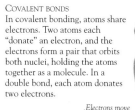

Electrons move freely between atoms

Metal filament

METALLIC BONDS

Electrons in the outer shell of metal atoms are loosely attached. These free-moving electrons form a common pool that bonds the atoms firmly together. They also make metals good conductors of heat and electricity.

LIGHT BULB

MOLECULE FACTS

• In 1811, the Italian Amedeo Avogadro was the first to distinguish molecules from atoms.

• At normal pressure and temperature, one liter of any gas contains 27,000 million million million molecules.

PARTICLES AND THEIR STRUCTURE FORMS			
STRUCTURE	COMPOSITION	TYPE OF SUBSTANCE	EXAMPLES
Metallic	Atoms	Metals	Sodium, iron, copper
Ionic	Ions	Compound of a metal with a nonmetal	Sodium chloride (salt), calcium hydroxide (lime)
Simple molecular	Small molecules	Nonmetal, or a nonmetal compound	Iodine, sulfur, water, carbon dioxide
Giant molecular	Large molecules	Nonmetal, or a nonmetal compound	Diamond, graphite, polythene, sand

CRYSTALS

MOST SOLIDS have a crystalline structure, in which particles link up in regular, repeating patterns. There are seven basic crystal shapes, or crystal systems. All have straight edges, regular corners, and smooth faces. Well-formed crystals are often prized for their beauty.

CRYSTAL FORMATION
• Crystals may form as a molten solid cools, or as a liquid evaporates from a solution.
• Atoms, ions, or molecules link up to form a framework called a lattice.
• A basic arrangement of particles, called a unit cell, can be identified in the lattice.
• The lattice is made up of identical unit cells repeated many times over.

Sulfur forms both orthorhombic and monoclinic crystals

SULFUR CRYSTALS

CRYSTAL FACTS

• Photographic film records images using special light-sensitive crystals of silver salts.

• Crystals of pure silicon are used in electronics. They are created artificially because they do not occur naturally.

• Diamonds are crystals of pure carbon.

This calculator displays figures using an LCD

LIQUID CRYSTALS
A liquid crystal can flow, but its particles line up in regular patterns. Heat or electricity can alter the pattern of the particles and change the passage of light through the crystal. This process forms letters or numbers on a liquid-crystal display (LCD).

CRYSTAL SYSTEMS

Crystal systems are based on the lengths of any three edges in the unit cell that meet at a corner, and the angles at which they meet.

CUBIC CRYSTALS OF GALENA (IRON ORE)

	CUBIC SYSTEM Every angle is 90°. All three edges are equal in length.
	TETRAGONAL SYSTEM Every angle is 90°. Two of the three edges are equal in length.
	ORTHORHOMBIC SYSTEM Every angle is 90°. None of the three edges are of equal length.
	MONOCLINIC SYSTEM Two of the three edges meet at 90°. None are equal in length.
	HEXAGONAL SYSTEM Edges form angles of 90° and 120°. Two are of equal length.
	TRIGONAL SYSTEM None of the three edges meet at 90°. All are of equal length.
	TRICLINIC SYSTEM None of the edges meet at 90°. None are equal in length.

PIEZOELECTRIC CRYSTALS

Some crystals produce an electric current when squeezed or made to vibrate. When an electric current is applied to them, they vibrate at a precise frequency. They are used in electronic devices and clocks.

Current from battery makes quartz crystal vibrate

Vibrating crystal controls watch hands

WATER OF CRYSTALLIZATION

Some crystals are "hydrates," meaning that they have water molecules trapped inside them. Heating blue copper sulfate crystals drives off this "water of crystallization," leaving white "anhydrous" crystals behind.

Adding water turns the white crystals blue again

MIXTURES AND COMPOUNDS

IN THE NATURAL WORLD, few elements exist alone. Most substances are made up of two or more elements, either mingled loosely as mixtures or, after chemical reactions, combined strongly as compounds. The main types of mixtures are solutions and colloids.

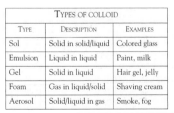

Potassium permanganate forms a solution in water

Water molecule attracts positively charged potassium ion

SOLUTIONS

A solution is a mixture of one substance (the solute) dissolved in another (the solvent). Many compounds break down in water into charged particles (ions) that form weak bonds with water molecules.

COLLOIDS

In a colloid, tiny particles of matter are dispersed evenly throughout a solid, liquid, or gas. Hair gel is a colloid of solid fat particles that are suspended in water.

HAIR GEL

TYPES OF COLLOID		
TYPE	DESCRIPTION	EXAMPLES
Sol	Solid in solid/liquid	Colored glass
Emulsion	Liquid in liquid	Paint, milk
Gel	Solid in liquid	Hair gel, jelly
Foam	Gas in liquid/solid	Shaving cream
Aerosol	Solid/liquid in gas	Smoke, fog

COMPARING MIXTURES AND COMPOUNDS
• A loose combination of sulfur and iron filings is a mixture. Heating the mixture causes a chemical reaction and forms a compound.
• The mixture separates easily with a magnet; the compound requires a chemical reaction.

Iron filings are attracted to a magnet

COMPOUND OF IRON SULFIDE

Magnet does not attract new compound

MIXTURE OF IRON FILINGS AND SULFUR

DIFFERENT COMPOUNDS

Copper and oxygen can form two different compounds. Copper(I) oxide contains twice as many copper atoms as oxygen atoms. Copper(II) oxide contains equal numbers of oxygen and copper atoms.

COPPER(I) OXIDE (Cu_2O)

COPPER(II) OXIDE (CuO)

PROPERTIES OF COMPOUNDS

CHLORINE

SODIUM

SODIUM CHLORIDE OR COMMON SALT

DANGEROUS ELEMENTS

Compounds often have different properties from those of the elements they contain. Common salt contains sodium, a dangerously reactive metal, and chlorine, a poisonous gas.

VITAL COMPOUND

In a chemical reaction, sodium and chlorine combine to form white crystals of salt – the compound sodium chloride. The sodium and chlorine lose their dangerous properties. The resulting compound is not only safe and edible, but also a vital part of our diet.

Separating mixtures

Scientists need to separate mixtures in order to investigate their components. Decanting involves pouring a liquid off from a solid sediment or a denser liquid. Centrifuging separates dense components from less dense ones by spinning them around. Other separation methods include distillation, evaporation, filtration, and desiccation.

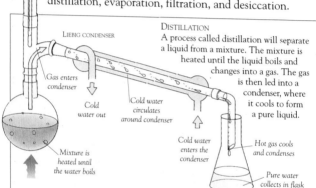

DISTILLATION

A process called distillation will separate a liquid from a mixture. The mixture is heated until the liquid boils and changes into a gas. The gas is then led into a condenser, where it cools to form a pure liquid.

LIEBIG CONDENSER

Gas enters condenser

Cold water out

Cold water circulates around condenser

Mixture is heated until the water boils

Cold water enters the condenser

Hot gas cools and condenses

Pure water collects in flask

FRACTIONAL DISTILLATION

This process is used to separate a mixture of liquids with different boiling points. To extract gases from air for industrial use, the air must be cooled first and liquefied. As the air warms, liquid gases boil off at different temperatures.

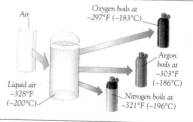

Air

Oxygen boils at −297°F (−183°C)

Argon boils at −303°F (−186°C)

Liquid air −328°F (−200°C)

Nitrogen boils at −321°F (−196°C)

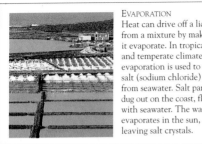

EVAPORATION
Heat can drive off a liquid from a mixture by making it evaporate. In tropical and temperate climates, evaporation is used to get salt (sodium chloride) from seawater. Salt pans, dug out on the coast, flood with seawater. The water evaporates in the sun, leaving salt crystals.

Filter paper holds back sulfur particles

FILTRATION
It is possible to separate large solid particles from a liquid mixture using a filter. A filter is a porous barrier that allows the liquid (the filtrate) to pass through, but holds back the solid particles (the residue).

Mixture of powdered sulfur and copper sulfate solution

Copper sulfate solution passes through filter paper

Airtight glass lid

Prism of rock salt to be kept dry

Silica gel desiccant absorbs moisture

DESICCATION
A desiccator removes water taken up by a solid mixture. It is a sealed glass dish containing a moisture-absorbing substance called a desiccant. Rock salt is stored in a desiccator to keep it dry for laboratory use.

WHAT ARE ELEMENTS?

AN ELEMENT IS a substance made of only one type of atom. Of the 114 known elements, 89 occur naturally on Earth. The rest are made artificially. A few "unreactive" elements, such as gold, occur in their pure state; most form compounds with other elements.

VEINS OF PURE
GOLD IN QUARTZ

ALLOTROPES OF CARBON

ALLOTROPES
Allotropes are different physical forms of the same element. The different arrangement of their atoms gives them different appearances and properties.

Diamond

Graphite

GRAPHITE
The atoms form huge sheets. Only weak bonds link the sheets together. Graphite is soft because the sheets can slide over each other easily.

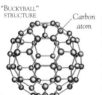

"BUCKYBALL"
STRUCTURE

Carbon
atom

DIAMOND
Each atom links strongly to four others in a rigid, compact framework that stretches throughout the diamond. This makes the diamond extremely hard.

Carbon atom

BUCKMINSTERFULLERENE
The molecules of this newly discovered carbon allotrope have 60 atoms linked in a sphere. It is called a "buckyball."

MOLECULAR STRUCTURE
OF A DIAMOND

Carbon atom

MOLECULAR STRUCTURE
OF GRAPHITE

COMPOSITION OF EARTH'S CRUST

The bulk of the Earth's crust is oxygen and silicon, mostly combined in rocks or sand (silicon dioxide). Clays are made of silicon and oxygen combined with the third most common element – aluminum.

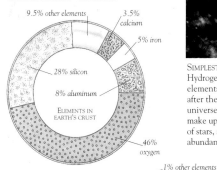

9.5% other elements

3.5% calcium

5% iron

28% silicon

8% aluminum

ELEMENTS IN EARTH'S CRUST

46% oxygen

SIMPLEST AND MOST ABUNDANT

Hydrogen and helium, the simplest elements, were the first to form after the Big Bang created the universe. Hydrogen and helium make up 97 percent of the mass of stars, and are by far the most abundant elements in the universe.

BODY ELEMENTS

The tissues of your body are made up of hydrogen, oxygen, carbon, and nitrogen, while bones contain calcium. Together, these five elements account for 98 percent of your body mass. Elements such as copper, iron, and zinc occur only in tiny amounts, but these "trace" elements are vital for good health.

1% other elements

1% phosphorus

2% calcium

3% nitrogen

10% hydrogen

18% carbon

65% oxygen

Over 50% of your body mass is water

ELEMENT FACTS

• Ancient Greek philosophers believed there were just four elements: earth, fire, air, and water.

• Astatine is the rarest element on Earth; the rarest metal is rhodium.

• Technetium was the first element to be made artificially.

• Earth's atmosphere is 78% nitrogen.

PERIODIC TABLE

CERTAIN ELEMENTS share similar chemical properties and atomic structures. These similarities become clear when all the known elements are set out in a chart called the periodic table. This chart arranges elements into "groups" (columns) and "periods" (rows).

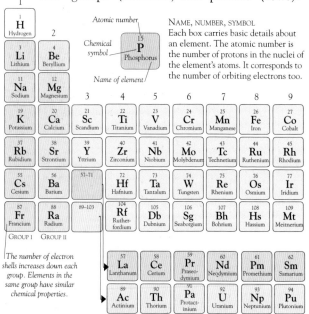

Atomic number

Chemical symbol

15
P
Phosphorus

Name of element

NAME, NUMBER, SYMBOL
Each box carries basic details about an element. The atomic number is the number of protons in the nuclei of the element's atoms. It corresponds to the number of orbiting electrons too.

GROUP I   GROUP II

The number of electron shells increases down each group. Elements in the same group have similar chemical properties.

1								
1 **H** Hydrogen	2							
3 **Li** Lithium	4 **Be** Beryllium							
11 **Na** Sodium	12 **Mg** Magnesium	3	4	5	6	7	8	9
19 **K** Potassium	20 **Ca** Calcium	21 **Sc** Scandium	22 **Ti** Titanium	23 **V** Vanadium	24 **Cr** Chromium	25 **Mn** Manganese	26 **Fe** Iron	27 **Co** Cobalt
37 **Rb** Rubidium	38 **Sr** Strontium	39 **Y** Yttrium	40 **Zr** Zirconium	41 **Nb** Niobium	42 **Mo** Molybdenum	43 **Tc** Technetium	44 **Ru** Ruthenium	45 **Rh** Rhodium
55 **Cs** Cesium	56 **Ba** Barium	57–71	72 **Hf** Hafnium	73 **Ta** Tantalum	74 **W** Tungsten	75 **Re** Rhenium	76 **Os** Osmium	77 **Ir** Iridium
87 **Fr** Francium	88 **Ra** Radium	89–103	104 **Rf** Ruther-fordium	105 **Db** Dubnium	106 **Sg** Seaborgium	107 **Bh** Bohrium	108 **Hs** Hassium	109 **Mt** Meitnerium

57 **La** Lanthanum	58 **Ce** Cerium	59 **Pr** Praseo-dymium	60 **Nd** Neodymium	61 **Pm** Promethium	62 **Sm** Samarium
89 **Ac** Actinium	90 **Th** Thorium	91 **Pa** Protact-inium	92 **U** Uranium	93 **Np** Neptunium	94 **Pu** Plutonium

TYPES OF ELEMENT KEY

▨ ALKALI METALS	▨ ACTINIDES
▨ ALKALINE-EARTH METALS	☐ POOR METALS
☐ TRANSITION METALS	▨ SEMIMETALS
▨ LANTHANIDES	▨ NONMETALS
	▨ NOBLE GASES

GROUPS AND PERIODS

Each period starts on the left with a highly reactive alkali metal with an outer shell of one electron. It ends on the right with a stable noble gas in group 18 (0) with eight electrons in its outer shell. Elements in the same group have the same number of electrons in their outer shells.

Two alternative systems are used to group the elements

As the atomic number increases by one along each period, the chemical properties of the element gradually change

			13	14	15	16	17	18
								2 **He** Helium
10	11	12	5 **B** Boron	6 **C** Carbon	7 **N** Nitrogen	8 **O** Oxygen	9 **F** Fluorine	10 **Ne** Neon
			13 **Al** Aluminum	14 **Si** Silicon	15 **P** Phosphorus	16 **S** Sulfur	17 **Cl** Chlorine	18 **Ar** Argon
28 **Ni** Nickel	29 **Cu** Copper	30 **Zn** Zinc	31 **Ga** Gallium	32 **Ge** Germanium	33 **As** Arsenic	34 **Se** Selenium	35 **Br** Bromine	36 **Kr** Krypton
46 **Pd** Palladium	47 **Ag** Silver	48 **Cd** Cadmium	49 **In** Indium	50 **Sn** Tin	51 **Sb** Antimony	52 **Te** Tellurium	53 **I** Iodine	54 **Xe** Xenon
78 **Pt** Platinum	79 **Au** Gold	80 **Hg** Mercury	81 **Tl** Thallium	82 **Pb** Lead	83 **Bi** Bismuth	84 **Po** Polonium	85 **At** Astatine	86 **Rn** Radon
110 **Uun** Unun-nilium	111 **Uuu** Unun-unium	112 **Uub** Unun-bium	GROUP III	114 **Uuq** Unun-quadium	GROUP V	116 **Uuh** Unun-hexium	GROUP VII	GROUP 0
				GROUP IV		GROUP VI		

63 **Eu** Europium	64 **Gd** Gadolinium	65 **Tb** Terbium	66 **Dy** Dysprosium	67 **Ho** Holmium	68 **Er** Erbium	69 **Tm** Thulium	70 **Yb** Ytterbium	71 **Lu** Lutetium
95 **Am** Americium	96 **Cm** Curium	97 **Bk** Berkelium	98 **Cf** Californium	99 **Es** Einsteinium	100 **Fm** Fermium	101 **Md** Mendelevium	102 **No** Nobelium	103 **Lr** Lawrencium

Elementary data

Most of the elements were first identified in the 18th and 19th centuries, but a few have been known since ancient times. Some can only be produced artifically. All are solids at room temperature, except for 11 gases, and mercury and bromine, which are liquids.

ANCIENT ELEMENTS	
ELEMENTS	KNOWN SINCE
Carbon	prehistoric times
Sulfur	prehistoric times
Gold	prehistoric times
Lead	prehistoric times
Copper	c.8000 BC
Silver	c.4000 BC
Iron	c.4000 BC
Tin	c.3500 BC
Mercury	c.1600 BC
Antimony	c.1000 BC

ELEMENTS PRODUCED ARTIFICIALLY		
ELEMENT	FIRST MADE	MAKER
Technetium	1937	C. Perrier (France) & E. Segré (Italy/US)
Astatine	1940	D.R. Corson (US)
Neptunium	1940	E.M. McMillan & P.H. Abelson (US)
Plutonium	1944	G. Seaborg (US)
Americium	1944	G. Seaborg (US)
Curium	1944	G. Seaborg (US)
Promethium	1947	J.A. Marinsky (US)
Berkelium	1949	S.G. Thompson (US)
Californium	1950	S.G. Thompson and others (US)
Einsteinium	1952	A. Ghiorso (US)
Fermium	1952	A. Ghiorso (US)
Mendelevium	1955	A. Ghiorso (US)
Nobelium	1958	A. Ghiorso (US)
Lawrencium	1961	A. Ghiorso (US)
Rutherfordium	1964	G. Flerov (USSR)
Dubnium	1967	A. Ghiorso (US)
Seaborgium	1974	A. Ghiorso (US); G. Flerov (USSR)
Bohrium	1976	G. Munzenburg (Germany)
Hassium	1982	P. Armbruster (Germany)
Meitnerium	1984	P. Armbruster (Germany)
Ununnilium	1994	P. Armbruster; S. Hofmann (Germany)
Unununium	1994	P. Armbruster; S. Hofmann (Germany)
Ununbium	1996	P. Armbruster; S. Hofmann (Germany)
Ununquadium	1998	Scientists in Dubna, Russia
Ununhexium	2000	Scientists in Dubna, Russia
(The discovery of elements in italics has yet to be confirmed.)		

BOILING POINTS

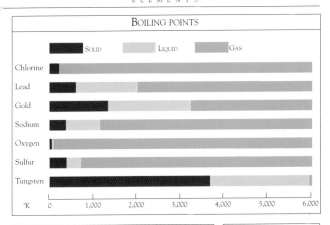

| | SOLID | LIQUID | GAS |

Chlorine
Lead
Gold
Sodium
Oxygen
Sulfur
Tungsten

°K   0   1,000   2,000   3,000   4,000   5,000   6,000

NAMING ELEMENTS

The names of many elements are derived from Greek words. They give clues about the elements' properties.

ELEMENT	GREEK WORD	MEANING
Argon (Ar)	*Argos*	Inactive
Astatine (At)	*Astatos*	Unstable
Barium (Ba)	*Barys*	Heavy
Bromine (Br)	*Bromos*	Stench
Chlorine (Cl)	*Chloros*	Pale green
Dysprosium (Dy)	*Dysprositos*	Hard to get
Hydrogen (H)	*Hydro genes*	Water-forming
Mercury (Hg)	*Hydragyrum*	Liquid silver
Phosphorus (P)	*Phosphoros*	Bringer of light
Technetium (Tc)	*Tekhnetos*	Artificial

MORE ELEMENT FACTS

• Helium has the lowest boiling point: –453.07°F (–268.93°C).

• Fluorine gas is the most reactive of all elements.

• At room temperature, osmium is the densest element and lithium the least dense metal. Radon is the densest gas and hydrogen the least dense.

SULFUR

METALS

MOST ELEMENTS are metals. Many are found in the Earth's crust, combined with other elements as deposits called ores. Metals in their pure form are either not very strong or they rust and tarnish easily. Most of the metals we use today are alloys. Alloys are solid mixtures of different metals. They provide hard, strong, long-lasting materials.

COMMON PROPERTIES OF METALS
- Most metals have high melting and boiling points.
- They conduct heat and electricity well.
- Metals have a high density, and are malleable (can be beaten) and ductile (can be drawn out into wire).
- Most metals react with air to form oxides, and with acids to release hydrogen.
- Metals form positive ions.

Blacksmith hammers hot iron into shape

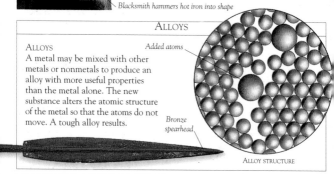

ALLOYS

ALLOYS
A metal may be mixed with other metals or nonmetals to produce an alloy with more useful properties than the metal alone. The new substance alters the atomic structure of the metal so that the atoms do not move. A tough alloy results.

Added atoms

Bronze spearhead

ALLOY STRUCTURE

COMPOSITION OF COMMON ALLOYS

ALLOY	TYPICAL COMPOSITION	PROPERTIES
Cast iron	Iron 97%, carbon 3%	Hard but brittle
Duralumin	Aluminum 96%, copper 4%	Strong and light
Pewter	Tin 73%, lead 27%	Fairly soft
Brass	Copper 70%, zinc 30%	Easy to shape
Solder	Tin 50%, lead 50%	Low melting point
Stainless steel	Iron 70%, chromium 20%, nickel 9.5%, carbon 0.5%	Hard and does not rust
Bronze	Copper 70%, tin 30%	Resists corrosion and wear

POOR METALS

A "tin" can may be made of steel coated with tin

Tankard made of pewter, a tin-lead alloy

The poor metals are aluminum, gallium, indium, thallium, tin, lead, bismuth, and polonium. They are softer and weaker than other metals, and melt more easily. Despite their name, they are very useful, especially in making alloys.

SEMIMETALS

Boron, silicon, germanium, arsenic, antimony, selenium, and tellurium are called semimetals because they have some of the properties of metals and some of nonmetals. Silicon and germanium are used to make electronic components because they are "semiconductors"; that is, they will conduct electricity, but not as well as true metals.

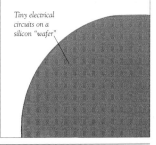

Tiny electrical circuits on a silicon "wafer"

Transition metals

In the middle of the periodic table lies the group of typical metals called the transition metals. They are less reactive than the alkali metals and alkaline-earth metals, and have higher melting and boiling points. Some transition metals, such as copper and nickel, are magnetic.

ZINC
A bluish gray metal, zinc often provides the casing for batteries. Its main use is as a protective coating that prevents iron or steel from rusting. With copper, it forms the alloy brass. Zinc oxides are used to make rubber and plastic compounds more stable.

PROPERTIES OF
TRANSITION METALS

• The transition metals form the center block of the periodic table.

• They are hard and dense.

• They are good conductors of heat and electricity.

• Many transition metals are good catalysts.

• They often form colored ions and compounds.

• They form alloys with other metals.

NICKEL
Nickel is a shiny metal that does not corrode or tarnish, and neither do its alloys. When alloyed with copper it forms cupronickel, which is used to make coins. In an alloy with chromium, iron, and carbon, it produces stainless steel.

SILVER
Apart from jewelry, silver is used mainly in the photographic industry. Black-and-white photographic film is coated with a compound of silver, and either iodine, chlorine, or bromine. The compound is sensitive to light.

Developing the film turns the light-affected areas into pure silver – the dark areas on the negative

IRON

Iron is the most important and cheapest of all the metals we use. However, when exposed to air it oxidizes – that is, it reacts with oxygen in the air to form rust (iron oxide). This problem is corrected by turning iron into steel.

PLATINUM

Rare and attractive platinum is used in jewelry. It never corrodes or wears away naturally.

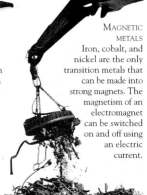

Platinum's main industrial use is as a catalyst. It is also used in electronic circuits.

MAGNETIC METALS

Iron, cobalt, and nickel are the only transition metals that can be made into strong magnets. The magnetism of an electromagnet can be switched on and off using an electric current.

INNER TRANSITION METALS

• The inner transition series consists of the lanthanide and actinide series.

• They are named after the first elements in their series: lanthanum and actinium.

• The lanthanides are so similar that chemists find it difficult to tell them apart.

• All the actinides are radioactive.

URANIUM

Uranium is a radioactive, silvery metal from the actinide series. It is extracted from the ores pitchblende and carnotite. Nuclear reactors use the isotope uranium–235 as a fuel.

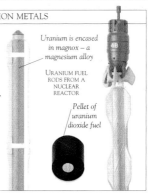

Uranium is encased in magnox – a magnesium alloy

URANIUM FUEL RODS FROM A NUCLEAR REACTOR

Pellet of uranium dioxide fuel

Other metals

At the beginning of the periodic table are two groups of highly reactive metals: the alkali metals and the alkaline-earth metals.

Our bodies need small amounts of some of these – potassium, sodium, magnesium, and calcium – to stay healthy. Francium and radium are radioactive metals.

DANGEROUS METALS
The alkali metals are very reactive. Potassium reacts violently with water, skidding across its surface and creating bubbles of hydrogen gas, which burn with a blue-pink flame. Cesium and rubidium will explode if they touch water.

Potassium reacts violently with water

PROPERTIES OF ALKALI METALS

• The alkali metals are: lithium, sodium, potassium, rubidium, cesium, and francium.

• They form the periodic table's Group 1(I).

• They are soft enough to cut with a knife.

• They are stored under oil to stop them from reacting with oxygen in the air.

• Their oxides and hydroxides dissolve in water to give strongly alkaline solutions.

• They form ions with a single charge.

• Alkali metals react with some nonmetals to form white, soluble, crystalline salts.

• They have low melting points, low boiling points, and low densities compared with other metals.

POTASSIUM FERTILIZER
Plants take in potassium from the soil because it is crucial for their healthy growth. Intensive farming depletes the soil, so farmers must replenish it by adding fertilizers that contain potassium and other nutrients.

SODIUM

Sodium, a silvery, soft
alkali metal, tarnishes
on exposure to the
air. An atom of
sodium has 11
electrons, but only
one in its outer
shell, which makes
it very reactive. It is
extracted from common
salt by electrolysis.

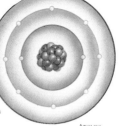

ATOMIC
STRUCTURE OF
SODIUM

PROPERTIES OF ALKALINE-EARTH METALS

• The alkaline-earth
metals are: beryllium,
magnesium, calcium,
strontium, barium, and
radium.

• They form Group 2
(II) of the periodic table.

• They react with
water to form alkaline
solutions. Their
compounds are widely
found in nature.

• Alkaline-earth
metals are reactive,
though less so than the
alkali metals.

MAGNESIUM

A magnesium atom has
12 electrons, but only
two in its outer shell.
This makes it reactive,
but less so than
sodium. Magnesium,
a light, alkaline-earth
metal, is used in alloys
with aluminum and zinc.

ATOMIC
STRUCTURE OF
MAGNESIUM

CALCIUM

Calcium is one of Earth's most
abundant metals. There are
vast deposits in the form of
limestone (also called calcium
carbonate). Calcium is also
present in bones, teeth, and the
shells of molluscs and other
sea creatures. The average
human contains 2.2 lb
(1 kg) of calcium.

RHESUS MONKEY
SKELETON

*Calcium,
in the form
of calcium
phosphate,
gives bone
its hardness*

NONMETALS

THE NONMETALS are phosphorus, sulfur, hydrogen, carbon, nitrogen, oxygen, the halogens, and the noble gases. Although they form a small part of the periodic table, they are vital to life on Earth. The nonmetals include elements that are gases at room temperature (68°F, 20°C) such as hydrogen and oxygen. Solid nonmetals include sulfur and phosphorus.

HYDROGEN
Hydrogen is at the top of the periodic table because it has the simplest atom, with just one proton orbited by a single electron. It is a colorless, odorless, tasteless, non-toxic gas, and is the least dense of all the elements.

Electron

Proton

HALOGENS

- The halogens are fluorine, chlorine, bromine, iodine, and astatine.
- They form group 17 (VII) of the periodic table.
- They are all poisonous and have a strong smell.
- Halogens form molecules of two atoms (Cl_2, Br_2, I_2, etc.).
- They react with metals to form salts (such as NaCl, LiF).
- Halogen ions have a single negative charge (F^-, Cl^-, Br^-, I^-, At^-).

NATURAL HALOGENS
The most widespread natural compound containing fluorine is the mineral fluorite (calcium fluoride). Iodine is found in seawater and was once extracted from certain types of seaweed.

Laminaria seaweed contains iodine

Pink fluorite crystal

NOBLE GASES

- The noble gases are helium, neon, argon, krypton, xenon, and radon.
- They form group 18 (0) of the periodic table.
- The noble gases have very low melting and boiling points.
- They all have a full outer shell of electrons, making them extremely unreactive.
- Noble gases exist as single atoms (He, Ne, Ar, Kr, Xe, Rn).

ATOMIC STRUCTURE OF NEON

SAFE GAS

Helium is a light noble gas that is used in balloons and blimps. It is very safe to use because it is so unreactive that it cannot catch fire. It is extracted from natural gas wells.

Helium-filled balloons

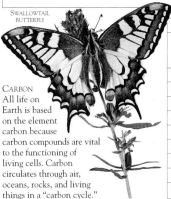

SWALLOWTAIL BUTTERFLY

CARBON

All life on Earth is based on the element carbon because carbon compounds are vital to the functioning of living cells. Carbon circulates through air, oceans, rocks, and living things in a "carbon cycle."

COMPOSITION OF AIR

Many of the nonmetallic elements are present in the air that we breathe.

ELEMENT	PERCENTAGE OF AIR
Nitrogen (N_2)	78%
Oxygen (O_2)	21%
Argon (Ar)	0.93%
Carbon dioxide (CO_2)	0.03%
Neon (Ne)	0.0018%
Helium (He)	0.0005%
Krypton (Kr)	0.00001%
Other gases	0.03769%

CHEMICAL REACTIONS

WHEN A CHEMICAL reaction occurs, new substances (called products) form from the substances taking part in the reaction (called reactants). The atoms of the reactants rearrange themselves to form the products.

As log gives off heat, the surrounding air becomes hotter

EXOTHERMIC REACTIONS
Burning is an exothermic reaction – more heat is given out during the reaction than is taken in. Oxidation occurs when a substance combines with oxygen. When a log burns, it combines with oxygen and gives out heat. Reduction occurs when a substance loses oxygen.

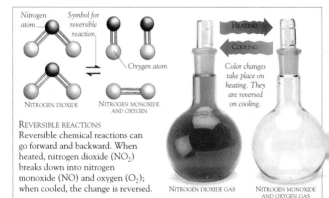

Nitrogen atom

Symbol for reversible reaction

Oxygen atom

NITROGEN DIOXIDE

NITROGEN MONOXIDE AND OXYGEN

HEATING

COOLING

Color changes take place on heating. They are reversed on cooling.

REVERSIBLE REACTIONS
Reversible chemical reactions can go forward and backward. When heated, nitrogen dioxide (NO_2) breaks down into nitrogen monoxide (NO) and oxygen (O_2); when cooled, the change is reversed.

NITROGEN DIOXIDE GAS

NITROGEN MONOXIDE AND OXYGEN GAS

MAKING AND BREAKING BONDS

Heat is absorbed during cooking

1 DURING A CHEMICAL REACTION
Energy is taken in when chemical bonds are broken, and it is released when new bonds are formed. When methane (CH_4) burns, it reacts with oxygen (O_2) in the air.

METHANE MOLECULE

Hydrogen atom

Carbon atom

Oxygen atom

OXYGEN MOLECULES

Bonds between atoms break

Bonds begin to rejoin to form carbon dioxide and water

2 BROKEN BONDS
During the reaction, all the bonds between the atoms are broken. New bonds form as the atoms join in different combinations.

ENDOTHERMIC REACTIONS
Some reactions take in more heat energy than they give off. These reactions are called "endothermic." When a reaction takes place during cooking, it is endothermic.

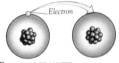

Electron

ELECTRON TRANSFER
During the oxidation process, atoms lose electrons and are "oxidized." During reduction, atoms gain electrons and are "reduced."

ACTIVATION ENERGY
Most reactions need some energy to get them started. This energy is called activation energy. Striking a match gives it the energy to ignite.

Chemicals in match head gain energy

CARBON DIOXIDE MOLECULE

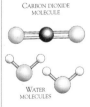

3 NEW BONDS FORM
The reaction produces carbon dioxide (CO_2) and water (H_2O). The new bonds have less stored energy than the original ones, so the reaction gives out energy as heat.

WATER MOLECULES

Describing reactions

Each element has a chemical symbol to identify it, and each compound a chemical formula. The formula indicates how the elements in the compound are combined. A chemical equation shows which substances react during a chemical reaction and the products that result.

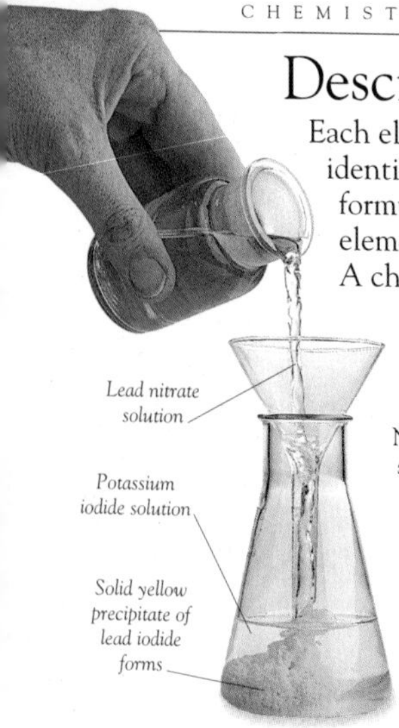

Lead nitrate solution

Potassium iodide solution

Solid yellow precipitate of lead iodide forms

CHEMICAL EQUATIONS ALWAYS BALANCE
No atoms are lost during a chemical reaction, so its chemical equation must balance, with equal numbers of atoms of each element on either side. Here, lead nitrate solution reacts with potassium iodide solution. The chemical equation for this reaction is shown below.

$$2KI \; + \; Pb(NO_3)_2 \; \longrightarrow \; PbI_2 \; + \; 2KNO_3$$

| Potassium iodide | + | Lead nitrate | $\longrightarrow$ | Lead iodide | + | Potassium nitrate |

Sodium is high in the activity series, and reacts violently with air

REACTION FACTS

• No mass is lost during any chemical reaction – this was first noted by French chemist Antoine Lavoisier in 1774.

• Cesium is the most reactive metal element.

• The present system of using letters to represent elements was devised in 1811.

THE ACTIVITY SERIES
The activity series compares the reactivity of different metals – that is, how readily they form compounds with other substances. Elements at the top of the series are highly reactive. Those at the bottom are very unreactive. Highly reactive metals cannot be found uncombined in nature.

Potassium
Calcium
Sodium
Magnesium
Aluminum
Zinc
Iron
Lead
Copper
Silver
Mercury
Platinum
Gold

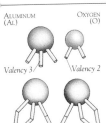

ALUMINUM
(AL)

OXYGEN
(O)

Valency 3

Valency 2

ALUMINUM OXIDE (AL₂O₃)

*Two aluminum atoms bond
with three oxygen atoms*

SI UNITS

The **mole** (mol) is a measure of the number of atoms, molecules, or ions in any substance.

• 1 mole contains 6 x 10²³ particles. This number is called Avogadro's constant, after Italian scientist Amedeo Avogadro.

• Although the number of particles in one mole of any element is the same, their masses vary due to different-sized nuclei. A mole of copper has a mass of 64 g, a mole of aluminum 27 g.

VALENCY

An atom's valency shows the number of chemical bonds it can form. It is the number of electrons the atom gains, loses, or shares when it makes bonds. When a compound has formed, the total valencies of the different atoms involved will be the same.

Copper crystals grow on the copper wire

Copper wire

DISPLACEMENT

A metal will displace (put out of place) a less reactive metal from a solution. Here, atoms from a "tree" of copper wire displace silver atoms from a clear solution of silver nitrate. The copper turns the solution blue, while the displaced silver forms crystals on the wire.

Blue copper nitrate solution forms

$$Cu + 2AgNO_3 \longrightarrow Cu(NO_3)_2 + 2Ag$$

Copper + Silver nitrate ⟶ Copper nitrate + Silver

SUFFIXES AND PREFIXES		
SUFFIX	DESCRIPTION	EXAMPLE
-ide	Contains just the two elements in the name	Iron sulfide (FeS)
-ite	Contains oxygen as well as the other elements in the name	Iron sulfite (FeSO₃)
-ate	Contains more oxygen than -ites	Iron sulfate (FeSO₄)
PREFIX	EXAMPLE	ATOMS IN PREFIX
Mono-	Carbon monoxide (CO)	1
Di-	Nitrogen dioxide (NO₂)	2
Tri-	Boron trichloride (BCl₃)	3

Controlling reactions

Chemists speed up reactions by making the reacting particles collide with each other more often or with greater energy. Substances called catalysts speed up reactions by helping substances react together. They remain unchanged by the chemical reaction.

Rate of reaction is slower with a weak dye solution

Strong dye solution reacts faster with material

CONCENTRATION
Increasing the concentration of a reactant speeds up a reaction. Dyeing a material is faster with a concentrated dye – there are more dye molecules to collide with the material.

SURFACE AREA
The surface area of a solid object is the size of its outer surface. Increasing the surface area of a reacting substance speeds up a chemical reaction. This is why chips fry faster than the potato from which they are made. The chips' greater surface area reacts with the hot cooking oil.

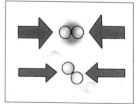

COLLISION THEORY
When particles collide, they usually bounce harmlessly off each other. But if the particles collide with enough force or energy, the bonds holding them together break, and a chemical reaction takes place.

CATALYSTS IN INDUSTRY		
PROCESS	REACTANTS	CATALYST
Manufacture of ammonia	Hydrogen and nitrogen	Iron and iron(III) oxide
Manufacture of nitric acid	Ammonia and oxygen	Platinum
Manufacture of sulfuric acid	Sulfur dioxide and oxygen	Vanadium(V) oxide
Manufacture of margarine	Vegetable oil and hydrogen	Nickel or platinum
Manufacture of methanol	Methane and oxygen	Chromium(III) oxide or zinc oxide

Sugar lump dropped in carbonated drink

SUGAR AS A CATALYST
Sugar makes a carbonated drink bubble harder. It acts as a catalyst for dissolved carbon dioxide gas to come out of the solution.

CATALYTIC CONVERTER
A car's catalytic converter provides a large surface area for chemical reactions to take place. Harmful gases formed when fuel burns are forced into close contact with catalysts in the converter. The substances react together to produce less harmful gases. The catalysts are unchanged by the reaction.

CATALYTIC CONVERTER

Polluting gases enter converter

Honeycomb structure gives large surface area

Coating of catalysts rhodium and platinum

Gas bubbles make dough expand

NATURAL CATALYSTS
Yeast is a fungus containing enzymes, which are biological catalysts. The enzymes in yeast make starches and sugars break down more rapidly into carbon dioxide gas and ethanol. In bread making, yeast helps the dough to rise.

Dough is left in warm place

Yeast mixture

MORE REACTION FACTS

• Raising temperature or pressure increases the rate of reaction.

• The human body contains over 1,000 different enzymes.

• Biodegradable plastics decompose faster in strong sunlight.

ACIDS AND ACIDITY

STRONG ACIDS are corrosive and burn clothes or skin. However, acids are found in fruit, ants, rain, and even our stomachs. Some acids dissolve metals. The strength of an acid is measured on the pH scale.

CORROSIVE WARNING SYMBOL FOR STRONG ACIDS

Hydrochloric acid poured over metal

Acid reacts furiously with metal chips, releasing hydrogen gas

Zinc chips

REACTION OF ACID ON METAL
Hydrochloric acid poured onto zinc chips causes a bubbling as the hydrogen (present in all acids) is released. The zinc replaces the hydrogen in the solution to form zinc chloride.

Water molecule (H_2O)

Hydrogen ion (H^+) splits from water molecule

Hydroxide ion (OH^-)

ACIDS IN WATER
Water (H_2O) can split into (OH^-) hydroxide and (H^+) hydrogen ions. Acidic compounds add more H^+ ions when they dissolve. A solution's pH is a measure of its H^+ ion concentration.

COMMON ACIDS				
ACID	FORMULA	STRENGTH	pH	OCCURRENCE
Hydrochloric	HCl	Strong	1	Human digestive system
Sulfuric	H_2SO_4	Strong	1–2	Car batteries
Nitric	HNO_3	Strong	1	Industrial processes
Acetic	CH_3COOH	Weak	3–4	Vinegar
Citric	$C_6H_8O_7$	Weak	3	Citrus fruit
Formic	HCOOH	Weak	4.5	Ant bites, nettle stings
Carbonic	H_2CO_3	Weak	4–5	Rainwater, bubbly drinks

UNIVERSAL INDICATOR COLOR/PH CHART OF ACIDS						
1	2	3	4	5	6	7
DIGESTIVE JUICES	CAR BATTERY ACID	LEMON JUICE	VINEGAR	ACID RAIN	TAP WATER	PURE WATER

MEASURING ACIDITY

The pH scale measures acidity (and alkalinity). On the pH scale, 1 is highly acidic, 7 neutral, and 14 highly alkaline. Acidity is measured with indicator papers or solutions, which change color in acids or alkalis, or with pH meters, which record the concentration of hydrogen ions.

Hydrochloric acid

Indicator paper shows pH of 1

ACID RAIN

Rainwater naturally contains weak carbonic acid, but pollution is now adding sulfuric acid and nitric acid to it. This creates a strong cocktail of acids that can kill trees and aquatic life, and erode statues and buildings.

USES OF SULFURIC ACID

Sulfuric acid is widely used in industry because it reacts readily with other compounds. It is produced in large quantities after a reaction between sulfur and oxygen.

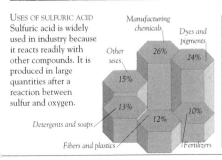

Manufacturing chemicals

Dyes and pigments

Other uses

26%

24%

15%

13%

12%

10%

Detergents and soaps

Fibers and plastics

Fertilizers

ACID FACTS

• pH or "potential of hydrogen," indicates the number of hydrogen ions a substance forms.

• The word "acid" comes from the Latin word for "sour."

• "Heartburn" is caused by excess hydrochloric acid in the stomach.

Alkalis, bases, and salts

Bases are compounds that cancel out, or neutralize, acidity. When a base reacts with an acid, a substance called a salt is created. Water (H_2O) is also produced. Pure water is neutral: it is neither acidic nor alkaline. Alkalis are bases that are soluble in water.

BEE

Painful stings contain acids or alkalis

WASP

USES OF AMMONIA

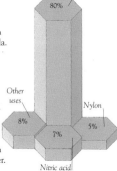

Fertilizers
80%

Other uses
8%

Nitric acid
7%

Nylon
5%

BEE STINGS AND WASP STINGS
A bee sting is acidic and can be neutralized by a weak alkali such as soap or bicarbonate of soda. Wasp stings are alkaline, so they can be neutralized by a weak acid such as vinegar.

AMMONIA
Fertilizers containing nitrogen are made from the alkali ammonia (NH_3). Ammonia is produced by the Haber process, which causes nitrogen and hydrogen to react together.

COMMON BASES				
BASE	FORMULA	STRENGTH	pH	OCCURRENCE
Sodium hydroxide	NaOH	Strong	14	Soap manufacture
Calcium hydroxide	$Ca(OH)_2$	Strong	12	Neutralizing soil acidity
Ammonium hydroxide solution	NH_4OH	Weak	10–11	Household cleaning fluids
Milk of magnesia	$Mg(OH)_2$	Weak	10	Neutralizing stomach acid
Sodium bicarbonate	$NaHCO_3$	Weak	8–9	Bicarbonate of soda
Blood		Weak	7.4	Human body

UNIVERSAL INDICATOR COLOR/PH CHART OF BASES

7	8	9	10	11	12	13	14
PURE WATER	SOAP	BICARBONATE OF SODA	DISINFECTANT	HOUSEHOLD CLEANER	CALCIUM HYDROXIDE	OVEN CLEANER	SODIUM HYDROXIDE

THE PH OF BASES
The pH scale for bases ranges from neutral pure water (pH 7) to strong alkalis such as sodium hydroxide (pH 14). Soaps are made by making weak organic acids react with a strong base. This makes soaps mildy alkaline, with a pH of 8–9.

Universal indicator paper dipped in calcium hydroxide shows pH of 12

COPPER SHAVINGS

ADD CARBONIC ACID

ADD HYDROCHLORIC ACID

ADD SULFURIC ACID

COPPER SULFATE

COPPER CHLORIDE

COPPER CARBONATE

MAKING SALTS
A salt is a compound of a metal and a nonmetal joined by ionic bonds. A salt forms when an acid reacts with a base or a metal. Like other metals, copper forms a variety of salts. Making it react with different acids produces very different salts.

CORROSIVE ALKALI WARNING
Alkalis are chemically opposite to acids. They dissolve in water to form negatively charged hydroxide ions (OH^-), making them as corrosive as acids.

BASE AND SALT FACTS
• In 1908, a German chemist named Fritz Haber devised the manufacturing process for ammonia.

• Alkalis, like acids, are good conductors of electricity. This is because they break up in water to form ions.

CHEMISTRY OF CARBON

THERE ARE MORE than ten million known carbon compounds. All living things contain some compounds of carbon. The study of substances containing carbon is known as organic chemistry.

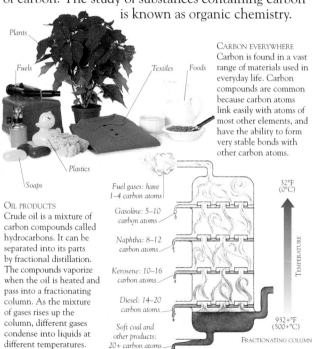

Plants

Fuels

Textiles

Foods

Plastics

Soaps

CARBON EVERYWHERE
Carbon is found in a vast range of materials used in everyday life. Carbon compounds are common because carbon atoms link easily with atoms of most other elements, and have the ability to form very stable bonds with other carbon atoms.

OIL PRODUCTS
Crude oil is a mixture of carbon compounds called hydrocarbons. It can be separated into its parts by fractional distillation. The compounds vaporize when the oil is heated and pass into a fractionating column. As the mixture of gases rises up the column, different gases condense into liquids at different temperatures.

Fuel gases: have 1–4 carbon atoms

Gasoline: 5–10 carbon atoms

Naphtha: 8–12 carbon atoms

Kerosene: 10–16 carbon atoms

Diesel: 14–20 carbon atoms

Soft coal and other products: 20+ carbon atoms

32°F (0°C)

TEMPERATURE

932+°F (500+°C)

FRACTIONATING COLUMN

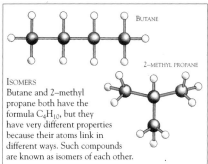

BUTANE

2–METHYL PROPANE

ISOMERS
Butane and 2–methyl propane both have the formula C_4H_{10}, but they have very different properties because their atoms link in different ways. Such compounds are known as isomers of each other.

AROMATIC COMPOUND
Benzene is a strong-smelling liquid obtained from coal. The molecular structure of benzene – a ring of six carbon atoms – is the basis of many useful "aromatic" compounds.

Hydrogen atom

MOLECULAR STRUCTURE OF BENZENE

Carbon atom

ORGANIC TERMS

TERM	MEANING	EXAMPLE
Hydrocarbon	Organic compound of hydrogen and carbon atoms only	Methane (CH_4)
Aromatic	Organic compound with a ring of carbon atoms	Benzene (C_6H_6)
Aliphatic	Organic compound with a chain of carbon atoms	Ethane (C_2H_6)
Alkane	Aliphatic hydrocarbon with single bonds between its carbon atoms	Octane (C_8H_{18})
Alkene	Aliphatic hydrocarbon with a double bond between two of its carbon atoms	Ethene (C_2H_4)
Alkyne	Aliphatic hydrocarbon with a triple bond between two of its carbon atoms	Ethyne (C_2H_2)
Alkyl group	Alkane that has lost one hydrogen atom	Methyl (CH_3–) forms from methane Ethyl (C_2H_5–) forms from ethane
Aryl group	Aromatic compound that has lost one hydrogen atom	Phenyl (C_6H_5–) forms from benzene
Alcohol	Organic compound with a hydroxyl (–OH) group	Ethanol (C_2H_5OH) – ethyl plus a hydroxyl group
Carbohydrate	Organic compound with hydrogen and oxygen atoms in the ratio of 2 to 1	Glucose ($C_6H_{12}O_6$)

POLYMERS

POLYMERS ARE giant
molecules made up of
winding chains of thousands
of smaller molecules called
"monomers." Rubber, starches, and
proteins are natural polymers, while
plastics and many artificial fibers are
made from synthetic polymers.

INFLATABLE
PVC (POLYVINYL
CHLORIDE) SNAKE

*PVC is a
"thermoplastic" –
it softens and melts
when heated*

*Double
bond*

Hydrogen atom

VINYL CHLORIDE
MONOMER

Carbon atom

*Double bond breaks to
join next molecule*

Chlorine atom

PVC POLYMER

MONOMERS AND POLYMERS
Vinyl chloride monomers are chemical compounds
of single molecules. They link end-to-end to form
a long PVC polymer. The double bond in the vinyl
chloride monomer breaks: one bond links to the chain
and the other is able to bond with the next monomer.

*Rug made from
woolen thread*

NATURAL POLYMERS
Wool and other natural fibers
are made of strong, flexible,
protein polymers. The
fibers are spun
into thread.

*Solutions
react in
beaker*

*Nylon is
drawn out as
a long strand*

MAKING NYLON POLYMERS
Hexanedioic acid and
1,6-diaminohexane react
together to produce nylon.
Their monomers join
to form long nylon
polymers, which can be
drawn out like thread.

TYPES OF POLYMER

POLYMER	PRODUCED FROM	USES
Polythene (polyethylene)	Ethene	Plastic bags, bottles, food wrappings, insulation
Polystyrene	Styrene (phenylethene)	Plastic toys, packaging, insulation, bowls, ceiling tiles
Polyvinyl chloride (PVC)	Vinyl chloride	Guttering and pipes, electrical insulation, waterproof clothing
Acrylic	Derivatives of acrylic acid	Synthetic fibers for clothing, paints
Nylon	Hexanedioic acid and 1,6-diaminohexane	Synthetic fibers for clothing, carpets, plastic ropes, engineering parts
Polyester	Organic acids and alcohols	Fiberglass, synthetic fibers for clothing, boat sails, photographic film
Polymethyl methacrylate (plexiglass)	Methyl methacrylate	Glass substitute
Polyurethane	Urethane resins	Packaging foam, adhesives, paints, varnishes
Polytetrafluoroethene (PTFE)	Tetrafluoroethene	Nonstick coating for cooking utensils, artificial body parts, machine bearings
Kevlar	Phenylenediamine, terephthalyl chloride	Bullet-proof vests and other high-strength materials

Polymerization is stopped by stabilizing molecules

Adhesive molecule

Moisture from the surface neutralizes the stabilizing molecules

Polymers form to create a strong bond

POLYMERIZING ADHESIVES

The molecules of an adhesive polymerize as they emerge from the tube to form strong bonds between materials. Stabilizing substances stop the adhesive from polymerizing in the tube.

POLYMER FACTS

• In 1862, English chemist Alexander Parkes made Parkesine, the first plastic.

• Kevlar fibers are stronger than steel, but much lighter.

• There are two types of plastic: thermosets are not changed by heat; thermoplastics soften and melt when heated.

ELECTROCHEMISTRY

USING ELECTRICITY to break
down a substance is called
electrolysis. It happens when
metal or carbon rods (called
electrodes) pass an electric
current through a dissolved or
molten compound containing
ions (called an electrolyte).

*Chlorine gas
collects in
test tube*

*Electrolyte of
copper(II)
chloride solution
loses its color*

*Copper forms
at cathode as
copper ions gain
electrons and
become atoms*

*Chloride ions
lose electrons
at anode and
become atoms
of chlorine*

ELECTROLYSIS OF COPPER(II) CHLORIDE
Electrolyzing a solution of copper(II)
chloride ($CuCl_2$) makes copper ions (Cu^{2+})
move to the negatively charged electrode
(cathode) where they become copper
atoms. Chloride ions (Cl^-) are attracted to
the positively charged electrode (anode)
where they become chlorine atoms.

BARE
NICKEL

SILVER-
PLATED

ELECTROPLATING
Using electricity to coat an
object with metal is called
electroplating. Here, a nickel
spoon is plated with silver.
Silver ions (Ag^+) in the
solution move to the nickel
cathode, where they gain
electrons and form a deposit
of silver. They are replaced by
atoms from the silver anode
that give up electrons and
go into the solution as ions.

*Spoon turns in
electrolyte of silver
nitrate solution*

*Silver dissolves
during
electrolysis*

FARADAY CONSTANT

The electricity needed to produce 1 mole of an element by electrolysis is always a multiple of 96,500 coulombs. This figure is the Faraday constant (F). The multiple depends on the charge carried by the element's ions.

For example:

- 96,500 (1 x F) coulombs produce 1 mole of iodine (I^-).
- 193,000 (2 x F) coulombs produce 1 mole of copper (Cu^{2+}).

1 MOLE OF COPPER
MASS OF 64 GRAMS

1 MOLE
OF IODINE
MASS OF
127 GRAMS

ELECTROLYSIS FACTS

- In 1807, English chemist Humphry Davy discovered the element potassium by electrolyzing molten potash (potassium carbonate).

- Electrorefining – using electrolysis to rid a metal of its impurities – can produce copper that is 99.99% pure.

GALVANIZING

A steel car body may be galvanized – that is, given a coating of zinc to guard against rust. The body is electrified and dipped in a bath of an electrolyte containing zinc. The body forms the cathode, so it attracts the zinc ions (Zn^{2+}) in the electrolyte.

MAKING ELECTRICITY

Chemical reactions can produce an electric current. In this cell, a reaction tears ions (Zn^{2+}) from the zinc plate, leaving it negatively charged. The copper plate loses electrons and becomes positively charged. A current flows as electrons move through the wire to the copper plate.

Electrons flow towards the copper anode

As the zinc electrode dissolves, electrons flow out of the cell and through the wire

Electrolyte of dilute sulfuric acid solution

Bulb lit by flow of electrons

CHEMICAL ANALYSIS

CHEMISTS USE various techniques to analyze
and identify substances. Qualitative analysis
reveals which elements or compounds
a substance contains; quantitative
analysis shows how much of each
element or compound is present.

TITRATION
A sample solution is made to react
with a chemical whose concentration
is known. When all the solution has
reacted, a color change occurs.
Measuring the amount of the
chemical used reveals the
concentration of the sample.

*Dyes travel
up paper at
different
speeds*

*Blotting
paper*

*The color of the test
solution changes as
the pink chemical
drops into the flask*

PAPER CHROMATOGRAPHY
The ingredients in a dissolved mixture
can be revealed by using absorbent
paper. They travel up the paper at
different speeds. Black ink, for
example, reveals a mixture of dyes.

*Black
ink*

FLAME TESTS
Metallic elements can be
identified by flame tests. A
small amount of a metal salt
is placed on the end of a
platinum wire and heated in
a flame. The metal burns and
gives the flame a particular
color. Fireworks use
metal compounds to
produce colored sparks.

*Sodium
burns with
an orange
flame*

FLAME TEST FOR IDENTIFYING METALS	
METAL	FLAME COLOUR
Barium	Brown-green
Calcium	Orange-red
Copper	Green-blue
Lithium	Red
Potassium	Lilac
Sodium	Orange

SPECTROSCOPY

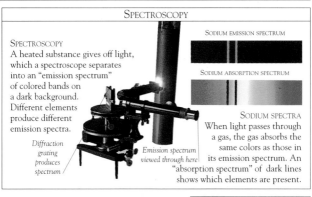

SPECTROSCOPY
A heated substance gives off light, which a spectroscope separates into an "emission spectrum" of colored bands on a dark background. Different elements produce different emission spectra.

Diffraction grating produces spectrum

Emission spectrum viewed through here

SODIUM EMISSION SPECTRUM

SODIUM ABSORPTION SPECTRUM

SODIUM SPECTRA
When light passes through a gas, the gas absorbs the same colors as those in its emission spectrum. An "absorption spectrum" of dark lines shows which elements are present.

MASS SPECTROSCOPY
Ions of a substance accelerate along a tube. Ions with a particular charge and mass are deflected by a magnetic field so that they strike a detector at the other end of the tube. One by one different ions are detected, producing a mass spectrum.

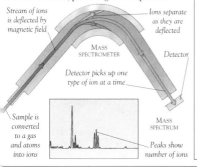

Stream of ions is deflected by magnetic field

Ions separate as they are deflected

MASS SPECTROMETER

Detector

Detector picks up one type of ion at a time

Sample is converted to a gas and atoms into ions

MASS SPECTRUM

Peaks show number of ions

DNA PROFILING
Fragments of the genetic material from skin, blood, or hair roots are analyzed using a technique known as electrophoresis. The result is a unique DNA profile that can be used to help identify individual people or animals.

FORCES AT WORK

WHAT MAKES a magnet attract iron filings or an arrow fly toward a target? The answer is force. You cannot see a force, though you feel its effects. Forces push, pull, stretch, or turn an object. Forces are measured in newtons (N).

Tension force applied by top half of bowstring

Arrow is thrust forward by the resultant of the two tension forces

Tension force applied by bottom half of bowstring

COMBINING FORCES
When more than one force acts on an object, the forces combine to produce a single force (the "resultant") that acts in one direction only. The force that fires an arrow from a bow is the resultant of tension forces applied by the two halves of the bowstring.

FORCE FACTS
• A jet engine produces a force of at least 200,000 newtons (N).

• Car brakes exert force of up to 5,000 N.

• It takes a force of 5 N to switch on a light.

• To squash an egg requires a force of 50 N.

TORQUE OR TURNING FORCE
Torque is the force that makes an object rotate. It helps a wrench turn a nut. Applying the force far from the nut increases the turning effect. The size of the torque is found by multiplying the force by its distance from the nut.

Extendable wrench

A long handle makes turning the nut easier

BALANCED FORCES

If the forces acting on an object are balanced, the object is said to be in equilibrium. It will either stay at rest, or continue moving at the same speed and in the same direction. These magnets exert exactly equal and opposite forces on the line of ball bearings.

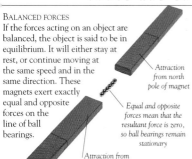

Attraction from north pole of magnet

Equal and opposite forces mean that the resultant force is zero, so ball bearings remain stationary

Attraction from south pole of magnet

TYPES OF FORCE

- Tension stretches objects.
- Compression squeezes objects.
- Torsion twists objects.
- Shear forces tear objects.
- Centripetal force keeps objects moving in a circle.
- Friction opposes motion.
- Upthrust acts on objects immersed in fluids.

FORCES ON IMMERSED OBJECTS

UPTHRUST IN WATER

Fluids (liquids and gases) exert pressure on immersed objects, producing an upward resultant force called "upthrust." The upthrust equals the weight of the fluid displaced (pushed aside) by the object. In this experiment, the upthrust of the water on the 1-kg mass is 1.2 N.

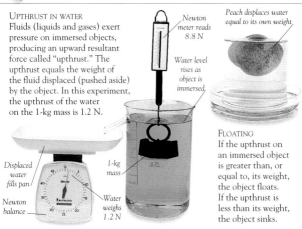

Newton meter reads 8.8 N

Water level rises as object is immersed

Peach displaces water equal to its own weight

Displaced water fills pan

Newton balance

1-kg mass

Water weighs 1.2 N

FLOATING

If the upthrust on an immersed object is greater than, or equal to, its weight, the object floats. If the upthrust is less than its weight, the object sinks.

The force of gravity

Gravity keeps our feet firmly on the ground. It is a force of attraction between all bodies of matter. All objects experience and exert a certain amount of gravity, depending on their mass. Most people are aware that Earth's gravity acts on us; few people realize that we pull on Earth with the same gravitational force.

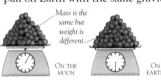

Mass is the same but weight is different

ON THE MOON

ON EARTH

WEIGHT AND MASS

Weight is the force exerted on an object by gravity. An object's mass is the same on the Moon as it is on Earth, but it weighs less, because the Moon's surface gravity is weaker.

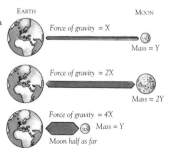

This apple weighs about 1 N

MEASURING FORCE

Gravity pulling on an object creates a force called weight. This force is measured in newtons. A simple instrument that measures force is the newton meter. (A spring balance works in the same way.)

NEWTON'S LAW OF GRAVITATION

According to Newton's law, to find the force of gravity between two objects, you multiply their masses and divide the result by the square of the distance between them. For example, if the Moon was only half as far from Earth, gravity between the two bodies would be four times as strong. If the Moon had twice its mass, the force of gravity between the Moon and Earth would be twice as great.

EARTH

MOON

Force of gravity = X

Mass = Y

Force of gravity = 2X

Mass = 2Y

Force of gravity = 4X   Mass = Y

Moon half as far

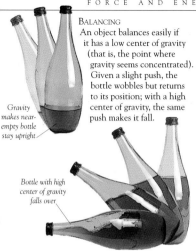

BALANCING

An object balances easily if it has a low center of gravity (that is, the point where gravity seems concentrated). Given a slight push, the bottle wobbles but returns to its position; with a high center of gravity, the same push makes it fall.

Gravity makes near-empty bottle stay upright

Bottle with high center of gravity falls over

SI UNITS

The **newton (N)** is the SI unit of force: 1 newton of force causes a mass of 1 kilogram to move with an acceleration of 1 meter per second per second.

EINSTEIN'S GENERAL THEORY OF RELATIVITY

Albert Einstein (1879–1955), the German–American physicist, suggested that gravity is a property of space rather than a force of attraction between bodies of matter. He argued that bodies of matter make space curve, causing other bodies to "fall" toward them, and even bend light as it passes around them.

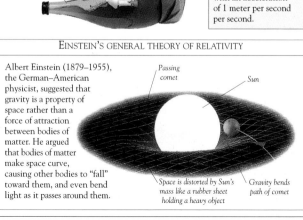

Passing comet

Sun

Space is distorted by Sun's mass like a rubber sheet holding a heavy object

Gravity bends path of comet

MOTION

FROM TINY PARTICLES to the huge planets, the whole universe is in motion. All objects tend to resist efforts to change their state of motion, whether they are actually moving or at rest. This is called inertia. On Earth, friction causes moving objects to stop; in space, objects move forever unless gravity forces are present.

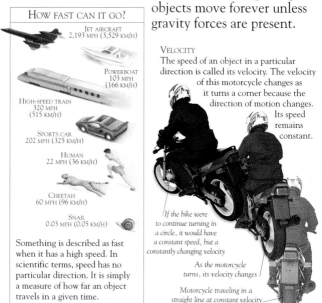

HOW FAST CAN IT GO?

JET AIRCRAFT
2,193 MPH (3,529 KM/H)

POWERBOAT
103 MPH
(166 KM/H)

HIGH-SPEED TRAIN
320 MPH
(515 KM/H)

SPORTS CAR
202 MPH (325 KM/H)

HUMAN
22 MPH (36 KM/H)

CHEETAH
60 MPH (96 KM/H)

SNAIL
0.03 MPH (0.05 KM/H)

Something is described as fast when it has a high speed. In scientific terms, speed has no particular direction. It is simply a measure of how far an object travels in a given time.

VELOCITY
The speed of an object in a particular direction is called its velocity. The velocity of this motorcycle changes as it turns a corner because the direction of motion changes. Its speed remains constant.

If the bike were to continue turning in a circle, it would have a constant speed, but a constantly changing velocity

As the motorcycle turns, its velocity changes

Motorcycle traveling in a straight line at constant velocity

MOTION FACTS

• Earth travels through space at 66,638 mph (107,244 km/h).

• Earth's gravity accelerates all falling objects at 32.1 ft (9.8 m) per second per second.

ACCELERATION
An object accelerates as its speed increases. Sprinters accelerate most as they pull out of the starting blocks. They decelerate as they cross the finish line, and their speed decreases.

OVERCOMING INERTIA AND FRICTION

OVERCOMING INERTIA
Pushing the pedals of a bicycle is harder at first, because you need to overcome both your own inertia and that of the bicycle. Once underway, inertia helps to keep you moving.

OVERCOMING FRICTION
Friction tries to oppose motion. It occurs where surfaces or materials rub together. Unless you keep pedaling, friction will bring your bicycle to a halt. Friction also helps the wheels to grip the road.

Friction helps hands grip handlebars

Brakes use friction to stop

Friction helps tires grip road

Friction helps feet grip pedals

Friction with air slows bicycle and rider

Friction slows pedals and gears

More motion

Not all motion is "linear" (in a straight line). An object may "oscillate" (move back and forth about a fixed point). It may also have circular motion, caused by "centripetal force," which keeps it moving in a circle. Moving objects have "momentum," which is velocity multiplied by mass.

Ball gains momentum when struck by cue

CONSERVATION OF MOMENTUM

When two objects collide, momentum is transferred between them. If a moving billiard ball strikes a stationary one, the first ball transfers some of its momentum to the second ball, which is set in motion. The total momentum of the two balls is the same as it was before the collision.

White ball strikes red ball, transferring momentum

Red ball gains momentum, and moves away

NEWTON'S LAWS OF MOTION

• **First law**
An object will remain at rest or continue traveling at a uniform velocity unless a force acts on it.

• **Second law**
The acceleration of an object is equal to the force acting on it, divided by the object's mass.

• **Third law**
When one object applies a force on another, the second object exerts an equal and opposite force on the first.

Weight is displaced to left

Weight swings towards equilibrium point

OSCILLATING PENDULUM

In an oscillation, such as a pendulum swing, an object is displaced and then pulled back to its equilibrium position (where no resultant force acts on it) by a force (gravity in the case of the pendulum).

Equilibrium point

Momentum takes weight past equilibrium

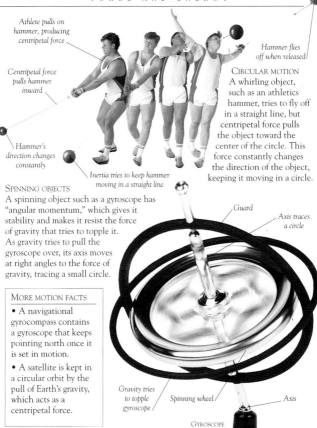

Athlete pulls on hammer, producing centripetal force

Centripetal force pulls hammer inward

Hammer's direction changes constantly

Hammer flies off when released

CIRCULAR MOTION
A whirling object, such as an athletics hammer, tries to fly off in a straight line, but centripetal force pulls the object toward the center of the circle. This force constantly changes the direction of the object, keeping it moving in a circle.

Inertia tries to keep hammer moving in a straight line

SPINNING OBJECTS
A spinning object such as a gyroscope has "angular momentum," which gives it stability and makes it resist the force of gravity that tries to topple it. As gravity tries to pull the gyroscope over, its axis moves at right angles to the force of gravity, tracing a small circle.

Guard

Axis traces a circle

MORE MOTION FACTS

• A navigational gyrocompass contains a gyroscope that keeps pointing north once it is set in motion.

• A satellite is kept in a circular orbit by the pull of Earth's gravity, which acts as a centripetal force.

Gravity tries to topple gyroscope

Spinning wheel

Axis

GYROSCOPE

PRESSURE

THE AIR AROUND us presses on us. At the same time, we push on the ground under our feet. Swimmers can feel the surrounding water press on their bodies. This is called pressure. Pressure measures how "concentrated" a force is when it presses on a particular area.

PINPOINT PRESSURE
It is much easier to push a drawing pin into a wall than a thick nail. This is because the drawing pin concentrates all the force exerted by your thumb onto a very small area.

Thumb presses on pin

2-kg (20-N) block exerts pressure of 80 Pa

Base covers 0.25 m² (25 squares)

MEASURING PRESSURE
It is possible to calculate the amount of pressure exerted by dividing the force applied by the area over which it acts. Increasing the area of the surface or reducing the force acting upon it reduces the pressure. Reducing the area or increasing the force acting upon it increases the pressure.

Base covers 0.50 m² (50 squares)

Base covers 0.25 m² (25 squares)

2-kg (20-N) block exerts pressure of 40 Pa

1-kg (10-N) block exerts pressure of 40 Pa

Grid has squares 0.01 m² in area

HOW AN AIRCRAFT FLIES

The curved upper surface of an aircraft's wing makes the air above it travel faster than the air under it. The faster the air moves, the lower its pressure. The difference in pressure creates "lift," a force that pushes the aircraft off the ground.

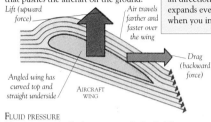

Lift (upward force)

Air travels farther and faster over the wing

Drag (backward force)

Angled wing has curved top and straight underside

AIRCRAFT WING

PASCAL'S LAW

Pascal's Law of Fluid Pressures (or Pascal's Principle) states that the pressure is transmitted equally through a fluid (a liquid or a gas) in all directions. This is why a balloon expands evenly in all directions when you inflate it with air.

SI UNITS

The **pascal** (Pa) is the SI unit of pressure: 1 pascal is equal to a force of 1 newton applied to an area of 1 square meter (1 N/m²).

FLUID PRESSURE

The pressure of a fluid increases with depth. This is why pressures in the deepest oceans are greater than they are just below the surface. Below, holes at different depths allow colored water out at different pressures.

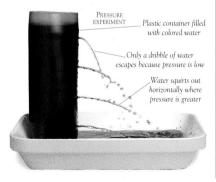

PRESSURE EXPERIMENT

Plastic container filled with colored water

Only a dribble of water escapes because pressure is low

Water squirts out horizontally where pressure is greater

PRESSURE FACTS

• The pressure at the bottom of the deepest ocean is 1.1×10^8 Pa.

• Standard atmospheric pressure at sea level is 101,325 Pa.

• Sharper knives cut better than blunt ones because their blades exert more pressure.

• Snowshoes help you walk on snow, spreading the weight and reducing the pressure underfoot.

SIMPLE MACHINES

MACHINES CAN CHANGE the direction or size of a force. For example, an axe is a machine called a wedge that splits a log easily. The effort used to wield the axe is sent a long way into the log, pushing it apart a short distance with a greater force.

Axe blade is a wedge

AXE SPLITTING A LOG

Turning effort spread over length of thread

SCREW
Less force is needed to turn the head of the screw than to pound it straight down.

Total length of screw thread

Effort applied to rim is magnified by axle

WHEEL AND AXLE
Applying a small effort to the rim of the wheel makes the axle turn with a greater force. A large effort at the axle means that the rim turns with less force, but travels farther.

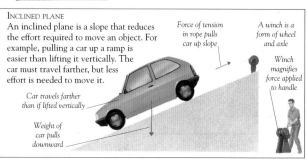

INCLINED PLANE
An inclined plane is a slope that reduces the effort required to move an object. For example, pulling a car up a ramp is easier than lifting it vertically. The car must travel farther, but less effort is needed to move it.

Force of tension in rope pulls car up slope

A winch is a form of wheel and axle

Winch magnifies force applied to handle

Car travels farther than if lifted vertically

Weight of car pulls downward

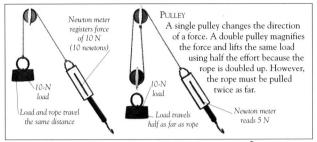

PULLEY
A single pulley changes the direction of a force. A double pulley magnifies the force and lifts the same load using half the effort because the rope is doubled up. However, the rope must be pulled twice as far.

Newton meter registers force of 10 N (10 newtons)

10-N load

Load and rope travel the same distance

10-N load

Load travels half as far as rope

Newton meter reads 5 N

SIMPLE LEVER

A lever is a bar that exerts a force by turning on a pivot, or "fulcrum." A small effort moved through a greater distance at one end moves a larger load through a shorter distance at the other end.

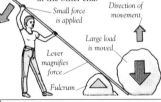

Small force is applied

Direction of movement

Large load is moved

Lever magnifies force

Fulcrum

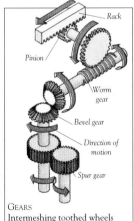

Rack

Pinion

Worm gear

Bevel gear

Direction of motion

Spur gear

MACHINE EQUATIONS

A machine's force ratio shows how effective the machine is as a force magnifier. The velocity ratio shows how effective the machine is as a distance magnifier.

Force ratio = $\dfrac{\text{load}}{\text{effort}}$

Velocity ratio = $\dfrac{\text{distance moved by effort}}{\text{distance moved by load}}$

GEARS

Intermeshing toothed wheels and bars that transmit force and motion are called gears. They can alter the force's size, and the motion's speed and direction.

ENERGY

EVERYTHING WE DO is fueled by energy. Our energy comes from food, which contains chemical energy stored in chemical compounds. Light, sound, heat, and electricity are forms of energy. Movement energy is called kinetic energy.

If the kitten falls, it will have kinetic energy

Jack has kinetic energy as he springs up

POTENTIAL ENERGY
An object gains potential energy if it is squeezed or stretched; the energy is stored until the object is released. The coiled spring of a jack-in-the-box has potential energy. When the box is opened and the jack leaps out, the energy becomes kinetic energy.

GRAVITATIONAL POTENTIAL
A raised object has gravitational potential energy – the potential to fall back to Earth. If the kitten loses its grip, this energy converts to kinetic energy as the kitten tumbles to the ground.

ENERGY FACTS
• There are about a quadrillion joules of heat and potential energy in a thunderstorm.

• A teenage girl needs about 10,000 kilojoules of energy each day.

CHEMICAL ENERGY
When we digest food, chemical compounds in the food are broken down and energy is released for our bodies to use. Different foods contain different amounts of energy. This chocolate has as much energy as all these tomatoes.

0.8 oz (24 g) of milk chocolate

2.2 lb (1 kg) of tomatoes

ENERGY USE	
ACTIVITY BY 154-LB PERSON	ENERGY USED IN JOULES PER SECOND (J/s)
Sleeping	60
Sitting reading	120
Playing the piano	160
Walking slowly	250
Running or swimming	800
Walking up stairs	800

SI UNITS

The **joule** (J) is the SI unit of energy and work: 1 joule of energy is needed to move a force of 1 newton through a distance of 1 meter. A kilojoule (kJ) is 1,000 J.

The **hertz** (Hz) is the SI unit of wave frequency: 1 hertz is one complete wave, or vibration, per second. A kilohertz (kHz) is 1,000 Hz.

WAVE ENERGY

TYPES OF WAVES

Energy often travels as moving vibrations called waves. Light and other forms of electromagnetic radiation travel as transverse waves: the vibration is at right angles to the wave's direction. Sound waves travel as longitudinal waves: the vibration is in the same direction as the wave.

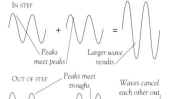

TRANSVERSE WAVE — Direction of motion ⟶ — Amplitude

Peak — Wavelength — Trough

LONGITUDINAL WAVE — Wavelength

Direction of motion ⟶

IN STEP

Peaks meet peaks + = Larger wave results

OUT OF STEP — Peaks meet troughs

Waves cancel each other out

+ =

INTERFERENCE

When waves overlap, they "interfere" with each other. Where two waves are in step, their peaks coincide and combine to form a bigger wave (constructive interference). Where two waves are out of step, the troughs of one cancel the peaks of the other, and there is no resulting wave (destructive interference).

Work, power, efficiency

Work is done when a force moves something.
Work cannot be done without energy. Energy
provides the ability to do work. When work is
done, energy converts from one form to another.
The rate at which work is done, or energy changed
from one form to another, is called power.

Bar carries two sets of 50-N weights

Weights are raised about 4.9 ft (1.5 m)

Total weight is 100 N

WEIGHTLIFTER RAISING WEIGHTS

Raised weights have gravitational potential energy

Weightlifter raises weights in two seconds

WORK AND POWER
When this man raises
a heavy weight, the power of
lifting the weight is calculated
by multiplying the weight by
the height to which it is raised,
and dividing the result by the
time taken to lift it. So if he lifts
100 newtons by 1.5 meters in
two seconds, the power is 75 W.

SI UNITS

The **watt** (W) is the SI
unit of power: 1 W is
the conversion of
1 joule of energy from
one form to another in
1 second. A kilowatt
(kW) is 1,000 watts,
and a megawatt (MW)
is 1,000,000 W.

The **kilowatt-hour**
(kWh) measures
electrical energy use:
1 kWh is energy used
when a 1-kW appliance
runs for 1 hour.

WORK FACTS

• The efficiency of
a 100-watt light bulb
is 15%, because 85
joules in every 100
are lost as heat.

• The first internal
combustion engine was
built by Étienne Lenoir,
a Belgian engineer.

ENERGY CONVERSION

Engines are "energy converters": they are machines that change energy from one form to another to do work. A car is powered by an internal combustion engine, which burns gasoline or diesel fuel. The chemical energy in the fuel is converted to the kinetic energy of moving pistons, which make the car move.

Fuel-air mixture sucked in

Explosion forces piston down

Chemical energy in fuel changes to kinetic energy of moving piston

INTERNAL COMBUSTION ENGINE

Piston rises, expelling waste gases, and process starts again

EFFICIENCY

Efficiency tells you how good a machine is as an energy converter. It compares the energy you put into a machine to the energy you get out of it.

MACHINE		ENERGY OUTPUT (% OF INPUT)
Car gasoline engine		15%
Rocket		about 15%
Steam train		15%
Jet engine		20%
Diesel train		35%
Electric train		35%
Coal-fired power station		35%
Wind farm		about 40%
Magnetic levitation train		about 60%
Hydroelectric plant		80%
Bicycle		90%

LAW OF CONSERVATION OF ENERGY

Energy can neither be created nor destroyed. The Law of Conservation of Energy states that energy can be converted into different forms, but the total amount of energy always stays the same. This law applies even to nuclear reactions, such as those that occur at the core of the Sun.

ENERGY EQUATIONS

Work (joules) = force (newtons) x distance moved (meters)

Power (watts) = $\dfrac{\text{work done (joules)}}{\text{time taken (seconds)}}$

Efficiency (%) = $\dfrac{\text{energy (or power) in}}{\text{energy (or power) out}}$ x 100

HEAT AND TEMPERATURE

THE MORE ENERGY an object's particles have, the hotter the object is. Heating an object increases the energy of its particles. Temperature is a measure of the average amount of heat energy possessed by the particles.

Height of liquid shows temperature

Liquid-crystal display

Heat-sensitive resistor in tip

Meter records temperature of filament

THERMOMETERS

Everyday thermometers measure temperature on the Fahrenheit and Celsius scales. Liquid thermometers use a column of mercury or alcohol that expands as the temperature rises. An electronic thermometer measures temperature with a tiny, heat-sensitive resistor.

PYROMETER

A pyrometer measures high temperatures. When pointed at a hot, glowing object, an electric current heats a filament until the color matches that of the object. Measuring the electric current reveals the temperature.

Light from glowing object

Electric filament is heated until its color matches light from hot object

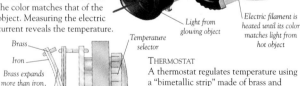

Brass

Iron

Brass expands more than iron, making strip bend and break contact

Flow of electric current

Temperature selector

THERMOSTAT

A thermostat regulates temperature using a "bimetallic strip" made of brass and iron. The metals expand at different rates, so the strip bends as it heats up. At the required temperature, the strip breaks an electrical contact and turns off a heater.

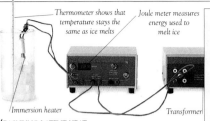

Thermometer shows that temperature stays the same as ice melts

Joule meter measures energy used to melt ice

Immersion heater

Transformer

MEASURING LATENT HEAT

This experiment measures the heat needed to melt ice. As a substance changes state, for example, from solid to liquid, it takes in or gives off heat without changing its temperature. This hidden heat is called "latent" heat.

RANGE OF TEMPERATURES	
TEMPERATURE	EXAMPLE
14 million K (25 million°F; 14 million°C)	Sun's core
30,000 K (53,540°F; 29,727°C)	Lightning bolts
5,800 K (9,980°F; 5,527°C)	Surface of the Sun
4,000 K (6,740°F; 3,727°C)	Core of Earth
523 K (482°F; 250°C)	Burning point of wood
373 K (212°F; 100°C)	Boiling point of water
331 K (136°F; 58°C)	Highest recorded air temperature on Earth
310 K (98.3°F; 37°C)	Normal human body temperature
273 K (32°F; 0°C)	Freezing point of water
184 K (−128°F; −89°C)	Lowest recorded air temperature on Earth
43 K (−382°F; −230°C)	Surface temperature of Pluto (most distant planet)
0 K (−459.67°F; −273.15°C)	Absolute zero

SI UNITS

The **kelvin (K)** is the SI unit of temperature. There are no minus values on the kelvin scale. This is because 0 K is "absolute zero" – the lowest possible temperature, at which the motion of all particles would cease. Absolute zero has never been attained.

SPECIFIC HEAT CAPACITIES

Specific heat capacity (symbol c) is the amount of heat energy needed to raise the temperature of 1 kilogram of a substance by 1 kelvin (or 1°C).

SUBSTANCE	SPECIFIC HEAT CAPACITY (J/KG/K)
Water	4,200
Alcohol	2,400
Ice	2,100
Nylon	1,700
Marble	880
Concrete	800
Glass	630
Steel	450
Copper	380
Lead	130

Heat transfer

Heat energy always passes from hot objects or materials to cooler ones. Heat travels by conduction through solids and fluids, and by convection through fluids only. Radiation is heat energy traveling as infrared rays of electromagnetic radiation.

Swirling color trails show how heat spreads through liquid

Hot, colored water floats to the top of the jar

Bottle contains hot, colored water

CONVECTION IN WATER

The hot, colored water is less dense than the cold water surrounding it. The hot water floats to the surface and loses heat to the air. As it cools it sinks once more. This circulation, or "convection current," spreads heat through the liquid.

Thermometer reads 18.7°C

Metal block at room temperature

MEASURING HEAT RADIATION

At room temperature, all objects emit infrared radiation: hotter objects emit more radiation than cooler ones. The lamp in the picture emits a lot of radiation, which travels through the air and heats the metal block below.

Radiation from lamp absorbed by particles in metal block

Desk lamp

Thermometer reads 31°C

Heat from feet conducts into stone, leaving feet feeling cold

CONDUCTION

When one part of a substance is heated, its particles vibrate faster. They "conduct" (pass on their heat energy) as they knock against neighboring particles.

CELSIUS & FAHRENHEIT

Temperatures are usually given in degrees Celsius (°C) or Fahrenheit (°F). The Celsius scale is based on the freezing point of water (32°F/0°C) and the boiling point of water (212°F/100°C). The kelvin scale is used in scientific work.

THERMAL CONDUCTIVITY

This constant tells you the rate at which a temperature difference makes heat flow through a standard sample of a material.

SUBSTANCE	CONDUCTIVITY (W/m·K)	
Copper	385	Good conductor
Gold	296	
Iron	72	
Glass	1	
Brick	0.6	
Water	0.6	
Nylon	0.25	
Wood (oak)	0.15	
Concrete	0.1	
Wool	0.040	Bad conductor
Air	0.025	

INSULATORS

Materials that are poor conductors of heat are called insulators. They include plastics, wood, cork, fiberglass, and air. Architects and builders use insulators in houses and offices to reduce the loss of heat through walls, roofs, ceilings, windows, and floors. A good insulating material is said to have a very low "U–value."

Cavity wall filled with insulating foam

Fiberglass insulation between ceiling beams

Air trapped between panes of a double-glazed window

Thick carpet on floor

U–VALUES (FOR HEAT CONDUCTION)

U–value (W/m²·K) is a measure of the rate of heat flow in watts (W) per square meter (m²) of a material produced by a temperature difference of 1 K (or 1°C).

MATERIAL	U–VALUE (W/M²/K)
Roof with no insulation	2.2
Insulated roof	0.3
Single brick wall	3.6
Double brick wall, air cavity between	1.7
Double brick wall filled with foam	0.5
Single-glazed window	5.6
Double-glazed window with air gap	2.7
Floor without carpets	1
Floor with carpets	0.3

ENERGY SOURCES

MOST OF THE WORLD'S electricity is generated by burning fossil fuels. But there are limited supplies of these fuels and they are only replaced over many millions of years. In the future, we will have to rely on renewable sources, such as wind and solar power, and hydroelectricity.

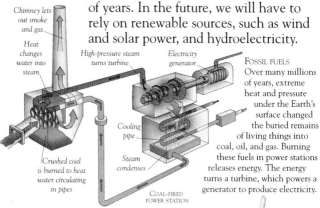

Chimney lets out smoke and gas

Heat changes water into steam

High-pressure steam turns turbine

Electricity generator

Cooling pipe

Steam condenses

Crushed coal is burned to heat water circulating in pipes

COAL-FIRED POWER STATION

FOSSIL FUELS
Over many millions of years, extreme heat and pressure under the Earth's surface changed the buried remains of living things into coal, oil, and gas. Burning these fuels in power stations releases energy. The energy turns a turbine, which powers a generator to produce electricity.

ENERGY SOURCE FACTS

• Hydroelectricity supplies about 3% of the world's energy needs.

• One gram of coal contains about 25 kJ of energy, and one gram of oil about 45 kJ.

• Most people in the world still use firewood.

WIND POWER
A wind turbine is a tall tower with large rotating blades that harness the wind's kinetic energy to produce electricity. A "wind farm" is a large group of wind turbines.

Blades can be up to 65 ft (20 m) long

As the blades turn in the wind, they power an electricity generator

Lightning conductor

Tower

HYDROELECTRIC POWER

Hydroelectricity is an efficient, pollution-free energy source. A hydroelectric power station is situated below a dam at the head of a reservoir. Water rushing down from above turns the power station's turbines at great speed. The turbines are connected to generators that produce electricity.

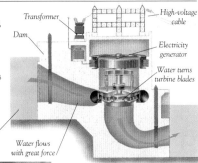

Transformer

High-voltage cable

Dam

Electricity generator

Water turns turbine blades

Water builds up behind dam at end of reservoir

Water flows with great force

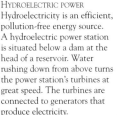

SOLAR POWER

Solar cells transform the energy of sunlight into electricity. To generate useful amounts of electricity, solar power stations use hundreds of large panels, each packed with solar cells. Controlled by computers, the panels can track the Sun across the sky.

ENERGY SOURCES THROUGH TIME

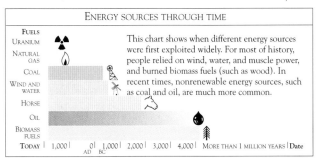

This chart shows when different energy sources were first exploited widely. For most of history, people relied on wind, water, and muscle power, and burned biomass fuels (such as wood). In recent times, nonrenewable energy sources, such as coal and oil, are much more common.

FUELS							
URANIUM							
NATURAL GAS							
COAL							
WIND AND WATER							
HORSE							
OIL							
BIOMASS FUELS							
TODAY	1,000	0 AD / 1,000 BC	2,000	3,000	4,000	MORE THAN 1 MILLION YEARS	Date

Nuclear energy

Atoms are tiny storehouses of energy. This energy comes from strong forces that hold the particles in the center, or nucleus, of an atom. Tremendous "nuclear" energy can be released when the nucleus of an atom splits (fissions), or when two nuclei fuse together (fusion). Nuclear reactors harness this energy to produce electricity.

INTERNATIONAL WARNING SYMBOL FOR RADIOACTIVITY

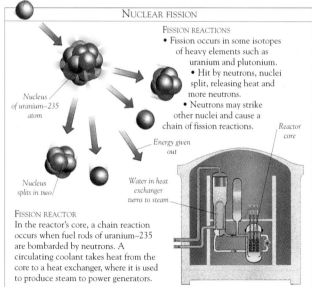

Neutron

NUCLEAR FISSION

FISSION REACTIONS
• Fission occurs in some isotopes of heavy elements such as uranium and plutonium.
• Hit by neutrons, nuclei split, releasing heat and more neutrons.
• Neutrons may strike other nuclei and cause a chain of fission reactions.

Nucleus of uranium–235 atom

Nucleus splits in two

Energy given out

Water in heat exchanger turns to steam

Reactor core

FISSION REACTOR
In the reactor's core, a chain reaction occurs when fuel rods of uranium–235 are bombarded by neutrons. A circulating coolant takes heat from the core to a heat exchanger, where it is used to produce steam to power generators.

NUCLEAR FUSION

FUSION REACTIONS

• Fusion occurs only with isotopes of light elements such as hydrogen.

• At high temperatures, fast-moving hydrogen nuclei smash into each other.

• A helium nucleus forms, and heat and neutrons are released.

Hydrogen nucleus with one neutron (deuterium)

Hydrogen nucleus with two neutrons (tritium)

Helium nucleus forms

Nuclei collide and fuse together

Powerful electromagnets

Energy given out

Neutron expelled

FUSION REACTOR

A practical fusion reactor has not yet been built. Experimental "tokamak" reactors contain a circular tube or "torus." Fusion occurs in the tube when hydrogen plasma is heated to very high temperatures. Powerful electromagnets confine the plasma.

Plasma circulates in the torus

NUCLEAR WEAPONS

The violent power of nuclear weapons comes from a fission or fusion reaction. The nuclear reaction in the bomb changes a tiny amount of mass into a vast amount of destructive energy.

Mushroom-shaped cloud of smoke and flames

NUCLEAR FACTS

• The first nuclear reactor was built by the physicist Enrico Fermi in the US in 1942.

• Nuclear fusion occurs in the heart of the Sun and other stars.

• The US has the most nuclear reactors (109) in the world.

ELECTROMAGNETIC RADIATION

LIGHT IS ONE of several types of wave energy called electromagnetic radiation. This radiation also includes radio waves, microwaves, infrared rays, ultraviolet rays, X-rays, and gamma rays. Together, they form the electromagnetic spectrum.

ELECTROMAGNETIC RADIATION AS WAVES AND PARTICLES

WAVES
Electromagnetic radiation travels as waves of oscillating (fluctuating) electric and magnetic fields. These are at right angles to each other and to the direction of travel.

PARTICLES
Electromagnetic radiation also travels as a stream of particles called photons – tiny "energy packets" given off when charged particles lose energy.

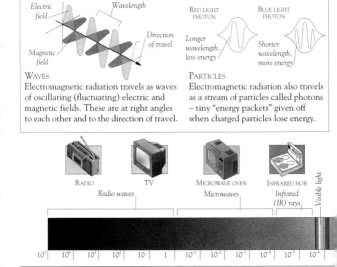

10^5 10^4 10^3 10^2 10 1 10^{-1} 10^{-2} 10^{-3} 10^{-4} 10^{-5} 10^{-6}

TABLE OF USEFUL X-RAYS	
WAVELENGTH (M) OF X-RAYS	USES AND APPLICATIONS
3×10^{-13}	Killing deep cancer tumors
3×10^{-12}	Inspecting welded joints in steel pipes
1.8×10^{-11}	Diagnostic chest X-rays
6×10^{-9}	Treatment of skin diseases

COMMON PROPERTIES OF ELECTROMAGNETIC WAVES

All types of electromagnetic radiation:

• Transfer energy from place to place

• Can be emitted and absorbed by matter

• Do not need a material medium to travel through

• Travel at 3×10^8 m/s in a vacuum

• Are transverse waves

• Can be polarized

• Can produce interference effects

• Can be reflected and refracted

• Can be diffracted

• Carry no electric charge.

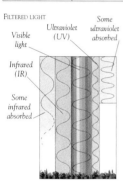

FILTERED LIGHT

Visible light

Ultraviolet (UV)

Some ultraviolet absorbed

Infrared (IR)

Some infrared absorbed

FILTERED LIGHT
Electromagnetic radiation reaches us from the Sun, stars, and galaxies. The Earth's atmosphere absorbs most types of electromagnetic radiation, but allows radio waves and light to pass through. Some wavelengths of IR and UV are filtered out before reaching the ground.

UV SUNBED
Ultraviolet (UV) rays

X-RAY MACHINE
X-rays

NUCLEAR EXPLOSION
Gamma rays

ELECTROMAGNETIC SPECTRUM

Waves at this end of the spectrum have more energy

WAVELENGTH (IN METERS)

| 10^{-8} | 10^{-9} | 10^{-10} | 10^{-11} | 10^{-12} | 10^{-13} | 10^{-14} | 10^{-15} | 10^{-16} | 10^{-17} |

LIGHT SOURCES

LIGHT IS A FORM of energy. It is produced
by two processes – incandescence
and luminescence. Incandescence
is the emission of light by hot
objects. Luminescence is
the emission of light
without using heat.

*Electron gives out photon as
it falls back to its original orbit*

LIGHT FROM THE SUN
Most of the light that reaches
us from space comes from the
Sun. Light is produced in the
Sun by incandescence. The light
travels through space at 186,000 miles per
second (300,000 km per second).

PHOTONS
If an atom gains energy, electrons
orbiting the nucleus jump to higher
orbits, or "energy levels." When the
electrons return to their original
orbits, they release photons of light,
or other electromagnetic radiation.

LUMINESCENCE	
TYPE	EXAMPLE
Triboluminescence Light released by friction	When some crystals, such as sugar, are suddenly crushed, the friction makes them briefly emit light.
Bioluminescence The emission of light without heat by living organisms	Creatures such as fireflies have chemicals in their bodies that combine to release light energy.
Phosphorescence The gradual emission of stored energy as light	Glow-in-the-dark paints absorb light energy and release it slowly. The light energy is especially noticeable in the dark.
Fluorescence The rapid reemission of light energy	Fluorescent dyes often contain fluorescent chemicals that briefly absorb ultraviolet light and then emit it as visible light.

Glowing filament

Unreactive gas

Bulb screws into electrical socket

INCANDESCENCE

An incandescent bulb contains a thin filament of tungsten wire. An electric current heats the filament so that it glows white and gives off light. The bulb is filled with an unreactive gas such as argon to stop the filament from burning, as it would do in air.

Beam leaves through partly silvered mirror

Light reflects up and down tube

Power supply

Photons of light

LASER LIGHT

A laser produces an intense beam of light of a single frequency. Light from a coiled tube "excites" atoms in a central tube of "lasing medium." The light that these "excited" atoms produce reflects between the tube's mirrored ends and escapes as a laser beam.

SI UNITS

• The **candela** (cd) is the SI unit of brightness (luminous intensity). A light source of 1 candela is approximately equal to the brightness of a burning candle.

• The **lux** (lx) is the SI unit of illumination. A 1-candela light source gives an illumination of 1 lux to a surface of 1 m² (10.8 sq ft) at a distance of 1 m (3.28 ft).

DISCHARGE TUBE

A discharge tube is a gas-filled tube fitted with two electrodes. When a powerful electric current flows between the electrodes, the vapor gives out, or "discharges," light. Most street lamps use sodium vapor discharge tubes.

Sodium vapor in discharge tube glows with yellow-orange light

Electrode

SODIUM VAPOR LAMP

LIGHT AND MATTER

A MATERIAL appears shiny, dull, or clear depending on whether it reflects, absorbs, or transmits light rays. Light may bend as it passes through materials, creating optical illusions such as mirages.

Transparent (clear)

Translucent (milky)

Opaque (dull)

Reflective (shiny)

LIGHT PASSING THROUGH MATTER
Light passes through transparent materials. Opaque materials block light. Translucent materials let light through, but scatter it. Light rays bounce off the surface of reflective materials.

REFRACTIVE INDEX

When a light ray passes through a material, its speed changes. If it enters the material at an angle, the difference in speed "refracts," or bends, the light ray. The refractive index shows how much a material refracts light:

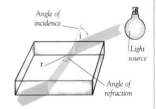

Angle of incidence

Light source

Angle of refraction

Refractive index = $\dfrac{\text{Speed of light in vacuum}}{\text{Speed of light in material}}$

MATERIAL	REFRACTIVE INDEX	SPEED OF LIGHT (ML/S)
Air	1.00	186,000 (300,000 km)
Water	1.33	140,000 (225,000 km)
Plexiglass	1.40	130,000 (210,000 km)
Glass (variable)	1.60	115,000 (185,000 km)
Diamond	2.40	78,000 (125,000 km)

The refractive index can also be calculated from the angles in the diagram, using an equation known as Snell's Law:

Refractive index = $\dfrac{\text{Sin i}}{\text{Sin r}}$

INTERNAL REFLECTION OF LIGHT

If light traveling through a material strikes a surface at a shallow angle, it reflects internally rather than refracts, and stays inside the material. The angle between the ray and a line at 90° to surface at which internal reflection occurs is called the critical angle.

INTERNAL REFLECTION	
SUBSTANCE	CRITICAL ANGLE
Water	49°
Glass	42°
Diamond	24°

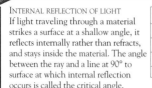

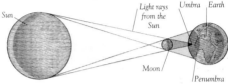

Light rays from the Sun

Sun

Umbra *Earth*

Moon

Penumbra

Ray hits surface at shallow angle

Ray reflects and stays inside material

SOLAR ECLIPSE

During a solar eclipse, the Moon, because it is opaque, casts a shadow over Earth. No rays reach the shadow's center (umbra); some rays reach its outer area (penumbra).

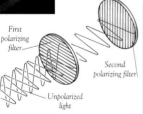

First polarizing filter

Second polarizing filter

Unpolarized light

POLARIZED LIGHT

Light rays vibrate in many different planes. A polarizing filter only allows light vibrating in one plane to pass. A second filter can be used to block out the remaining light. Sunglasses may use polarizing filters to cut out glare.

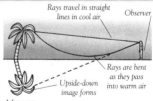

Rays travel in straight lines in cool air

Observer

Rays are bent as they pass into warm air

Upside-down image forms

MIRAGE

Light is refracted as it passes through layers of air at different temperatures. Light rays traveling from the palm tree to the ground are bent upward by the warm air so that it seems to an observer that the tree has a watery reflection.

LENSES AND MIRRORS

LENSES ARE CURVED transparent materials that make light rays converge (come together) or diverge (spread out). Mirrors are shiny materials that reflect light. Curved mirrors can also make light rays converge or diverge.

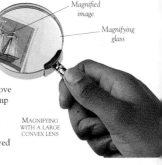

Magnified image

Magnifying glass

MAKING LARGER

This stamp looks much bigger when an outwardly curving convex lens is held above it. The lens bends light rays from the stamp inward before they reach your eyes. Your brain assumes that the rays have traveled in a straight line, as if they were coming from a much larger stamp. The more curved a lens, the more it magnifies an object.

MAGNIFYING WITH A LARGE CONVEX LENS

MAKING SMALLER

An inwardly curving concave lens gives a reduced image of the squares. It makes light rays from the squares spread, but your brain assumes they have traveled in a straight line, as if they were coming from much smaller squares.

CONVEX AND CONCAVE LENSES

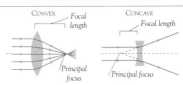

CONVEX — Focal length

CONCAVE — Focal length

Principal focus

Principal focus

A convex lens converges parallel light rays at the principal focus. The distance from here to the center of the lens is the focal length. A concave lens spreads out light rays so that they appear to come from a principal focus behind the lens. The focal length is the distance from here to the lens's center.

VIRTUAL IMAGE

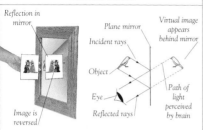

Reflection in mirror

Plane mirror

Incident rays

Virtual image appears behind mirror

Object

Eye

Path of light perceived by brain

Reflected rays

Image is reversed

When you see an object in a mirror, light rays from the object reflect from the mirror's surface into your eyes. Your brain assumes that the rays have reached your eyes by traveling in a straight line, so you see a "virtual" image that appears to be behind the mirror.

LAW OF REFLECTION

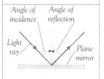

Angle of incidence

Angle of reflection

Light ray

Plane mirror

According to the Law of Reflection, the angle at which a light ray is reflected from a surface (the angle of reflection) is equal to the angle at which the light ray strikes the surface (the angle of incidence).

REAL IMAGES
Convex lenses and concave mirrors can focus light to form an inverted "real" image on a surface. In a movie projector, light shines through an inverted film. This is so that the image projected onto the screen appears the right way up.

CONVEX AND CONCAVE MIRRORS

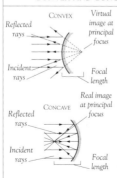

CONVEX

Reflected rays

Virtual image at principal focus

Incident rays

Focal length

CONCAVE

Reflected rays

Real image at principal focus

Incident rays

Focal length

When parallel light rays strike an outwardly curving convex mirror, they spread out as they are reflected. The rays appear to the brain to come from a principal focus behind the mirror. Parallel rays striking an inwardly curving concave mirror will reflect so that they converge at a principal focus in front of the mirror.

VISIBLE SPECTRUM

LIGHT IS WAVES of electromagnetic radiation. "White light" is a mixture of many different colors of light, each with its own frequency and wavelength. These colors make up the visible spectrum. Our eyes and brains detect colors by recognizing the different wavelengths of visible light.

SPLITTING LIGHT

A beam of white light is refracted (bent) as it enters and leaves a prism. The prism refracts different wavelengths of light by different amounts, splitting the beam of white light into the visible spectrum.

LIGHT, COLOR, AND HEAT

The atoms of a hot object give out infrared radiation and some red light. As the object gets hotter, its atoms give out shorter and shorter wavelengths and it appears orange and then yellow. Very hot objects give out the whole spectrum, and appear white.

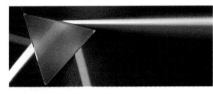

Atoms emit light at red end of spectrum

Hotter atoms emit orange light

Heated further, atoms emit yellow light

The hottest atoms now emit white light

DIFFRACTION COLORS

All forms of wave energy "diffract," or spread out, when they pass through gaps or around objects. A diffraction grating is a glass slide engraved with narrow slits. Light rays diffract as they pass through the slits, and interference between the bent rays produces streaks of different colors.

SKY COLOR

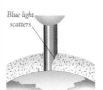

Blue light scatters

Sunlight passes through atmosphere

BLUE SKIES

The Sun gives off white light, which is scattered by air molecules as it enters the Earth's atmosphere. Blue light is scattered more than other colors, making the sky appear blue.

RED SKIES

When the setting Sun is low in the sky, light from the blue end of the spectrum is scattered. The Sun appears orange-red because colors from this end of the spectrum pass through to our eyes but blue colors are lost.

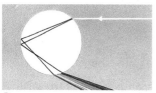

PRIMARY RAINBOW

A rainbow is visible during rain, when the Sun is shining behind you. As rays of sunlight pass through raindrops in the sky, the raindrops act like tiny prisms. The white light is split into a spectrum inside the raindrops and reflected back as an arc of colors.

COLOR WAVELENGTHS AND FREQUENCIES

The wavelengths and frequencies of the different colors vary according to the energy they carry. For example, red light has less energy than violet light.

COLOR	WAVELENGTH (M)	FREQUENCY (Hz)
Violet	$3.9–4.5 \times 10^{-7}$	$6.7–7.7 \times 10^{14}$
Blue	$4.5–4.9 \times 10^{-7}$	$6.1–6.7 \times 10^{14}$
Green	$4.9–5.8 \times 10^{-7}$	$5.3–6.1 \times 10^{14}$
Yellow	$5.8–6.0 \times 10^{-7}$	$5.1–5.3 \times 10^{14}$
Orange	$6.0–6.2 \times 10^{-7}$	$4.8–5.1 \times 10^{14}$
Red	$6.2–7.7 \times 10^{-7}$	$3.9–4.8 \times 10^{14}$

Mixing color

Paints, dyes, inks, and colored objects get their particular colors because they absorb some light wavelengths but reflect others. This is called the subtractive process. In the additive process, colors are created by mixing different-colored light. Each process has three pure "primary" colors, which cannot be produced by mixing other colors.

RED LIGHT

Red and blue give magenta

Red, blue, and green give white

THE ADDITIVE PROCESS
Red, green, and blue are the primary additive colors. Mixing the three together gives white light. When two primary colors are mixed, the eye sees a mixture of colors that the brain interprets as a single color, called a secondary color. In the additive process, the secondary colors are yellow, cyan, and magenta.

GREEN LIGHT

BLUE LIGHT

Red and green give yellow

Blue and green give cyan

In white light, shoes reflect only red light and absorb all the other colors

In blue light, red pigment absorbs blue light and shoes look nearly black

WHITE LIGHT

BLUE LIGHT

COLOR FILTERS
A color filter will absorb some colors but let others pass through. Placing a blue filter over a spotlight gives blue light. The filter absorbs the green and red parts of the spectrum, and allows only blue light to pass. These shoes look very different in blue light.

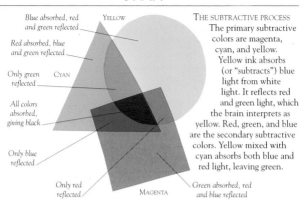

Blue absorbed, red and green reflected

YELLOW

Red absorbed, blue and green reflected

Only green reflected — CYAN

All colors absorbed, giving black

Only blue reflected

Only red reflected

MAGENTA

Green absorbed, red and blue reflected

THE SUBTRACTIVE PROCESS

The primary subtractive colors are magenta, cyan, and yellow. Yellow ink absorbs (or "subtracts") blue light from white light. It reflects red and green light, which the brain interprets as yellow. Red, green, and blue are the secondary subtractive colors. Yellow mixed with cyan absorbs both blue and red light, leaving green.

FOUR-COLOR PRINTING

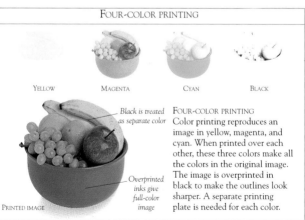

YELLOW

MAGENTA

CYAN

BLACK

Black is treated as separate color

Overprinted inks give full-color image

PRINTED IMAGE

FOUR-COLOR PRINTING
Color printing reproduces an image in yellow, magenta, and cyan. When printed over each other, these three colors make all the colors in the original image. The image is overprinted in black to make the outlines look sharper. A separate printing plate is needed for each color.

OPTICAL INSTRUMENTS

TELESCOPES BRING distant stars into view, while microscopes enable us to examine minute objects in great detail. Optical instruments use lenses and mirrors to reveal a world that would be impossible to see with the naked eye alone.

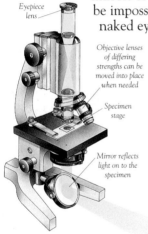

Eyepiece lens

Objective lenses of differing strengths can be moved into place when needed

Specimen stage

Mirror reflects light on to the specimen

COMPOUND MICROSCOPE
A compound microscope has more than one lens. First, it magnifies an object with a powerful "objective" lens. Then, the magnified image is enlarged by the eyepiece lens, which acts as a simple magnifying glass. The microscope may be fitted with extra lenses to give greater clarity.

TYPES OF TELESCOPE

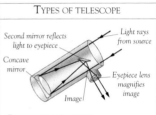

Second mirror reflects light to eyepiece

Concave mirror

Light rays from source

Eyepiece lens magnifies image

Image

REFLECTING TELESCOPES
A reflecting telescope forms an image using a large concave mirror that gathers and concentrates light rays.

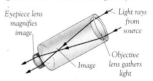

Eyepiece lens magnifies image

Light rays from source

Objective lens gathers light

Image

REFRACTING TELESCOPES
A refracting telescope uses a convex lens to refract light and form an upside-down image of a distant object.

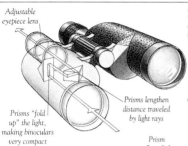

Adjustable
eyepiece lens

Prisms "fold
up" the light,
making binoculars
very compact

Prisms lengthen
distance traveled
by light rays

BINOCULARS

A pair of binoculars consists of
two compact refracting telescopes
joined together. Each telescope
contains two prisms. The prisms
reflect light rays focused by the
objective lenses, forming images
that are viewed through the
eyepiece lenses.

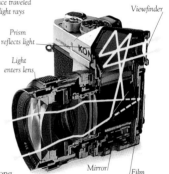

Viewfinder

Prism
reflects light

Light
enters lens

Mirror

Film

SLR CAMERA

In an SLR (single-lens reflex)
camera, light enters the camera
through the main lens. A mirror
reflects the light up through a prism
and out of the viewfinder. Pressing
the shutter release button raises the
mirror, so that light strikes the film
at the back of the camera.

ENDOSCOPE

Doctors look inside the body using a long
tube called an endoscope. One end of the
tube is fed into the body. Optical fibers in the
tube carry light to and from the area being
examined, which is seen with an eyepiece lens.

Doctor sees
image in
eyepiece lens

Light is internally reflected
in the optical fibers

Light enters body
through optical fibers

MAGNIFICATION

A telescope with a
magnification of 100x forms
an image that is 100 times
larger than the object appears
without the telescope.
Magnification equals the
focal length of the objective
lens divided by the focal
length of the eyepiece.

SOUND WAVES

SOUND WAVES ARE the vibrations that occur in a
material as a sound passes through it. When we listen
to someone speak, our ears detect sound waves in the
air around us caused by the person's vibrating vocal
chords. Sound waves can travel through solids, liquids,
and gases, but not through a vacuum, because there
are no particles of matter to transmit the vibrations.

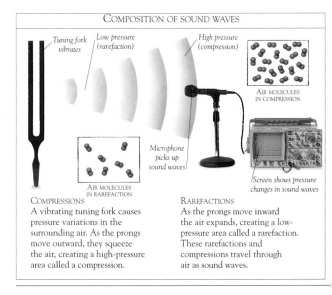

COMPOSITION OF SOUND WAVES

Tuning fork vibrates

Low pressure (rarefaction)

High pressure (compression)

AIR MOLECULES
IN COMPRESSION

Microphone picks up sound waves

AIR MOLECULES
IN RAREFACTION

Screen shows pressure changes in sound waves

COMPRESSIONS
A vibrating tuning fork causes
pressure variations in the
surrounding air. As the prongs
move outward, they squeeze
the air, creating a high-pressure
area called a compression.

RAREFACTIONS
As the prongs move inward
the air expands, creating a low-
pressure area called a rarefaction.
These rarefactions and
compressions travel through
air as sound waves.

Echoes bounce back from wall

Clapping sets off sound waves

HOW SONAR WORKS

A ship's sonar system emits ultrasound waves, which have a frequency above 20,000 Hz. The sound waves bounce off underwater objects. The time between sending the wave and receiving its echo reveals the depth of the object.

Ultrasound pulse reflected by wreck

MAKING ECHOES

Sounds bounce off hard surfaces and return to their source as echoes. Most sounds we hear are a combination of the original sound and echoes bouncing off nearby objects.

THE SPEED OF SOUND		
Sound travels at different speeds through different materials. Sound also travels faster at higher temperatures. Unless stated, all figures are for substances at 68°F (20°C).		
SUBSTANCE	SPEED FT/SEC	SPEED M/SEC
Rubber	177	54
Carbon dioxide	853	260
Air at 32°F (0°C)	1,086	331
Air at 68°F (20°C)	1,125	343
Air at 212°F (100°C)	1,280	390
Cork	1,640	500
Water at 32°F (0°C)	4,213	1,284
Hydrogen	4,219	1,286
Water at 68°F (20°C)	4,865	1,483
Wood (oak)	12,631	3,850
Steel	16,601	5,060

Sound waves pile up when a jet travels at speed of sound

Shock wave released as jet breaks sound barrier

SONIC BOOM

When an aircraft breaks the sound barrier, sound waves build up in front of the aircraft. The sound forms as a massive shock wave. It is heard on the ground as a "sonic boom."

Measuring sound

The loudness of a sound depends on changes in pressure. The greater the pressure changes between the highest and lowest points of the sound wave, the louder the sound. The loudness of a sound is measured in decibels. The pitch of a sound describes how high or low a sound is. It depends on the frequency (vibrations per second) of the sound waves. The frequency of waves, including sound, light, and radio waves, is measured in hertz (Hz).

WAVEFORMS

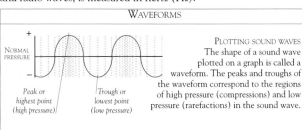

NORMAL PRESSURE

Peak or highest point (high pressure)

Trough or lowest point (low pressure)

PLOTTING SOUND WAVES
The shape of a sound wave plotted on a graph is called a waveform. The peaks and troughs of the waveform correspond to the regions of high pressure (compressions) and low pressure (rarefactions) in the sound wave.

SOFT SOUNDS
The waveform produced by a quiet sound shows little difference between the low- and high-pressure regions.

LOUD SOUNDS
As a sound gets louder, the difference between the low- and the high-pressure regions becomes much greater.

LOW-PITCHED SOUNDS
The waveform of a low-pitched sound shows few waves per second, because it has a low frequency.

HIGH-PITCHED SOUNDS
As the pitch of a sound increases, its frequency rises and the waveform shows more waves per second.

EXAMPLES ON THE DECIBEL SCALE			
LOUDNESS IN DECIBELS (DB)	AMPLITUDE IN PASCALS (PA)	POWER (INTENSITY) IN WATTS PER SQUARE METER (W/M²)	SOUND
140	300	100	Permanent ear damage; rocket taking off 328 ft (100 m) away
120	30	1	Pain threshold; jet aircraft taking off 328 ft (100 m) away
100	3	10^{-2}	Rock concert
80	0.3	10^{-4}	Door slamming in room; busy traffic in street
60	0.03	10^{-6}	Normal conversation
30	0.0009	10^{-9}	People whispering 3.28 ft (1 m) away
10	0.00009	10^{-11}	Falling leaves 3.28 ft (1 m) away
0	0.00002	10^{-12}	Threshold of human hearing; sound just audible

ANIMAL SOUNDS

Most animals hear more frequencies of sound than they can produce. Compared with many animals, the range of sounds produced by humans is very limited. Sound below the range of human hearing is called infrasound.

BAT MAKES 10,000–120,000 Hz
HEARS 1,000–120,000 Hz

DOG MAKES 450–1,080 Hz
HEARS 15–50,000 Hz

HUMAN MAKES 85–1,100 Hz
HEARS 20–20,000 Hz

GRASSHOPPER MAKES 7,000–100,000 Hz
HEARS 100–15,000 Hz

THE DECIBEL

Loudness is measured in decibels. The decibel scale is logarithmic, meaning that a sound increase of 10 dB multiplies the intensity by 10 times. So a 20-dB increase corresponds to a sound 10 x 10 = 100 times louder.

Sound quality

If you play the same note on a piano and a guitar, the notes have a different sound, because they have a different "tone," or quality. Tone depends on the way an instrument vibrates. "Pitch" is used to describe how high or low a sound is. The "acoustics" of a building refers to the way it preserves the quality of sounds made within it.

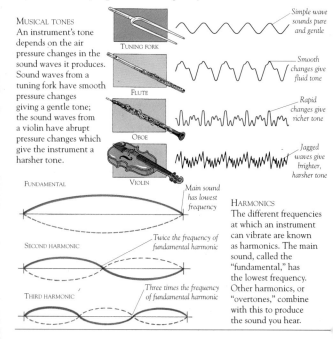

MUSICAL TONES
An instrument's tone depends on the air pressure changes in the sound waves it produces. Sound waves from a tuning fork have smooth pressure changes giving a gentle tone; the sound waves from a violin have abrupt pressure changes which give the instrument a harsher tone.

TUNING FORK

Simple wave sounds pure and gentle

FLUTE

Smooth changes give fluid tone

OBOE

Rapid changes give richer tone

VIOLIN

Jagged waves give brighter, harsher tone

FUNDAMENTAL

Main sound has lowest frequency

SECOND HARMONIC

Twice the frequency of fundamental harmonic

THIRD HARMONIC

Three times the frequency of fundamental harmonic

HARMONICS
The different frequencies at which an instrument can vibrate are known as harmonics. The main sound, called the "fundamental," has the lowest frequency. Other harmonics, or "overtones," combine with this to produce the sound you hear.

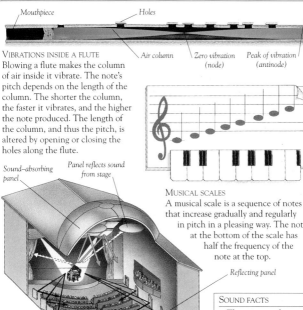

VIBRATIONS INSIDE A FLUTE
Blowing a flute makes the column
of air inside it vibrate. The note's
pitch depends on the length of the
column. The shorter the column,
the faster it vibrates, and the higher
the note produced. The length of
the column, and thus the pitch, is
altered by opening or closing
the holes along the flute.

MUSICAL SCALES
A musical scale is a sequence of notes
that increase gradually and regularly
in pitch in a pleasing way. The note
at the bottom of the scale has
half the frequency of the
note at the top.

ARCHITECTURAL ACOUSTICS
To preserve the quality of musical sounds, concert
halls are built so that the echoes of sound waves can
be controlled. The building materials absorb just the
right amount of sound, while special sound panels inside
the hall are used to direct the sound toward listeners.

SOUND FACTS
• The science of
architectural acoustics
was founded by an
American physicist
named Wallace Sabine
(1868–1919).

• On a piano, the note
called "middle C" has a
frequency of 256 Hz.

SOUND RECORDING

ALL SOUND RECORDING systems store sound by making copies of sound waves, either as magnetic patterns on tape, a spiral groove on a record, or as tiny pits in a compact disc. A recording system uses a microphone to convert sound waves into electrical signals.

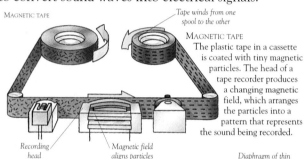

MAGNETIC TAPE

Tape winds from one spool to the other

MAGNETIC TAPE
The plastic tape in a cassette is coated with tiny magnetic particles. The head of a tape recorder produces a changing magnetic field, which arranges the particles into a pattern that represents the sound being recorded.

Recording head

Magnetic field aligns particles

Wire coil forms electromagnet

Permanent magnet

Diaphragm of thin plastic or metal foil

RECORDING FACTS
• The first sound recording was made by the American inventor Thomas Edison in 1877. His "phonograph" recorded sound as grooves cut into a wax-coated cylinder.

• The first magnetic recording was made in Denmark in 1898.

MICROPHONE
In a moving-coil microphone, sound waves cause a wire coil to vibrate within a magnetic field. This makes an electric current flow through the coil. The current fluctuates in strength as the sound waves change, producing electrical signals that mirror the sound waves.

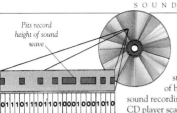

Pits record height of sound wave

`01110111101010001000101`

COMPACT DISC

A compact disc (CD) is a plastic disc with pits pressed into its surface. The pits store sound waves as a sequence of binary numbers created by digital sound recording. As the disc spins, a laser in the CD player scans the disc and "reads" the sequence of pits. The CD player translates the sequence into an electrical signal and feeds it to a loudspeaker.

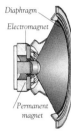

Diaphragm

Electromagnet

Permanent magnet

LOUDSPEAKER

Feeding electrical signals to a loudspeaker generates a varying magnetic field around an electromagnet. The magnet is attached to a diaphragm. The varying field causes the diaphragm to vibrate, producing sound waves.

RECORDS

Stylus   Pick-up head

Sound can be stored as a continuous wobbling groove around a vinyl record. The stylus of a record player vibrates as it moves along the groove, setting up electrical signals in the pick-up head. The signals are then fed to loudspeakers.

SAMPLING

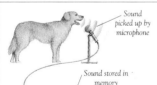

Sound picked up by microphone

Sound stored in memory

Sound played back on keyboard

A sampling system records sounds and stores them digitally. The sounds are played back through a keyboard. Pressing a key makes the system alter the pitch of a sound to match the pitch of that key. This means that the same sound can be played across a whole musical scale.

MAGNETISM

THERE IS AN invisible force exerted by magnets and electric currents called magnetism. Magnets attract iron and a few other metals, and attract or repel other magnets. Every magnet has two ends, called its north and south poles, where the forces it exerts are strongest.

MAGNETIC FORCES AT WORK

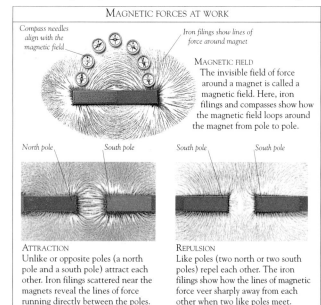

Compass needles align with the magnetic field

Iron filings show lines of force around magnet

MAGNETIC FIELD
The invisible field of force around a magnet is called a magnetic field. Here, iron filings and compasses show how the magnetic field loops around the magnet from pole to pole.

North pole   *South pole*

South pole   *South pole*

ATTRACTION
Unlike or opposite poles (a north pole and a south pole) attract each other. Iron filings scattered near the magnets reveal the lines of force running directly between the poles.

REPULSION
Like poles (two north or two south poles) repel each other. The iron filings show how the lines of magnetic force veer sharply away from each other when two like poles meet.

MAGNETIC INDUCTION

Magnetic objects contain "domains" – tiny regions of magnetism, each with two poles. The domains' poles point in all directions, so there is no overall magnetism. A magnetic field lines up the domains, magnetizing the object.

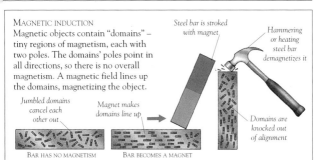

Steel bar is stroked with magnet

Hammering or heating steel bar demagnetizes it

Jumbled domains cancel each other out

Magnet makes domains line up

Domains are knocked out of alignment

BAR HAS NO MAGNETISM

BAR BECOMES A MAGNET

THE EARTH – A GIANT MAGNET

Earth's core of molten iron gives the planet its own magnetic field. The magnetic north and south poles are located near the geographic poles. The north pole of a magnet always points magnetic north.

Earth's axis runs through geographic poles

Magnetic south is near geographic south

Magnetic field is strongest near magnetic poles

MAGNETIC FACTS

• Earth's magnetic poles are at 70° N, 100° W and 68° S, 143° E, but they change constantly.

• The most magnetic substance is neodymium iron boride ($Nd_2Fe_{14}B$).

• The ancient Chinese may have made magnets by heating iron bars and letting them cool while aligned north–south.

NATURALLY MAGNETIC

Lodestone is a natural magnet. It is a form of the mineral magnetite (iron oxide). Its name means "guiding stone," and it was used in compasses 1,500 years ago.

STATIC ELECTRICITY

ELECTRICITY THAT <u>does not flow</u> is static electricity. A static charge can be produced by rubbing a balloon against an object such as a sweater. Electrons are transferred from the sweater's atoms onto the balloon's atoms. The balloon gains a negative electric charge and the sweater a positive one.

BALLOON CHARGED BY RUBBING (FRICTION)

ELECTROSTATIC INDUCTION

This charged balloon can induce a static electric charge in these pieces of paper. The balloon's negative charge repels electrons from the paper's surface, giving the paper's surface a positive charge. Since unlike charges attract, the balloon picks up the paper.

Balloon induces charge in paper

ELECTRIC FIELD

The area in which a charged object exerts a force on other objects is called an electric field. Here, a charged plastic spoon induces an opposite charge in a nearby flow of water. Force of attraction causes the flow to bend.

Flow of water moves toward spoon

Unlike charges attract

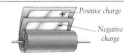

Positive charge

Negative charge

CAPACITOR

Many electronic devices use capacitors to build up charge and store it until it is needed. Inside a capacitor are two metal plates separated by an insulator.

VAN DE GRAAFF GENERATOR

This machine generates static electricity. A charged metal comb sprays positive charge onto a moving belt. When the belt reaches the metal dome, it strips electrons from the metal, giving the dome a huge positive charge.

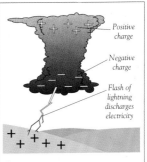

Positive charge

Negative charge

Flash of lightning discharges electricity

LIGHTNING

The tremendous build-up of static electricity inside a thundercloud induces a positive charge in the ground below. Eventually, electricity discharges from the cloud's base to the ground and back again (forked lightning), or within clouds (usually sheet lightning).

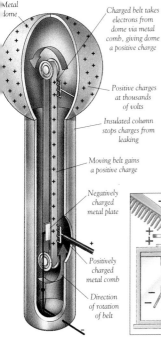

Metal dome

Charged belt takes electrons from dome via metal comb, giving dome a positive charge

Positive charges at thousands of volts

Insulated column stops charges from leaking

Moving belt gains a positive charge

Negatively charged metal plate

Positively charged metal comb

Direction of rotation of belt

A gold-leaf electroscope detects electric charge

ELECTROSCOPE

A negatively charged comb touching the rod repels the rod's electrons to the leaves, which then have more electrons than protons; since like charges repel, the leaves push each other apart.

CURRENT ELECTRICITY

AN ELECTRIC CURRENT is a flow of electric charge. In a simple circuit a battery moves negatively charged electrons through metal wires. Electricity can only flow through materials called conductors. Metals are good conductors – they contain free electrons that can move easily.

INSULATED ELECTRIC CABLE

INSULATORS
Electrical insulators block the flow of electric current, because their atoms have no free electrons. Plastics are good insulators and are used to cover conducting wires.

Electrons stay with atoms in insulator

Free electrons in copper wire conductor

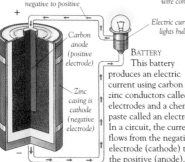

Current flows from negative to positive

Carbon anode (positive electrode)

Zinc casing is cathode (negative electrode)

Electric current lights bulb

BATTERY
This battery produces an electric current using carbon and zinc conductors called electrodes and a chemical paste called an electrolyte. In a circuit, the current flows from the negative electrode (cathode) to the positive (anode).

CURRENT FACTS
• "Semiconductors" are materials that are insulators when cold, and become conductors when warm.

• "Superconductors" are metals and some ceramics that become very good conductors at temperatures close to absolute zero.

SI UNITS
The **ampere** or **amp** (A) is the SI unit of electric current.

The **coulomb** (C) is the SI unit of electric charge. A current of 1 amp carries a charge of 1 coulomb per second.

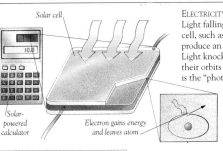

Solar cell

18.0

Solar-powered calculator

Electron gains energy and leaves atom

ELECTRICITY FROM SUNLIGHT
Light falling onto a "photovoltaic" cell, such as a solar cell, can produce an electric current. Light knocks electrons out of their orbits around atoms. This is the "photoelectric effect." The electrons move through the cell as an electric current.

TYPES OF CURRENT
Electric current is either direct (d.c.), in which electrons flow in one direction only, or alternating (a.c.), in which electrons change direction many times each second. A battery produces d.c. current.

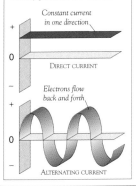

Constant current in one direction

DIRECT CURRENT

Electrons flow back and forth

ALTERNATING CURRENT

RECHARGEABLE BATTERY
A car battery can be recharged by passing an electrical current through it. This reverses the chemical changes that have occurred inside.

Dissolved metal electrodes are restored in recharging

CONDUCTIVITY OF SELECTED SUBSTANCES	
Conductivities are given in units of siemens per meter (S/m): 1 S is the conductance of a material with a resistance of 1 ohm (Ω).	
SUBSTANCE	CONDUCTIVITY S/M
Copper	58,000,000
Gold	45,000,000
Tungsten	19,000,000
Graphite	70,000
Water (at 20°C)	0.0000025
Diamond	0.00000000001
Air (at sea level)	0.000000000000025

Electrical circuits

An electrical circuit is the path around which an electric current flows. A simple circuit will include a source of electrical energy, such as a battery, and conducting wires linking components, such as switches, bulbs, and resistors, that control the flow of the current.

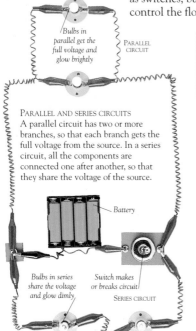

Bulbs in parallel get the full voltage and glow brightly

PARALLEL CIRCUIT

PARALLEL AND SERIES CIRCUITS

A parallel circuit has two or more branches, so that each branch gets the full voltage from the source. In a series circuit, all the components are connected one after another, so that they share the voltage of the source.

Battery

Bulbs in series share the voltage and glow dimly

Switch makes or breaks circuit

SERIES CIRCUIT

CIRCUIT SYMBOLS

–o⌒o–	Switch
–┤├–	Single cell
–┤│┤├–	Battery
–(A)–	Ammeter
–(V)–	Voltmeter
–⊃○	Bulb
∿∿∿	Resistor
∿∿∿	Variable resistor

SI UNITS

• The **volt** (V) is the SI unit of electromotive force (emf) and potential difference (pd). An emf of 1 volt transfers 1 joule of energy per second to a current of 1 amp.

• The **ohm** (Ω) is the SI unit of resistance. The resistance is 1 ohm when a pd of 1 volt produces a current of 1 amp.

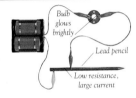

Bulb glows brightly

Lead pencil

Low resistance, large current

RESISTANCE OF A CIRCUIT

Resistance is the degree to which materials resist the flow of current. It can be used to control the flow of current through a circuit. In this circuit, the resistance of a graphite pencil lead controls current flow.

ELECTROMOTIVE FORCE

Electrons are propelled around a circuit by electromotive force (emf). The emf comes from a source of electrical energy, such as a cell or battery. Electromotive force is measured in volts.

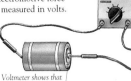

Voltmeter shows that emf of cell is 1.5 volts

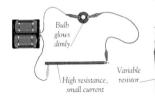

Bulb glows dimly

High resistance, small current

Variable resistor

POTENTIAL DIFFERENCE

The difference in emf between any two points in a circuit is called potential difference (pd) or voltage. Current flows because electrons always move from a point of high potential to a point of low potential.

CIRCUIT EQUATIONS

Several equations can be used to calculate the resistance (R), voltage (V), or current (I) across a conductor in an electrical circuit. These equations are:

- To calculate resistance: $R = V/I$
- To calculate voltage: $V = IR$
- To calculate current: $I = V/R$

Voltage (pd) across bulb is 2.2 volts

This "multimeter" can measure current, voltage, or resistance

ELECTROMAGNETISM

MOVING A WIRE in a magnetic field causes a current to flow through the wire. An electric current flowing through a wire generates a magnetic field around the wire. This is electromagnetism.

Electrical connection

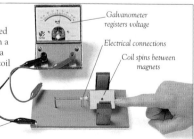

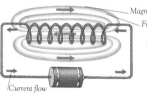

Magnetic field

Field has magnetic poles like a normal magnet

Current flow

Coils of copper wire around iron core

FIELD PRODUCED BY A WIRE COIL
A coil of current-carrying wire produces a stronger magnetic field than a straight wire. The coil creates a type of electromagnet called a solenoid.

POWERFUL ELECTROMAGNET
Winding a solenoid around an iron core creates a more powerful magnetic field. Here, iron filings show the strong field created by this electromagnet.

GENERATORS
Electric current can be produced by rotating a wire coil between a magnet's poles. Alternatively, a magnet may rotate while the coil remains static. Generators called dynamos give either direct or alternating current; alternators give only alternating current.

Galvanometer registers voltage

Electrical connections

Coil spins between magnets

Wires run under board

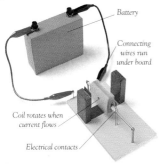

Battery

Connecting wires run under board

Coil rotates when current flows

Electrical contacts

FLEMING'S RIGHT-HAND RULE

Motion

Field

Current

FLEMING'S RULES

Fleming's rules are used to work out the directions of current, magnetic field, and motion. Fleming's right-hand rule shows the direction a current flows along a wire when the wire moves in a magnetic field (in a generator). Fleming's left-hand rule shows the direction a current-carrying wire will move in a magnetic field (in a motor).

Motion

Field

Current

FLEMING'S LEFT-HAND RULE

ELECTRIC MOTORS

In an electric motor, a current flows through a coil of wire between the poles of a magnet. The magnetic field that the coil produces interacts with the field of the magnet, forcing the coil to turn. The rotating coil can be attached to a drive shaft or flywheel to power a machine.

ELECTRIC BELL

Current induces a magnetic field in the electromagnets in this bell, pulling the hammer up to strike the gong. As the hammer moves, it breaks the circuit, then falls back to its original position.

Make-and-break circuit contact

Electromagnets

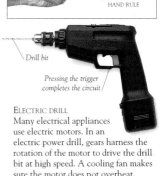

Drill bit

Pressing the trigger completes the circuit

ELECTRIC DRILL

Many electrical appliances use electric motors. In an electric power drill, gears harness the rotation of the motor to drive the drill bit at high speed. A cooling fan makes sure the motor does not overheat.

ELECTRICITY SUPPLY

ELECTRICITY PRODUCED BY generators in power stations reaches homes via a network of cables known as a grid. Resistance causes some power to be wasted as heat. To sidestep this, electricity is distributed at high voltage and low current to minimize power loss.

THE ELECTRICITY GRID

PRODUCING ELECTRICITY
Power stations send electricity to substations, where "step-up" transformers increase the voltage for distribution. The power travels along underground cables or overhead lines.

CONSUMING ELECTRICITY
At "step-down" substations, the voltage is reduced by transformers to supply suitable voltages for use in industry or in the home. A local grid takes electricity to these consumers.

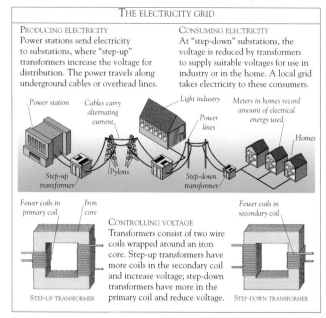

Power station

Cables carry alternating current

Light industry

Power lines

Meters in homes record amount of electrical energy used

Homes

Step-up transformer

Pylons

Step-down transformer

Fewer coils in primary coil

Iron core

Fewer coils in secondary coil

CONTROLLING VOLTAGE
Transformers consist of two wire coils wrapped around an iron core. Step-up transformers have more coils in the secondary coil and increase voltage; step-down transformers have more in the primary coil and reduce voltage.

STEP-UP TRANSFORMER

STEP-DOWN TRANSFORMER

CIRCUIT BREAKER

FUSE

Fuse wire melts and breaks circuit

CIRCUIT BREAKERS AND FUSES
An electrical fault may allow too much current to flow and cause wires to catch fire. Domestic circuit breakers cut off the current if it reaches dangerous levels. Fuses are the weakest link in a circuit, and burn out if the current is too strong.

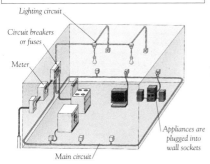

Lighting circuit

Circuit breakers or fuses

Meter

Appliances are plugged into wall sockets

Main circuit

DOMESTIC CIRCUITS
Modern houses have various circuits to supply power for different purposes. For example, lighting and most appliances usually take power from different circuits to heavier appliances, such as electric stoves and air conditioning units, which use a lot more current.

TYPES OF PLUG
Electrical appliances are connected to the grid by fitting plugs into sockets. Electrical earth wires direct dangerous currents safely into the ground.

2-PIN PLUG

Ground wire

3-PIN PLUG

Fuse

3-PIN FUSED PLUG

ELECTRICITY FACTS

• In 1887, American Nikola Tesla patented an electricity supply system that transmitted alternating current.

• In homes, shops, and offices, voltage must be at 110 V in the US (240 V in some countries).

ELECTRONICS

USING COMPONENTS to control electricity is known as electronics. Integrated circuits and other electronic components are made of semiconducting materials, such as silicon. Adding impurities creates two types of silicon: n-type silicon has extra, free-roaming electrons; p-type silicon has fewer electrons, leaving "holes."

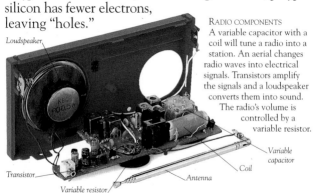

RADIO COMPONENTS
A variable capacitor with a coil will tune a radio into a station. An aerial changes radio waves into electrical signals. Transistors amplify the signals and a loudspeaker converts them into sound. The radio's volume is controlled by a variable resistor.

Loudspeaker

Transistor

Variable resistor

Antenna

Coil

Variable capacitor

CONTROLLING CURRENT

Electronic circuits amplify electric current, change one-way (direct) current to an oscillating (alternating) current, or switch the current on and off.

Transmitters are oscillators which produce an oscillating current

Amplifier circuits make a stronger copy of a weak current

Computer circuits use pulses of on/off current to represent data

SEMICONDUCTORS

Hole moves
Boron atom

P-TYPE SILICON
Adding boron leaves "holes" in the silicon, since boron atoms have fewer electrons in their outer shell. The current is carried by the moving holes.

Free electron moves
Arsenic atom

N-TYPE SILICON
Arsenic gives free electrons to the silicon, since arsenic atoms have more electrons in their outer shell. Current is carried by these free electrons.

TRANSISTOR
A transistor is a sandwich of n- and p-type silicon in a p-n-p or n-p-n arrangement. It can boost current or act as a switch. In computers, transistors switch on and off many times each second, enabling rapid calculations to be carried out.

ELECTRICAL COMPONENTS		
COMPONENT	FUNCTION	SYMBOL
Capacitor	Stores charge	
Variable capacitor	Stores varying amounts of charge	
Diode	Permits current to flow in one direction only; can also be used to convert a.c. signals to d.c. signals (a "rectifier")	
Light-emitting diode (LED)	Emits light when current flows through it	
Thermistor	Registers temperature changes by changing resistance	
Aerial	Converts radio waves into a.c. signals (and vice versa)	
Microphone	Converts sound waves into a.c. current/voltage	
Loudspeaker	Converts a.c. signals into sound waves	
n-p-n transistor	Amplifies electric current, and turns it on and off	NPN
p-n-p transistor	Amplifies electric current, and turns it on and off	PNP

Integrated circuits

An integrated circuit is a tiny "wafer" of silicon that contains a complete circuit with thousands of components such as transistors and diodes. Integrated circuits, or "microchips," have made electronic devices both smaller and more efficient.

MANUFACTURING

The components of an integrated circuit are made by building up layers of p-type and n-type semiconductors and other materials on a silicon wafer. They are linked by fine conducting wires. A detailed overlay plan is made for each layer and checked for accuracy.

Each plan is a different color

Transparent overlays

Tiny chip is dwarfed by packaging

ENCASED CHIP

An integrated circuit is also called a microchip. The chip is encased in a tough plastic or ceramic capsule, with pins that can be soldered or plugged into a circuit board. Many chips have logic gates, which are transistor circuits that process electrical signals. Logic gates (see right) add up numbers in calculators.

BINARY CODE

Microchips store data as electrical signals in binary code. Binary numbers use only the digits 0 and 1. The decimal number 13, for example, is 1101 in binary form (8+4+0+1). This converts into a binary sequence of on (1) and off (0) electrical pulses. So 1101 is on-on-off-on in binary code.

| (ON) | (ON) | (OFF) | (ON) |
| (1x8) | (1x4) | (0x2) | (1x1) |

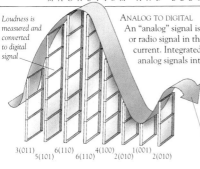

Loudness is measured and converted to digital signal

ANALOG TO DIGITAL

An "analog" signal is a copy of a sound, light, or radio signal in the form of a varying electric current. Integrated circuits are used to convert analog signals into "digital" signals, which are in binary code. A digital signal made of on/off electrical pulses is much easier to store than a varying electric current.

Analog copy of sound wave

3(011) 6(110) 4(100) 1(001) 2(010)
  5(101)   6(110)   2(010)   2(010)

LOGIC GATES

Logic gates work with digital signals. They switch on or off depending on the type of signal they receive. "Truth tables" show what happens when signals are either applied (1) or not applied (0) to the gates.

OUTPUT

INPUT A	INPUT B	OUTPUT
0	0	0
1	0	0
0	1	0
1	1	1

A   B

AND GATE
Gives an output signal when a signal is applied to one input AND to the other input.

OUTPUT

INPUT A	INPUT B	OUTPUT
0	0	0
1	0	1
0	1	1
1	1	1

A   B

OR GATE
Gives an output signal when a signal is applied to one input OR to the other input, OR to both.

OUTPUT

INPUT	OUTPUT
0	1
1	0

A symbol used in
INPUT *designing computer circuits*

NOT GATE
The NOT gate gives an output signal when a signal is NOT applied to its input.

Weight display

MICROPROCESSOR
A microprocessor is a chip that can store instructions in an electronic memory and act on them. These scales are controlled by a single microchip. The chip converts the weight on the scales into a digital readout. It can convert the weight to or from metric or imperial units.

COMPUTERS

A COMPUTER contains thousands of electronic circuits that enable it to store and process vast amounts of information. Although a computer cannot "think" for itself, it can perform a wide variety of tasks extremely quickly. Each task is broken down into a series of simple mathematical calculations.

PERSONAL COMPUTER
The most familiar type of computer is the personal computer (PC), which can only be used by one person at a time. Most PCs consist of a keyboard and mouse, a disk drive, and a monitor screen. Machinery such as this is called "hardware."

Monitor screen displays results

Disk drive contains software programs

Keyboard and mouse for inputting data

COMPUTER PROGRAMS
A program is a set of instructions that tells a computer to carry out a specific task. The instructions may be written as "machine code" (long sets of numbers) or in a computer language such as BASIC or FORTRAN. Computer programs are called "software."

INTERNET

The Internet is a global web of interconnected computer networks. It enables people all over the world to exchange data and send electronic mail (email). The worldwide web is an Internet service that provides a wide range of information in the form of user-friendly websites. The Internet can be used for banking, shopping (e-commerce), listening to the radio, watching videos, or even playing chess with an opponent thousands of miles away.

The alpha sign @ means "at," and is part of each email address

CAD BUILDING PLANS

COMPUTER-AIDED DESIGN (CAD)

Information fed into a computer "builds" an object on the screen using computer graphics. CAD allows architects and engineers to test new ideas.

VIRTUAL REALITY

A virtual-reality system enables you to interact with a computer-generated world. A headset supplies you with 3-D images, while a "data glove" lets you "touch" what you see.

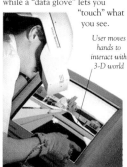

User moves hands to interact with 3-D world

COMPUTER GENERATIONS		
GENERATION	DATE	CHARACTERISTIC
1st	1944–59	Valves (vacuum tubes)
2nd	1959–64	Transistors
3rd	1964–75	Large Scale Integrated circuits (LSIs)
4th	1975–	Very Large Scale Integrated circuits (VLSIs)
5th	Under development	"Artificial Intelligence"-based computers

Inside computers

Memory is crucial to the operation of computers because they need to be able to remember sequences of instructions in order to carry out specific tasks. In a personal computer (PC), there are two memories: read-only memory (ROM) and random-access memory (RAM), each consisting of a number of microchips.

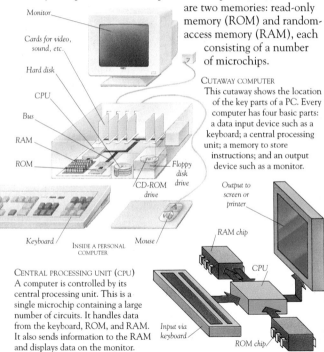

CUTAWAY COMPUTER
This cutaway shows the location of the key parts of a PC. Every computer has four basic parts: a data input device such as a keyboard; a central processing unit; a memory to store instructions; and an output device such as a monitor.

Monitor

Cards for video, sound, etc.

Hard disk

CPU

Bus

RAM

ROM

Floppy disk drive

CD-ROM drive

Keyboard

INSIDE A PERSONAL COMPUTER

Mouse

Output to screen or printer

RAM chip

CPU

Input via keyboard

ROM chip

CENTRAL PROCESSING UNIT (CPU)
A computer is controlled by its central processing unit. This is a single microchip containing a large number of circuits. It handles data from the keyboard, ROM, and RAM. It also sends information to the RAM and displays data on the monitor.

Disk coated with magnetic material

Read/write head

Track selector mechanism

DISKS

A hard disk stores data when a computer is off. A floppy disk is used to transfer data to other computers. The disks record data as magnetic patterns in binary code. Data is read from a disk by a disk drive.

HELPER BOARDS

Computers contain special circuit boards, or "cards," to carry out specific tasks needing a lot of memory. The computer passes the job on to the card, and is free to handle other tasks.

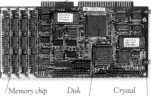

Edge connectors plug into slots

Memory chip

Disk controller

Crystal controls timing

CD-ROM AND DVD
Large amounts of data, such as pictures, sounds, text, and video, can be permanently stored on CD-ROM and DVD. A laser reads the data from the disc. The CD-R and DVD-R formats allow the user to record new data onto the discs.

CD PAGE

COMPUTER TERMS	
TERM	MEANING
ROM	A computer's permanent memory, whose contents cannot be changed.
RAM	The memory used to store programs being run on the computer.
Buffer	A region of memory that stores data temporarily.
Bus	A set of wires or metal strips that carries information from one part of the computer to another.
Operating system	The program that controls how a computer functions.
Bit	A digit of binary information (1 or 0).
Byte	A piece of data consisting of eight bits.
Megabyte	One million bytes.
Modem	A device that allows computers to share information via a telephone network.

TELECOMMUNICATIONS

RADIO AND TELEVISION programs – and even some telephone conversations – are broadcast by radio waves. The waves must first be "modulated" (coded) so that they can carry the sound and picture signals.

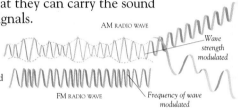

AM RADIO WAVE

Wave strength modulated

MODULATION
A steady radio (high frequency) signal is modulated by a sound signal in one of two ways. Its amplitude (strength) may be modulated (AM) or its frequency may change (FM). The resulting signal is transmitted as a radio wave.

FM RADIO WAVE

Frequency of wave modulated

COMMUNICATION FACTS

• In 1926, Scottish engineer John Logie Baird demonstrated the first television system.

• Italian inventor Guglielmo Marconi made the first radio transmission in 1894.

• US communications satellite "Telstar" was launched in 1962.

LONG-RANGE COMMUNICATIONS
Low-frequency radio waves are sent long distances by bouncing them between the ionosphere (an ion-laden region of the atmosphere) and the ground. High-frequency waves pass through the ionosphere and are transmitted to receiving stations on Earth by orbiting communications satellites.

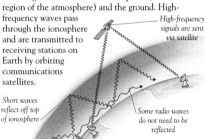

High-frequency signals are sent via satellite

Short waves reflect off top of ionosphere

Some radio waves do not need to be reflected

Low-frequency waves bounce between ionosphere and ground

TRANSMITTING RADIO WAVES

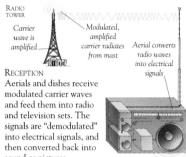

RADIO
TOWER

*Carrier
wave is
amplified*

*Modulated,
amplified
carrier radiates
from mast*

*Aerial converts
radio waves
into electrical
signals*

RECEPTION

Aerials and dishes receive
modulated carrier waves
and feed them into radio
and television sets. The
signals are "demodulated"
into electrical signals, and
then converted back into
sound or pictures.

HOW A TELEVISION WORKS

A demodulated picture
signal is sent to the picture
tube (a cathode-ray tube).
This tube contains three
"electron guns" that fire
beams of electrons at the
TV screen. Magnetic fields
cause the beams to scan
the screen. The screen is
coated with materials called
phosphors, which glow red,
green, or blue
when hit by the
electron beams.

TELEVISION SET

*Input from TV
aerial*

Electromagnets

Electron beams

*Screen coated
with phosphors*

*Red, green,
and blue
electron guns*

*Circuits
amplify signal*

*Picture builds as
beams scan screen*

TELEPHONES

TELEPHONE

A telephone uses a microphone to change
the sound waves from a person's voice into
electrical signals. The signals are sent by
cable to a receiving telephone, and
changed back into
sound. Telephone
signals are also
sent as pulses
of light along
optical fibers.

Microphone

OPTICAL FIBER

TIMELINE OF SCIENTIFIC DISCOVERIES

THIS CHART CHRONICLES some of the important discoveries in the history of science – from early ideas about the universe and the nature of force and energy to the modern world of particle physics.

C.1000 BC			AD 1650
C.1000 BC–C.260 BC	C.259 BC–AD 1599	1600–1640	1641–1650
MATTER •c.400 BC Greek scientist Democritus suggests that matter is made out of tiny indivisible particles, which he calls atoms. •c.350 BC Aristotle, a Greek philosopher, proposes that matter is made out of four elements: earth, fire, air, and water.	•2 BC Alchemy studied in Egypt, China, and India. Alchemists try to change "base" metals such as lead into precious metals such as gold. Alchemy was the first systematic study of matter. It later reaches Europe.	•1620 A Dutch scientist called Jan van Helmont coins the word "gas." •1620s Francis Bacon, an English philosopher, develops scientific method – science based on experiment.	•1649 French philosopher Pierre Gassendi translates ancient Greek texts on the atomic theory, making the idea of the atom popular once again. •c.1650 German physicist Otto von Guericke perfects his vacuum pump.
FORCE AND ENERGY •c.1000 BC Early civilizations rely on wind and muscle power for work and transport, and burn wood and plant matter for heat. •c.260 BC Greek scientist Archimedes discovers principle of flotation and establishes principles of mathematics.	•AD 100 Hero of Alexandria, a Greek engineer, invents the aeolipile, a forerunner of the steam turbine. It uses steam from a boiler to make a metal ball rotate.	•1600 William Gilbert, doctor to Queen Elizabeth I of England, claims that the Earth's core is like a huge magnet. •1638 Italian scientist Galileo Galilei founds mechanics (the study of force and motion). He is the first person to use a telescope.	•1643 Italian physicist Evangelista Torricelli discovers atmospheric pressure, and measures it with a mercury barometer – his own invention. •1650 Blaise Pascal, a French scientist, develops his law of fluid pressures.

1651			1820
1651–1700	1701–1770	1771–1800	1801–1820

MATTER

- **1661** Irish scientist Robert Boyle realizes the nature of elements and compounds. He suggests that the existence of small particles explains chemical reactions.
- **1670** English physicist Robert Hooke develops the compound microscope.

- **1755** Scottish chemist Joseph Black identifies carbon dioxide. Also discovers latent heat.
- **1766** English chemist Henry Cavendish discovers hydrogen.
- **1770s** French physicist and inventor Charles Coulomb studies electrostatic forces.

- **1779** French chemist Antoine Lavoisier names oxygen and shows its role in burning. Proves that air is a mixture of gases, and water a compound of oxygen and hydrogen.
- **1780s** Jean Antoine Chaptal, a chemist from France, sets up a factory to produce sulfuric acid.

- **1807–8** Discovery by British chemist Humphry Davy of potassium, sodium, magnesium, barium, and strontium.
- **1811** Italian physicist Amedeo Avogadro formulates his law, which states that equal volumes of different gases contain the same number of particles.

FORCE AND ENERGY

- **1665** English mathematician Isaac Newton formulates laws of motion and gravitation. Later discovers that light is made up of a spectrum of colors.
- **1675** Danish astronomer Olë Römer measures the speed of light by observing Jupiter's moons.
- **1683** French engineer John Desaguliers introduces the words "conductor" and "insulator."

- **1701** French scientist Joseph Sauveur distinguishes between sound waves and vibrations.
- **1706** English scientist Francis Hawksbee develops a friction machine to generate sparks of electricity.
- **1752** American scientist Benjamin Franklin proves that lightning is electrical. Also suggests that electricity consists of two types of charge.
- **1765** James Watt, a Scottish engineer, builds first efficient steam engine.

- **1798** Henry Cavendish, English chemist, measures the mass of the Earth with a torsion balance.
- **1799** Italian chemist Alessandro Volta devises his "voltaic pile" – the world's first battery – using different metals separated by paper discs soaked in salt solution.
- **1800** André Marie Ampère, a French physicist, explores links between electric current and voltage.

- **1803** Englishman John Dalton proposes modern atomic theory – that elements and compounds are made up of atoms and molecules.
- **1820** Hans Christian Oersted, a Danish physicist, discovers electromagnetism when he notices how a compass needle is deflected by a current-carrying wire.

1821			1899
1821–1840	1841–1860	1861–1880	1881–1899

MATTER

•1830 German chemists concentrate their studies on carbon as the basis of the "organic" chemistry of living things. •1833 English physicist and chemist Michael Faraday discovers the laws of electrolysis.	•1841 Swedish chemist Jöns Jacob Berzelius discovers allotropy. •1842 French scientist Eugene-Melchor Pellgot discovers uranium. •1852 English chemist Edward Franklin introduces the concept of valency.	•1868 Helium discovered by spectroscopic studies of the Sun. •1869 The Russian schoolteacher Dmitri Mendeleyev classifies elements into groups by atomic weight, and devises the periodic table.	•1896 Radioactivity discovered by French physicist Antoine Henri Becquerel. •1897 British physicist Joseph John Thompson discovers the electron. •1898 Polish–French chemist Marie Curie and her French husband Pierre Curie isolate radium and polonium.

FORCE AND ENERGY

•1831 Scientists Michael Faraday of England and Joseph Henry of the US independently discover how to use magnetism to create electricity. •1836 English chemist John Frederic Daniell invents the Daniell cell, the first practical and reliable source of electricity. •1839 Englishman William Fox Talbot and Frenchman Louis Daguerre independently devise a practical photographic process.	•1843 English scientist James Joule describes the relationship between heat, power, and work. •1846 Laws of thermodynamics are established by William Thomson, a British scientist. •1849 French physicist Hippolyte Fizeau makes an accurate measurement of the speed of light. •1859 Étienne Lenoir, a Belgian engineer, invents the internal combustion engine.	•1864 James Maxwell, a Scottish physicist, introduces the idea of the electromagnetic field. Also identifies light as a form of electromagnetic radiation. •1876 Scottish-born inventor Alexander Graham Bell makes the first telephone. •1879 American Thomas Edison and Englishman Joseph Swan independently produce the first electric light bulbs. Edison's is the more successful.	•1884 Charles Parsons, an English engineer, invents the steam turbine for generating electricity. •1888 Heinrich Hertz, a German physicist, proves the existence of radio waves. •1888 Croatian-born physicist Nikola Tesla invents the first practical electrical induction motor. •1894 Young Italian inventor Guglielmo Marconi makes the first radio communication.

1900			2002
1900–1911	1912–1930	1931–1945	1946–2002

MATTER

•1909 Leo Henrick Baekeland, an American chemist, produces the first stable, fully synthetic plastic – "Bakelite." •1911 The atomic nucleus is discovered by New Zealand-born physicist Ernest Rutherford. Later, he learns to convert one element into another.	•1913 Niels Bohr, a Danish physicist, discovers that electrons orbit the nucleus of an atom in shells. •1915 William Bragg and his son Lawrence Bragg invent X-ray crystallography – a way of using X-rays to explore the structure of crystals.	•1931 The neutron is discovered by James Chadwick, a British physicist. •1931 German physicist Ernst Ruska invents the electron microscope. •1939 American chemist Linus Pauling explains the nature of chemical bonds between atoms and molecules.	•1964 American physicist Murray Gell-Mann proposes the existence of quarks. •1984 Genetic fingerprinting is developed by British scientist Alec Jeffreys. •1995 Fifth state of matter, called the "superatom," is found at temperatures close to absolute zero.

FORCE AND ENERGY

•1900 Max Planck, a German physicist, proposes quantum theory – that energy is made up of small units called "quanta." From this theory, scientists deduce that light acts both as waves and as particles. •1905 German-born physicist Albert Einstein publishes his *Special Theory of Relativity*. Together with his *General Theory of Relativity* (1915), it revolutionizes the world of science and shows that mass can be converted to energy.	•1911 Dutch physicist Heike Onnes discovers superconductivity in mercury at near absolute zero. •1912 German physicist Max von Laue discovers that X-rays are electromagnetic radiation, by studying their reflection from crystals. •1912 Austrian-born American physicist Victor Hess discovers high energy cosmic radiation during high-altitude balloon flights.	•1937 First working jet engine is built by British engineer Frank Whittle. •1938 German scientist Otto Hahn and Austrian physicist Lise Meitner discover nuclear fission. •1939 German scientist Hans Bethe explains that the Sun and stars are powered by nuclear fusion. •1942 Enrico Fermi, an Italian–American physicist, builds the first nuclear reactor. •1945 The first electronic computer, ENIAC, is devised in the US.	•1947 US physicists John Bardeen, Walter Brattain, and William Shockley invent the transistor. •1958 The first integrated circuit is produced by US electronics engineer Jack Kilby. •1960 US physicist Theodore Maiman invents the laser. •1971 The first microprocessor, the Intel 4004, is manufactured in the US. •1990 The world-wide web is devised by British software engineer Tim Berners-Lee.

EARTH AND WEATHER

HOW THE EARTH WAS FORMED

ABOUT 5 BILLION years ago our solar system began
to take shape. The Sun and the nine planets formed
from a cloud of dust and gas swirling in space. Some
scientists believe that the center of this cloud cooled
and contracted to form the Sun. Gravity pulled the
planets from the rest of the cloud. Other scientists
suggest that the dust cloud formed
asteroids that joined together to
make the Sun and planets.

1 FORMING THE SUN
A spinning cloud of
gas and dust contracted
to form the Sun. Cooler
matter from this dust
cloud combined to shape
the planets.

*A dense atmosphere
of cosmic gases
surrounded the Earth.*

2 FORMING THE EARTH
The Earth's radio-
activity caused the surface
to melt. Lighter minerals
floated to the surface and
heavier elements, such as
iron and nickel, sank to
form the Earth's core.

3 THE EARTH'S CRUST
About 4 billion years
ago, the Earth's crust began
to form. Blocks of cooling,
solid rock floated on a
molten rock layer. The rock
sometimes sank and remelted
before rising again.

• The Earth orbits the Sun at 18.5 miles/sec (29.8 km/sec).

• Oceans cover 70.8% of the Earth's surface.

• Earth is not a sphere – it bulges in the middle.

• The Earth completes a turn on its axis every 23 hours, 56 minutes.

COMPOSITION OF THE EARTH
The elements here are divided by weight. Earth's crust consists mostly of oxygen, silicon, and aluminum. Heavier metals such as iron and nickel are found in the core.

Other elements less than 1%
Aluminum 1.1%
Sulfur 1.9%
Nickel 2.4%
Magnesium 13%
Silicon 15%
Oxygen 30%
Iron 35%

4 MAKING THE ATMOSPHERE
The Earth's crust thickened. It took several million years for volcanic gases to form the atmosphere. Water vapor condensed to make oceans.

6 THE EARTH TODAY
Earth's unique conditions are just right to support a variety of life. Our planet, though, continues to change. Tectonic plates are moving, pulling some continents nearer and pushing others farther apart.

5 LAND FORMS
About 3.5 billion years ago protocontinents formed on the crust. Today's continents look very different.

THE EARTH IN SPACE

EARTH IS A DENSE rocky planet, third nearest to the
Sun, and tiny compared with Jupiter and Saturn.
While Earth rotates on its axis once each day, it
also orbits the Sun once each year, held in orbit
by the Sun's gravity. One moon revolves around
the Earth. From space the Earth looks blue and
calm but under its oceans, deep beneath the
crust, intense heat melts metal and rock.

MERCURY
- 88 days to orbit Sun
- diameter 3,032 miles
  (4,879 km)

EARTH
- 365.25 days to orbit Sun
- diameter 7,926 miles
  (12,756 km)
- 1 moon

MERCURY   EARTH

VENUS   MARS

MARS
- 687 days to orbit Sun
- diameter 4,220 miles
  (6,792 km)
- 2 moons

VENUS
- 224.7 days to orbit Sun
- diameter 7,521 miles
  (12,104 km)

SUN
- diameter 865,121 miles (1,391,980 km)

THE SOLAR SYSTEM
Our solar system consists of nine plan
ets, as well as moons, asteroids,
comets, meteorites, dust, and gas. Al
of these orbit a central star – the Sun

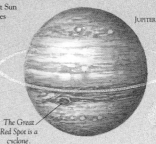

JUPITER

*The Great
Red Spot is a
cyclone.*

JUPITER
- 11.86 years to orbit Sun
- diameter 88,846 miles
  (142,984 km)
- 40 moons
- 1 ring

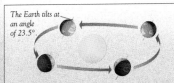

The Earth tilts at an angle of 23.5°.

EARTH'S ORBIT

As the Earth turns on its axis, it also orbits the Sun. When the Northern Hemisphere faces the Sun it has its summer. At the same time the Southern Hemisphere faces away from the Sun and has its winter. The equator faces towards the Sun most of the time and there are no significant seasonal changes there.

DISTANCE FROM THE SUN

PLANET	MILLION MILES	MILLION KM
Mercury	36	57.9
Venus	67.2	108.2
Earth	93	149.6
Mars	141.6	227.9
Jupiter	483.7	778.4
Saturn	886.9	1,427
Uranus	1,784	2,871
Neptune	2,795	4,498
Pluto	3,670	5,906

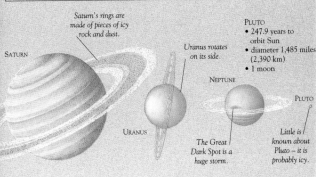

Saturn's rings are made of pieces of icy rock and dust.

SATURN

Uranus rotates on its side.

URANUS

NEPTUNE

The Great Dark Spot is a huge storm.

PLUTO
- 247.9 years to orbit Sun
- diameter 1,485 miles (2,390 km)
- 1 moon

PLUTO

Little is known about Pluto – it is probably icy.

SATURN
- 29.45 years to orbit Sun
- diameter 74,897 miles (120,536 km)
- 30 moons
- 7 rings

URANUS
- 84 years to orbit Sun
- diameter 31,763 miles (51,118 km)
- 21 moons
- 11 rings

NEPTUNE
- 164.8 years to orbit Sun
- diameter 30,775 miles (49,528 km)
- 11 moons
- 4 rings

EARTH'S MAGNETIC FIELD

THE EARTH BEHAVES like a giant magnet. Molten nickel and iron flowing in the molten outer core of the Earth produce an electric current. This electricity creates a magnetic field, or magnetosphere, that extends into space. Like a magnet, the Earth has two magnetic poles. From time to time, the magnetic poles reverse polarity. The last time they changed was about 700,000 years ago. No one knows why this happens.

MAGNETIC POLES

North and south geographical poles lie at either end of the Earth's axis (the invisible line around which the Earth turns). The magnetic poles' position varies over time. It is the Earth's magnetic field that causes a compass needle to point north.

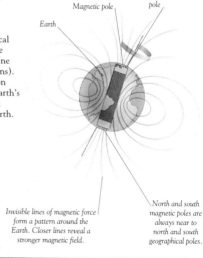

Earth

Magnetic pole

Geographic pole

Invisible lines of magnetic force form a pattern around the Earth. Closer lines reveal a stronger magnetic field.

North and south magnetic poles are always near to north and south geographical poles.

MAGNETIC FACTS

• Whales and birds use the Earth's magnetic field to help them navigate.

• Every second the Sun sheds at least a million tons (tonnes) of matter into the solar wind.

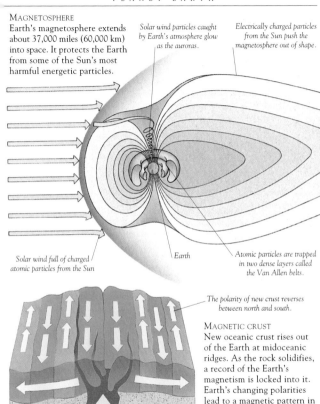

MAGNETOSPHERE
Earth's magnetosphere extends about 37,000 miles (60,000 km) into space. It protects the Earth from some of the Sun's most harmful energetic particles.

Solar wind particles caught by Earth's atmosphere glow as the auroras.

Electrically charged particles from the Sun push the magnetosphere out of shape.

Solar wind full of charged atomic particles from the Sun

Earth

Atomic particles are trapped in two dense layers called the Van Allen belts.

The polarity of new crust reverses between north and south.

MAGNETIC CRUST
New oceanic crust rises out of the Earth at midoceanic ridges. As the rock solidifies, a record of the Earth's magnetism is locked into it. Earth's changing polarities lead to a magnetic pattern in the rock, symmetrical either side of the spreading ridge.

EARTH'S ATMOSPHERE

THE EARTH IS WRAPPED in a blanket of gases called the atmosphere. This thin layer protects the Earth from the Sun's fierce rays and from the hostile conditions of outer space. There are five layers in the Earth's atmosphere before the air merges with outer space. The lowest layer holds air and water vapor that support life, and our weather and climate.

A THIN LAYER
The Earth's atmosphere is actually a thin blanket around the planet. If the Earth were an orange, the atmosphere would be as thin as the skin of the orange.

EXOSPHERE
• begins at 560 miles (900 km)
• thin layer before spacecraft reach outer space

THERMOSPHERE
• 50-280 miles (80-450 km)
• reaches 3,600°F (2,000°C)
• contains the ionosphere – electrically charged air that reflects radio waves

MESOSPHERE
• 30-50 miles (50-80 km)
• meteors burn up and cause shooting stars

STRATOSPHERE
• 12-30 miles (20-50 km)
• ranges from -76°F (-60°C) to just about freezing point at the top
• calm layer where airplanes fly
• contains the ozone layer that protects us from the Sun's harmful rays

TROPOSPHERE
• up to 12 miles (20 km) above the Earth
• weather layer, where rain clouds form

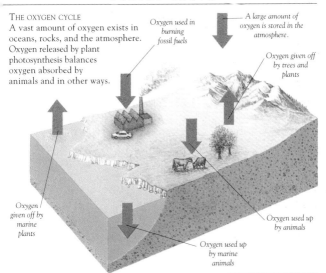

THE OXYGEN CYCLE
A vast amount of oxygen exists in oceans, rocks, and the atmosphere. Oxygen released by plant photosynthesis balances oxygen absorbed by animals and in other ways.

Oxygen used in burning fossil fuels

A large amount of oxygen is stored in the atmosphere.

Oxygen given off by trees and plants

Oxygen given off by marine plants

Oxygen used up by animals

Oxygen used up by marine animals

ATMOSPHERE FACTS

• The troposphere is the densest layer of the atmosphere.

• Ozone is a type of oxygen that absorbs damaging ultraviolet rays from the Sun.

• Humans can live and breathe normally only in the troposphere layer.

COMPOSITION OF THE LOWER ATMOSPHERE
Although nitrogen makes up most of the air we breathe, oxygen is the essential gas for all animal and human life. Nitrogen is simply breathed in and out. Other gases, such as argon and carbon dioxide, make up less than 1 percent.

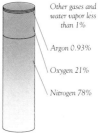

Other gases and water vapor less than 1%

Argon 0.93%

Oxygen 21%

Nitrogen 78%

MAPPING THE EARTH

MAPS HELP US SEE what the Earth looks like. A map uses symbols to represent different features of the Earth. A technique called projection can transfer the curved surface of the globe onto a flat sheet of paper. Aerial photographs help make maps that show valleys and hills. On a larger scale, satellite photographs help mapmakers show how the Earth looks from space.

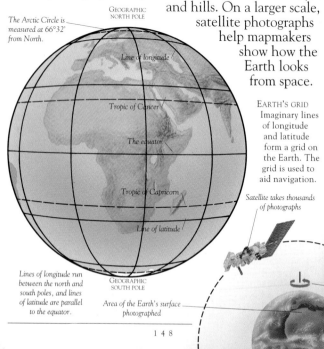

The Arctic Circle is measured at 66°32' from North.

GEOGRAPHIC NORTH POLE

Line of longitude

Tropic of Cancer

The equator

Tropic of Capricorn

Line of latitude

GEOGRAPHIC SOUTH POLE

Lines of longitude run between the north and south poles, and lines of latitude are parallel to the equator.

EARTH'S GRID
Imaginary lines of longitude and latitude form a grid on the Earth. The grid is used to aid navigation.

Satellite takes thousands of photographs

Area of the Earth's surface photographed

MERCATOR'S PROJECTION

PETERS' PROJECTION

MAP PROJECTIONS
Mercator's map of 1569 distorted the land area of the continents – Greenland appeared larger than Africa. Peters' map shows the right land area but the shape of the continents is incorrect.

THE WORLD'S CONTINENTS
The Earth is divided into seven land masses or continents.

Asia is larger than Europe and Africa combined. It takes up 30% of the Earth's land.

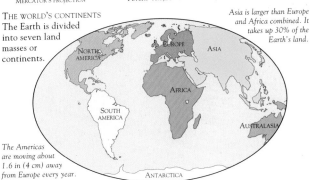

The Americas are moving about 1.6 in (4 cm) away from Europe every year.

SATELLITE MAPPING
While orbiting the Earth, satellites photograph the planet in sections. The separate images are combined to give a clear picture of the Earth.

Satellite's orbit around the poles

Direction of the Earth's rotation

THE SIZE OF THE CONTINENTS		
CONTINENT	AREA IN SQ KM	AREA IN SQ MILES
Asia	44,485,900	17,176,100
Africa	30,269,680	11,687,180
North America	24,235,280	9,357,290
South America	17,820,770	6,880,630
Antarctica	13,209,000	5,100,020
Europe	10,530,750	4,065,940
Australasia	8,924,100	3,445,610

THE EARTH'S CRUST

EARTH'S SURFACE IS covered by a thin layer of rock called crust. Rocky crust standing above sea level forms islands and continents. The lithosphere is in pieces, or plates, that move slowly all the time. When two plates meet they may slide past each other or one may go under another. New crust forms at ocean ridges and old crust melts into the mantle.

PLATE FACTS

• Earth's plates "float" on a layer of mantle called asthenosphere.

• The size of the Earth doesn't change – new crust produced equals older crust consumed.

EARTH'S SKIN
Earth's crust, like the skin of an apple, is a thin covering for what is inside. Under the ocean the crust, called oceanic crust, is 4 miles (6 km) thick, but under mountain ranges the continental crust can be 40 miles (64 km) thick.

The rock plates of the Earth's crust fit together like pieces of a jigsaw puzzle.

CROSS-SECTION THROUGH THE EARTH'S CRUST
This section through the Earth's crust at the Equator shows the landscape and the direction of plate movement at plate boundaries.

AFRICA

African Rift Valley

INDIAN OCEAN

Indo-Australian plate

African plate

African plate

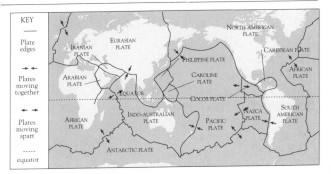

PLATES OF THE WORLD
The surface of the Earth has 15 large plates. A plate can include both continental lithosphere and oceanic lithosphere. Areas such as Australia lie in the middle of a plate, while others, like Iceland, have a plate boundary through them.

MOVEMENT OF THE EARTH'S PLATES

PLATE NAMES	DIRECTION OF MOVEMENT	RATE OF MOVEMENT	
		CM PER YEAR	IN PER YEAR
Pacific/Nazca	apart	18.3	7.2
Cocos/Pacific	apart	11.7	4.6
Nazca/South American	together	11.2	4.4
Pacific/Indo-Australian	together	10.5	4.1
Pacific/Antarctic	apart	10.3	4.0

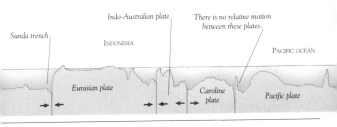

MOVING CONTINENTS

EARTH'S CONTINENTS can be rearranged to fit together like pieces of a jigsaw puzzle. This idea made scientists think that they once formed a giant landmass, Pangaea. This "supercontinent" broke up and the continents drifted, over millions of years, to where they are now. This is continental drift, or plate tectonics, theory. Continents move as the Earth's plates move, sliding along on the asthenosphere, a layer of soft mantle.

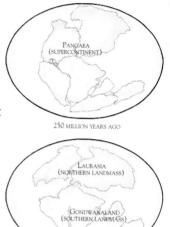

PANGAEA (SUPERCONTINENT)

250 MILLION YEARS AGO

LAURASIA (NORTHERN LANDMASS)

GONDWANALAND (SOUTHERN LANDMASS)

120 MILLION YEARS AGO

CONTINENTAL DRIFT
When Pangaea broke up, new continents emerged. The outlines of South America and Africa appeared.

CROSS-SECTION THROUGH THE EARTH'S CRUST

PACIFIC OCEAN

Pacific plate

Nazca plate

PLATE BOUNDARIES

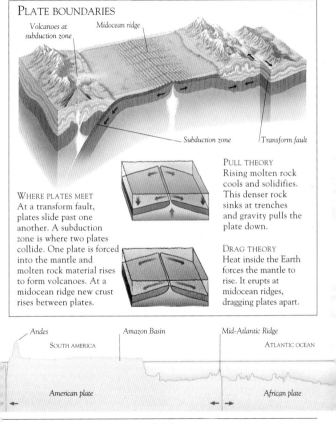

Volcanoes at subduction zone

Midocean ridge

Subduction zone

Transform fault

WHERE PLATES MEET
At a transform fault, plates slide past one another. A subduction zone is where two plates collide. One plate is forced into the mantle and molten rock material rises to form volcanoes. At a midocean ridge new crust rises between plates.

PULL THEORY
Rising molten rock cools and solidifies. This denser rock sinks at trenches and gravity pulls the plate down.

DRAG THEORY
Heat inside the Earth forces the mantle to rise. It erupts at midocean ridges, dragging plates apart.

Andes

Amazon Basin

Mid-Atlantic Ridge

SOUTH AMERICA

ATLANTIC OCEAN

American plate

African plate

INSIDE THE EARTH

THE INTERIOR OF the Earth has four major layers. On the outside is the crust made of familiar soil and rock. Under this is the mantle, which is solid rock with a molten layer at the top. The inside or core of the Earth has two sections: an outer core of thick fluid, and a solid inner core.

The atmosphere stretches about 400 miles (640 km) into space.

The crust varies between about 4 to 40 miles (6 to 64 km) thick.

The crust and rigid upper part of the mantle are called the lithosphere.

The crust floats on semifluid layer of the mantle called the asthenosphere.

The mantle is 1,800 miles (2,900 km) thick.

The outer core is 1,240 miles (2,000 km) thick.

The inner core is 1,700 miles (2,740 km) thick.

LAYERS OF THE EARTH
Earth's outer shell is called the lithosphere. It includes the crust and part of the upper mantle. The crust floats on the asthenosphere, like an iceberg on the sea. Earth's outer core is mostly oxygen, liquid iron, and nickel. Its inner core, about 7,232°F (4,000°C), is solid iron and nickel.

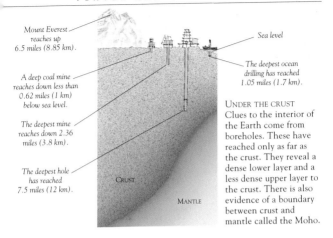

Mount Everest reaches up 6.5 miles (8.85 km).

A deep coal mine reaches down less than 0.62 miles (1 km) below sea level.

The deepest mine reaches down 2.36 miles (3.8 km).

The deepest hole has reached 7.5 miles (12 km).

Sea level

The deepest ocean drilling has reached 1.05 miles (1.7 km).

CRUST

MANTLE

UNDER THE CRUST
Clues to the interior of the Earth come from boreholes. These have reached only as far as the crust. They reveal a dense lower layer and a less dense upper layer to the crust. There is also evidence of a boundary between crust and mantle called the Moho.

CRUST FACTS
• If an excavator could dig a hole through the Earth at 39 in (1 m) per minute, it would take 24 years to reach the other side.

• Western Deep Gold Mine in South Africa is the world's deepest mine. It is 2.36 miles (3.8 km) deep.

• The Earth's crust is mainly granitelike rock.

COMPOSITION OF THE EARTH'S CRUST
Light elements such as silicon, oxygen, and aluminum make up the Earth's crust. Oceanic crust is mostly basalt (which also contains magnesium and iron). Continental crust is composed of granitelike rocks. These may have formed from recycled basaltic ocean crust.

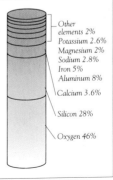

Other elements 2%
Potassium 2.6%
Magnesium 2%
Sodium 2.8%
Iron 5%
Aluminum 8%
Calcium 3.6%

Silicon 28%

Oxygen 46%

EXTINCT VOLCANO
Castle Rock, Edinburgh is an extinct volcano. It has not erupted for 340 million years. An extinct volcano such as this is not expected to erupt again.

DORMANT VOLCANO
If scientists believe a volcano may erupt again, perhaps because it gives off volcanic gases, it is called dormant. Mt. Rainier, WA, is considered dormant.

THE EARTH'S VOLCANOES

MOST VOLCANOES are found at plate boundaries near the Pacific coast or at mid-ocean ridges. Here fractures in the lithosphere allow molten rock, called magma, to rise from the mantle inside the Earth. Magma is known as lava when it flows out of a volcano. Ash, steam, and gas also spew out from a volcano and can cause a great deal of destruction.

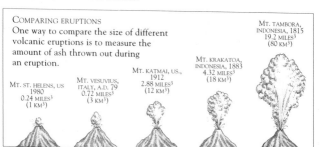

COMPARING ERUPTIONS
One way to compare the size of different volcanic eruptions is to measure the amount of ash thrown out during an eruption.

MT. ST. HELENS, US
1980
0.24 MILES^3
(1 KM^3)

MT. VESUVIUS,
ITALY, A.D. 79
0.72 MILES^3
(3 KM^3)

MT. KATMAI, US.,
1912
2.88 MILES^3
(12 KM^3)

MT. KRAKATOA,
INDONESIA, 1883
4.32 MILES^3
(18 KM^3)

MT. TAMBORA,
INDONESIA, 1815
19.2 MILES^3
(80 KM^3)

VOLCANO SITES

In general, volcanoes, like earthquakes, occur near plate boundaries. Volcanoes are formed by plate destruction or the presence of a hot spot underneath the plate.

The chain of volcanoes around the edge of the Pacific Ocean is known as the "Ring of Fire."

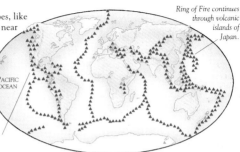

Ring of Fire continues through volcanic islands of Japan.

PACIFIC OCEAN

POMPEII
In A.D 79 Mt. Vesuvius erupted, burying the town of Pompeii under dust and ash. The two-day eruption killed 2,000 people with poisonous gases and hot ash.

LARGEST VOLCANIC EXPLOSIONS

The Volcanic Explosivity Index (V.E.I.) grades eruptions from 0 to 8. The scale is based on the height of the dust cloud, the volume of tephra (debris ejected by a volcano), and an account of the severity of the eruption. Any eruption above 5 on the scale is very large and violent. So far, there has never been an eruption of 8.

VOLCANO	DATE	V.E.I.
Crater Lake, Oregon	c.4895 B.C.	7
Towada, Honshu, Japan	915	5
Oraefajokull, Iceland	1362	6
Tambora, Indonesia	1815	7
Krakatoa, Indonesia	1883	6
Santa Maria, Guatemala	1902	6
Katmai, US	1912	6
Mt. St. Helens, Washington	1980	5

VOLCANO SHAPES

NOT ALL VOLCANOES are the same. Some are cone-shaped and others are almost flat. The shape of the volcano depends on the kind of lava that erupts. Soupy, nonviscous lava spreads quickly before hardening, but stiff, viscous lava piles up near the volcanic vent. Volcanoes usually appear near plate boundaries, but they also form at hot spots such as in Hawaii. Volcanoes also exist under the ocean at plate edges.

ICELAND'S RIFT
Skaftar fissure in Iceland lies where two plates are moving apart. It is part of a 16-mile (27-km) rift along the plates' edges.

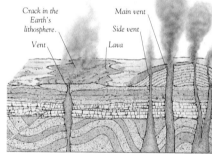

Crack in the Earth's lithosphere

Vent

Main vent

Side vent

Lava

FISSURE VOLCANO
This type of volcano arises from a long crack in the lithosphere. Nonviscous lava flows out to form a plateau.

SHIELD VOLCANO
A large, gently sloping volcanic cone. It grows when nonviscous lava erupts from a central vent or side vents.

WORST VOLCANIC ERUPTIONS		
VOLCANO	DATE	HUMAN DEATHS
Tambora	1815	92,000
Mt. Pelée	1902	40,000
Krakatoa	1883	36,000
Nevado del Ruiz	1985	23,000

COMPOSITE VOLCANO
Cone-shaped volcanoes build up from viscous lava. Inside are layers of thick lava and ash from previous eruptions. Gas pressure inside the volcano magma chamber causes violent eruptions.

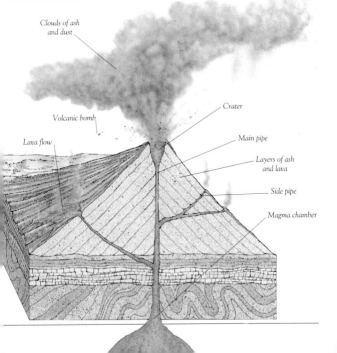

Clouds of ash and dust

Volcanic bomb

Lava flow

Crater

Main pipe

Layers of ash and lava

Side pipe

Magma chamber

EXPLOSIVE VOLCANOES

SOMETIMES VOLCANOES explode violently. Volcanoes that form from viscous lava are most likely to do this.

Viscous lava tends to plug up volcanic vents. When pressure in the magma chamber increases, the lava is blown out. Pieces of rock and a great deal of ash are hurled high into the air. Clouds of ash and pumice flow like hot avalanches down the sides of the volcano. Mudflows (also called lahars) are a mixture of water and ash. They travel at great speed and engulf everything in their paths.

NUÉE ARDENTE
An explosive eruption can cause a glowing ash cloud or *nuée ardente*.

BEFORE MT. ST. HELENS ERUPTED

MT. ST. HELENS
In the Cascades a peaceful-looking volcano erupted after 123 years of dormancy. A warning came when one side of the volcano began to bulge as the magma rose. A gas explosion lasting 9 hours and a landslide ensued. An ash cloud over 580 miles^2 (1,500 km^2) caused darkness. Melted snow and ash made mudflows.

ERUPTION ON MAY 18TH 1980

DEVASTATING MUDFLOWS
When Ruiz volcano in Colombia erupted in 1985, the snow melted around its summit. A mixture of water, dust, and ash fast turned to mud and buried the nearby city of Armero. More than 22,000 people were drowned in the mud.

PUMICE FACTS
• Pumice is really light-weight frothed glass that is able to float on water.

• Pumice is used in industry as an abrasive for soft metals. It is also used for insulation in some buildings.

PRODUCTS OF EXPLOSIVE VOLCANOES

ASH
Lava particles larger than dust cover the land.

LAPILLI
Lava ejected in pea-sized pieces is called lapilli.

PUMICE
Pumice is light-weight lava filled with holes.

BOMB
Bomb-shaped lava forms as it flies in the air.

PELE'S HAIR
Sometimes drops of liquid lava blow into fine spiky strands. The threads form needles of volcanic glass. They are named Pele's hair after Pele, the Hawaiian goddess of volcanoes.

NONEXPLOSIVE VOLCANOES

SOME VOLCANOES arise from fissures. Nonviscous lava flows for long distances before cooling. It builds broad plateaus or low-sided volcanoes. This kind of volcano forms at plate edges, mostly under the ocean. A hot spot volcano bursts through the middle of a plate; it is not related to plate margins.

SPREADING RIDGES
Flows of basalt lava from fissures form mountains along the edges of separating plates. These spreading ridges are usually underwater. In some places, such as Iceland, lava erupts along the crack forming rift mountains above sea level.

TYPES OF LAVA

PAHOEHOE LAVA
Lava with a wrinkled skin is called pahoehoe. This nonviscous lava cools to form a "ropy" surface. Such flows of basalt pahoehoe lava are common in Hawaii.

AA LAVA
This is an Hawaiian word for slow-moving, viscous lava. When aa lava solidifies it has a rough, jagged surface that is also described as blocky.

HAWAIIAN VOLCANOES
At places called hot spots, notably in Hawaii, magma rises to create fire fountains and fire curtains.

HOT SPOT VOLCANOES
The Earth's plates move slowly over hot spots in the crust. Magma rises, punching through the lithosphere to form a new island. In Hawaii, hot spots have built a chain of islands.

BASALT COLUMNS
Northern Ireland's Giant's Causeway is made of mostly hexagonal columns of basalt rock. They formed as thick lava flows cooled and vertical shrinkage cracks developed.

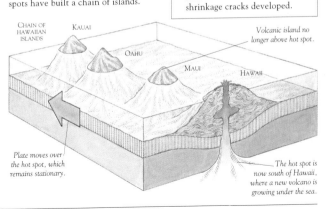

CHAIN OF HAWAIIAN ISLANDS

KAUAI

OAHU

MAUI

HAWAII

Volcanic island no longer above hot spot.

Plate moves over the hot spot, which remains stationary.

The hot spot is now south of Hawaii, where a new volcano is growing under the sea.

VOLCANIC LANDSCAPES

MOVEMENT IN ROCKS underground can cause changes to the landscape above. The combination of heat and water in the Earth's rocks produces various phenomena. Molten rock erupting out of the Earth brings gases, mineral deposits, and water with it. Mud pools, hot springs, and geysers form when the gases and water escape. Minerals dissolved in the hot waters precipitate to form cone-like or terraced deposits of rocks.

OLD FAITHFUL
This geyser is in Yellowstone Park, Wyoming. It has shot out a column of boiling water and steam every hour for the last 100 years.

THE LANDSCAPE AROUND VOLCANOES

Steaming hot water

Volcanic gases bubble through liquid mud

HOT SPRINGS
Magma warms water in cracks in the rock. Water returns to the surface as a hot spring.

MUD POOLS
Steam, particles of rock, and volcanic gases bubble through pools of liquid mud.

FUMAROLES
Vents, or fumeroles, allow steam and other gases to escape from cooling rocks.

PILLOW LAVA

When lava erupts underwater it can produce these rounded shapes, which are known as pillow lava. The seawater cools the lava rapidly, so that as it solidifies a crust forms around each lump. The lava formed is typically an igneous rock called basalt.

A NEW ISLAND

In 1963, off the southern coast of Iceland, a new volcanic island rose from the ocean floor. This island, Surtsey, formed from the buildup of lava flows. Seawater interacting with lava produced explosions and huge amounts of steam.

GEYSERS

Heat from magma chambers causes ground water to boil, erupting as jets of steam and water.

TERRACES

Minerals, dissolved in heated ground water, are deposited in layers that rise around a vent.

GEYSER FACTS

• The tallest geyser is Yellowstone National Park's Steamboat Geyser in Wyoming. It reaches 195–380 ft (60–115 m).

• Strokkur Geyser in Iceland spurts every 10 to 15 minutes.

• In 1904, Waimangu Geyser, New Zealand erupted to a height of 1,500 ft (460 m).

WHEN THE EARTH SHAKES

MORE THAN A million times a year, the Earth's crust suddenly shakes during an earthquake. Most of the world's earthquakes are fairly slight. A mild earthquake can feel like a truck passing; a severe one can destroy roads and buildings and cause the sea to rise in huge waves. Earthquakes often happen near volcanoes and young mountain ranges: at the edges of the Earth's plates.

Surface waves radiate from the epicenter.

The focus is below the epicenter.

Shock waves go through the Earth and up to the surface.

A SEVERE EARTHQUAKE
The city of San Francisco was shaken by a devastating earthquake in 1906. Only the chimney stacks were left standing.

CENTER OF AN EARTHQUAKE
The earthquake is strongest at the focus. At the epicenter, the point on the surface above the focus, the crust shakes and sends out shock waves. Internal waves bend as they travel through the Earth.

EARTHQUAKE FAULT ZONES

Earthquakes occur at cracks in the lithosphere called faults. Deep earthquakes take place where one plate is sliding under another.

Many earthquakes occur on the northeast coast of Asia. This is at the boundary of two of the Earth's plates.

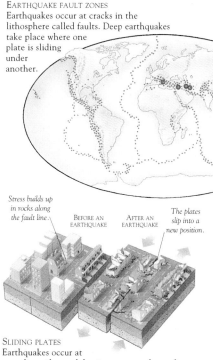

Stress builds up in rocks along the fault line.

BEFORE AN EARTHQUAKE

AFTER AN EARTHQUAKE

The plates slip into a new position.

SLIDING PLATES

Earthquakes occur at spreading ridges, subduction zones, and transform faults, where two plates slide past each other. Stress builds up in rock and causes a sudden movement as the rock jolts into a new position. Foreshocks may precede an earthquake, and aftershocks follow it.

EARTHQUAKE FACTS

• Before some earthquakes it is reported that dogs howl, pandas moan, and well water bubbles.

• A strong earthquake can cause the ground to roll like waves at sea.

• The 1755 earthquake in Lisbon, Portugal lasted 10 minutes. It was felt as far away as North Africa.

• About 90 percent of earthquakes occur in the Ring of Fire around the Pacific Ocean.

MEASURING EARTHQUAKES

SCIENTISTS WHO STUDY earthquakes are known as seismologists (*seismos* is the Greek word for earthquakes). Seismologists monitor the vibrations or shock waves that pass through the Earth using an instrument called a seismometer. Predicting earthquakes is very difficult. Scientists look for warnings such as bulges or small cracks on the surface of the ground.

EARTHQUAKE DESTRUCTION
In 1994 in the city of Los Angeles an earthquake caused devastation. Roads and buildings collapsed, water mains and gas pipes burst, and fires began in the city. Many buildings in Los Angeles were built to be earthquake-proof and so did not suffer very much damage. The earthquake measured 5.7 on the Richter scale.

MERCALLI SCALE
Giuseppe Mercalli (1850–1914) devised a method of grading earthquakes based on the observation of their effects. Using this scale enables the amount of shaking, or intensity, of different earthquakes to be easily compared. On Mercalli's scale earthquakes are graded from 1 to 12.

1 • detected by instruments
2 • felt by people resting
3 • hanging lamps sway
4 • felt by people indoors
  • plates, windows rattle
  • parked cars rock

5 • buildings tremble
  • felt by most people
  • liquids spill
6 • movement felt by all
  • pictures fall off wall
  • windows break

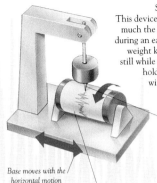

SEISMOMETER
This device records how much the Earth shakes during an earthquake. A weight keeps the pen still while the machine holding it moves with the Earth.

A pen records the movement on a rotating drum.

Base moves with the horizontal motion of the Earth.

The recording from a seismometer is called a seismogram. It shows an amplified wave form, resulting from the motion of the Earth's surface.

RICHTER SCALE

The amount of energy released by an earthquake can be measured on the Richter scale. An increase of 1.0 on the scale represents a tenfold increase in energy.

EARTHQUAKE	DATE	RICHTER SCALE
North Peru	1970	7.7
Mexico City	1985	7.8
Erzincan	1939	7.9
Tangshan	1976	8.0
Tokyo	1923	8.3
Kansu	1920	8.6

7 • bricks and tiles fall
  • chimneys crack
  • difficult to stand
8 • steering cars difficult
  • tree branches snap
  • chimneys fall

9 • some buildings collapse
  • ground cracks
  • mud oozes from ground
10 • underground pipes burst
  • river water spills out
  • most buildings collapse

11 • bridges collapse
  • railroad tracks buckle
  • landslides occur
12 • near total destruction
  • rivers change course
  • waves seen on ground

EARTHQUAKE DAMAGE

IN GENERAL, great loss of life during an earthquake can be avoided. It is often not the Earth's shaking that kills people but falling buildings, particularly poorly constructed ones. Landslides and tsunamis also cause a lot of damage. During an average earthquake, it is best to stay indoors in a doorway or under a sturdy table. Falling masonry is a hazard outdoors.

ESTIMATED LIVES LOST AS A RESULT OF RECENT EARTHQUAKES		
PLACE	YEAR	ESTIMATED DEATHS
Tangshan, China	1976	695,000
Kansu, China	1920	100,000
Tokyo, Japan	1976	99,000
Messina, Italy	1908	80,000
Armenia	1988	55,000
Northwest Iran	1990	40,000
Erzincan, Turkey	1939	30,000

FIRE HAZARD
Fire poses a great danger following an earthquake. Gas leaks and oil spills can lead to large fires like this in San Francisco in 1989.

JAPANESE PRINT SHOWING
A GREAT TSUNAMI WITH
MT. FUJI, JAPAN, IN THE
BACKGROUND

TSUNAMIS

An earthquake on the continental shelf can start a wave at sea. Such waves have low height in deep water. As the wave nears shore its front slows and water behind builds up to form a huge tsunami.

TSUNAMI FACTS

• The highest tsunami wave was 279 ft (85 m) high. It struck Ishigaki Island, Japan in 1971.

• In the open ocean, a tsunami can travel at speeds of 370 miles (600 km) per hour.

EARTHQUAKE-PROOF BUILDINGS

A great deal of damage is caused by buildings collapsing during earthquakes. In earthquake-prone San Francisco and Japan there are safety guidelines that all new buildings must meet. Wooden buildings are replaced with concrete and concrete and steel foundations are used.

LANDSLIDES

Loose rock and debris may be dislodged by an earthquake and cause landslides as in Alaska in 1964. Avalanches too may be triggered by the ground shaking. Mudflows or lahars can result from rain or snow mixing with loosened soil.

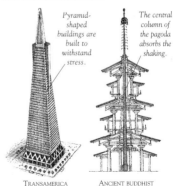

Pyramid-shaped buildings are built to withstand stress.

The central column of the pagoda absorbs the shaking.

TRANSAMERICA
BUILDING, SAN FRANCISCO

ANCIENT BUDDHIST
PAGODA, JAPAN

LANDSCAPES AND SOIL

WEATHERING PROCESSES are primarily responsible for soil development. These processes take thousands of years. Climate, vegetation, and rock type determine what type of soil forms. Soil contains organic matter from decaying plants and animals (humus) as well as sand, silt, and clay. It covers the landscape and provides a medium for plants to grow in.

PEAT LANDSCAPE
This landscape is green and low-lying. Spongy peat soil is rich in humus from decayed bog plants. It retains water and nutrients easily.

SANDY LANDSCAPE
In arid (dry) sandy landscapes there is little vegetation. The soil contains hardly any organic material. Winds blow away small particles, leaving sand and stones.

TYPES OF SOIL
Chalky soil is thin and stony; water passes through it quickly. Water drains easily through sandy soil, washing out nutrients. Clay soil retains nutrients and moisture but is difficult for plants to take root in. Peat soil is acidic. It holds water and minerals.

CLAY

SAND

PEAT

CHALK

SOIL FACTS

• 35 ft³ (1 m³) of soil may contain more than one billion animals.

• Some soils in India, Africa, and Australia are 2 million years old.

• It can take 500 years for 1 in (2.5 cm) of topsoil to form.

SOIL PROFILE

A slice of soil down to the bedrock is called a soil profile. The profile shows several layers, or horizons. The number and thickness of horizons vary with the soil type.

HORIZON O
• humus layer
• contains live and decaying plants and soil animals

HORIZON A
• topsoil
• dark and fertile
• rich in humus

HORIZON B
• subsoil
• contains minerals washed down from topsoil
• little organic matter
• lighter colored

HORIZON C
• infertile layer
• composed of weathered parent rock

HORIZON D
• bedrock (parent rock)
• source of soil's minerals

SOIL CREEP AND EROSION

Gravity and water pull soil down a slope particle by particle. This is called soil creep. Plant roots bind soil and help to prevent it from wearing away, or eroding. Overgrazing and felling forests both lead to soil erosion.

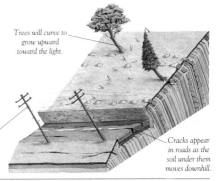

Trees will curve to grow upward toward the light.

Soil creep is indicated by leaning structures such as walls and telegraph poles.

Cracks appear in roads as the soil under them moves downhill.

EROSION IN WET CLIMATES

AS SOON AS ROCK is exposed on the Earth's surface, it is attacked by wind, water, or ice – a process known as weathering. This prepares for erosion, when rock is broken down and removed. Weathering can be either physical (wearing away the rock itself) or chemical (attacking the minerals in the rock). Climate and rock type determine the kind of weathering that occurs. In wet climates chemical weathering, mainly by rainwater, is dominant.

MOUNTAIN STREAM
Cascading over steep gradients, a swift-flowing stream wears away softer rocks. Harder rocks remain and create rocky outcrops. These become steep rapids or waterfalls.

TREE-ROOT ACTION
As trees and other plants grow, their roots push down into small cracks in the rock. The cracks widen as the roots grow and eventually the rock breaks up.

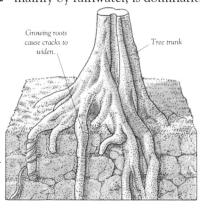

Growing roots cause cracks to widen.

Tree trunk

FROST SHATTERING

This type of weathering occurs when water in cracks in the rock freezes and expands. Joints in the rock widen and the rock shatters.

Shattering leaves sharp broken edges on the rock's surface.

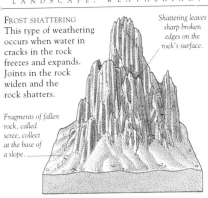

Fragments of fallen rock, called scree, collect at the base of a slope.

EROSION FACTS

• Acid rain can dissolve rock as deep as 98 ft (30 m) below the surface.

• Erosion is fastest in steep, rainy areas and semiarid areas with little vegetation.

• The rate of erosion for the whole of the world's land area is estimated to be 3.3 in (8.6 cm) every 1,000 years.

CLINTS AND GRIKES

Acid in rainwater seeps into limestone joints and dissolves the calcite in the rock. Ridges known as clints and grooves known as grikes form in the rock.

ACID RAIN

Rainwater naturally contains a weak acid called carbonic acid. However, the burning of fossil fuels produces gases such as sulfur dioxide. When this combines with rainwater it produces sulfuric acid – an ingredient of "acid rain." Acid rain damages trees and lake life.

Acid rain slowly dissolves rocks such as limestone and marble.

LIMESTONE STATUES SUFFER EROSION BY ACID RAIN

EROSION IN ARID CLIMATES

IN HOT, DRY, DESERT areas extremes of temperature cause rocks to fragment. By day rock expands in the heat and by night it contracts in the cold. It is mainly physical weathering that occurs in arid climates, chiefly caused by wind. The sand-filled wind helps to erode rocks and build shifting sand dunes.

Some rocks break away and fall to the ground.

Larger rock masses split into blocks.

BLOCK DISINTEGRATION
Acute temperature changes can cause rocks to break up. Joints in the rock grow wider with the rock's cycle of expansion and contraction. Large pieces split into small blocks.

ONION-SKIN LAYERING
In the heat of the desert, a rock's surface may expand though the interior stays cool. At night, the surface of the rock cools and contracts. This daily process causes flaking on the surface of the rock, and the outer layers begin to peel and fall away.

SAND DUNES

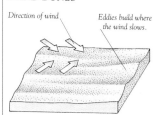

Direction of wind

Eddies build where the wind slows.

LINEAR OR SEIF DUNE
This type of dune has long parallel ridges. It forms where the wind blows continually in one direction.

ZEUGENS

Sand carried by the wind sculpts these strange forms called zeugens. Sand wears away soft rock leaving behind areas of harder rock, worn into jagged shapes.

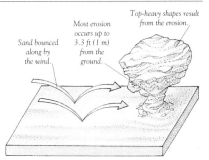

Top-heavy shapes result from the erosion.

Most erosion occurs up to 3.3 ft (1 m) from the ground.

Sand bounced along by the wind

MUSHROOM ROCKS (PEDESTAL ROCKS)

The desert wind contains a great deal of sand which scours away the surface of rocks. Mushroom-shaped rocks are a result of this action. Rocks are worn away most at their base by the sand, leaving behind a landscape of rock pedestals.

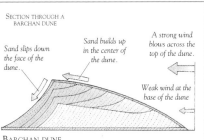

SECTION THROUGH A BARCHAN DUNE

Sand slips down the face of the dune.

Sand builds up in the center of the dune.

A strong wind blows across the top of the dune.

Weak wind at the base of the dune

BARCHAN DUNE

A sand dune with a cresent-shaped front and a long, sloping rear is called a barchan dune. This is the most common dune shape for sandy deserts.

SAND DUNE FACTS

• Sand is composed mostly of the hard mineral quartz.

• Linear or seif dunes can reach 700 ft (215 m) high.

• Not all dunes are made of sand – dunes can form from salt crystals, gypsum, or shell fragments.

• Black sand dunes form in volcanic areas.

IGNEOUS ROCKS

MAGMA THAT COOLS solidifies into igneous rocks. The rock material of the lower lithosphere and mantle is semimolten. Sudden release of confining pressure allows this material to change to liquid magma. Magma that cools and solidifies under the Earth's surface forms intrusive igneous rock. If it erupts as lava from a volcano and cools on the Earth's surface it forms extrusive igneous rock.

INTRUSIVE IGNEOUS ROCK
Sugar Loaf Mountain, Brazil formed from magma that solidified underground. Eventually, the surrounding rock eroded, leaving this dome

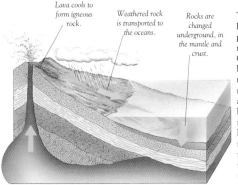

Lava cools to form igneous rock.

Weathered rock is transported to the oceans.

Rocks are changed underground, in the mantle and crust.

THE ROCK CYCLE
Rocks constantly pass through a recycling process. Crustal movements bring igneous rocks to the surface. The rocks weather away and the particles build sedimentary rocks. Pressure and heat underground may change, or metamorphose, rocks before they reemerge.

SYDNEY HARBOR BRIDGE
The supporting pylons of this famous bridge in Sydney, Australia are built from granite. The span of the bridge is 1,650 ft (503 m) and the arch is made of steel. Granite is often used as a building material because of its strength and availability.

IGNEOUS ROCK FACTS
• Basalt makes up most of the ocean floor.

• Obsidian was used in early jewelry and tools.

• Most continental igneous rocks are quartz, feldspar, and mica.

• Earth's first rocks were igneous rocks.

TYPES OF IGNEOUS ROCK

Shell-like, curved fracture

OBSIDIAN
This natural glass forms from rapid cooling of granitic lava.

Granite has coarse grains

GABBRO
This intrusive, coarse-grained rock forms from slow-cooled lava.

BASALT
Nonviscous lava that flows great distances forms fine-grained basalt.

PINK GRANITE
Granite is a common intrusive rock. Crystals of pink feldspar, black mica, and gray quartz minerals are visible.

SEDIMENTARY ROCKS

ROCK IS GRADUALLY weakened by the weather. Particles of rock are then carried off by rain or wind. These particles build up into layers of sediment. Evaporation of ground water may leave behind minerals, such as silica, calcium carbonate, and iron oxides, that cement the sediment grains (a process known as lithification). Studying sedimentary rock layers can reveal ancient environments.

STRATA
Over millions of years, layers of sediment are cemented into bands of rock called strata. Strata in the Grand Canyon, Arizona preserve a record of the region's history.

FLINT TOOLS
Prehistoric people fashioned tools from a sedimentary rock called flint. Flint was chipped into shape using a stone. It is a common rock that flakes easily, leaving a sharp edge. Prehistoric tools such as hand axes and adzes (for shaping wood) have been found.

FLINT ADZE

CHALK CLIFFS
These cliffs in Sussex, England are a type of limestone. They are calcium carbonate (chalk) and contain fossils of microorganisms.

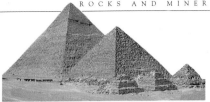

EGYPTIAN PYRAMIDS AT GIZA
Elaborate tombs (begun c. 2686) for the Egyptian pharaohs were constructed at Giza, Egypt. They were built from nummulitic limestone which contains many large marine fossils called *nummulites*.

SEDIMENTARY FACTS
• Chalk consists of tiny shells, visible only under a microscope.

• Mudstone forms from compressed mud grains, and sandstone from compressed sand grains.

• Oil is usually found in permeable and porous sandstones.

TYPES OF SEDIMENTARY ROCK

BRECCIA
Angular fragments of rock are cemented together to form a breccia.

CHALK
Skeletons of tiny sea animals form this type of limestone. Chalk is fine-grained and soft.

RED SANDSTONE
Cemented sand grains coated with iron oxide make up this sedimentary rock.

SHELLY LIMESTONE
This rock contains a great many fossils cemented together with calcite. Limestone usually forms in a shallow sea, though it can come from a freshwater environment. It is possible to find the source of a specimen by studying the fossils it contains.

FOSSILS

PLANTS AND ANIMALS that lived millions of years ago are preserved in rocks as fossils. A fossil is the remains of an organism, a cast of an animal or plant made from minerals, or even burrows or tracks left by animals and preserved in rock. Sedimentary rocks such as limestone or chalk hold fossils. Paleontologists are scientists who study fossils.

PLANT FOSSIL
Seed ferns like this one were widespread in the hot swamps of the late Carboniferous period. These primitive land plants, with some adaptations, still exist today.

THE FOSSILIZATION PROCESS

1 When an animal or plant dies underwater, it falls to the seabed. The soft parts of its body decay or are eaten by animals.

2 The organism is buried in layers of sediment. Hard parts of the animal, such as the shell, bones, or teeth, are preserved.

3 Minerals in the seabed react with the animal's shell to harden it. Some animals decay, leaving a space where a cast forms.

SEED FERN
(ALETHOPTERIS)

INSECT FOSSIL
Early dragonflies, preserved in limestone, have been found in Europe and Australasia. This one dates from the Jurassic period.

DRAGONFLY
(PETALURA)

FISH FOSSIL
Fish are the most primitive vertebrates (animals with backbones). This fish first appeared 30 to 24.5 million years ago, long after the dinosaurs had died out.

FISH FROM THE OLIGOCENE PERIOD

4 Further sediments cover the fossil. Uplift of the lithosphere or erosion may eventually expose the fossil.

TRACE FOSSILS
Fossilized droppings or tracks are called trace fossils. This dinosaur footprint was left in mud 135 million years ago.

FOSSIL FACTS
• The oldest dinosaur fossils, of prosauropods, date back 230 million years. They were found in Madagascar in 1999.

• The largest fossil footprint was left by a hadrosaurid. It is 4 ft 6 in (1.36 m) long.

• Fossils of cells are the first evidence of life, 3,500 million years ago.

THE AGES OF THE EARTH

THE LARGEST DIVISIONS of Earth's history are eras, periods, and epochs. The timescale is marked by the appearance of new life-forms. Life on Earth is never static – it constantly changes and evolves. Creatures become extinct and others appear. Some types of creatures may be short-lived and others survive unchanged for millions of years. Fossils can build up a picture of life in the past.

JELLYFISH FOSSIL

PRECAMBRIAN FOSSIL
This fossil is about 570 million years old. It is a kind of primitive jellyfish that lived in Australia.

MORE FOSSIL FACTS

• Our species, *Homo sapiens*, appeared between 100,000 and 400,000 years ago.

• A million Ice Age fossils were found in tar pits at La Brea, California.

CARBONIFEROUS SWAMP
Extensive swamps covered Earth during the Carboniferous period (354–290 million years ago). It was during this time that forests, containing seed plants and ferns, flourished. Some of these were preserved and now form coal deposits. The first reptiles and giant dragonflies lived in these swamps.

DILOPHOSAURUS
(TWO-RIDGED LIZARD)

*Distinguishing tall,
double crest on
the skull*

THE DINOSAUR AGE
The first land-dwelling
dinosaurs appeared in the
Triassic period. The age
of the dinosaurs
lasted through
the Jurassic and Cretaceous periods.
This skeleton is from *Dilophosaurus*,
an agile, predatory Jurassic dinosaur.

HOMO
HABILIS

EARLY HUMANS
Homo habilis (handy man) is an
early human, dating from the
Quaternary period. The name of
this ancestor comes from the fossil
evidence that the early human was
skilled in using crude tools.

GEOLOGICAL TIMESCALE		
ERA	PERIOD: MILLIONS OF YEARS AGO (MYA)	
CENOZOIC	QUATERNARY 2 MYA–PRESENT	
	TERTIARY 65–2 MYA	
MESOZOIC	CRETACEOUS 142–65 MYA	
	JURASSIC 206–142 MYA	
	TRIASSIC 248–206 MYA	
PALEOZOIC	PERMIAN 290–248 MYA	
	CARBONIFEROUS 354–290 MYA	
	DEVONIAN 417–354 MYA	
	SILURIAN 443–417 MYA	
	ORDOVICIAN 495–443 MYA	
	CAMBRIAN 545–495 MYA	
	PRECAMBRIAN 4,600–545 MYA	

METAMORPHIC ROCKS

SEDIMENTARY, metamorphic, or igneous rocks are remade into new metamorphic rocks. The rock doesn't melt but it is changed underground by pressure and heat. During mountain building, in particular, intense pressure over millions of years alters the texture and nature of rocks. Igneous rocks such as granite change into gneiss and sedimentary rocks like limestone into marble.

SLATE MOUNTAINS
Fine-grained slate forms from sedimentary rocks. Rocks such as shale or mudstone are compressed during mountain building and changed into slate. Slate's aligned crystals let it split, or cleave, easily into flat sheets.

Carved white marble

MARBLE SCULPTURE
Michelangelo's statue of David is carved in marble. Marble comes in many varieties. It is a relatively soft rock that is often sculpted.

> METAMORPHIC FACTS
>
> • The oldest rock on Earth is a metamorphic rock. It is Amitsoc gneiss from Amitsoc Bay, Greenland.
>
> • Rubies are found in metamorphic limestone in the Himalayas. They formed during mountain building.

REGIONAL METAMORPHISM
Extreme pressure and heat created during mountain building lead to regional metamorphism. Metamorphism on this scale can cover a vast area.

Intrusive igneous rock exposed by weathering.

Aureole (area where metamorphism has taken place)

Migmatite showing swirls of folded rock

CONTACT METAMORPHISM
Rocks near to a lava flow or to an intrusion of igneous rock can be altered by contact metamorphism. This metamorphism affects a small area and is generated by heat alone.

TYPES OF METAMORPHIC ROCK

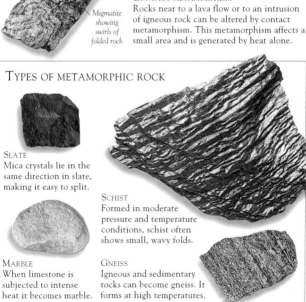

SLATE
Mica crystals lie in the same direction in slate, making it easy to split.

SCHIST
Formed in moderate pressure and temperature conditions, schist often shows small, wavy folds.

MARBLE
When limestone is subjected to intense heat it becomes marble.

GNEISS
Igneous and sedimentary rocks can become gneiss. It forms at high temperatures.

CALCITE

Perfect cleavage plane through the crystal.

CLEAVAGE AND FRACTURE
Diamond and calcite cleave when they break. Cleavage is a smooth break between layers of atoms in a crystal. A fracture is an uneven break, not related to the internal atomic structure. Most minerals fracture and cleave.

MINERALS

ROCKS ARE MADE from non-living, natural substances called minerals, which may be alone or in combination. Marble is pure calcite, for example, but granite is a mixture of quartz, feldspar, and mica. Most minerals are silicates (compounds of oxygen and silicon). Minerals with regular arrangements of atoms may form large, regular crystals. To identify a mineral, properties such as crystal structure, color, and hardness are tested.

MOHS' SCALE	1	2	3	4
A German mineralogist named Friedrich Mohs devised a scale to compare the hardness of different minerals. A mineral is able to scratch any others below it on the scale and can be scratched by any mineral above it.	TALC	GYPSUM	CALCITE	FLUORITE

MINERAL FACTS

- Only a diamond will scratch a diamond.
- Quartz is found in igneous, sedimentary, and metamorphic rock.
- The word "crystal" comes from a Greek word *kyros* meaning "icy cold."

PLAGIOCLASE FELDSPAR

FELDSPAR
This type of rock-forming mineral is in both basalt and granite.

QUARTZ OR ROCK CRYSTAL

QUARTZ
A common mineral, quartz comes in many different colors. Amethyst and citrine are varieties of quartz.

COLOR STREAKS
Scratching a mineral on an unglazed tile produces a colored streak. The color of the powder left behind is known as the mineral's streak.

ORPIMENT · GOLDEN   HEMATITE · RED/BROWN

A light aluminum-rich mica

MUSCOVITE

MICA
Found in metamorphic rocks such as schists and slate, flaky mica is also in igneous rocks like granite.

5	6	7	8	9	10
APATITE	ORTHOCLASE FELDSPAR	QUARTZ	TOPAZ	CORUNDUM	DIAMOND

GEMSTONES

ONLY ABOUT 50 OF Earth's
3,000 minerals are valued as
gemstones. Minerals such as
diamonds, sapphires, emeralds,
and rubies are commonly used
as gems. They are chosen for
their rarity, durability, color,
and optical qualities. Gems may
be found embedded in rocks
or washed into the gravel of a
river. Organic gemstones have
a plant or animal origin. They
include pearl, amber, and coral.

Red spinels were often mistaken for rubies.

The crown contains more than 3,000 stones.

CROWN JEWELS
The British Imperial State
Crown contains the Black
Prince's ruby (in fact a
170-carat spinel) and the
famous Cullinan II diamond.

EMERALD
Green beryl crystals called
emeralds contain chromium
to make them green. Most
emeralds are mined in
Colombia. They have a
hardness of 7.5 on
Mohs' scale.

Emerald is found in granites and pegmatites.

KIMBERLITE
Diamonds used
to be found mainly in
river gravels in India.
In 1870 diamonds were
discovered in volcanic
rock, called kimberlite,
in South Africa.

BRILLIANT
Skilled gem cutters, known
as lapidaries, cut a rough
crystal into a sparkling stone.
A diamond has 58 facets, or
faces, cut and polished on its
surface to make it a "brilliant."

SYNTHETIC GEMS
Some gems can be reproduced almost exactly in a laboratory. Dissolved minerals and coloring agents crystallize under strictly controlled conditions to produce perfect crystals. Synthetic crystals are used in medicine and the electronics industry.

NATURAL RUBY

SYNTHETIC RUBY

GEMSTONE FACTS
• The Cullinan is the largest diamond ever found. It weighed 3,106 carats (1.37 lb/0.6 kg).

• About one in every 1,000 oysters contains a pearl, and about one in every 3,000 mussels.

• A carat equals 0.007 oz (0.2 g).

IMITATION TURQUOISE

REAL TURQUOISE

IMITATION GEMS
Glass or plastic may be used to imitate gems. The optical properties of such imitations are different from those of the genuine gem.

PEARL
Shellfish, such as mussels and oysters, grow pearls in their shells. When a grain of sand lodges in its shell, the animal covers it with nacre, a substance to stop irritation. This creates a pearl.

AMBER
Fossilized resin from coniferous trees is called amber. The trees that yielded this amber existed more than 300 million years ago and are extinct. Amber may contain insects trapped in the tree sap.

ORE MINERALS

A ROCK THAT yields metal in sufficient amounts is a metallic ore. Gold and platinum are found as pure metals – that is, uncombined with any other elements. Most other metals, such as iron and tin, are extracted from ores. Mined or quarried rock is crushed. The ore is separated and purified.

IRON ORE
(HEMATITE)

ALUMINUM ORE
(BAUXITE)

ALUMINUM
FOIL

ALUMINUM
Lightweight aluminum is a good conductor of electricity and resists corrosion. It is extracted from its main ore (bauxite) by passing an electric current through molten bauxite and chemical fluxes.

GOLD FACTS

• The largest pure gold nugget weighed 142.5 lb (70.9 kg). It was found in Victoria, Australia.

• 60 percent of the world's gold is mined in South Africa.

• Gold never loses its luster or shine.

• It is said that all the gold ever mined would fit into an average four-bedroom house.

MERCURY ORE
(CINNABAR)

IRON
Hematite is an important iron ore. Iron can be cast, forged, and alloyed with other metals. Steel, used in ship-building and industry, is produced using iron.

MERCURY
THERMOMETER

MERCURY
The primary mercury ore is called cinnabar. It is found near volcanic vents and hot springs, mostly in China, Spain, and Italy. Mercury is liquid at room temperature.

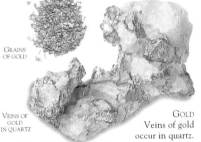

GRAINS
OF GOLD

VEINS OF
GOLD
IN QUARTZ

GOLD GRIFFIN
BRACELET

MINING
Blasting and boring rock in underground mines allows recovery of ores such as gold or tin. Dredging gravel or quarrying rock also retrieves ores.

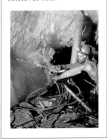

GOLD
Veins of gold occur in quartz. Panning or larger-scale dredging can retrieve gold grains from sand or river gravel deposits. About 1,500 tons (tonnes) of gold are produced each year.

FOSSIL FUELS: COAL

PLANTS THAT GREW millions of years ago slowly changed to form coal. Vegetation in swamp areas, buried under layers of sediment, forms a substance called peat. Peat, in turn, is pressed into a soft coal called lignite. Soft, bituminous coal forms under further pressure. Anthracite is the hardest and most compressed coal. When coal burns, the energy of the ancient plants is released. Coal is used to fuel power stations that produce electricity. Coal supplies, like oil, are finite.

PEAT

LIGNITE

BITUMINOUS COAL

ANTHRACITE

FROM PEAT TO COAL
Heat and pressure change crumbly brown peat into hard black anthracite coal.

COAL FORMATION

Vegetation

PEAT LAYER
In swamps, when plants decay they form a compact layer called peat. This material is 60 percent carbon and can be burned as a fuel.

Layers of sediment

Temperature and pressure increases.

COAL LAYER
Buried beneath sediment layers compacted peat forms coal. Lignite is the softest coal and anthracite the hardest coal.

INSIDE A COAL MINE

To reach a seam, or layer, of coal underground, rock must be blasted and bored away. Shafts go down from the surface to tunnels at different levels. Rock pillars and walls support the roof.

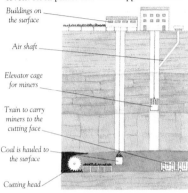

Buildings on the surface

Air shaft

Elevator cage for miners

Train to carry miners to the cutting face

Coal is hauled to the surface

Cutting head

COAL MINING

People have mined coal since about 500 B.C. Today's miners use drills and computer-controlled machines. Special cutting machines dig out the coal at the coal face. Deep coal mines deliver 2,000 tons (tonnes) of coal a day.

MAP OF COAL DEPOSITS

Swampy forests covered parts of Europe, Asia, and North America, which were low-lying during the Carboniferous period (360-286 million years ago). These tropical forest areas provide most of the coal deposits that are mined today.

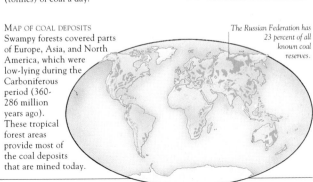

The Russian Federation has 23 percent of all known coal reserves.

FOSSIL FUELS: OIL AND GAS

MOST SCIENTISTS believe oil and gas are derived from the remains of ancient, single-cell marine animals. The organic remains were decomposed over millions of years to form oil and gas. The source rocks were compressed and heated to form liquid and gas hydrocarbons. Then they migrated to porous reservoir rocks that form oil and gas traps.

OIL RIG
An oil production platform floats but is tethered to the seabed. Oil is pumped up long pipelines to the oil platform.

OIL AND GAS FORMATION

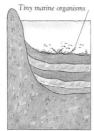

Tiny marine organisms

New layers of sediment

Oil and gas rigs

Fuels collect under solid caprock

1 Decaying plants and animals sink to the sea floor. They lie buried by accumulating layers of sediment.

2 Heat and pressure increase as the sediments sink deeper. The organic remains become oil and gas.

3 Molecules of gas and oil rise through permeable rock and are held in porous rock.

PRODUCTS MADE FROM OIL

Crude oil is separated into products such as paraffin, gasoline, and propane gas in a refinery. Further processing (cracking) produces chemicals used to manufacture paints, textiles, plastics, and many other products.

SWEATER MADE FROM
SYNTHETIC FIBERS

INFLATABLE TOY MADE
FROM THIN PLASTIC

PAINT

PLASTIC TOY

OIL USED IN MACHINERY AND VEHICLES

MAP OF OIL AND GAS DEPOSITS

Oil has been found in places such as the Middle East and the Arctic. North and Central America also have large oil and gas fields.

There are large oil deposits in the North Sea.

Most gas fields lie in the US, especially Alaska, and in the Russian Federation, usually close to oil deposits.

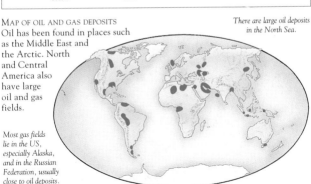

OTHER SOURCES OF ENERGY

MOST OF THE energy the world uses for cooking, heating, or industry is produced by burning fossil fuels. These fuels cause pollution and will eventually run out. The Sun, wind, or water can be used to create pollution-free energy. This energy is renewable for as long as the Sun shines, the wind blows, and the tides rise and fall. Some of the electrical energy we use in our homes is generated by nuclear fuels.

SOLAR ENERGY
The Sun's light energy is concentrated by huge mirrors. The energy is used to generate electricity.

TIDAL POWER
Inexpensive power can be generated in estuaries that have a large height difference between low and high tide, such as the Bay of Fundy in the US and Canada. Power can be generated both as the tide rises and as it falls.

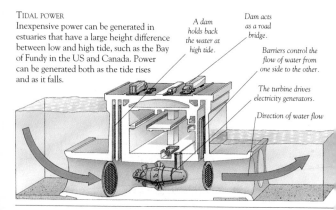

A dam holds back the water at high tide.

Dam acts as a road bridge.

Barriers control the flow of water from one side to the other.

The turbine drives electricity generators.

Direction of water flow

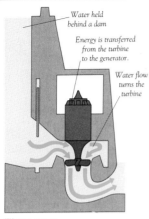

Water held behind a dam

Energy is transferred from the turbine to the generator.

Water flow turns the turbine

WATER POWER
A hydroelectric power station uses water power to produce electricity. The energy created by falling water turns a turbine that turns an electric generator.

NUCLEAR ENERGY
Elements such as plutonium and uranium are used in nuclear power stations to generate energy. An atom of uranium can be split using a particle called a neutron. This produces heat and other neutrons. In turn, these neutrons split more atoms, generating further energy.

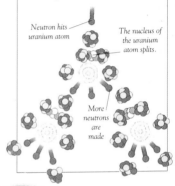

Neutron hits uranium atom

The nucleus of the uranium atom splits.

More neutrons are made

ENERGY FACTS
• The first tidal power station opened in La Rance, France in 1966.

• Nuclear power first produced electricity in the US in 1951.

• Hydroelectric power stations generate five percent of all electricity.

WIND POWER
California has wind farms that contain thousands of windmills. Persistent winds spin the propellers, which drive electric generators. Each windmill can produce up to 300 kilowatts of power.

THE WORLD'S MOUNTAINS

SOME MOUNTAIN ridges on land result from the collision of continental masses riding on tectonic plates. The Alps and Himalayas formed in this way. These lofty peaks continue to form as the Indian plate pushes the Eurasian plate. As the rocky plates fracture and crumple (or fault and fold) a mountain range takes shape. Our planet has had several mountain-building episodes during its history. Some mountains are rising faster than they are being weathered away.

ANCIENT MOUNTAINS
The Scottish Highlands have been eroded into low rounded hills. These ancient mountains formed more than 250 million years ago.

YOUNG MOUNTAINS
Mountains such as the Himalayas continue to rise. The mountains are about 50 million years old and have jagged peaks.

TYPES OF MOUNTAIN

FAULT-BLOCK MOUNTAIN
When Earth's plates push into one another, faults or cracks in the crust appear. Huge blocks of rock are forced upward.

FOLD MOUNTAIN
At the meeting of two continents, the crust buckles and bends. The rocky crust is forced up into a mountain range.

MOUNTAINS AND MOUNTAIN RANGES

The world's longest mountain ranges usually follow the edges of the Earth's plates.

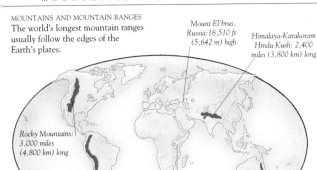

Mount El'brus, Russia: 18,510 ft (5,642 m) high

Himalaya-Karakoram Hindu Kush: 2,400 miles (3,800 km) long

Rocky Mountains: 3,000 miles (4,800 km) long

Andes: 4,500 miles (7,200 km) long

Mt. Kilimanjaro, Tanzania: 19,340 ft (5,895 m) high

Trans-Antarctic: 2,200 miles (3,500 km) long

Great Dividing Range: 2,240 miles (3,600 km) long

VOLCANO
Lava from a deep magma chamber may erupt to form a volcano. A tall cone builds up from lava, ash, and rock ejected from the volcano.

DOME MOUNTAIN
Rising magma forces up rocks near the surface. A dome-shaped mountain results.

MOUNTAIN FACTS

• The ten highest mountains on land are all in the Himalayas.

• Europe's Alps are part of a mountain belt that stretches from the Pyrenees in Europe to the Himalayas in Asia.

• The Himalayas grow at a rate of 3.3 ft (1 m) every 1,000 years.

• The Alps are the youngest of the world's great mountain ranges.

MOUNTAIN FEATURES

CONDITIONS ON MOUNTAINS can be harsh. As altitude increases temperature drops, air becomes thinner, and winds blow harder. Animal and plant life has adapted to survive in this environment. Mountains can be divided into several separate zones. The zones are similar whether the mountain lies in a tropical or temperate area and whether it is an isolated volcanic peak or part of a mountain range.

MOUNT KILIMANJARO
Africa's tallest mountain is Mount Kilimanjaro in Tanzania. It is a solitary peak, not part of a range. In fact, it is a dormant volcanic cone. Despite lying near the equator, Kilimanjaro is permanently snow-capped.

WORLD'S HIGHEST MOUNTAINS PER CONTINENT			
MOUNTAIN	CONTINENT	HEIGHT IN METERS	HEIGHT IN FEET
Mt. Everest, Nepal	Asia	8,848	29,028
Mt. Aconcagua, Argentina	South America	6,960	22,834
Mt. McKinley, Alaska	North America	6,194	20,320
Mt. Kilimanjaro, Tanzania	Africa	5,895	19,340
Mt. El'brus, Russia	Europe	5,642	18,510
Vinson Massif	Antarctica	5,140	16,863
Mt. Wilhelm, Papua New Guinea	Australasia	4,884	16,024

THE ANDES
The world's longest range of mountains on land is the Andes in South America. The chain stretches for 4,500 miles (7,200 km).

UNDERSEA MOUNTAIN
Measured from the ocean floor, Mauna Kea, Hawaii is taller than Mount Everest. Rising 13,796 ft (4,205 m) above sea level, its base lies in a trough under the sea.

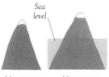

Sea level

MT. EVEREST
29,028 FT
(8,848 M)

MAUNA KEA
33,480 FT
(10,205 M)

MORE MOUNTAIN FACTS
• On a mountain, the temperature drops 1.1°F (0.7°C) for every 330 ft (100 m) climbed.
• In warm Equatorial regions trees can grow at heights of 13,124 ft (4,000 m).

MOUNTAIN VEGETATION
As the altitude increases the temperature falls. This effect produces distinct vegetation and climate zones. The plant and animal life of each zone varies. These are the zones of the European Alps.

Rocks permanently covered with snow support no plant or animal life.

Permanent snowline

Loose rock, or scree, fractured by the weathering process

Alpine plants and flowers in pastureland have adapted to survive in the cold air.

Coniferous forest

Deciduous forests grow at the base of the mountain.

VALLEYS

FORCES OF EROSION, especially water, control the shape of the landscape. Steep-sided valleys can be cut by fast-flowing mountain streams. Larger rivers wear a path through the land, shaping wide, flat valleys as they near the sea. Frozen water in glaciers also erodes rock, forming deep, icy gullies. Valleys sometimes form as a result of crustal movements that pull rocks apart at steep faults in the Earth's surface rocks.

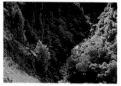

GORGE
A ravine with steep sides is called a gorge. A canyon is similar to a gorge but it is usually found in desert areas.

The lithosphere drops between the plate

RIFT VALLEY
Faults occur in the Earth's crust where two plates are moving apart. A long, straight valley, such as the African Rift Valley, forms between the faults.

Rivers shed their sediments

A fan-shaped delta forms at the river mouth.

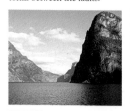

FJORD
Steep-sided estuaries such as those in Norway and New Zealand, are caused by glaciers deepening river valleys. As the ice melts and the sea level rises the fjords flood.

VALLEY FACTS
• Africa's Rift Valley stretches for 2,500 miles (4,000 km).
• The longest fjord, in Nordvest, Greenland, is 194 miles (313 km) long.

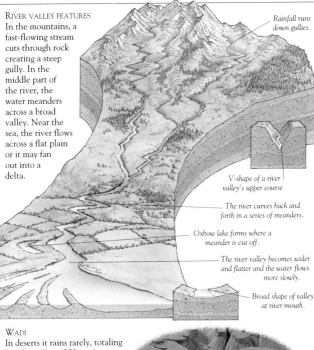

RIVER VALLEY FEATURES

In the mountains, a fast-flowing stream cuts through rock creating a steep gully. In the middle part of the river, the water meanders across a broad valley. Near the sea, the river flows across a flat plain or it may fan out into a delta.

Rainfall runs down gullies.

V-shape of a river valley's upper course

The river curves back and forth in a series of meanders.

Oxbow lake forms where a meander is cut off.

The river valley becomes wider and flatter and the water flows more slowly.

Broad shape of valley at river mouth.

WADI

In deserts it rains rarely, totaling less than 10 in (250 mm) a year. A torrential downpour in such an arid area can cause a flash flood. The rain carves out a channel called a wadi. Water runs down these dry river valleys carrying rocks and debris with it.

205

CAVES

UNDERGROUND CAVERNS and caves occur in several types of landscape. Different processes are responsible for the development of caves. The action of ice, lava, waves, and rainwater cause subterranean openings. In particular, rainwater has a spectacular effect on limestone, producing vast caverns full of unusual shapes.

ICE CAVE
Beneath a glacier there is sometimes a stream of water that has thawed, called meltwater. The water can wear away an ice cave full of icicles in the glacier.

INSIDE A LIMESTONE CAVE
Carbonic acid in rain seeps into cracks in limestone and dissolves the rock. Underground tunnels and caves form as water dissolves the rock. Streams may flow down sinkholes in the rock into a cave system and emerge in another place.

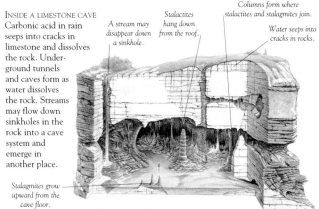

A stream may disappear down a sinkhole.

Stalactites hang down from the roof.

Columns form where stalactites and stalagmites join.

Water seeps into cracks in rocks.

Stalagmites grow upward from the cave floor.

LAVA CAVE
Some lava cools to form a thick crust. Below the crust a tube of molten lava flows. When it empties a cave remains.

SEA CAVE
Caves may form at the base of cliffs undercut by erosion. A cave can be worn through to form an arch. The top of this arch may eventually collapse and leave an isolated stack to be buffeted by the waves.

CAVE FACTS
• Jean Bernard cave in France is the deepest in the world. It is 5,256 ft (1,602 m) deep.

• The longest stalactite – 20.4 ft (6.2 m) long – is in Co. Clare, Ireland.

• The tallest stalagmite is 105 ft (32 m) high. It is in the Czech Republic.

• America's Mammoth Cave system, Kentucky, is the world's longest cave system. It is 348 miles (560 km) long.

STALAGMITES AND STALACTITES

STALACTITE
In limestone caves, deposits of calcite left by dripping water create distinctive features, such as stalactites. These grow from the ceiling of the cave toward the floor.

COLUMNS
Mineral deposits construct stalactites and stalagmites in caves. If the two shapes meet, they form a column.

STALAGMITE
It may take several thousand years for a stalagmite to grow 1 in (2.5 cm) – drip by drip from a cave floor to the roof.

THE WORLD'S GLACIERS

A GLACIER IS a mass of moving ice that originates in mountainous regions (mountain glaciers) or large, cold regions (ice caps). Ice builds up where there is more winter snow than melts in summer. The thick snow is compressed into ice. When the ice becomes very thick it begins to flow under its weight. Mountain glaciers are ice streams that follow former river valleys as they carry rock debris downhill.

GLACIAL DEBRIS
Rocks are smoothed when they are plucked up and carried along by a glacier. This rock has scratches, or striae, too.

Ridge or arête between two glaciers

Medial moraine – debris carried in the middle of the glacier

When the ice moves over a sharp incline, it cracks to form crevasses.

THE WORLD'S LONGEST GLACIERS		
GLACIERS	LENGTH IN KM	LENGTH IN MILES
Lambert-Fisher Ice Passage, Antarctica	515	320
Novaya Zemlya, Russia	418	260
Arctic Institute Ice Passage, Antarctica	362	225
Nimrod-Lennox-King, Antarctica	289	180
Denman Glacier, Antarctica	241	150
Beardmore Glacier, Antarctica	225	140
Recovery Glacier, Antarctica	200	124

BEFORE GLACIATION
The mountain valley carved out by a river is usually steep and shaped like a letter V.

AFTER GLACIATION
A mountain glacier flows along the path of a river. The V-shape is eroded by the glacier into a U-shape.

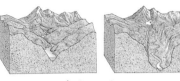

GLACIER FACTS

• Eight of the ten longest glaciers in the world are found in the Antarctic.

• About 10 percent of Earth's land surface is permanently glaciated.

• The fastest-moving glacier is the Quarayaq glacier in Greenland. It flows 65–80 ft (20–24 m) per day.

• Most glaciers move at a rate of about 6 ft (2 m) per day.

CROSS-SECTION OF A GLACIER

Cirque or corrie – hollow where glacier begins

Compact snow called firn

FEATURES OF A GLACIER
A glacier begins high in the mountains in hollows called cirques. New snow builds up and becomes compacted, forming denser ice called firn. As the glacier moves downhill it collects soil and rock from the floor and sides of the valley and carries it along. The rock debris carried by the glacier erodes the valley. The debris accumulates as moraine at the front of the melting glacier.

The snout or front of the glacier

Meltwater flows from the snout

Pile of rocks and boulders called terminal moraine

ICE CAPS AND ICE AGES

ANTARCTICA AND GREENLAND are blanketed in ice sheets up to 11,500 ft (3,500 m) thick. Many winters of snowfall accumulate to produce an ice cap, which eventually moves downhill as a broad glacial mass. In Earth's history, periods of extreme cold, called ice ages, brought glacial conditions as far south as Europe and North America. Our mild climate may only be an interval between ice ages.

ICE CAP
Vast ice sheets covering Antarctica and Greenland are known as ice caps.

FORMATION OF AN ICE CAP
Layers of snow build up during the winter months and become icy firn. Over many years, the result is a thick ice cap. Gravity pulls the ice down to the edges of the land.

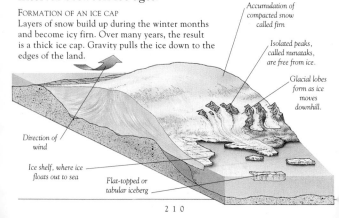

Accumulation of compacted snow called firn

Isolated peaks, called nunataks, are free from ice.

Glacial lobes form as ice moves downhill.

Direction of wind

Ice shelf, where ice floats out to sea

Flat-topped or tabular iceberg

GRAPH OF THE EARTH'S TEMPERATURE
The low points on the graph show the
time when the average earth
temperature was cold enough to allow
major glacial advances.

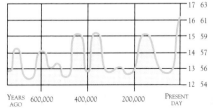

CLIMATE
°C °F

- 17 63
- 16 61
- 15 59
- 14 57
- 13 56
- 12 54

YEARS 600,000   400,000   200,000   PRESENT
AGO   DAY

ICE FACTS

- Most of the world's freshwater – 75 percent of it – is stored in ice caps and glaciers.

- About 12 percent of the sea and 10 percent of the land is presently covered in ice.

- Almost 90 percent of the world's ice lies in the continent of Antarctica.

ICE AGES

During the last ice age, about
30,000 years ago, ice sheets
covered much of the planet,
particularly North America
and northern Europe. All ice
ages are interspersed with
warmer periods called
interglacials. Ice advanced
and retreated with each
major temperature change.

PLEISTOCENE EPOCH
– THE LAST ICE AGE

EXTENT OF ICE IN
THE WORLD TODAY

SCIENTISTS EXAMINE
A BABY MAMMOTH
FOUND IN THE ICE

WOOLLY MAMMOTH

In Siberia, the remains of extinct
animals called mammoths have
been found in ice. They froze so
quickly that their bodies were
preserved virtually intact. These
elephant-like mammals had
curled tusks and woolly coats and
lived during the last ice age.

AVALANCHES AND ICEBERGS

MOUNTAINS ARE inhospitable places. Winter snowstorms pile up layers of ice and snow. The layers may become unstable and swoop down the mountain in an avalanche, destroying anything in their path. Icebergs form when large chunks of ice break off (calve) from coastal glaciers or ice shelves. These are carried out to sea by ocean currents and are a hazard to ships.

SEA ICE
Seawater freezes when it reaches 28°F (−1.9°C). Sea ice is never more than about 16 ft (5 m) thick. It can be used as a source of freshwater because the salt is left behind in the sea.

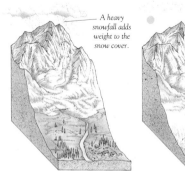

A heavy snowfall adds weight to the snow cover.

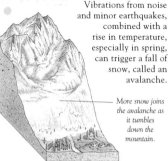

AVALANCHE
Vibrations from noise and minor earthquakes, combined with a rise in temperature, especially in spring, can trigger a fall of snow, called an avalanche.

More snow joins the avalanche as it tumbles down the mountain.

SNOWLINE

There is an elevation on a mountainside, called the snowline, below which snow melts during summer. Above this elevation the snow remains throughout the year. The snowline is higher in more equatorial regions.

The snowline in the European Alps is at about 9,000 ft (2,700 m) high.

In Antarctica, the snowline is at or near sea level.

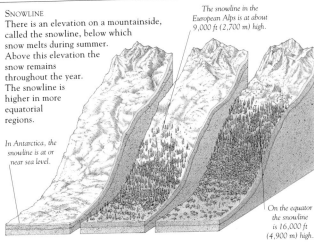

On the equator the snowline is 16,000 ft (4,900 m) high.

ICEBERGS

Glaciers and the floating edges of ice caps lose chunks of ice called icebergs into the sea, a process known as calving. All icebergs are frozen freshwater, rather than frozen seawater.

ICEBERG FACTS

• Only 12 percent of an iceberg can be seen above the ocean. 88 percent is under the water.

• The tallest iceberg was sighted in 1958 off Greenland. It was 550 ft (167 m) high.

• The largest iceberg, spotted in the Pacific Ocean in 1956, had an area of 12,500 miles^2 (32,500 km^2).

THE WORLD'S OCEANS

SEEN FROM SPACE, the Earth looks blue and watery. This is because two-thirds of it is covered with water. The water is held in oceans and seas. (Seas are surrounded by land.) There are five oceans: three are in the Southern Hemisphere. Major currents circulate the oceans counter-clockwise in the Southern Hemisphere and clockwise in the Northern Hemisphere.

THE WORLD'S LARGEST OCEANS AND SEAS		
OCEAN OR SEA	AREA IN KM²	AREA IN MILES²
Pacific Ocean	166,229,000	64,181,000
Atlantic Ocean	86,551,000	33,417,000
Indian Ocean	73,422,000	28,348,000
Arctic Ocean	13,223,000	5,105,000
South China Sea	2,975,000	1,149,000
Caribbean Sea	2,516,000	917,000
Mediterranean Sea	2,509,000	969,000
Bering Sea	2,261,000	873,000

FORMATION OF OCEANS

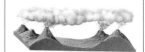

THE ATMOSPHERE FORMS
The semimolten surface of the Earth was covered by volcanoes. Hot gases and water vapor emitted by volcanoes formed the Earth's early atmosphere.

THE RAINS FALL
The water vapor in this early atmosphere condensed as rain. Rainstorms poured down on the planet and filled the vast hollows on the Earth's surface.

THE OCEANS FORM
These huge pools became the oceans. The water was hot and acidic. Later, plant life evolved and modified the chemical composition of the atmosphere and oceans.

OCEAN ZONES
Oceanographers split
the oceans into zones
according to depth.
Only near-surface
waters are sunlit.
Generally the coldest
water is at the bottom
of the ocean. Water
pressure increases with
depth, but sea
creatures have adapted
to the different zones.

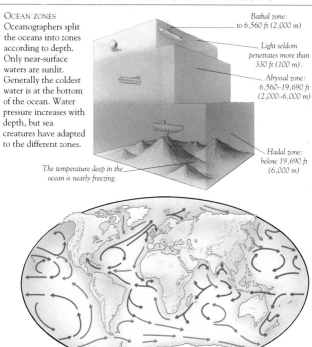

Bathal zone:
to 6,560 ft (2,000 m)

Light seldom
penetrates more than
330 ft (100 m).

Abyssal zone:
6,560–19,690 ft
(2,000–6,000 m)

Hadal zone:
below 19,690 ft
(6,000 m)

The temperature deep in the
ocean is nearly freezing.

THE OCEANS' CURRENTS
Currents may be warm or cold. They flow across the
surface or deep beneath it. The wind controls surface
currents, which flow in circular directions. Currents
carry some of the Sun's heat around the planet,
warming polar areas and cooling tropical areas.

KEY	
COLD CURRENT	→
WARM CURRENT	→

WAVES AND TIDES

THE OCEANS AND seas are always moving. Buffeted by the wind and heated by the Sun, waves and currents form in the oceans. Ripples on the surface of the water may grow into waves that pound the shore and shape the coastlines. The Moon's and Sun's gravity pull the oceans, causing a daily and monthly cycle of tides.

WHIRLPOOL
An uneven channel can cause several tidal flows to collide. The currents surge upwards and rush into each other. Eddies and whirlpools form on the surface.

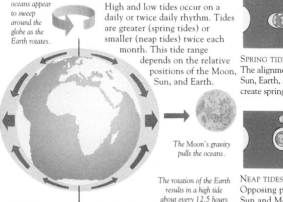

Bulges in the oceans appear to sweep around the globe as the Earth rotates.

MONTHLY TIDES
High and low tides occur on a daily or twice daily rhythm. Tides are greater (spring tides) or smaller (neap tides) twice each month. This tide range depends on the relative positions of the Moon, Sun, and Earth.

The Moon's gravity pulls the oceans.

The rotation of the Earth results in a high tide about every 12.5 hours in the open ocean.

Earth's spinning on its axis affects the tides.

SPRING TIDES
The alignment of the Sun, Earth, and Moon create spring tides.

NEAP TIDES
Opposing pulls of Sun and Moon cause neap tides.

GULF STREAM

A current of warm water called the Gulf Stream moves from the Gulf of Mexico across the Atlantic, bringing mild winter weather to the western coasts of Europe. Like a huge river at sea, the Gulf Stream flows 100 miles (160 km) a day. This current or gyre is 37 miles (60 km) wide and 2,000 ft (600 m) deep. As the Gulf Stream nears Europe it is called the North Atlantic Drift.

EUROPE

NORTH AMERICA

Gulf Stream

GULF OF MEXICO

The warm water slows out and spreads out as it nears Europe.

The top part of the wave, the crest, continues up the beach.

Particles near the surface turn over and over

The beach slows down the base of the wave.

WAVE MOVEMENT

Waves travel toward the shore from large storms at sea. But it is not the water particles that travel, only the wave form. The particles rotate as each wave passes and return to their original position.

WAVE FACTS

• The highest recorded wave was seen in the western Pacific. It was 112 ft (34 m) high from trough to crest.

• The Antarctic Circumpolar Current flows at a rate of 4.3 billion ft³ (130 million m³) per second.

• Hawaiian tides rise 12 in (45 cm) a day.

COMPOSITION OF SEAWATER

The oceans contain dissolved minerals, some washed from the land by rivers. The predominant constituents of seawater are sodium and chloride which together form salt. About 3.5 percent of the weight of ocean water is salt.

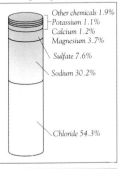

Other chemicals 1.9%
Potassium 1.1%
Calcium 1.2%
Magnesium 3.7%

Sulfate 7.6%

Sodium 30.2%

Chloride 54.3%

THE OCEAN FLOOR

THE WORLD UNDER the oceans has both strange and familiar features. Similar to a landscape on dry ground, mountains, valleys, and volcanoes dot the ocean floor. Once scientists had equipment to explore the ocean bed, they discovered that tectonic plate movement had caused many ocean floor features, including trenches, seamounts, and submarine canyons.

MAPPING THE OCEAN
Oceanographers use precision echo-sounding, which bounces signals off the ocean bed, to map the ocean floor's contours.

FEATURES OF THE OCEAN FLOOR

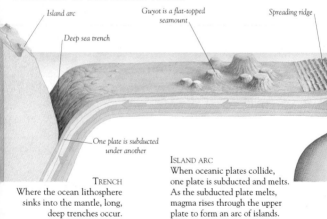

Island arc

Deep sea trench

Guyot is a flat-topped seamount

Spreading ridge

One plate is subducted under another

ISLAND ARC
When oceanic plates collide, one plate is subducted and melts. As the subducted plate melts, magma rises through the upper plate to form an arc of islands.

TRENCH
Where the ocean lithosphere sinks into the mantle, long, deep trenches occur.

DEEP-SEA EXPLORATION

DIVERS AND VEHICLES	DEPTH IN METERS	DEPTH IN FEET
Sponge diver holding breath	15	49
Air/SCUBA sports diver	50	164
Oil rig divers with diving bell	250	820
Deepest experimental dive	500	1,640
Barton's benthoscope	1,370	4,494
Cousteau diving saucer	3,350	11,000
Shinkai submersible	6,500	21,325
Trieste bathyscape	10,911	35,800

BATHYSCAPE
The deepest dive was made by the bathyscape *Trieste* in 1960. It dived in the world's deepest trench, the Mariana Trench.

SEAMOUNT
An underwater volcano that rises over 3,280 ft (1,000 m) is a seamount.

ABYSSAL PLAIN
This sediment-covered plain lies at a depth of about 15,000 ft (4,000 m).

SUBMARINE CANYON
Dense sediment flows from the continental shelf have eroded deep canyons.

Two of the Earth's tectonic plates are moving apart

Seamount

Submarine canyon

Continental shelf

Abyssal plain

Continental slope

Magma rises between the plates

Continental rise

MIDOCEANIC RIDGE
Magma rising between two tectonic plates forms a ridge.

CONTINENTAL SLOPE
The continental slope is the edge of the continent. It descends from the edge of the continental shelf to the rise, or into a trench.

CONTINENTAL SHELF
Stretching from the edge of the land like a vast plateau under the sea, the continental shelf averages 43 miles (70 km) wide. The ocean here is about 1,600 ft (250 m) deep.

OCEAN FEATURES

OCEANS ARE a rich source of many useful mineral substances. Seawater contains nutrients for phytoplankton and both metallic and nonmetallic minerals. Deposits of oil and gas are found in continental shelf sediment layers where tectonic paltes are rifting apart.

BLACK SMOKERS
In 1977, scientists discovered strange chimneys, formed from minerals on the ocean floor, called black smokers. In rift valleys between spreading ridges, they eject water as hot as 572°F (300°C), containing manganese and sulfur.

The vent minerals color the water black.

Jets of hot water shoot from the chimneys.

Smokers can grow as tall as 33 ft (10 m).

Tubeworms and giant clams live on bacteria near the vents.

THE WORLD'S DEEPEST SEA TRENCHES		
Trench	Depth in meters	Depth in feet
Mariana Trench, West Pacific	10,920	35,827
Tonga Trench, South Pacific	10,800	35,433
Philippine Trench, West Pacific	10,057	32,995
Kermadec Trench, South Pacific	10,047	32,961
Izu-Ogasawara Trench, West Pacific	9,780	32,087

OCEAN PRODUCT FACTS
• There are 0.000004 parts per million of gold in the ocean.

• It takes a million years for a manganese nodule to grow 0.08 in (2 mm) in diameter.

OCEAN PRODUCTS

MANGANESE
Nodules from the seabed are used in industry.

OIL
This is a non-renewable fossil fuel. It is pumped from rocks in the continental shelf.

SAND
Rock pounded by waves becomes sand. In volcanic areas it is black.

CORAL
Like sand, coral is found in coastal waters.

Diamond

Diamonds in gravel are known as alluvial diamonds.

DIAMONDS IN GRAVEL
Off the coasts of Africa and Indonesia, diamonds can be found in continental shelf gravels. Most have been washed down by rivers into the sea.

OCEAN FLOOR SEDIMENT
The continental shelf is covered with sand, mud, and silt washed onto it from rivers. In the deep ocean, the floor is coated with ooze. This contains the remains of dead marine life.

Rock is carried 311 miles (500 km) from the ridge over 5 million years. Sediment gathers.

After 10 million years the rock has moved farther from the ridge. It is now covered with thick sediment.

New rock erupted from the mantle at mid-ocean ridges has no sediment cover.

ISLANDS

A PIECE OF LAND smaller than a continent and surrounded by water is called an island. Magma rising from volcanic vents in the oceanic lithosphere creates islands in the sea. An arc of islands appears where a tectonic plate is subducted. Some islands exist only when the tide is high; at low tide it is possible to walk to these islands. Small islands may exist in rivers and lakes. In warmer regions coral reefs may grow from the sea, built by living organisms.

Causeway

A narrow strip of land links the island to the shore.

CAUSEWAY
A change in sea level can create an island. Land may be accessible only at low tide by a causeway. At high tide the island is cut off.

ISLAND FACTS
• Bouvet Island is the most remote island – about 1,056 miles (1,700 km) from the nearest landmass (Antarctica).

• Kwejalein in the Marshall Islands, in the Pacific Ocean, is the largest coral atoll. Its reef measures 176 miles (283 km) long.

ISLAND ARC
On one side of a subduction zone, a curved chain or arc of volcanic islands may be pushed up from under the ocean floor. From space the numerous volcanic peaks on the islands of Indonesia are clearly visible.

THE WORLD'S LARGEST ISLANDS		
ISLAND	AREA IN KM²	AREA IN MILES²
Greenland	2,175,219	839,852
New Guinea	792,493	305,981
Borneo	725,416	280,083
Madagascar	587,009	226,644
Baffin Island, Canada	507,423	195,916
Sumatra, Indonesia	427,325	104,990
Honshu, Japan	227,401	87,799
Great Britain	218,065	84,195

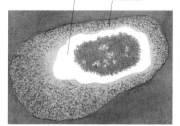

Sand builds up more on one side of the reef.

New coral organisms grow on old coral skeletons.

CORAL

Islands such as the Maldives in the Indian Ocean are known as coral. Tiny marine organisms called corals grow on submerged rock formations such as undersea volcanoes (seamounts) in warm, salty seas. The coral grows slowly up to the ocean's surface and, when the sea level drops, creates a firm platform above sea level.

FORMATION OF A CORAL ATOLL

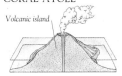

Volcanic island

1 A FRINGING REEF
Where a volcano has emerged from under the ocean, coral begins to grow on its fringes, around the base of the volcano.

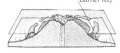

Barrier reef

2 A BARRIER REEF
When volcanic activity subsides, the peak erodes and sinks. The coral forms a reef around the edge of the volcano.

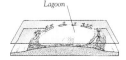

Lagoon

3 AN ATOLL FORMS
Eventually, the volcano sinks beneath the sea. A ring of coral known as an atoll remains on the surface.

COASTS

WHERE THE LAND meets the sea there is the coast. Coasts may be bordered by cliffs, dunes, or pebble beaches. There is a continual battle between sea and coast as rock is broken down by pounding waves, and sand carried about by wind. Some coasts retreat but new coast is always being created in other areas. Beaches alter their height and width with the seasons.

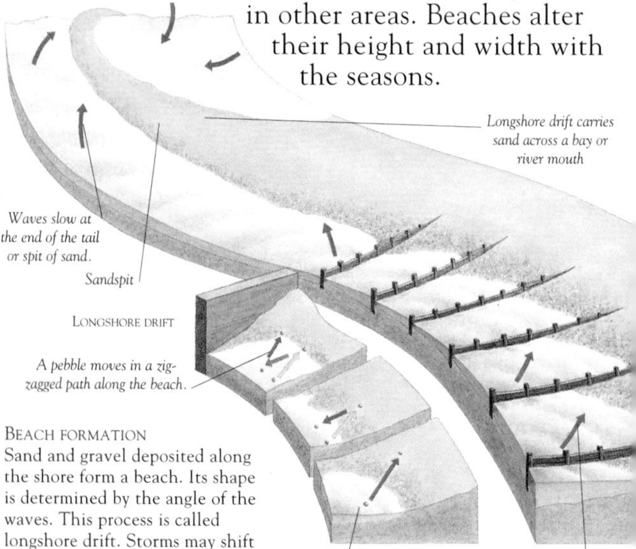

Longshore drift carries sand across a bay or river mouth

Waves slow at the end of the tail or spit of sand.

Sandspit

LONGSHORE DRIFT

A pebble moves in a zig-zagged path along the beach.

BEACH FORMATION
Sand and gravel deposited along the shore form a beach. Its shape is determined by the angle of the waves. This process is called longshore drift. Storms may shift or cut through barrier islands.

Waves strike the beach at an angle.

Wind and wave direction

COAST FACTS

• The largest pleasure beach is Virginia Beach, with an area of 310 miles² (803 km²).

• The world has about 312,000 miles (504,000 km) of coastline.

• The highest sea cliffs are at Molokai, Hawaii. They descend 3,300 ft (1,010 m) to the sea.

• At Martha's Vineyard, Mass., the cliffs retreat 5.6 ft (1.7 m) per year.

TYPES OF COAST

Direction of waves

TOMBOLO
This type of coastline links an island to the shore by a strip of sand.

BARRIER BEACH
A lagoon forms behind a barrier of sand built by onshore waves.

Direction of waves

BAYHEAD BEACH
Waves striking a headland at an angle leave a protected arc of sand.

FJORD COASTLINE
A submerged glacial valley with steep sides forms a fjord coastline.

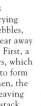

Groynes or fences built into the sea prevent longshore drift.

Sand builds up against the groin.

Sand and shingle

SEA STACKS
Waves, carrying sand and pebbles, gradually wear away a headland. First, a cave appears, which is enlarged to form an arch. Then, the arch falls, leaving an isolated stack.

Sea cave eroded by sea until arch forms

Top of arch collapses leaving pillar or stack

THE WORLD'S RIVERS

WHEREVER THEY occur, rivers are a key part of the Earth's water cycle. They carry snowmelt and rainwater from high areas down to the sea, filling up marshes and lakes where the land surface is uneven. In arid regions small rivers may be intermittent. They dry up and reappear after heavy rains or during an annual wet season.

PERENNIAL RIVER
In temperate and tropical areas a reliable supply of rainwater creates perennial rivers. Rivers such as the Nile, in Africa, flow all year.

THE WATER CYCLE
Water is constantly circulating between land, sea, and air. The Sun's heat causes evaporation from seas, lakes, and rivers. Water vapor rises and cools. Tiny droplets of water condense to form clouds. The droplets grow and eventually fall as rain. The water fills rivers and lakes, and flows to the sea.

RIVER FACTS
• The Nile River is longer, but the Amazon carries more water.
• China's Yangtze carries 1,600,000 tons (tonnes) of silt a year.

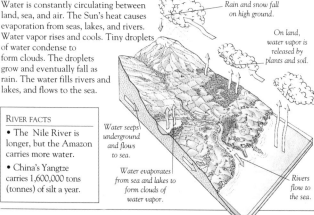

Rain and snow fall on high ground.

On land, water vapor is released by plants and soil.

Water seeps underground and flows to sea.

Water evaporates from sea and lakes to form clouds of water vapor.

Rivers flow to the sea.

SEASONAL RIVER
This dry river bed belongs to a
Spanish river. In the hot
summer many rivers dry up, but
rain will fill them up during the
wet winter season.

THE WORLD'S LONGEST RIVERS		
RIVER AND CONTINENT	LENGTH IN KM	LENGTH IN MILES
Nile, Africa	6,695	4,160
Amazon, S. America	6,437	4,000
Yangtze/Chang Jiang, Asia	6,379	3,964
Mississippi-Missouri, N. America	6,264	3,892
Ob-Irtysh, Asia	5,411	3,362
Yellow/Huang He, Asia	4,672	2,903
Congo/Zaire, Africa	4,662	2,897
Amur, Asia	4,416	2,744
Lena, Asia	4,400	2,734
Mackenzie-Peace, N. America	4,241	2,635

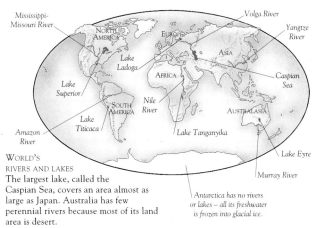

WORLD'S
RIVERS AND LAKES
The largest lake, called the
Caspian Sea, covers an area almost as
large as Japan. Australia has few
perennial rivers because most of its land
area is desert.

Antarctica has no rivers
or lakes – all its freshwater
is frozen into glacial ice.

RIVER FEATURES

FROM ITS SOURCE in the mountains, the snow or rainwater that fills a stream cuts a path through sediment and bedrock on its way to the sea. Streams join and form a river that flows more slowly, meandering across the land. A river may carry a large amount of sediment, which it deposits on its floodplain or in a delta.

DELTA
At the river's mouth, it sheds its sediment to form a broad fan of swampy land.

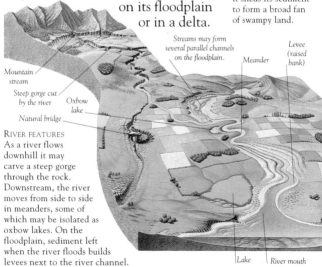

Streams may form several parallel channels on the floodplain.

Meander

Levee (raised bank)

Mountain stream

Steep gorge cut by the river

Oxbow lake

Natural bridge

Lake

River mouth

RIVER FEATURES
As a river flows downhill it may carve a steep gorge through the rock. Downstream, the river moves from side to side in meanders, some of which may be isolated as oxbow lakes. On the floodplain, sediment left when the river floods builds levees next to the river channel.

MELTWATER
A river may begin its life in a glaciated part of the world. Melting ice and snow from a glacier feed mountain streams.

OVERLAND FLOW
Rainwater running downhill gathers into small streams called tributaries, which join to form a river.

SPRING
A rock layer called the aquifer stores rainwater. Springs form where streams cut into aquifer rock layers.

MORE RIVER FACTS
• The Ganges and Brahmaputra delta, India, is the largest in the world. Its area is about 30,000 miles^2 (75,000 km^2).

• The widest waterfall is Khone Falls in Laos. They are 6.7 miles (10.8 km) wide.

• Each year rivers unload 20 billion tons (tonnes) of sediment into the sea.

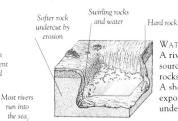

Softer rock undercut by erosion

Swirling rocks and water

Hard rock

Flood plain where sediment is deposited

Most rivers run into the sea

Sediment on seabed

WATERFALLS
A river flows swiftly near its source, cutting through soft rocks more easily than hard. A sheer face of hard rock is exposed where water plunges, undercutting the rock below.

THE WORLD'S HIGHEST WATERFALLS

WATERFALL AND COUNTRY	HEIGHT IN METERS	HEIGHT IN FEET
Angel Falls, Venezuela	979	3,212
Tugela Falls, S. Africa	853	2,799
Utgaard, Norway	800	2,625
Mongefossen, Norway	774	2,539
Yosemite Falls, US	739	2,425

LAKES

AN INLAND BODY of freshwater or brackish water, collected in a basin, is called a lake. In geological terms, lakes are short-lived; they can dry up or become clogged in a few thousand years. Lakes form when depressions resulting from lithosphere movement, erosion, or volcanic craters fill up with water. The Caspian Sea, the world's largest lake, and Lake Baikal, Siberia, the deepest lake, were both produced when shifts of the lithosphere cut off large arms of the sea.

SWAMP
The Everglades, Florida, are mangrove swamps. In warm climates, mangrove trees grow in the salty (brackish) water of muddy estuaries. The trees form islands in the mud.

TYPES OF LAKE

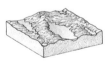

KETTLE LAKE
Ice left behind by a melting glacier may be surrounded by moraine. When the ice melts the depression forms a kettle lake.

TARN
A circular mountain lake is known as a tarn. These lakes form in hollows worn by glacial erosion or blocked by ice debris.

VOLCANIC LAKE
The craters of ancient volcanoes fill up with water and produce lakes such as Crater Lake, Oregon.

VANISHING LAKES

SEDIMENT BUILDS

Lakes begin to fill up with sediment, washed into them by rivers. The mud and silt create a delta in the lake, which has areas of dry land.

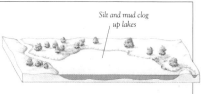

Silt and mud clog up lakes

Channels become narrow

SWAMP FORMS

The lake area gets smaller and shallower. Islands of dry land fan out into the lake. Reeds grow, turning the lake into a swamp.

LAKE DISAPPEARS

Eventually, the lake area is colonized by plants, forming a wetland environment.

Plants grow in the sediment

OXBOW LAKE

This curved lake appears when a river cuts off a meander loop. Eventually, the isolated lake fills with sediment and vegetation.

THE WORLD'S LARGEST LAKES AND INLAND SEAS

LAKE AND CONTINENT	AREA IN KM^2	AREA IN MILES^2
Caspian Sea, Asia/ Europe	370,980	143,236
Lake Superior, N. America	82,098	31,698
Lake Victoria, Africa	69,480	26,826
Lake Huron, N. America	59,566	22,999
Lake Michigan, N. America	57,754	22,299
Aral Sea, Asia	37,056	14,307
Lake Tanganyika, Africa	32,891	12,699
Lake Baikal, Asia	31,498	12,161
Great Bear Lake, N. America	31,197	12,045

WEATHER AND CLIMATE

CLIMATE IS A LONG-ESTABLISHED PATTERN of weather.
This pattern may vary, or it may remain the same
throughout the year. Climate
is usually defined in terms
of temperature and rainfall.

WORLD CLIMATES:
TEMPERATURE

ALWAYS HOT

HOT SUMMER
WARM WINTER

HOT SUMMER
MILD WINTER

WARM SUMMER
COLD WINTER

COOL SUMMER
COLD WINTER

ALWAYS
COLD

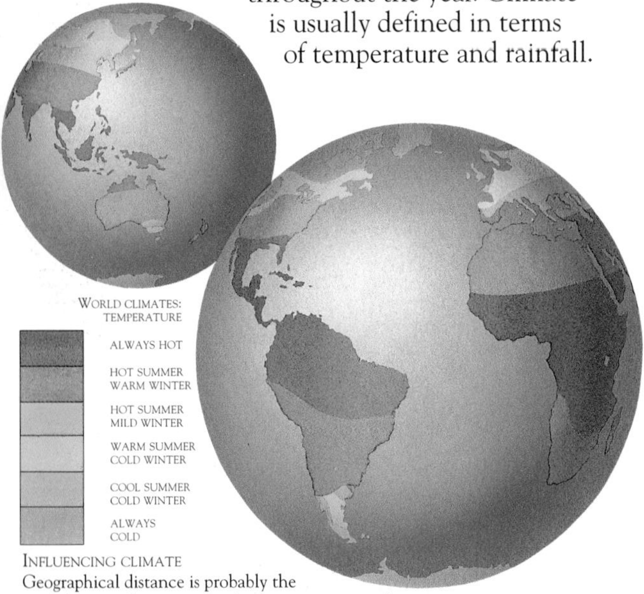

INFLUENCING CLIMATE
Geographical distance is probably the
main factor influencing the climate in any particular part
of the world. Distance from the equator affects temperature,
as does altitude (distance above sea level). Distance from a
coastline affects both temperature and rainfall, while distance
from a mountain range can increase or decrease rainfall.

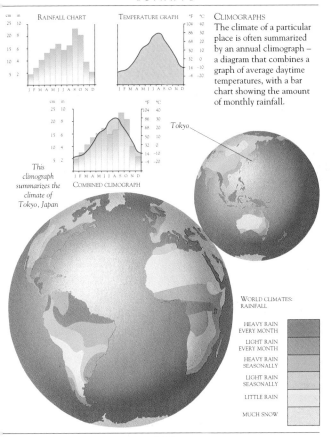

RAINFALL CHART

TEMPERATURE GRAPH

CLIMOGRAPHS
The climate of a particular place is often summarized by an annual climograph – a diagram that combines a graph of average daytime temperatures, with a bar chart showing the amount of monthly rainfall.

This climograph summarizes the climate of Tokyo, Japan

COMBINED CLIMOGRAPH

Tokyo

WORLD CLIMATES:
RAINFALL

HEAVY RAIN
EVERY MONTH

LIGHT RAIN
EVERY MONTH

HEAVY RAIN
SEASONALLY

LIGHT RAIN
SEASONALLY

LITTLE RAIN

MUCH SNOW

TROPICAL

YEAR-ROUND HIGH TEMPERATURES combined with heavy rainfall are characteristic of a tropical climate. Near the equator, the rainfall is distributed fairly evenly throughout the year. Warm, moist air rising over high ground produces frequent thunderstorms and dense cloud cover. Farther to the north and south, the rainfall tends to be concentrated into a distinct wet season.

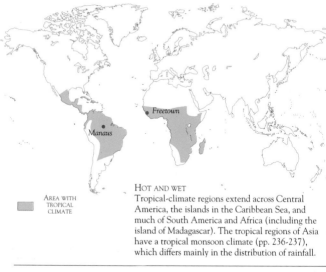

AREA WITH
TROPICAL
CLIMATE

HOT AND WET
Tropical-climate regions extend across Central America, the islands in the Caribbean Sea, and much of South America and Africa (including the island of Madagascar). The tropical regions of Asia have a tropical monsoon climate (pp. 236-237), which differs mainly in the distribution of rainfall.

TROPICAL CONDITIONS

High temperatures, heavy rainfall, and lush vegetation make most tropical regions extremely humid (humidity measures the amount of water vapor in the air). Frequent rainfall means that the sky is often filled with clouds, and sunshine is fairly limited. In general, winds are light but tropical thunderstorms and cyclones (hurricanes) can cause considerable destruction.

LANDSCAPE

Tropical climates produce a characteristic natural vegetation known as tropical rain forest. The largest remaining rainforest is in the Amazon Basin, Brazil.

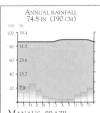

ANNUAL RAINFALL
74.8 IN (190 CM)

MANAUS, BRAZIL

With consistently high year-round temperatures, Manaus experiences a brief "dry" season during the months of July, August, and September.

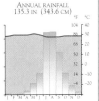

ANNUAL RAINFALL
135.3 IN (343.6 CM)

FREETOWN, SIERRA LEONE

Situated on the coast, Freetown has six months of heavy rain each year. During the wet season, sunshine is limited to only 2–3 hours per day.

CLIMATE FACTS

• The kinetic energy of the raindrops in a tropical rainstorm is equivalent to 2,200 watts per acre (5,500 watts per hectare).

• In geography, the "Tropics" lie between the Tropic of Cancer (23°30N) and the Tropic of Capricorn (23°30S). Tropical climates extend beyond this strict geographical definition.

TROPICAL MONSOON

TORRENTIAL MONSOON rains
dominate the climate in the
tropical regions of Asia and
Australasia. Twice a year, the
prevailing winds reverse their
direction completely. This shift
in the wind divides the year into
a rainy season followed by a
predominantly dry season.

WET SEASON
In parts of India, the
monsoon rains regularly
produce flooding.

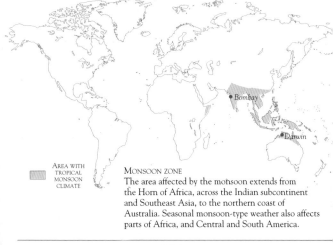

AREA WITH
TROPICAL
MONSOON
CLIMATE

MONSOON ZONE
The area affected by the monsoon extends from
the Horn of Africa, across the Indian subcontinent
and Southeast Asia, to the northern coast of
Australia. Seasonal monsoon-type weather also affects
parts of Africa, and Central and South America.

NORTHEAST MONSOON
With the onset of winter (below), Central Asia becomes a high-pressure region, and the winds reverse direction. Cool dry winds blow from the northeast toward the equator, lowering temperatures.

SOUTHWEST MONSOON
During early summer (above), low pressure over Central Asia creates southwesterly winds that carry warm moisture-laden air from the Indian Ocean. These winds bring the heavy monsoon rains.

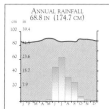

ANNUAL RAINFALL
68.8 IN (174.7 CM)

BOMBAY, INDIA
Nearly all of Bombay's rainfall occurs in the four months of the monsoon wet season – June, July, August, and September.

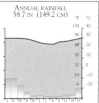

ANNUAL RAINFALL
58.7 IN (149.2 CM)

DARWIN, AUSTRALIA
Because it is situated south of the equator, Darwin has a dry season at the same time as Bombay has a wet season.

CLIMATE FACTS

• The word monsoon comes from the Arabic word *mausim*, which means "seasonal wind."

• Monsoon rains advance across Asia at a rate of about 60 miles (100 km) per day.

• At Cherrapungi in northern India, 864 in (22 m) of rain fell during the 1861 monsoon season.

DRY

LITTLE OR NO RAINFALL is the main characteristic
of the dry climate found in desert and semidesert
regions. Most deserts also experience high daytime
temperatures, but some are cool or even cold. The
large midlatitude deserts – the Sahara and Arabian
deserts – are the result of the global pattern of air
circulation. Dry air descends on these regions,
bringing clear skies and hot sunshine.

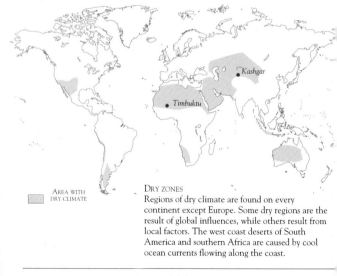

AREA WITH
DRY CLIMATE

DRY ZONES
Regions of dry climate are found on every
continent except Europe. Some dry regions are the
result of global influences, while others result from
local factors. The west coast deserts of South
America and southern Africa are caused by cool
ocean currents flowing along the coast.

DRY CONDITIONS

Desert skies are usually cloudless with strong sunlight. Although the air above the desert surface heats up, it remains relatively cool compared with the ground. Sand or rocks in direct sunlight will easily reach 140–160°F (60–70°C). Dry air loses heat more quickly at night than moist air, so nighttime temperatures may drop to below freezing point.

LANDSCAPE

Large areas of the driest deserts are seas of sand dunes. The constantly shifting dunes prevent even the most drought-resistant plants from gaining a foothold.

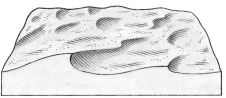

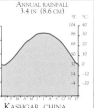

ANNUAL RAINFALL
9.1 IN (23.2 CM)

ANNUAL RAINFALL
3.4 IN (8.6 CM)

TIMBUKTU, MALI

Located in the southern Sahara, Timbuktu has high temperatures year-round. All of the rainfall occurs during the summer months.

KASHGAR, CHINA

Situated more than 1,000 miles (1,600 km) from the sea, Kashgar is hot in summer, cold in winter, and very dry throughout the year.

CLIMATE FACTS

• The world's driest place is the Atacama Desert in northern Chile. Between 1903 and 1917, the town of Arica received no rain at all for a period of 5,206 days.

• The sunniest place in the world is the town of Yuma, in Arizona, with an average of 4,127 hours of bright sunshine each year.

WARM

COMFORTABLE TEMPERATURES and moderate rainfall throughout the year are found in warm-climate regions. Some of these regions are described as having a "Mediterranean" climate, but this term can be misleading. Geographical conditions around the Mediterranean Sea have created an especially mild climate. Some warm-climate regions have more extreme temperatures in both winter and summer.

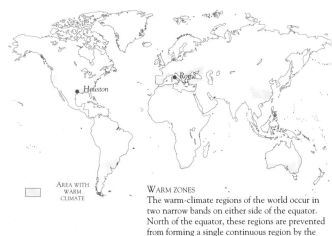

Rome

Houston

AREA WITH
WARM
CLIMATE

WARM ZONES
The warm-climate regions of the world occur in two narrow bands on either side of the equator. North of the equator, these regions are prevented from forming a single continuous region by the presence of geographical barriers, such as the Rocky Mountains and the Himalayas.

WARM CONDITIONS

With mild winters and a long frost-free growing period, warm-climate regions are ideally suited to most types of agriculture. In California and the Mediterranean region, citrus fruits, grapes, and olives are important cash crops. In China, the warm-climate region is the most productive rice-growing area.

LANDSCAPE

Most of the natural vegetation has been cleared from warm-climate regions to make way for human settlements and agriculture.

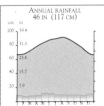

ANNUAL RAINFALL
46 IN (117 CM)

HOUSTON, TEXAS
The climograph for Houston shows a short, mild winter and a long, warm summer. Rainfall is distributed fairly evenly over the year.

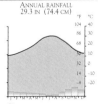

ANNUAL RAINFALL
29.3 IN (74.4 CM)

ROME, ITALY
Situated slightly farther north, Rome has a shorter summer than Houston. Rainfall is more seasonal, and is highest during autumn.

CLIMATE FACTS

• A warm climate is no guarantee of a mild winter. In January 1932, 2 in (5 cm) of snow fell on Los Angeles, California.

• Europe's highest temperature of 123°F (50.5°C) was recorded in southern Portugal.

• The Mediterranean region has more than 30 individually named local winds.

Cool

COLD WINTERS with frequent nighttime frosts are characteristic of cool-climate regions. These regions have much more changeable weather than elsewhere. Cool-climate regions are strongly influenced by large moving weather systems called depressions, or "lows," and anticyclones, or "highs." As one of these systems passes over a particular location, it produces a series of changing weather conditions.

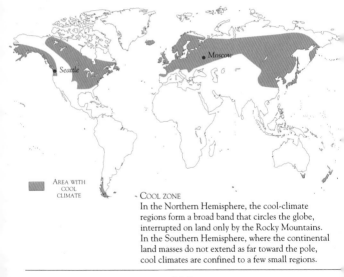

AREA WITH COOL CLIMATE

COOL ZONE
In the Northern Hemisphere, the cool-climate regions form a broad band that circles the globe, interrupted on land only by the Rocky Mountains. In the Southern Hemisphere, where the continental land masses do not extend as far toward the pole, cool climates are confined to a few small regions.

COOL CONDITIONS

There is considerable variation across cool-climate regions because of their great geographical extent. Coastal regions often have a less extreme climate than regions farther inland. Deciduous trees, which lose their leaves in winter, are confined to the warmer regions. In general, human settlement and agriculture are similarly restricted by temperature.

LANDSCAPE

In most cool-climate regions, the landscape is still dominated by natural vegetation. Forests of needleleaf (coniferous) trees encircle the globe.

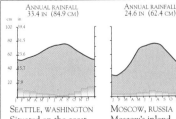

ANNUAL RAINFALL
33.4 IN (84.9 CM)

ANNUAL RAINFALL
24.6 IN (62.4 CM)

SEATTLE, WASHINGTON
Situated on the coast, Seattle's climate is moderated by the sea, which keeps temperatures relatively high during the winter months.

MOSCOW, RUSSIA
Moscow's inland climate is more extreme than that of Seattle. Rainfall also follows a different pattern, with a summer maximum.

CLIMATE FACTS

• The lowest recorded temperature in the Northern Hemisphere, −96°F (−71°C), was measured inside the cool-climate region at Oimyakon, Siberia.

• The highest recorded temperature in Britain is 98.8°F (37.1°C) in August 1990; and the lowest on record is −17.0°F (−27.2°C) in January 1982.

MOUNTAIN AND POLAR

MOUNTAINS CREATE THEIR OWN CLIMATE, no matter where they are located. The climate of a mountain or mountain range can be divided vertically into a number of subzones. While foothills may have a tropical climate, peaks may be covered in ice. Near the North and South Poles, the polar climate is dominated by low temperatures, strong winds, and year-round snow cover.

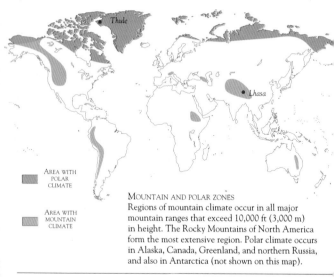

AREA WITH
POLAR
CLIMATE

AREA WITH
MOUNTAIN
CLIMATE

MOUNTAIN AND POLAR ZONES
Regions of mountain climate occur in all major mountain ranges that exceed 10,000 ft (3,000 m) in height. The Rocky Mountains of North America form the most extensive region. Polar climate occurs in Alaska, Canada, Greenland, and northern Russia, and also in Antarctica (not shown on this map).

MOUNTAIN CONDITIONS

The subzones of a mountain climate get progressively colder with increased altitude. The vegetation on the lower slopes largely depends upon which climate zone the mountain is in. On the upper slopes, needleleaf trees reach to the tree line. Above this level are found alpine plants which can withstand the harsh conditions. The uppermost level is bare rock and snow.

POLAR LANDSCAPE
Polar regions are dominated by snow and ice. Some parts of Antarctica are covered with a layer of ice more than 10,000 ft (3,000 m) thick.

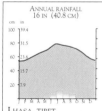

ANNUAL RAINFALL
16 IN (40.8 CM)

cm	in
100	39.4
80	31.5
60	23.6
40	15.7
20	7.9

J F M A M J J A S O N D

LHASA, TIBET
Situated some 12,000 ft (3,600 m) above sea level, Lhasa has surprisingly warm summers thanks to clear skies and strong sun.

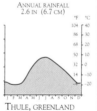

ANNUAL RAINFALL
2.6 IN (6.7 CM)

°F	°C
104	40
86	30
68	20
50	10
32	0
14	-10
	-20

J F M A M J J A S O N D

THULE, GREENLAND
Temperatures at Thule only rise above freezing during the middle of summer. The annual "rainfall" consists entirely of snow.

CLIMATE FACTS

• The highest recorded temperature inside the Arctic Circle is 100°F (37.8°C), at Fort Yukon, Alaska, in June 1915.

• The highest recorded Antarctic temperature is 58°F (14.4°C) in October 1958.

• Mount Kilimanjaro in Tanzania is the only permanent snowcap within sight of the equator.

WEATHER AND SEASONS

IN SOME PARTS OF THE WORLD, weather is seasonal; it changes according to the time of year. Seasons depend on varying amounts of sunlight reaching different parts of the Earth's surface. These variations are the result of the Earth's orbit around the Sun on a tilted axis. In general, seasons become more noticeable with increasing distance from the equator.

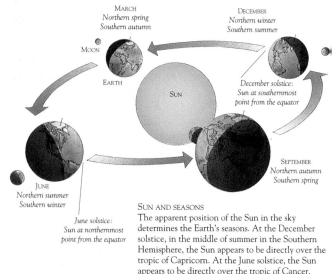

MARCH
Northern spring
Southern autumn

DECEMBER
Northern winter
Southern summer

MOON

EARTH

SUN

December solstice:
Sun at southernmost
point from the equator

SEPTEMBER
Northern autumn
Southern spring

JUNE
Northern summer
Southern winter

June solstice:
Sun at northernmost
point from the equator

SUN AND SEASONS
The apparent position of the Sun in the sky determines the Earth's seasons. At the December solstice, in the middle of summer in the Southern Hemisphere, the Sun appears to be directly over the tropic of Capricorn. At the June solstice, the Sun appears to be directly over the tropic of Cancer.

GRAPHS OF AVERAGE DAYTIME TEMPERATURE

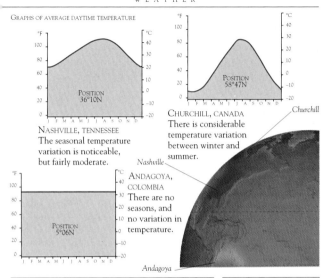

NASHVILLE, TENNESSEE
The seasonal temperature variation is noticeable, but fairly moderate.

CHURCHILL, CANADA
There is considerable temperature variation between winter and summer.

ANDAGOYA, COLOMBIA
There are no seasons, and no variation in temperature.

DATA: SEASONS AND DAYLIGHT (HOURS AND MINUTES)			
Date	Andagoya	Nashville	Churchill
1/15	11:51	10:00	6:38
2/15	11:58	10:56	9:11
3/15	12:06	11:55	11:41
4/15	12:14	12:45	14:31
5/15	12:20	14:00	17:04
6/15	12:23	14:32	18:49
7/15	12:21	14:26	17:31
8/15	12:17	13:32	15:46
9/15	12:09	12:27	13:00
10/15	12:01	11:19	10:11
11/15	11:53	10:21	7:37
12/15	11:49	9:46	5:54

SOLSTICE FACTS

• The June solstice (midsummer in the Northern Hemisphere) takes place around June 21–22.

• The December solstice (midwinter in the Northern Hemisphere) takes place around December 22–23.

WIND AND WEATHER

WINDS CIRCULATE air around the planet. They carry warm air from the equator to the poles and cold air in the opposite direction. This process balances the Earth's temperature. Some global winds (known as prevailing winds), such as polar casterlies and trade winds, are an important part of the world's weather systems.

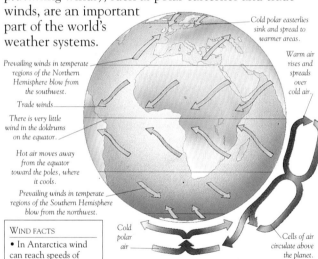

Cold polar easterlies sink and spread to warmer areas.

Warm air rises and spreads over cold air.

Prevailing winds in temperate regions of the Northern Hemisphere blow from the southwest.

Trade winds

There is very little wind in the doldrums on the equator.

Hot air moves away from the equator toward the poles, where it cools.

Prevailing winds in temperate regions of the Southern Hemisphere blow from the northwest.

Cold polar air

Cells of air circulate above the planet.

WIND FACTS

• In Antarctica wind can reach speeds of 200 mph (320 km/h).

• Highest wind speed recorded at ground level is 230 mph (371 km/h).

WINDS OF THE WORLD

Three prevailing winds blow around the planet at ground level, on either side of the equator. Trade winds bring dry weather, westerly winds are damp and warm, and polar easterlies carry dry, cold polar air.

FORMATION OF A ROSSBY WAVE

A SNAKING WIND
The Earth's rotation causes curling, high altitude winds called Rossby waves.

DEEPENING WAVE
The wave deepens along the polar front. It forms a meander 1,250 miles (2,000 km) long.

DEVELOPED LOOPS
The curls become loops and the hot and cold air separate to produce swirling frontal storms.

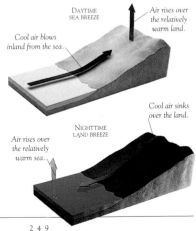

Earth's rotation deflects winds on the ground.

Trade winds near the equator

SEA BREEZES AND LAND BREEZES
On sunny days the land warms up during the day. Warm air rises from the land and cool air is drawn in from the sea. At night the land cools down quickly and cold air sinks out to sea.

DAYTIME SEA BREEZE

Air rises over the relatively warm land.

Cool air blows inland from the sea.

Cool air sinks over the land.

NIGHTTIME LAND BREEZE

Air rises over the relatively warm sea.

TRADE WINDS
In the area on either side of the equator (the tropics) the prevailing winds are called the trade winds. In the Northern Hemisphere the winds blow from the northeast, and in the Southern Hemisphere they blow from the southeast.

TEMPERATURE AND PRESSURE

WE THINK OF temperature in terms of whether it is a hot or cold day – the temperature close to the Earth's surface. We cannot feel air pressure in the same way, but it is equally important. The distribution of temperature and pressure throughout the atmosphere is crucial to the working of the weather machine.

A WARM DAY?
On the beach it is warm. Some 10,000 ft (3,000 m) overhead, however, the temperature is well below the freezing point.

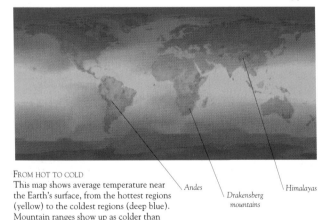

FROM HOT TO COLD
This map shows average temperature near the Earth's surface, from the hottest regions (yellow) to the coldest regions (deep blue). Mountain ranges show up as colder than the surrounding areas.

Andes

Drakensberg mountains

Himalayas

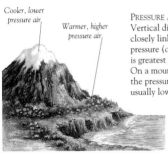

Cooler, lower pressure air

Warmer, higher pressure air

PRESSURE AND TEMPERATURE

Vertical differences in air temperature are closely linked to air pressure. In general, air pressure (often called atmospheric pressure) is greatest at sea level, where the air is densest. On a mountain peak, the air is less dense and the pressure is lower. The air temperature is usually lower than it would be at sea level.

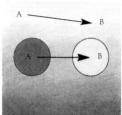

A pressure gradient exists between high pressure at A and low pressure at B

ATMOSPHERIC MOTION

Like other fluids, air tends toward a state where all regions at the same altitude have equal pressure. As a result, air flows from regions of high pressure to regions of low pressure. The difference between two adjoining regions can be described as a pressure gradient, and air flows "down" the gradient.

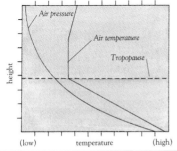

Air pressure

Air temperature

Tropopause

height

(low) temperature (high)

LAPSE RATE

Air pressure and air temperature both decrease away from the Earth's surface. The pressure decreases smoothly, but the temperature decrease is variable and depends on the water content (humidity) of the air. The rate of decrease is known as the lapse rate. The lapse rate for dry air is about 5.5°F per 1,000 ft (1.0°C per 100 m).

AIR MASSES

PROLONGED HIGH PRESSURE can cause parts of the atmosphere to become stagnant. The resulting air masses take on the weather characteristics of the region in which they formed. When these air masses start moving, they carry their weather with them, especially to the midlatitudes.

AIR MASS MARKERS
Cumulus clouds like these are typical of a maritime polar air mass.

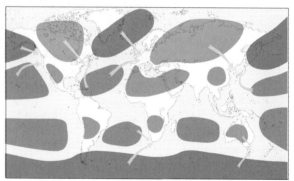

MAIN MASSES
This map shows the basic distribution of the different air masses that influence the weather. The size and locations of individual air masses are approximate because they change constantly.

MARITIME POLAR
CONTINENTAL POLAR
CONTINENTAL TROPICAL
MARITIMEL TROPICAL

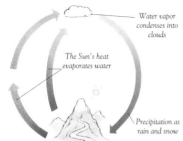

Water vapor condenses into clouds

The Sun's heat evaporates water

Precipitation as rain and snow

CLOSED CYCLE

Water circulates through the atmosphere as vapor, evaporating from land and oceans, and condensing to fall as precipitation. The amount of water vapor in a given air mass is called its humidity. Warm air can hold more water vapor than cold air. Air that cannot hold any more water vapor is said to be saturated.

ITCZ

The ITCZ (intertropical convergence zone) is marked by a narrow zone of cloud clusters that bring heavy rainfall. The ITCZ occurs because air streams from higher latitudes converge near the equator, forcing warm moist air to rise, cool, and condense into rain-bearing clouds.

DATA: AIR MASSES	
Air Mass	Description
Maritime tropical (mT)	warm and very moist
Maritime polar (mP)	cool and fairly moist
Maritime arctic (mA)	cold and quite moist
Maritime antarctic (mAA)	very cold and fairly dry
Continental tropical (cT)	hot and dry
Continental polar (cP)	cold and dry
Continental arctic (cA)	very cold and dry
Continental antarctic (cAA)	very cold and dry

ATMOSPHERE FACTS

• Water has an average "residence period" in the atmosphere of 11 days before it falls as rain or snow.

• A tropical air mass contains about 5–10 times more water than a polar air mass of similar size.

HIGHS AND LOWS

WEATHER IN THE midlatitudes is
controlled by a sequence of high-
pressure and low-pressure frontal
weather systems. High-pressure
systems, called anticyclones or
"highs," usually bring fair weather.
Low-pressure systems, called
depressions or "lows," usually
bring rain, or other precipitation,
and very changeable conditions.

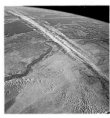

JET-STREAM CLOUDS
These clouds have been
blown into elongated
shapes by the jet stream.

FAMILY OF DEPRESSIONS
This illustration shows a family of three depressions
at different stages of development. The upper picture
shows the shape of the depressions viewed from above.
The lower picture shows the systems in
cross-section along the
line A–B.

A

Cold front

Jet stream

Rain
(green shading)

Cloud
(brown shading)

Low pressure
at center of
depression

A

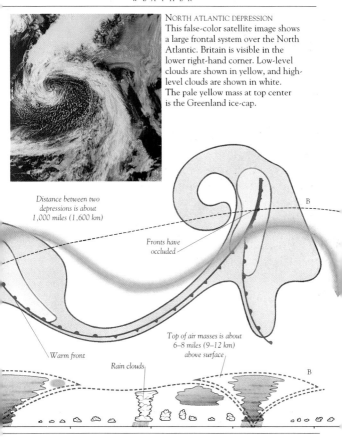

NORTH ATLANTIC DEPRESSION
This false-color satellite image shows
a large frontal system over the North
Atlantic. Britain is visible in the
lower right-hand corner. Low-level
clouds are shown in yellow, and high-
level clouds are shown in white.
The pale yellow mass at top center
is the Greenland ice-cap.

B

*Distance between two
depressions is about
1,000 miles (1,600 km)*

*Fronts have
occluded*

*Top of air masses is about
6–8 miles (9–12 km)
above surface*

Warm front

Rain clouds

B

CLOUDS

AIR RISES as it warms, as it passes over mountains, or as it is pushed over air masses near the ground. Rising air cools, water vapor condenses, and clouds of water droplets form. There are three cloud levels: cirrus form at the highest level, alto in the middle, and stratus at the lowest level.

FOGGY AIR
Clouds that form at ground level are known as fog. Fog, mixed with smoke from burning fuels, produces smog. Earlier this century, London, England suffered from severe smog.

CLOUD FORMATION

THE LAND WARMS
The Sun warms the land on a clear day. Air near the ground is warmed and rises.

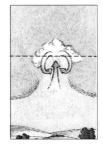

A CLOUD FORMS
As the warm air rises, it cools. The moisture it contains condenses and forms a cloud.

GROWING CLOUDS
Fleecy clouds appear in the sky. They get bigger and cool air circulates inside them.

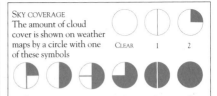

CLOUD AND AIR FACTS

• Cirrus are the highest clouds – they may reach 39,370 ft (12,000 m).

• Glider pilots and birds use pockets of rising air called thermals to help them stay in the air.

SKY COVERAGE

The amount of cloud cover is shown on weather maps by a circle with one of these symbols

CLEAR 1 2

3 4 5 6 7 8

Freezing level

CLOUD TYPES

CIRRUS (A)
• wisps of cloud made of ice crystals
• about 39,372 ft (12,000 m) high

CIRROCUMULUS (B)
• forms at about 29,529 ft (9,000 m)
• rippled ice crystal cloud

CUMULONIMBUS (C)
• dark, storm cloud with large vertical development

ALTOCUMULUS (D)
• layers or rolls of fluffy cloud

ALTOSTRATUS (E)
• gray or white sheet of cloud
• forms between 6,562 ft and 19,685 ft (2,000 m and 6,000 m)

STRATOCUMULUS (F)
• layer at the top of cumulus cloud

CUMULUS (G)
• large, heaped white fluffy cloud

NIMBOSTRATUS (H)
• low, rain cloud
• under 6,562 ft (2,000 m)

STRATUS (I)
• low-level, flat gray sheet of cloud

RAIN AND THUNDERSTORMS

EARTH'S WATER CYCLE relies on rain. Rain fills rivers
and lakes and provides water for plants and animals. Tiny
water droplets in the air form rain when they gather into
larger drops inside clouds. Raindrops can be moved
around by air currents. Light
rain or snowfall may
come from altostratus
clouds, heavy rain from
stratus clouds, and
torrential rains, or
thunderstorms, from
cumulonimbus clouds.

*Droplets of more
than 0.2 in
(0.5 mm) fall
as rain.*

*Smaller drops
of water fall as
drizzle.*

Rising air

HOW RAIN FORMS
In warm regions, rising air currents agitate the water
droplets in clouds until they join into raindrops. In
temperate regions, ice crystals in the clouds above
freezing level melt on their way down and form rain.

MONSOON
Seasonal winds called
summer monsoons draw
moist air inland, bringing
rain to southern Asia. In
winter, a cold, dry wind
(winter monsoon) blows
over land and out to sea.

RAIN FACTS

• A record 73.62 in (1,870 mm) of rain fell in one month in 1861 in Cherrapunji, India.

• Tutunendo, Colombia, the world's wettest place, has an annual rainfall of 463.4 in (11,770 mm).

LIGHTNING

Turbulence and collision of ice particles and water droplets inside a storm may cause electric charges. Positive charges gather at the top of the cloud and negative ones at the base. When the electricity is released it flashes between clouds or sparks to the ground and back.

Positive charges

Negative charges

RAINBOWS

Sunlight striking raindrops is refracted, reflected by the backs of the droplets, and refracted again. This causes the white light to split into its seven constituent colors: red, orange, yellow, green, blue, indigo, and violet.

RAINFALL MAP

Around the world rainfall varies greatly. Warm seas in the tropics evaporate and bring lots of rain. Near the sea land is wetter but mountains may block rain.

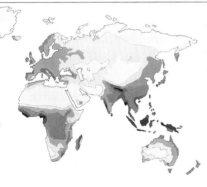

KEY TO ANNUAL RAINFALL

◯ Less than 10 in (250 mm)

◯ 10–20 in (250–500 mm)

◯ 20–39 in (500–1,000 mm)

◯ 39–79 in (1,000–2,000 mm)

◯ 79–118 in (2,000–3,000 mm)

● More than 118 in (3,000 mm)

SNOW, HAIL, AND SLEET

WHEN THE WEATHER is very cold, snow, hail, or sleet leave a white coating on the landscape. Snow and hail result from water freezing in the clouds. Snow falls from the altostratus clouds, and hail from thunderstorm clouds. Sleet forms when partially frozen rainwater freezes completely as it touches any cold surface.

SNOWY WEATHER
In the European Alps the snow in the winter months does not melt because the ground temperature is low. Strong winds sometimes blow the snow into deep snowdrifts.

HOW SNOW FORMS
High up in the atmosphere, above the freezing level, water droplets in clouds form ice crystals, which collide and combine. As they fall, the ice crystals form snowflakes or hail.

SNOW FACTS
• The largest recorded hailstone weighed 1.7 lb (765 g) and fell in Kansas in 1970.

• In 1921, 76 in (1,930 mm) of snow fell in Colorado in one day.

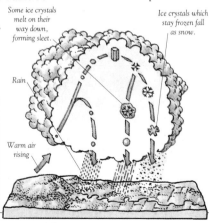

Some ice crystals melt on their way down, forming sleet.

Ice crystals which stay frozen fall as snow.

Rain

Warm air rising

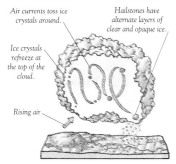

Air currents toss ice crystals around.

Hailstones have alternate layers of clear and opaque ice.

Ice crystals refreeze at the top of the cloud.

Rising air

HOW HAIL FORMS

In cumulonimbus clouds above 6 miles (10 km) the temperature is freezing. Water droplets blown to the top of the cloud freeze. Layers of ice build up around the hailstone as it repeatedly melts and refreezes in its motion through the cloud.

FROZEN RIVER

The Zanskar River in the Himalayas is frozen during the winter months. The frozen river makes traveling in the region easier, since local people can walk up and downstream on the ice. Under the ice fish can survive in the unfrozen water. In summer, the river is a fast-flowing torrent.

ICICLES

Spectacular ice shapes such as icicles form when water freezes in cold weather. Icicles grow as drips of melting snow or ice refreeze.

The outside of an icicle freezes before the inside.

Icicles often hang from leaking pipes.

HOAR FROST

Below freezing point, water vapor in the air freezes. It leaves spiky crystals of hoar frost on cold surfaces.

HURRICANES AND TORNADOES

FIERCE WINDS such as hurricanes and tornadoes occur when warm air masses encounter cold air masses. Winds reach high speeds and bring torrential rain and huge dark clouds. A tornado concentrates its havoc on a fairly narrow trail whereas a hurricane destroys a much larger area and can last for many days.

BEAUFORT SCALE	
NUMBER	DESCRIPTION
0	Calm, smoke rises straight up
1	Light air, smoke drifts gently
2	Light breeze, leaves rustle
3	Gentle breeze, flags flutter
4	Moderate wind, twigs move
5	Fresh wind, small trees sway
6	Strong wind, large branches move
7	Near gale, whole tree sways
8	Gale, difficult to walk in wind
9	Severe wind, slates and branches break
10	Storm, houses damaged, trees blown down
11	Severe storm, buildings seriously damaged
12	Hurricane, devastating damage

SATELLITE PHOTOGRAPH
Hurricanes can be tracked easily using hurricane hunter planes and weather satellites. The small central eye develops as the hurricane reaches full intensity.

HURRICANE
Low-lying coasts are endangered by the high winds that generate large waves and also push water onshore as a destructive storm surge.

Cirrus and cirrostratus clouds around the edge of the storm.

Hurricanes can be as wide as 480 miles (800 km).

Bands of wind and rain spiral.

At the eye the sky is clear and winds light.

Currents rise and spread outward.

HOW A HURRICANE FORMS

A cluster of tropical storms can become a hurricane. Bands of cumulonimbus and cumulus clouds spiral toward the center of the storm. Warm air rises and cools, building huge storm clouds that bring rain. At the center, or eye, of the hurricane, the pressure is low and the weather is calm.

WATERSPOUT

If a tornado occurs over the ocean it is known as a waterspout. Water spray from the sea swirls around the base of the spout. Higher up, water vapor condenses in a whirling tubular cloud.

A violent updraft sucks up soil and debris.

Winds in the tornado may reach speeds of 200 mph (320 km/h).

HURRICANE FACTS

• Winds up to 100 mph (160 km/h) have been recorded in a hurricane.

• Hurricanes spin counterclockwise north of the equator and clockwise south of the equator.

• Waterspouts are usually between 164 and 330 ft (50–100 m) high.

TORNADO

If a mass of cool, dry air collides with a mass of warm, damp air it may form a squall line of tornado-generating thunderstorms. The storm may last only a few minutes but its spinning winds are very destructive. Tornados are most frequent in midwest US.

BLIZZARDS AND SANDSTORMS

WINDBLOWN PARTICLES of snow
and sand are a normal part of
weather in polar and desert
regions. In remote areas, they
cause little disruption. However,
when blizzards and sandstorms
occur in highly populated areas,
they can cause chaos. Visibility
is greatly reduced, and most forms
of transportation are paralyzed.

BLIZZARD
A blizzard is snow blown
by winds that have an
average speed of at least
32 mph (52 km/h).

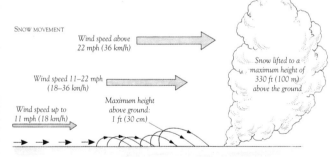

SNOW MOVEMENT

Wind speed above
22 mph (36 km/h)

Wind speed 11–22 mph
(18–36 km/h)

Wind speed up to
11 mph (18 km/h)

Maximum height
above ground:
1 ft (30 cm)

Snow lifted to a
maximum height of
330 ft (100 m)
above the ground

SNOW CREEP
Under gentle winds,
snow particles roll along
the ground, rising no
more than 1 in (2.5 cm)
above the surface.

SALTATION
Under moderate winds,
snow particles jump and
bounce along the ground
in a form of movement
called saltation.

TURBULENT DIFFUSION
In strong winds, the wind
has enough force to lift
fallen snow back into the
air in a process called
turbulent diffusion.

SANDSTORM

A sandstorm darkens the sky in sub-Saharan Africa. There are two types of storm. A small sandstorm (*haboob*) is formed by the downdraft winds of a thunderstorm. A large sandstorm (*khamsin*) is formed by strong winds that blow for several days.

DUST STORM

With dramatic suddenness, a dust storm sweeps across a Canadian airport. Dust particles are smaller and lighter than sand and are lifted into the atmosphere more easily. This particular storm was raised by the strong winds at the leading edge of a cold front.

DATA BOX: WIND CHILL EFFECT

Air temperature	Wind speed	
	10 mph (6 km/h)	20 mph (32 km/h)
32°F (0°C)	27°F (−3°C)	21°F (−6°C)
24°F (−4°C)	19°F (−7°C)	10°F (−12°C)
20°F (−7°C)	14°F (−10°C)	5°F (−15°C)
16°F (−9°C)	10°F (−12°C)	0°F (−19°C)
12°F (−12°C)	6°F (−14°C)	−5°F (−20°C)

Explanation: with air temperature 32°F (0°C), the cooling effect of a wind of 10 mph (6 km/h) is the same as still air at 27°F (−3°C).

FREEZING RAIN
Rain falling through very cold air, or onto cold objects, can freeze into a coating of clear ice. This is also known as glaze.

WEATHER MAPPING

MILLIONS OF PEOPLE listen to the
weather forecast each day. The
forecast is compiled using data
collected from all around the world
and from weather satellites in
space. Meteorologists study the
movements of warm and cold air
masses and the fronts where they
meet. Using this information
they plot weather charts and
predict the coming weather.

SATELLITE IMAGES
From space, the Earth appears
to be surrounded by swirling
clouds. Deserts, however, often
have no cloud cover at all.

WEATHER MAP
A picture of the
weather at a given
time can be shown
on a weather map,
known as a synoptic
chart. Standard
symbols are used, such
as lines to show fronts
(where one body of
air – an air mass –
meets another).

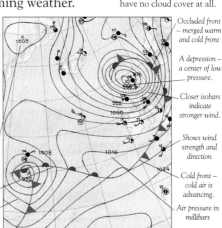

*Occluded front
– merged warm
and cold front*

*A depression –
a center of low
pressure.*

*Closer isobars
indicate
stronger wind.*

*Shows wind
strength and
direction*

*Cold front –
cold air is
advancing.*

*Air pressure in
millibars*

Center of high pressure

*Warm front – warm
air is advancing.*

*Isobars link points with
the same air pressure.*

FORMATION OF A DEPRESSION

AIR MASSES
Air masses are a vast area of wet or dry, warm or cold air. At the polar front, a warm air mass and a cold one collide.

FORMING A BULGE
The warm tropical air mass pushes into the cold polar air along the polar front. The front begins to bulge.

DIVIDING INTO TWO
The Earth's rotation spins the air masses. Cold air pursues warm air in a spiral formation. The polar front splits.

OCCLUDED FRONT
When the cold front catches up with the warm front, it pushes under the warm air. An occluded front results.

BAROMETER
The air around the Earth has mass and exerts pressure. A barometer measures air pressure in units called millibars.

TEMPERATURE PEAKS
Troughs in the temperature graph show when ice sheets advanced to cover high latitude and land masses. These cold periods were separated by interglacials when the average temperature rose and the ices sheets retreated.

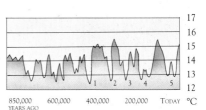

850,000 YEARS AGO   600,000   400,000   200,000   TODAY   °C

17
16
15
14
13
12

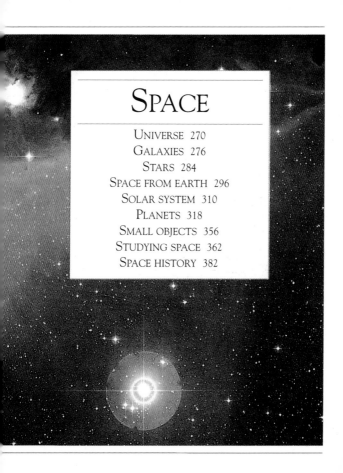

SPACE

WHAT IS THE UNIVERSE?

THE UNIVERSE IS EVERYTHING that exists. From the Earth beneath our feet to the farthest stars, everything is a part of the universe. The universe is so large that it contains countless billions of stars. However, most of it consists of nothing but empty space.

Galaxies

Galaxy containing billions of stars

Comet – a dirty snowball

Quasar – the brilliant center of a distant galaxy

Supernova – the death of a large star

LOOKING TO THE SKIES

From Earth, we can look into space and study the universe. In every direction we look there are stars. There are more stars in the universe than any other type of object – stars at different stages of their lives in enormous groups called galaxies, including at least one star that has planets. Despite the huge size of the universe, we know of only one place where life exists – planet Earth.

UNIVERSE FACTS

• There are at least a trillion galaxies in the universe; large ones contain more than a trillion stars.

• The most distant objects we can detect are 87,000 million million million miles (139,000 million million million km) away.

HORSEHEAD IN SPACE
Looking like a chess knight, the Horsehead
Nebula (right) is a gigantic cloud of dark-colored
dust. It is visible because the dust blocks out light
from behind the nebula, so that we see it in
silhouette. The universe contains many similar
clouds that block our view of different regions.

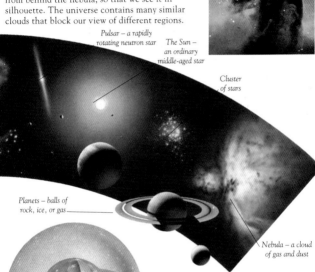

*Pulsar – a rapidly
rotating neutron star*

*The Sun –
an ordinary
middle-aged star*

*Cluster
of stars*

*Planets – balls of
rock, ice, or gas*

*Nebula – a cloud
of gas and dust*

VISUALIZING THE UNIVERSE
The easiest way to think of the universe
is as a sphere which is constantly
expanding so that everything is getting
farther away from everything else. There
is nothing beyond the universe, because
the universe contains all of time and
space within it.

SCALE OF THE UNIVERSE

DISTANCES IN THE UNIVERSE are so great that the light-year is used as a unit of measurement. Light travels at about 186,000 miles/sec (300,000 km/s), and a light-year (ly) is the distance light travels in one year. A galaxy can measure thousands of light-years across and be millions of light-years distant.

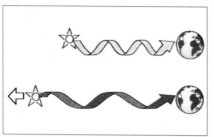

LIGHT AND MOTION
A star's light can tell us about its motion. If the star is moving away from Earth, its light is stretched by comparison with stationary stars. Light from a star moving away is also shifted toward the red end of the spectrum. Stars approaching Earth have compressed light shifted toward blue.

SCALE OF SIZES
The human world, the world of everyday experience, is dwarfed by the scale of the universe. Earth is one of nine planets orbiting the Sun, which is one of about 200 billion stars in the Milky Way galaxy.

The Sun is just one star among billions in the Milky Way galaxy.

Earth is the third of nine planets orbiting the Sun.

More than 5,000 million people live on Earth.

The human scale is the familiar one of everyday objects.

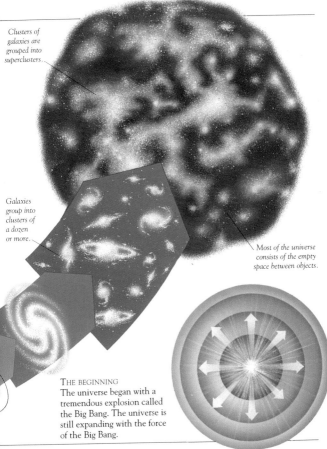

Clusters of galaxies are grouped into superclusters.

Galaxies group into clusters of a dozen or more.

Most of the universe consists of the empty space between objects.

THE BEGINNING
The universe began with a tremendous explosion called the Big Bang. The universe is still expanding with the force of the Big Bang.

LIFE STORY OF THE UNIVERSE

ALL MATTER, ENERGY, space, and time were created in the Big Bang around 14 billion years ago. At first the universe was small and very hot. As the universe expanded and cooled, atomic particles joined to form hydrogen and helium. Over billions of years these gases have produced galaxies, stars, planets, and us.

The Big Bang creates the universe

Universe keeps expanding

The universe will slowly cool as it gets ever larger and less dense.

WHAT HAPPENS NEXT?

The universe has been expanding since the Big Bang, and will probably go on expanding for ever. Recent observations indicate that the expansion is speeding up as the universe gets older and bigger.

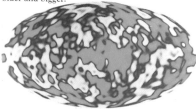

BIG BANG RIPPLES

This map of the whole sky is based on tiny variations in the temperature of space. Red is warmer than average and blue is colder. These tiny variations are irregularities of the Big Bang explosion. The information for the map was obtained by the Cosmic Background Explorer Satellite (COBE).

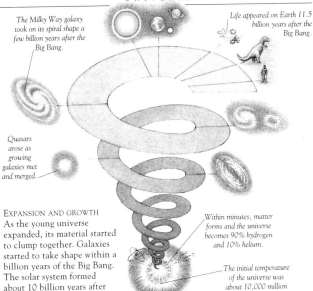

The Milky Way galaxy took on its spiral shape a few billion years after the Big Bang.

Life appeared on Earth 11.5 billion years after the Big Bang.

Quasars arose as growing galaxies met and merged.

EXPANSION AND GROWTH
As the young universe expanded, its material started to clump together. Galaxies started to take shape within a billion years of the Big Bang. The solar system formed about 10 billion years after the Big Bang.

Within minutes, matter forms and the universe becomes 90% hydrogen and 10% helium.

The initial temperature of the universe was about 10,000 million million million degrees

UNIVERSE: COOLING DATA	
Time after Big Bang	Temperature
10^{-6} secs	1.8×10^{13}°F (10^{13}°C)
3 minutes	1.8×10^8°F (10^8°C)
300,000 years	18,000°F (10,000°C)
1 million years	5,400°F (3,000°C)
1 billion years	−275°F (−170°C)
15 billion years	−454°F (−270°C)

UNIVERSE FACT
• Scientists can trace the life story of the universe back to what is called the Planck time, 10^{-43} seconds after the Big Bang. 10^{-43} means a decimal point followed by 42 zeros and then a one.

WHAT IS A GALAXY?

A GALAXY IS an enormous
group of stars. A large galaxy
may have a billion, a small
galaxy only a few hundred
thousand. Even small galaxies
are so big that it takes light
thousands of years to cross
them. Galaxies are formed from
vast spinning clouds of gas.
Many continue to spin.
Galaxies come in a number
of different shapes.

DISTANT STAR CITY
The Andromeda galaxy is so
far away that its light takes
2,500,000 years to travel to
Earth. We see the galaxy as
it was 2,500,000 years ago.

GALAXIES: THE FOUR
BASIC TYPES

ELLIPTICAL
These range from ball-
shaped to egg-shaped.
They contain mainly
old stars, and are the
most common type.

SPIRAL
These are disk-shaped.
Most material is in the
spiral arms where new
stars are formed. Old
stars are in the nucleus.

BARRED-SPIRAL
These are like spiral
galaxies, but the nucleus
is elongated into a bar.
The spiral arms extend
from the ends of the bar.

BRIGHTEST LIGHTS
This is an X-ray image of a quasi-stellar object, one of the brightest, and remotest objects. The most distant are about 15 billion light-years away. Known as quasars, they are probably the cores of the first galaxies to be formed.

BRIGHT GALAXIES: DATA		
Galaxy	Distance	Type
Andromeda (M31)	2,500,000 ly	Sb
M33	2,800,000 ly	Sc
NGC 300	4,200,000 ly	Sc
NGC 55	5,800,000 ly	Sc
NGC 253	8,000,000 ly	Sc
M81	14,000,000 ly	Sb
M82	14,000,000 ly	peculiar
Centaurus A	16,000,000 ly	E (peculiar)
M83	16,000,000 ly	SBc
M101	17,000,000 ly	Sc
M64	18,000,000 ly	Sab
Whirlpool (M51)	27,000,000 ly	Sbc
M104	44,000,000 ly	Sa/b
M87	55,000,000 ly	E0
M100	55,000,000 ly	Sc
M77	62,000,000 ly	Sb
NGC 1316 (Fornax A)	66,000,000 ly	Sa (peculiar)

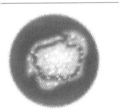

IRREGULAR
Some of these have a hint of spiral structure, while others do not fit any known pattern. They are the rarest type.

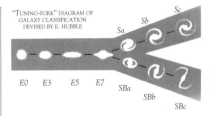

"TUNING-FORK" DIAGRAM OF GALAXY CLASSIFICATION DEVISED BY E. HUBBLE

E0   E3   E5   E7   SBa   Sa   Sb   Sc   SBb   SBc

CLASSIFYING GALAXIES BY SHAPE
Elliptical galaxies are classified from E0 (spherical) to E7 (very flattened). Spirals (S) and barred spirals (SB) are graded from a to c, according to the compactness of the central nucleus and the tightness of the arms. Irregular galaxies (Irr) are not shown here, but can be divided into types I and II.

CLUSTERS AND SUPERCLUSTERS

GALAXIES OCCUR TOGETHER in clusters that range in size from a few to a few thousand galaxies. Clusters themselves also occur in groups called superclusters, which are the largest structures in the universe.

NEIGHBORING CLUSTER
The Virgo cluster is about 55 million light-years away, but it is the nearest major cluster to our own Local Group.

Milky Way

M31

M33

THE LOCAL GROUP
Our own cluster is about five million light-years across and contains about 36 galaxies. The largest galaxies in the Local Group are Andromeda (M31), Triangulum (M33), and our own Milky Way galaxy.

SUPERCLUSTER FACTS

• The average distance between galaxies in a cluster is about ten galaxy diameters.

• The Local Group is just one small part of a giant supercluster about 100 million light-years in diameter.

SOME LOCAL GROUP GALAXIES: DATA

Name	Diameter	Distance
Andromeda	150,000 ly	2,500,000 ly
M33	40,000 ly	2,800,000 ly
Large Magellanic Cloud (LMC)	30,000 ly	170,000 ly
Small Magellanic Cloud (SMC)	20,000 ly	190,000 ly
NGC 6822	15,000 ly	1,650,000 ly
NGC 205	11,000 ly	2,700,000 ly

HONEYCOMB SPACE

Superclusters tend to be flattened into disks or sheets, or elongated into filaments. These shapes cannot be seen through a telescope, but scientists now know that the large-scale structure of the universe is basically a honeycomb arrangement. Superclusters are arranged on the surface of immense "bubbles." These bubbles are almost completely empty of matter. They are huge voids that contain only a few atoms of gas.

Coma cluster

Ursa Major cluster

Local Group

Virgo cluster

Leo cloud

THE LOCAL SUPERCLUSTER

THE MILKY WAY

THE SUN IS JUST ONE of the more than 100 billion stars in our own galaxy – the Milky Way. Ours is a spiral galaxy, with a nucleus of old stars surrounded by a halo of even older stars. All the young stars are located in the spiral arms. The Milky Way is so large that it takes light 100,000 years to travel from edge to edge. All the stars we see at night are in the Milky Way.

SAGITTARIUS STAR CLOUD
This infrared image shows young stars in Sagittarius, looking toward the Milky Way's center. Infrared reveals millions of stars that are obscured by dust clouds when viewed in visible light.

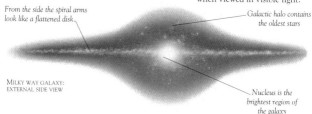

From the side the spiral arms look like a flattened disk.

Galactic halo contains the oldest stars

MILKY WAY GALAXY:
EXTERNAL SIDE VIEW

Nucleus is the brightest region of the galaxy

SIDE-ON SPIRAL
Viewed from the side, from a distance of about a million light-years, the Milky Way galaxy would look like a giant lens – with flattened edges and a bright central nucleus. Around the nucleus is a roughly spherical halo that contains the oldest stars in the galaxy.

THE MILKY WAY
AS SEEN FROM
EARTH

ABOVE THE SPIRAL
From above, or below, the spiral arms of
the Milky Way galaxy would be clearly
visible. These contain most of the galaxy's
gas and dust, and this is where
star-forming regions
are found.

MILKY WAY FACTS
• The Milky Way is
now thought to be a
barred spiral galaxy.

• Our galaxy rotates.
The Sun takes about
220 million years to
make one revolution –
a period sometimes
known as a "cosmic
year." Stars in other
parts of the galaxy
travel at different rates.

Galactic
nucleus

Crux-Centaurus arm

Location of
the solar system

Orion arm
(Local Arm)

Sagittarius
arm

MILKY WAY GALAXY:
EXTERNAL OVERHEAD VIEW

THE LOCAL ARM

THE SOLAR SYSTEM is situated about two-thirds of the way from the galaxy's center, at the edge of a spiral arm called the Local Arm or the Orion Arm. From this viewpoint, we see the galaxy as a great milky river of stars across the night sky.

The galactic nucleus is about 6,000 ly across.

POSITION OF THE
LOCAL ARM IN
THE GALAXY

SEVEN STARRY SISTERS
The Pleiades is a cluster of bright stars, seven of which can be seen with the naked eye, hence their popular name – the Seven Sisters – which has been in use for at least 2,000 years. In fact there are more than 200 stars in the cluster, which formed about 60 million years ago – shortly after the dinosaurs died out on Earth.

SPECTACULAR END

The Dumbbell Nebula, located about 1,000 light-years from the Sun, is a single star nearing the end of its life. Spherical shells of gas are blown out from the star's surface, making a spectacular sight. Gradually the gas will disperse, and will eventually be used to form new stars elsewhere in the galaxy.

LOCAL ARM FACTS

• From edge to edge the Dumbbell Nebula is two light-years in diameter.

• Some stars in Taurus and Orion are less than 1 million years old – mere star babies compared with our own Sun, which is 5 billion years old.

• The nearest bright star cluster to the Sun is the Hyades about 150 light-years away. The Hyades forms the V-shape of the bull's head in the constellation of Taurus.

THE LOCAL REGION OF SPACE WITHIN 1,000 LIGHT-YEARS OF THE SUN

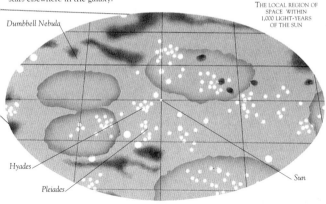

Dumbbell Nebula

Hyades

Pleiades

Sun

WHAT IS A STAR?

A STAR IS an enormous spinning ball of hot and luminous gas. Most stars contain two main gases – hydrogen and helium. These gases are held together by gravity, and at the core they are very densely packed. Within the core, immense amounts of energy are produced.

STAR CLUSTER
The cluster M13 in the constellation of Hercules contains hundreds of thousands of stars arranged in a compact ball.

Temperature and pressure increase toward the core.

STRUCTURE OF A STAR

Energy is released at the surface as light and heat.

Energy is produced by nuclear reactions in the core.

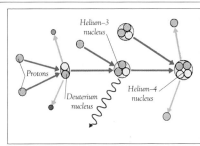

CORE FUSION

A star produces energy by
nuclear fusion. Within the
core, hydrogen nuclei
(protons) collide and fuse to
form first deuterium (heavy
hydrogen) and then two forms
of helium. During fusion,
energy is given off. This type
of reaction, which is found in
most stars, is called the
proton-proton chain.

VARYING SIZES

Stars differ greatly in
the amount of gas they
contain, and in their
size. The largest stars
are 1,000 times the
diameter of the Sun,
while the smallest are
just a fraction of its size
– not much bigger than
the planet Jupiter.

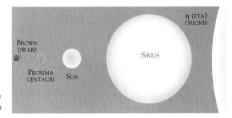

PROMINENT STARS: DATA		
Name	Designation	Distance
Vega	α Lyrae	25 ly
Pollux	β Geminorum	34 ly
Capella	α Aurigae	42 ly
Aldebaran	α Tauri	65 ly
Regulus	α Leonis	77 ly
Spica	α Virginis	262 ly
Canopus	α Carinae	313 ly
Betelgeuse	α Orionis	427 ly
Polaris	α Ursae Minoris	431 ly

STAR FACTS

• All the chemical
elements heavier than
hydrogen, helium, and
lithium were made by
nuclear reactions
inside stars.
• The mass of the Sun
– 1 solar mass – is
used as a standard for
measuring other stars.

STAR BIRTH

STARS FOLLOW a life cycle that lasts millions to billions of years. All stars begin in the same way – as material in a nebula, a cloud of gas and dust. Stars are not born individually, but in groups called clusters. Initially, the stars in a cluster have roughly the same composition. Despite these early similarities, the stars usually develop at different rates, and most clusters drift apart before very long.

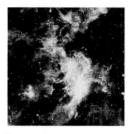

STELLAR BIRTHPLACE
In the Orion Nebula light from new stars illuminates the dust clouds. The stars themselves remain hidden by the dust. One of these young stars is 10,000 times brighter than the Sun.

FORMATION AND EARLY DEVELOPMENT OF A STAR

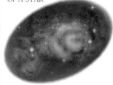

Inside a nebula, gravity causes spinning balls of gas to form – these are known as protostars.

The protostar (seen here in cross-section) shrinks, and its core becomes denser. An outer halo of gas and dust develops.

When the core reaches a critical density, nuclear reactions start. The energy released blows away most of the halo.

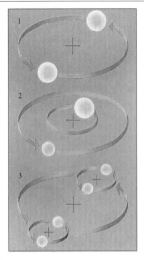

SINGLE OR DOUBLE

The Sun is unusual – it is a solitary star.
Most stars come in pairs or even larger
families. Multiple stars may orbit around a
common center of gravity (diagrams 1 and 2,
left), and may also orbit around one another
(3). Double stars often appear to be variable
in their light output (below) because one
star regularly blocks the light of the other.

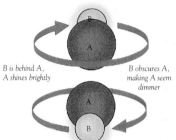

B is behind A,
A shines brightly

B obscures A,
making A seem
dimmer

As the young star
continues to spin
rapidly, the remaining
gas and dust become
flattened into a disk.

In some cases, such as
around the star we call the
Sun, this disk of gas and
dust has formed into a
system of orbiting planets.

With or without planets,
the new star now shines
steadily, converting
hydrogen to helium by
nuclear fusion.

LIFE CYCLE OF A STAR

A STAR'S LIFE CYCLE depends on its mass. Stars of the same mass as the Sun shine steadily for about 10 billion years. More massive stars convert their hydrogen more quickly, and have shorter lives. The Sun is halfway through its life. In about 5 billion years, it will expand to become a red giant star, and then collapse and end as a dwarf star.

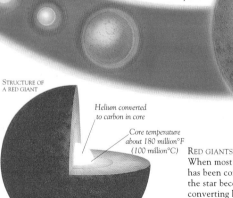

Star converting hydrogen i.e. in the main sequence

STRUCTURE OF
A RED GIANT

Helium converted to carbon in core

Core temperature about 180 million°F (100 million°C)

Cooler outer layers glow red

RED GIANTS
When most of the hydrogen has been converted to helium, the star becomes a red giant – converting helium to carbon. The core heats up causing the surface to expand and cool. A red giant may expand to more than 100 times its former size.

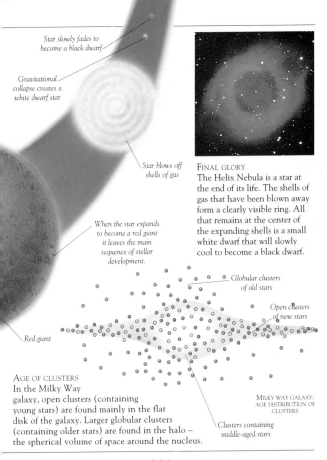

Star slowly fades to become a black dwarf

Gravitational collapse creates a white dwarf star

Star blows off shells of gas

When the star expands to become a red giant it leaves the main sequence of stellar development.

Red giant

FINAL GLORY
The Helix Nebula is a star at the end of its life. The shells of gas that have been blown away form a clearly visible ring. All that remains at the center of the expanding shells is a small white dwarf that will slowly cool to become a black dwarf.

Globular clusters of old stars

Open clusters of new stars

AGE OF CLUSTERS
In the Milky Way galaxy, open clusters (containing young stars) are found mainly in the flat disk of the galaxy. Larger globular clusters (containing older stars) are found in the halo – the spherical volume of space around the nucleus.

MILKY WAY GALAXY: AGE DISTRIBUTION OF CLUSTERS

Clusters containing middle-aged stars

DEATH OF MASSIVE STARS

THE WAY A STAR DIES depends on its mass. The most massive stars end their lives by simply exploding. This huge explosion is called a supernova, and may be bright enough to briefly outshine an entire galaxy. What happens next depends on how much stellar material is left after the supernova.

EXPLOSIVE COLLAPSE
Stars of at least eight solar masses end as supernovae. Gravity causes them to collapse with incredible force producing shock waves.

SUPERNOVA
EXPLOSION

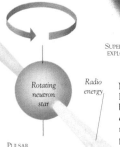

Rotating neutron star

Radio energy

PULSAR

Temperature at core
18 billion°F
(10 billion°C)

NEUTRON SPINNER
If the core that remains after a supernova is between 1.4 and 3.0 solar masses, it forms what is called a neutron star. Composed of super-dense material, neutron stars spin very quickly and produce beams of radio energy that appear to flash on and off very rapidly. These are called pulsars.

A RARE AND SPECTACULAR SIGHT

Although supernovae are fairly common in the universe, they are rarely visible to the naked eye. In 1987 a supernova was observed in the Large Magellanic Cloud, a nearby galaxy. The left-hand photograph shows the normal appearance of the star (arrowed). The supernova (designated SN 1987A) is clearly visible in the right-hand picture. After shining brightly for a few months, it slowly faded from view.

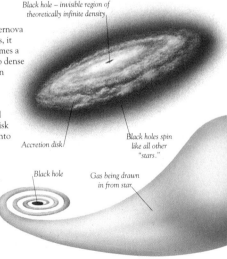

BLACK HOLES

If the core left after a supernova exceeds three solar masses, it will collapse until it becomes a black hole – something so dense that its gravity will suck in even light. By definition black holes are invisible, but they are believed to be surrounded by a spinning accretion disk of material being drawn into the black hole.

Black hole – invisible region of theoretically infinite density

Accretion disk

Black holes spin like all other "stars."

STELLAR THEFT

If a black hole forms near another star, it may suck in gas from the star, gradually stealing its mass. Astronomers believe that the object known as Cygnus X-1 is a star/black hole pair.

Black hole

Gas being drawn in from star

STELLAR CLASSIFICATION

THE MASS OF A STAR affects its other properties – its color, temperature, and luminosity. Each star is different, but by studying their properties, astronomers have been able to devise a system that enables them to classify all stars.

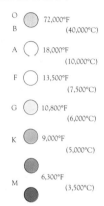

O		72,000°F
B		(40,000°C)
A		18,000°F
		(10,000°C)
F		13,500°F
		(7,500°C)
G		10,800°F
		(6,000°C)
K		9,000°F
		(5,000°C)
		6,300°F
M		(3,500°C)

HEAT AND LIGHT

A star's color is usually a good indicator of its temperature. Blue stars are the hottest, and red the coolest. The Harvard system uses letters of the alphabet to classify stars according to their surface temperature. This diagram shows the color and temperature range of the main types.

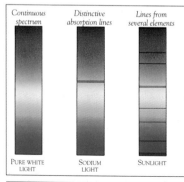

Continuous spectrum

Distinctive absorption lines

Lines from several elements

PURE WHITE LIGHT

SODIUM LIGHT

SUNLIGHT

CHEMICAL LINES

Each star emits its own particular light. Splitting this light into a spectrum reveals the chemical elements that make up the star. The different elements are indicated by dark absorption lines that run across the spectrum. Sodium atoms absorb light only in the yellow part of the spectrum. Sunlight displays hundreds of absorption lines, but only the most prominent are shown here.

HERTZSPRUNG-RUSSELL (HR) DIAGRAM OF STELLAR CLASSIFICATION

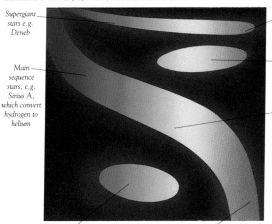

Supergiant stars e.g. Deneb

Main sequence stars, e.g. Sirius A, which convert hydrogen to helium

Betelgeuse is a red supergiant.

Arcturus is a red giant.

The Sun is a main sequence yellow dwarf.

White dwarf stars e.g. Sirius B

Barnard's Star is a main sequence red dwarf.

COLOR-CODED DIAGRAM

The HR diagram plots a star's temperature against its absolute magnitude (the amount of light it gives off). The brightest stars are at the top, and the dimmest are near the bottom. The hottest stars are to the left and the coolest to the right. Most stars spend some part of their lives in the main sequence which runs from top left to bottom right across the diagram. Giant stars are found above the main sequence and white dwarf stars below.

STAR FACTS

• Hot, bright young stars are found in large groups known as OB associations.

• By the standards of space, the Sun is very small. Astronomers refer to it as a type G dwarf star.

• The smallest stars, cooler and fainter than red dwarfs, are known as brown dwarfs.

BRIGHTNESS

HOW BRIGHTLY A STAR shines in
the sky depends on its luminosity
(amount of light energy produced),
and on its distance from Earth.
Astronomers use two different
scales to measure a star's magnitude
(brightness). Absolute magnitude
compares stars from a standard
distance. Apparent magnitude
describes how bright a star appears
as viewed from Earth.

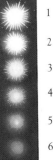

OBSERVED BRIGHTNESS
The scale of apparent
magnitude for naked-eye
stars. Brighter stars have
lower numerical values.

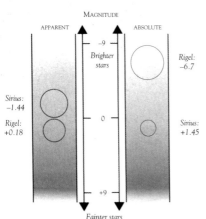

MAGNITUDE

APPARENT — ABSOLUTE

Brighter stars

Rigel:
−6.7

−9

0

Sirius:
−1.44

Rigel:
+0.18

Sirius:
+1.45

+9

Fainter stars

APPARENT VS ABSOLUTE
Sirius is the brightest star
in our sky (apparent
magnitude −1.46) brighter
than Rigel (apparent
magnitude +0.12). Yet in
reality, Rigel is by far the
brighter star with an
absolute magnitude of
−7.1, as opposed to Sirius
which has an absolute
magnitude of +1.4.

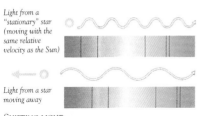

Light from a "stationary" star (moving with the same relative velocity as the Sun)

Light from a star moving away

SHIFTING LIGHT

All objects in the universe are moving. In light from stars moving away from the Sun, the dark absorption lines are shifted toward the red end of the spectrum – the so-called "red shift."

HOW FAR?

Calculating a star's absolute magnitude means knowing its distance. For fairly close stars (within a few hundred light-years) astronomers can measure distance using the parallax method. Earth's orbit around the Sun enables astronomers to take two sightings of a star from opposite sides of the orbit. The apparent shift in position of the star between the two sightings is called the parallax. The greater the parallax, the nearer the star. In this case, star A has the greater shift and is the closer.

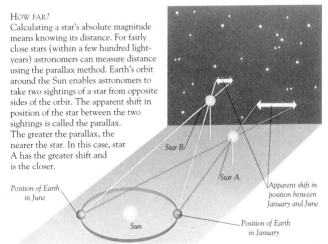

Star B

Star A

Apparent shift in position between January and June

Position of Earth in June

Sun

Position of Earth in January

ABOVE OUR HEADS

OUR KNOWLEDGE of the universe has been gained from our unique position on Earth. By day the sky is dominated by the Sun. At night the blackness of space is studded with stars and galaxies which form an unchanging backdrop. However, our view of them changes throughout the year as Earth orbits the Sun.

CIRCULAR STAR TRAILS
Earth's daily rotation causes the stars to appear to circle around the sky. This effect can be captured by a long-exposure photograph.

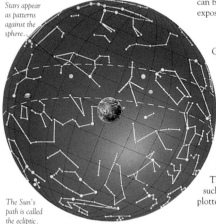

Stars appear as patterns against the sphere.

The Sun's path is called the ecliptic.

CELESTIAL SPHERE
From Earth the stars appear to be set against a giant celestial sphere. As the Earth travels on its yearly orbit around the Sun, different sections of the sphere are exposed to our view. At any particular time, about half the sphere is hidden by the Sun's glare. The motion of other objects, such as the planets, are also plotted against the sphere.

GALAXY

All the stars we
can see in the sky, including
the Sun, are in the Milky Way galaxy.
This panoramic view of the Milky
Way (looking toward the center of
the galaxy), was photographed from
Christchurch, New Zealand.

MARTIAN MOTION

Planets, which have their own
orbits around the Sun, appear to
move across the sky against the
backdrop of stars. The name
"planet" is in fact taken from an
ancient Greek word meaning
"wanderer." Of all the planets,
Mars seems to wander the most –
sometimes it appears to change
direction and move backward
across Earth's sky. This backward
motion is in fact an optical
illusion caused by the Earth
overtaking Mars as it travels
around the Sun.

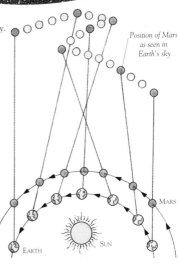

*Position of Mars
as seen in
Earth's sky*

MARS

EARTH

SUN

297

SPECIAL EFFECTS

FROM EARTH it is possible to see several "special effects" in the sky. Some of these effects are due to peculiarities of the Earth's magnetic field and atmosphere. Other effects depend on the position of the objects in the solar system, especially the Sun, Earth and Moon. Meteor showers are an effect produced by space dust burning up in the atmosphere.

AURORA BOREALIS
Charged particles from the Sun, carried by the solar wind, cause dramatic light shows when they enter Earth's atmosphere.

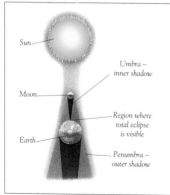

Sun

Umbra – inner shadow

Moon

Region where total eclipse is visible

Earth

Penumbra – outer shadow

ECLIPSE OF THE SUN
Occasionally, the Moon comes into perfect alignment between the Sun and the Earth. When this occurs, the Moon blocks out the Sun's light causing what is called a solar eclipse. From some parts of Earth's surface, the disc of the Moon appears to cover completely the Sun's face, and there is a brief period of darkness. Although the Moon is a great deal smaller than the Sun, it is able to block the light totally because it is so much nearer to the Earth.

HALO AROUND THE MOON
On some winter nights a halo appears around the Moon, but this has nothing to do with the Moon itself. Sunlight reflected toward Earth by the Moon is refracted (bent) by ice crystals high in Earth's atmosphere. This refraction of light creates a circular halo.

SPECIAL EFFECT FACTS
• Aurora borealis ("northern lights") are best observed near the north pole. Similar displays in the southern hemisphere are called aurora australis.

• A lunar eclipse occurs when the Earth comes directly between the Sun and the Moon, and the Earth's shadow can be seen crossing the Moon's surface.

• A meteor radiant is an optical illusion. In fact the meteors travel along parallel tracks.

METEOR RADIANT
Dust particles from space are seen as meteors when they burn up in the atmosphere. In a meteor shower, all the meteors appear to come from a single point in the sky which is called the radiant.

CONSTELLATIONS

SEEN FROM EARTH, the stars seem to form patterns in the sky. These patterns are known as constellations. The skies around Earth have been divided into 88 different constellations, each one of which is supposed to represent a mythological person, creature, or object.

CONSTELLATION OF ORION
In Greek myth, Orion was a mighty hunter. The row of three bright stars (center left) forms Orion's Belt, an easily located "skymark."

CELESTIAL SPHERE AS SEEN FROM THE NORTHERN HEMISPHERE

AROUND THE SPHERE
As the Earth makes its yearly orbit around the Sun, different portions of the celestial sphere come into view, presenting the constellations in an annual sequence.

Position of Earth in March

Constellations visible from Earth in March

100,000 YEARS AGO

TODAY

100,000 YEARS FROM NOW

CHANGING SHAPE
The constellations appear fixed, but
in fact they change very slowly. The
changes to the Big Dipper can only
be seen over very long periods of time.

CONSTELLATION FACTS
• A constellation is a
two-dimensional view
of objects in three-
dimensional space.
• The Big Dipper is
not a separate
constellation but is
part of Ursa Major
(the Great Bear).
• The Aboriginal
people of Australia have
their own view of
constellations – they see
patterns in the dark
spaces between stars.

STARS IN THE
BIG DIPPER

Dubhe

Alkaid   Alioth   Megrez   Phad   Merak

Mizar

LINES OF SIGHT
The constellations are a
human invention. We see
them as flat patterns
against the blackness of
space, but in fact the stars
may be farther in distance
from each other than they
are from Earth. The stars
in the Big Dipper seem to
be close together.
However, they are more
scattered than they appear.

*Dubhe, the
farthest star, is
124 ly away;
Mizar, the nearest
star, is 78 ly
from Earth.*

*The Big
Dipper as seen
from Earth*

CATALOGING STARS

STARS ARE cataloged according to
the constellation in which
they appear. Within each
constellation, the individual
stars are identified by means of
letters or numbers. Other
objects are cataloged separately.

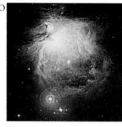

The constellation
"figure" is drawn
around the stars.

ORION

ORION NEBULA
In Earth's sky, the nebula
appears as a faint, fuzzy patch
of light just below Orion's Belt.

POSSESSIVE NAMES
All the constellations have been
given Latin names. When referring to
a particular star, the possessive case of
the Latin name is used. For example,
stars in the constellation of Orion are
designated Orionis.

MAPPING THE SKIES
The constellations fit
together to map the sky.
All the stars inside
a constellation's
boundaries belong to
that constellation,
even if they appear
to be unconnected to
the star making up
the main "title" figure.

GALAXIES AND NEBULAE

Nonstellar objects, such as bright star clusters, nebulae, and other galaxies, are classified separately according to the Messier catalog (numbers prefixed by letter M), or the New General Catalog (numbers prefixed by the letters NGC).

GREEK LETTERS

The brighter stars in a constellation are identified by Greek letters. The brightest star is usually designated alpha (α), the next brightest beta (β) and so on, but this rule is not always followed.

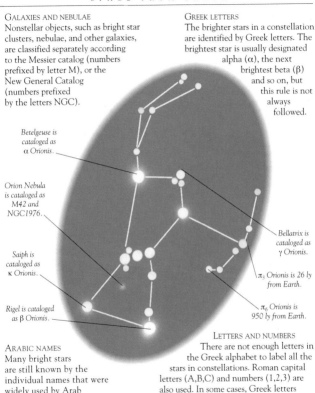

Betelgeuse is cataloged as α Orionis.

Orion Nebula is cataloged as M42 and NGC1976.

Saiph is cataloged as κ Orionis.

Rigel is cataloged as β Orionis.

Bellatrix is cataloged as γ Orionis.

π_3 Orionis is 26 ly from Earth.

π_6 Orionis is 950 ly from Earth.

ARABIC NAMES

Many bright stars are still known by the individual names that were widely used by Arab astronomers more than 800 years ago – e.g. Betelgeuse. Saiph, and Rigel.

LETTERS AND NUMBERS

There are not enough letters in the Greek alphabet to label all the stars in constellations. Roman capital letters (A,B,C) and numbers (1,2,3) are also used. In some cases, Greek letters are used with subscript numbers to identify stars that are near to each other, for example π_3 and π_6 Orionis.

NEAR OR FAR?

STARS ARE VAST DISTANCES from
us and from each other. Light,
which travels faster than
anything else, takes 8.3 minutes
to travel from the Sun to the
Earth. Light from the next
nearest star, Proxima Centauri,
takes 4.2 years. People cannot
tell the distances to stars just by
looking at them. But they can
see subtle differences in color
and apparent brightness.

LIGHT-YEARS APART
All the stars in this distant
cluster may look as if they
are the same distance from
Earth. Yet in fact the stars
are many light-years apart.

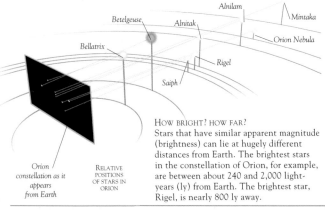

Alnilam

Betelgeuse

Alnitak

Mintaka

Bellatrix

Orion Nebula

Rigel

Saiph

Orion
constellation as it
appears
from Earth

RELATIVE
POSITIONS
OF STARS IN
ORION

HOW BRIGHT? HOW FAR?
Stars that have similar apparent magnitude
(brightness) can lie at hugely different
distances from Earth. The brightest stars
in the constellation of Orion, for example,
are between about 240 and 2,000 light-
years (ly) from Earth. The brightest star,
Rigel, is nearly 800 ly away.

STELLAR DATA: NEAREST STARS TO THE SUN		
Name	Distance	Color
Proxima Centauri	4.2 ly	red
α Centauri A	4.4 ly	yellow
α Centauri B	4.4 ly	orange
Barnard's Star	5.9 ly	red
Wolf 359	7.8 ly	red
Lalande 21185	8.3 ly	red
Sirius A	8.6 ly	white
Sirius B	8.6 ly	white

STAR FACTS

• Proxima Centauri is part of a triple star system along with α Centauri A and α Centauri B.
• The brightest star, Sirius A, has a faint white dwarf companion Sirius B.

NEIGHBOURING STARS

Many of the stars within 40 light-years of the Sun are dim red dwarfs like Barnard's Star, which cannot be seen with the naked eye. Others, such as Vega, are 50 times more luminous than the Sun.

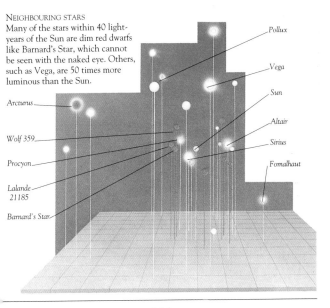

Pollux

Vega

Sun

Arcturus

Altair

Wolf 359

Sirius

Procyon

Fomalhaut

Lalande 21185

Barnard's Star

THE NORTHERN SKY

AT RIGHT ARE THE MAIN STARS that lie north of the celestial equator. The stars seen on a particular night by people living in the northern hemisphere depend on the observer's latitude, the time of year, and the time of night. The stars near the center of the sky-map are called circumpolar and can be seen throughout the year. Polaris (the North Star) appears to remain directly over the North Pole.

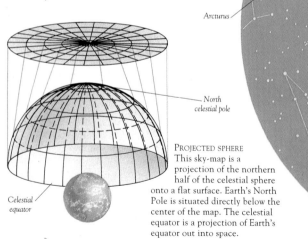

Arcturus

North celestial pole

Celestial equator

PROJECTED SPHERE
This sky-map is a projection of the northern half of the celestial sphere onto a flat surface. Earth's North Pole is situated directly below the center of the map. The celestial equator is a projection of Earth's equator out into space.

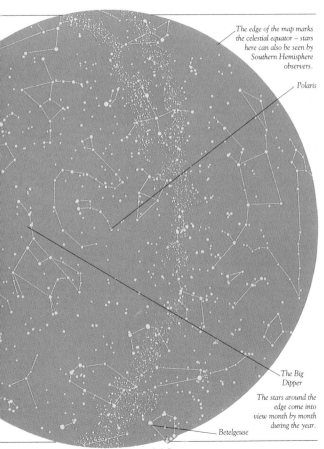

The edge of the map marks the celestial equator – stars here can also be seen by Southern Hemisphere observers.

Polaris

The Big Dipper

The stars around the edge come into view month by month during the year.

Betelgeuse

THE SOUTHERN SKY

AT RIGHT ARE THE MAIN STARS that lie south
of the celestial equator. The stars seen on a
particular night by people living in the southern
hemisphere depend on the observer's latitude,
the time of year, and the time of night.
The stars near the center of the sky-map
are called circumpolar and can be seen
all year round. Alpha Centauri, one
of the nearest stars to the Sun, is
a southern hemisphere star.

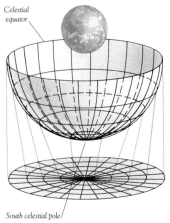

Celestial equator

Alpha Centauri

Antares

South celestial pole

PROJECTED SPHERE
This sky-map is a
projection of the
southern half of the
celestial sphere onto a
flat surface. Earth's South
Pole is situated directly
below the center of the
map. The celestial equator
is a projection of Earth's
equator out into space.

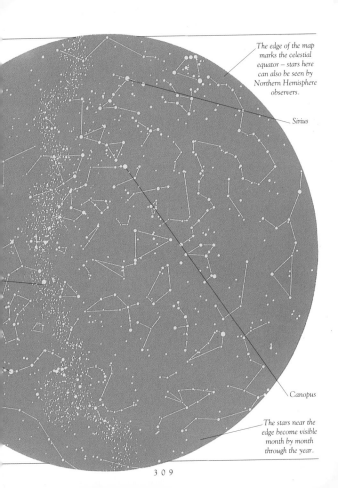

The edge of the map marks the celestial equator – stars here can also be seen by Northern Hemisphere observers.

Sirius

Canopus

The stars near the edge become visible month by month through the year.

WHAT IS THE SOLAR SYSTEM?

THE SOLAR SYSTEM consists of the Sun and the many objects that orbit around it – nine planets, more than 100 moons, and countless asteroids and comets. The system occupies a disk-shaped volume of space more than 7.45 billion miles (12 billion kilometers) across. At the center is the Sun which contains more than 99 percent of the solar system's mass.

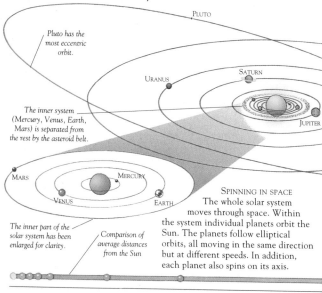

PLUTO

Pluto has the most eccentric orbit.

URANUS

SATURN

The inner system (Mercury, Venus, Earth, Mars) is separated from the rest by the asteroid belt.

JUPITER

MARS

MERCURY

VENUS

EARTH

The inner part of the solar system has been enlarged for clarity.

Comparison of average distances from the Sun

SPINNING IN SPACE
The whole solar system moves through space. Within the system individual planets orbit the Sun. The planets follow elliptical orbits, all moving in the same direction but at different speeds. In addition, each planet also spins on its axis.

MERCURY

VENUS

EARTH

MARS

JUPITER

SATURN

URANUS

NEPTUNE

PLUTO

SOLAR SYSTEM FACTS

• Images obtained with the latest telescopes strongly suggest that some other stars (e.g. β Pictoris) are forming planetary systems.

• The solar system has more than 100 moons by the latest count. Future space probes are almost certain to discover extra moons orbiting the outer planets.

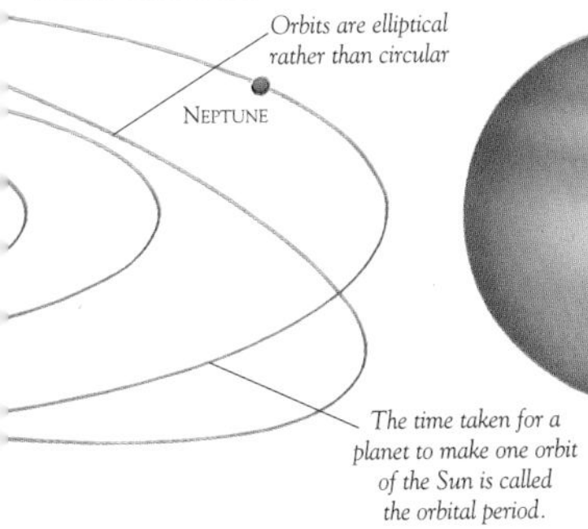

Each of the four gas planets has a ring system around it – the rings have been omitted from this illustration for ease of comparison.

Orbits are elliptical rather than circular

NEPTUNE

The time taken for a planet to make one orbit of the Sun is called the orbital period.

NINE PLANETS

The planets form two main groups – the inner four are composed of rock, while the next four are larger and are composed mostly of liquefied gas. The outermost planet, Pluto, is composed of rock and ice.

Pluto is the smallest and least-known planet.

SOLAR GRAVITY

ABOUT 4.6 BILLION years ago, the solar system formed from a cloud of gas and dust. The Sun formed first and the other objects formed from the leftovers. The Sun's gravity dominates the system because it is so massive by comparison with the planets.

CONDENSING INTO PLACE

The young Sun was surrounded by a disk of dust, gas, and snow. Dust clumped together to form the four inner rock planets. The giant outer planets formed from a mixture of gas, snow, and dust. Pluto and the comets formed from the icy leftovers.

ORBITAL PATHS

Most of the planets orbit close to the plane of the Earth's orbit (the ecliptic). Pluto has the most inclined orbit, possibly because it is the most distant planet and is the least influenced by the Sun's gravity. However the next most inclined planet is Mercury (7°), which is the nearest planet to the Sun.

THE PLANETS:
ORBITAL INCLINATION
TO THE ECLIPTIC

Pluto: 17.2°
Mercury: 7°
Venus: 3.39°
Saturn: 2.49°
Mars: 1.85°
Neptune: 1.77°
Jupiter: 1.3°
Uranus: 0.77°
Earth: 0°

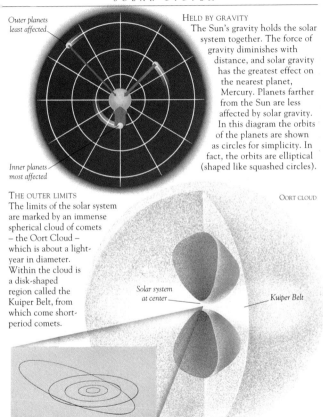

Outer planets least affected

Inner planets most affected

HELD BY GRAVITY

The Sun's gravity holds the solar system together. The force of gravity diminishes with distance, and solar gravity has the greatest effect on the nearest planet, Mercury. Planets farther from the Sun are less affected by solar gravity. In this diagram the orbits of the planets are shown as circles for simplicity. In fact, the orbits are elliptical (shaped like squashed circles).

THE OUTER LIMITS

The limits of the solar system are marked by an immense spherical cloud of comets – the Oort Cloud – which is about a light-year in diameter. Within the cloud is a disk-shaped region called the Kuiper Belt, from which come short-period comets.

OORT CLOUD

Solar system at center

Kuiper Belt

THE SUN

LIKE OTHER STARS, the Sun is a huge ball of spinning gas. Nuclear reactions take place at its core, giving off energy. The Sun is the only star close enough to be studied in detail. Its surface features, such as sunspots and prominences, can be observed from Earth. Satellites and space probes are able to get a closer view and obtain even more information.

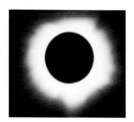

ECLIPSE OF THE SUN
During an eclipse, the outer layer of the Sun, the corona, becomes visible. Normally the corona is hidden by glare.

Year 1   Year 4   Year 7   Year 10   Year 12

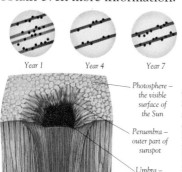

Photosphere – the visible surface of the Sun

Penumbra – outer part of sunspot

Umbra – coolest and darkest part

COOL AND DARK
Sunspots, dark patches on the surface, are regions of cooler gas caused by disturbances in the Sun's magnetic field. Sunspots follow an 11-year cycle that begins with the Sun being spot-free. The spots appear at high latitude and gradually increase in number, moving toward the Sun's equator during the cycle.

SOLAR DATA

Average distance from Earth	93,026,724 miles
	(149,680,000 km)
Distance from center of galaxy	30,000 light-years
Diameter (at equator)	865,121 miles
	(1,391,980 km)
Rotation period (at equator)	25.04 Earth days
Mass (Earth = 1)	330,000
Gravity (Earth = 1)	27.9
Average density (water = 1)	1.41
Absolute magnitude	4.83

SOLAR FACTS

• **Never look directly at the Sun. Even with sunglasses, camera film, or smoked glass you risk damaging your eyesight.**

• The safe way is to project the Sun's image onto a piece of paper using a hand lens.

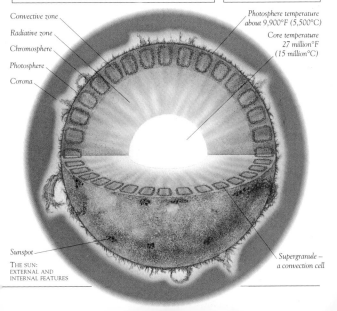

Convective zone

Radiative zone

Chromosphere

Photosphere

Corona

Photosphere temperature about 9,900°F (5,500°C)

Core temperature 27 million°F (15 million°C)

Sunspot

THE SUN:
EXTERNAL AND
INTERNAL FEATURES

Supergranule – a convection cell

SOLAR ENERGY AND INFLUENCE

AT ITS CORE, the Sun converts hydrogen to helium at a rate of 600 million tons (tonnes) every second. The energy produced eventually reaches the surface and travels through space.

Nuclear reactions at core produce gamma rays

Gamma rays take up to two million years to travel to surface, losing energy in the process

Visible light and other radiation travels from the Sun's surface to Earth in about 8 minutes.

SOLAR PROMINENCES
Enormous jets of hot gas shoot out from the Sun's surface stretching for many thousands of miles (kilometers). The largest jets, called prominences, can last for several months. The Sun's magnetic field holds some prominences in gigantic loops.

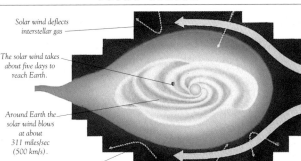

Solar wind deflects interstellar gas

The solar wind takes about five days to reach Earth.

Around Earth the solar wind blows at about 311 miles/sec (500 km/s).

Solar wind deflects most cosmic rays

EXTENT OF INFLUENCE

The Sun influences an enormous volume of space around it. Gases streaming from the corona become the high-speed solar wind. The solar wind carries a magnetic field from the Sun. As the Sun rotates, the field takes on a spiral shape. The volume of space swept by the solar wind is called the heliosphere.

ULYSSES
SOLAR PROBE

Sensors located on hinged boom

TO THE SOLAR POLES

Earth's orbit in the Sun's equatorial plane means that the Sun's poles cannot be studied from Earth. The Ulysses probe was launched in 1990 to study these hard-to-observe regions.

SOLAR ENERGY FACTS

• Converting hydrogen to helium means that the Sun loses at least a million tons (tonnes) of its mass every second.

• The amount of the Sun's energy reaching Earth's surface (known as the solar constant) is equivalent to 1.37 kw (kilowatts) of electricity per square yard (meter) per second.

MERCURY

A SMALL ROCK WORLD with a large dense core, Mercury is the closest planet to the Sun. There is no real atmosphere, and much of the surface is marked by numerous impact craters. Dominated by the Sun, Mercury experiences the greatest variation in surface temperature of any planet in the solar system. Differences between day and night can be more than 1,080°F (600°C).

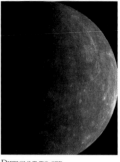

DIFFICULT TO SEE
Photographs taken from Earth show Mercury as a fuzzy disk, difficult to observe against the Sun. This image was put together from photographs taken by the Mariner 10 probe.

Earth

Mercury

MERCURY: PLANETARY DATA	
Average distance from the Sun	36 million miles (57.9 million km)
Orbital period	88 Earth days
Orbital velocity	29.7 miles/sec (47.9 km/s)
Rotation period	58.7 Earth days
Diameter at equator	3,032 miles (4,879 km)
Surface temperature	−292°F to +806°F (−180°C to +430°C)
Mass (Earth = 1)	0.055
Gravity (Earth = 1)	0.38
Number of moons	0

MERCURY FACTS

• Mercury was named after the fleet-footed messenger of the Roman gods because it travels so quickly across Earth's sky.

• Mercury's largest crater, Caloris Planitia, measures 875 miles (1,400 km) across.

42% oxygen

29% sodium

22% hydrogen

6% helium

MERCURY:
COMPOSITION OF ATMOSPHERE

THIN AIR
Mercury's atmosphere is
extremely thin – less
than one trillionth of
Earth's. Sodium and
potassium occur in the
daytime only, as the
Sun's energy releases
them from the
planet's surface.

PROBE'S EYE VIEW
Craters cover about 60
percent of Mercury's surface.
The other 40 percent consists
of relatively smooth plains.

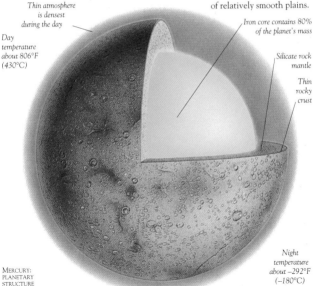

*Thin atmosphere
is densest
during the day*

*Day
temperature
about 806°F
(430°C)*

*Iron core contains 80%
of the planet's mass*

*Silicate rock
mantle*

*Thin
rocky
crust*

*Night
temperature
about −292°F
(−180°C)*

MERCURY:
PLANETARY
STRUCTURE

LONG DAYS

Mercury rotates very slowly on an upright axis at 90° to the plane of its orbit. A single day on Mercury (sunrise to sunrise) lasts for 176 Earth days. Although days are very long, the Mercurian year is very short. Mercury takes only 88 Earth days to complete one orbit around the Sun. This is the shortest obital period of all the planets.

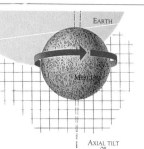

EARTH

MERCURY

AXIAL TILT
0°

ECCENTRIC ORBIT

A combination of long days and short years would create strange effects for any inhabitants. While Mercury completes two orbits of the Sun (shown here separately for clarity), an observer on the surface (marked by a dot) would experience only one Mercurian day. Birthdays would happen more often than sunrise.

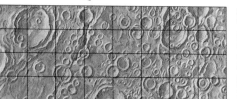

SURFACE MAP

The Mariner 10 photographs were used to produce maps of Mercury. Each square of the grid covers about 50 x 50 miles (80 x 80 km).

IMPACT CRATER FORMATION ON ROCK PLANETS

A meteorite impact blasts out a circular crater, and ejected material falls back to form a circular rim.

Rock compressed by the initial impact may bounce back from the sides to form a roughly conical central peak.

The crater profile is gradually reduced as rock fragments and debris slip from the walls and peak.

SOLITARY VISITOR

Mariner 10 is the only probe to have made a detailed study of Mercury. Launched in November 1973, the probe took five months to reach the planet. During three close approaches the probe photographed about 40 percent of the surface area. At its closest approach, Mariner 10 was 187 miles (300 km) above the surface.

High resolution cameras

MARINER 10 PROBE

MERCURY: CREATIVE CRATER NAMES			
Mercury's craters commemorate creative people:			
Writers	Composers	Painters	Architects
Bronte	Bach	Brueghel	Bernini
Cervantes	Chopin	Cezanne	Bramante
Dickens	Grieg	Dürer	Imhotep
Goethe	Handel	Holbein	Mansart
Li Po	Liszt	Monet	Michelangelo
Melville	Mozart	Renoir	Sinan
Shelley	Stravinsky	Titian	Sullivan
Tolstoy	Verdi	Van Gogh	Wren

FACTS

• Mercury can only be seen from Earth at twilight – either just before dawn or just after sunset.

• Parts of Mercury's surface have a wrinkled appearance – the result of the planet shrinking as its core cooled.

VENUS

A ROCK PLANET with a dense
atmosphere, Venus is almost
the same size as the Earth.
The two share some surface
features, but conditions on
Venus are very different from
those on Earth. The surface
environment of Venus is
extremely hostile – intense
heat, crushing pressure, and
unbreathable air. Overhead
there are thick clouds of
sulfuric acid droplets.

OBSCURED BY CLOUDS
The surface features of Venus
are hidden by a permanent
blanket of thick cloud. The
dark swirls are high-altitude
wind systems.

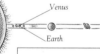

Venus

Earth

VENUS: PLANETARY DATA	
Average distance from the Sun	67.2 million miles (108.2 million km)
Orbital period	224.7 Earth days
Orbital velocity	21.7 miles/sec (35 km/s)
Rotation period	243 Earth days
Diameter at equator	7,521 miles (12,104 km)
Surface temperature	860°F (460°C)
Mass (Earth = 1)	0.81
Gravity (Earth = 1)	0.91
Number of moons	0

VENUS FACTS

• Venus shines brightly
in Earth's sky because
the cloud layer reflects
most of the sunlight.

• Venus has phases like
the Moon. You need a
telescope to see them
clearly, but binoculars
will enable you to see
the crescent phase.

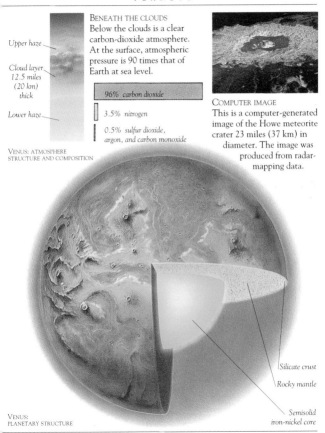

Upper haze

Cloud layer
12.5 miles
(20 km)
thick

Lower haze

BENEATH THE CLOUDS
Below the clouds is a clear
carbon-dioxide atmosphere.
At the surface, atmospheric
pressure is 90 times that of
Earth at sea level.

96% carbon dioxide

3.5% nitrogen

0.5% sulfur dioxide,
argon, and carbon monoxide

VENUS: ATMOSPHERE
STRUCTURE AND COMPOSITION

COMPUTER IMAGE
This is a computer-generated
image of the Howe meteorite
crater 23 miles (37 km) in
diameter. The image was
produced from radar-
mapping data.

VENUS:
PLANETARY STRUCTURE

Silicate crust

Rocky mantle

Semisolid
iron-nickel core

BACKWARD ROTATION

Venus is one of only three planets
to rotate on its axis in a backward
direction (the others are Pluto and
Uranus). Venus' backward rotation
is so slow that a Venusian day lasts
longer (243 Earth days) than a
Venusian year (224.7 Earth days).
Driven by powerful winds, Venus'
atmosphere moves at its own, much
faster, pace. The upper levels of the
cloud layer take just four Earth days
to travel right around the planet.

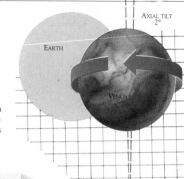

EARTH

AXIAL TILT
2°

VENUS

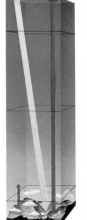

62 miles
(100 km)

*Sunlight reflected
by cloud layer*

EARTH   VENUS

GREENHOUSE PLANET

Venus has a higher average surface
temperature (860°F/460°C) than
any other planet in the solar
system. The heating of Venus is the
result of a "greenhouse effect" run
wild. Although the cloud layer
reflects much of the sunlight that
hits it, some solar heat energy does
reach the surface. But instead of
being radiated back into space, this
heat energy is trapped by the cloud
layer causing temperatures to rise.
On Earth the cloud layer allows
much more heat to escape.

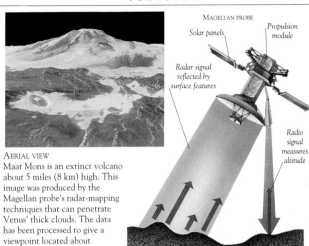

MAGELLAN PROBE

Propulsion module

Solar panels

Radar signal reflected by surface features

Radio signal measures altitude

AERIAL VIEW
Maat Mons is an extinct volcano about 5 miles (8 km) high. This image was produced by the Magellan probe's radar-mapping techniques that can penetrate Venus' thick clouds. The data has been processed to give a viewpoint located about 1 mile (1.6 km) above the planet's surface.

VENUS: SELECTED EXPLORATION EVENTS		
Probe	Date	Result
Mariner 2	14/12/62	Successful flyby
Venera 4	18/10/67	Sampled atmosphere
Venera 7	15/12/70	Sent data from surface
Mariner 10	5/2/74	Flyby on way to Mercury
Venera 9	23/10/75	First orbit and soft landing and first surface image
Venera 15	10/10/83	First radar mapping
Pioneer-Venus 2	9/12/78	Multiple descent probes investigate atmosphere
Magellan	10/8/90	Complete radar mapping

MORE FACTS
• The facts that Venus has a small axial tilt and backward rotation is just popular convention. According to the rules of the IAU (International Astronomical Union), Venus rotates in a normal direction around an axis tilted at 177.4° to the vertical.

EARTH

THE THIRD PLANET from the
Sun, Earth, is unique in the
solar system and is possibly
unique in the universe.
Only Earth has the surface
conditions that permit
liquid water to exist, and
Earth alone has developed
an oxygen-rich atmosphere.
These two factors have
enabled the rocky planet
Earth to evolve myriad
varieties of life.

JEWEL IN SPACE
Photographed by Apollo
astronauts returning from the
Moon, planet Earth looks like a
brightly colored jewel – blue
oceans, white clouds, and green-
brown land masses.

Earth

EARTH: PLANETARY DATA	
Average distance from the Sun	93 million miles (149.6 million km)
Orbital period	365.25 days
Orbital velocity	18.5 miles/sec (29.8 km/s)
Rotation period	23.93 hours
Diameter at equator	7,926 miles (12,756 km)
Surface temperature	–94°F to +131°F (–70°C to +55°C)
Gravity (Earth = 1)	1
Number of moons	1

EARTH FACTS
• The oldest rocks so
far discovered in the
Earth's crust date back
3.9 billion years.
• The oxygen in
Earth's atmosphere
is the result of life.
The process of
oxygenation began
with bacteria about
2 billion years ago.

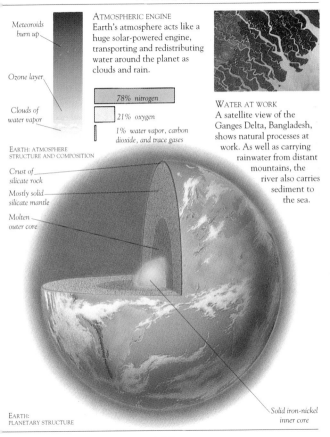

Meteoroids
burn up

Ozone layer

Clouds of
water vapor

ATMOSPHERIC ENGINE
Earth's atmosphere acts like a
huge solar-powered engine,
transporting and redistributing
water around the planet as
clouds and rain.

| 78% nitrogen |
| 21% oxygen |
| 1% water vapor, carbon dioxide, and trace gases |

EARTH: ATMOSPHERE
STRUCTURE AND COMPOSITION

WATER AT WORK
A satellite view of the
Ganges Delta, Bangladesh,
shows natural processes at
work. As well as carrying
rainwater from distant
mountains, the
river also carries
sediment to
the sea.

Crust of
silicate rock

Mostly solid
silicate mantle

Molten
outer core

Solid iron-nickel
inner core

EARTH:
PLANETARY STRUCTURE

UNEQUAL HEATING

Earth's axis of rotation is tilted at 23.5° to the vertical. As the planet travels around the Sun during the year, the tilt causes seasonal variations in climate. These variations are most noticeable in the high latitudes away from the equator. Spinning on a tilted axis gives rise to unequal heating of the surface by the Sun. This differential heating produces differences in atmospheric pressure which create the wind systems that drive Earth's climate.

AXIAL TILT 23.5°

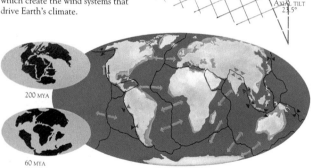

200 MYA

60 MYA

200 MILLION YEARS AGO
The continents were grouped closer together.

60 MILLION YEARS AGO
The landmasses had moved some way toward their present locations.

CONTINENTS IN MOTION

The continents "float" on the surface of the Earth's crust, which is made up of a number of separate plates. These plates are in constant slow-motion, pushed apart as new crust is produced at mid-ocean ridges. The result is that the continents are also gradually moving. Areas where plates are in collision have many volcanoes and earthquakes.

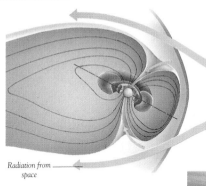

Radiation from space

SPINNING MAGNET

Earth has a much stronger magnetic field than any of the other rock planets. Produced by the rapid rotation of the nickel-iron core, the magnetic field extends far into space and deflects harmful radiation away from the planet. Despite its elongated ovoid shape, this magnetic field is called the magnetosphere.

THE WATER OF LIFE

Water only exists in its liquid form between 32°F (0°C) and 212°F (100°C), which is about the same range of temperatures found on Earth. Liquid water is absolutely essential to practically all forms of life. Along with carbon dioxide, it is one of the two raw materials used by plants to produce their own food and provide the oxygen upon which animal life depends.

EARTH: PHYSICAL LIMITS	
Age	4.6 billion years
Mass	6,571 million million million tons
Surface area	317 million sq miles
	(510 million km²)
Covered by water	70.8 percent
Highest mountain	29,028 ft (8,848 meters)
Deepest ocean trench	35,800 ft (10,924 meters)
Oldest evidence of life	3.5 billion years ago
Total number of living species	at least 10 million

MORE FACTS

• The Atlantic Ocean increases in width by about 1.2 in (3 cm) each year.

• Earth has periodic magnetic reversals when the north pole becomes the south pole, and the south becomes north.

EARTH'S MOON

EARTH HAS A single satellite, the Moon, which is about one-quarter the size of our planet. Although the Earth and the Moon are closely linked, there are many striking contrasts. The Moon is a waterless, airless, and lifeless place. Its surface is covered by craters, the scars of a massive meteorite bombardment that took place billions of years ago.

FAMILIAR SIGHT
Some of the features on the Moon can be identified with the naked eye. Binoculars, or a small telescope, will reveal a considerable amount of detail.

 The Moon's distance from Earth varies during its orbit.

Minimum   Average   Maximum

THE MOON: DATA	
Average distance from the Earth	238,855 miles (384,400 km)
Orbital period	27.3 Earth days
Orbital velocity	0.6 miles/sec (1 km/s)
Rotation period	27.3 Earth days
Diameter at equator	2,159 miles (3,475 km)
Surface temperature	−247°F to +221°F (−155°C to +105°C)
Mass (Earth = 1)	0.012
Gravity (Earth = 1)	0.16
Escape velocity	1.48 miles/sec (2.38 km/s)

MOON FACTS

• The Moon has approximately the same surface area as the continents of North and South America.

• The pull of the Moon's gravity is largely responsible for the twice daily rise and fall of tides in Earth's seas and oceans.

Figure in a Moonscape
The Moon remains unique as the only
extraterrestrial object upon which
human beings have walked. Protected
by a spacesuit from the airless lunar
environment, one of the Apollo 17
astronauts investigates a large boulder.
Undisturbed by the effects of wind or
rain, his footprints should remain
visible for millions of years.

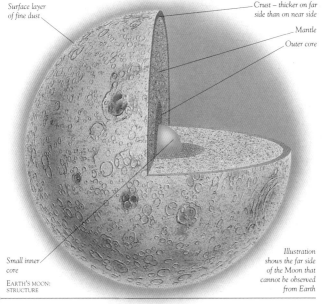

Surface layer
of fine dust

Crust – thicker on far
side than on near side

Mantle

Outer core

Small inner
core

Earth's Moon:
structure

Illustration
shows the far side
of the Moon that
cannot be observed
from Earth

HELD IN PLACE

Earth is larger and more massive than the Moon, and has a powerful effect on its smaller neighbor. Under the influence of Earth's gravity the Moon's motion through space has been moderated so that its rotation period is the same as its orbital period – 27.3 days. This synchronization of motion means that the same face of the Moon is always turned toward the Earth – the near side. The other side is always turned away from us – the far side.

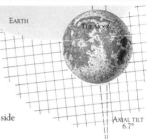

EARTH

THE MOON

AXIAL TILT
6.7°

BATTERED SURFACE

About 3.8 billion years ago, the Moon's surface received an intense meteorite bombardment.

Some 1 billion years later, the largest craters gradually filled up with dark lava, and formed the lunar seas.

Since that time, the appearance of the lunar surface has hardly changed apart from a few recent ray craters.

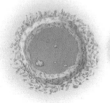

OLD CRATER

RAY CRATER

CHANGING MOONSCAPE
Most of the craters were made about 3 billion years ago, and many are only faintly visible. Some newer craters are identifiable by conspicuous rays of pale ejected material fanning out from the crater wall.

MOON ROCK

About 836 lb (380 kg) of moon rock have been brought back to Earth. There are no sedimentary or metamorphic rocks on the Moon – all the samples brought back are either igneous lavas (mainly basalt) or breccias produced by the heat and force of meteorite impacts. Most of the Moon's surface is covered with a layer of crushed and broken rock (called "regolith") which is about 65 ft (20 m) deep .

MOON ROCK COLLECTED BY APOLLO ASTRONAUTS

PHASES OF THE MOON

The Moon shines by reflected sunlight. As it travels around the Earth, the visible amount of sunlit area changes day by day. Viewed from Earth's surface, this produces a cycle of lunar phases – waxing from New Moon to Full Moon, and then waning back to New Moon once more.

Waning

SUNLIGHT

Full Moon

New Moon

Waxing

EARTH'S MOON: SELECTED EXPLORATION EVENTS		
Vehicle	Date	Result
Luna 3	10/10/59	First images of far side
Luna 9	3/2/66	First soft landing
Surveyor 3	17/4/67	Landing site soil studies
Apollo 11	20/7/69	Humans first land on Moon
Luna 16	24/9/70	Robot returns with samples
Luna 17	17/11/70	Mobile robot landed
Apollo 15	30/7/71	Lunar Roving Vehicle used
Apollo 17	11/12/72	Last Apollo mission lands

MORE FACTS

• The first person to step on to the Moon was the astronaut Neil Armstrong early on July 21, 1969.

• His historic first words were, " That's one small step for man, one giant leap for mankind."

MARS

A RED-HUED ROCKY PLANET, Mars is a cold, barren world with a thin atmosphere. There are many Earthlike features, such as polar ice caps and water-carved valleys, but there are many important differences. Temperatures rarely rise above the freezing point, the air is unbreathable, and dust-storms occasionally scour the surface. The planet's red color is caused by the presence of iron oxide.

LONG RANGE VIEW
This image was obtained by the Earth-orbiting Hubble Space Telescope at a distance of about 43 million miles (69 million km) from Mars. Bluish clouds can be seen near the poles.

Earth

Mars

MARS: PLANETARY DATA	
Average distance from the Sun	141.6 million miles (227.9 million km)
Orbital period	687 Earth days
Orbital velocity	15 miles/sec (24.1 km/s)
Rotation period	24.62 hours
Diameter at equator	4,220 miles (6,792 km)
Surface temperature	–184°F to +77°F (–120°C to +25°C)
Mass (Earth = 1)	0.107
Gravity (Earth = 1)	0.38
Moons:	2

MARS FACTS

• Mars was named after the Roman god of war because it appears the color of spilled blood.

• The south polar ice cap on Mars is much larger than the north polar ice cap, and the southern winter is considerably longer.

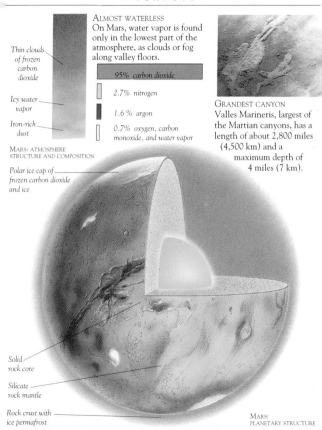

ALMOST WATERLESS
On Mars, water vapor is found only in the lowest part of the atmosphere, as clouds or fog along valley floors.

95% carbon dioxide
2.7% nitrogen
1.6 % argon
0.7% oxygen, carbon monoxide, and water vapor

Thin clouds of frozen carbon dioxide

Icy water vapor

Iron-rich dust

MARS: ATMOSPHERE STRUCTURE AND COMPOSITION

GRANDEST CANYON
Valles Marineris, largest of the Martian canyons, has a length of about 2,800 miles (4,500 km) and a maximum depth of 4 miles (7 km).

Polar ice cap of frozen carbon dioxide and ice

Solid rock core

Silicate rock mantle

Rock crust with ice permafrost

MARS: PLANETARY STRUCTURE

EARTHLIKE SEASONS
Mars is smaller than
the Earth, but turns
on its axis more
slowly, so that the
day lengths are almost
identical. A day on
Mars is just 41 minutes
longer. A similar axial
tilt gives Mars the same
pattern of seasons as we
experience on Earth. However,
because of the greater orbital
period (687 Earth days), the length
of each season is nearly twice as long.

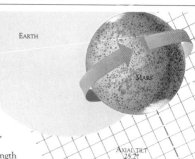

EARTH

MARS

AXIAL TILT
25.2°

DESERT SURFACE
This is a view of the Martian surface
photographed by the Mars Pathfinder
lander. Part of the lander is seen here in
the foreground. The hills on the horizon,
nicknamed Twin Peaks, are 0.6-1.2 miles
(1-2 km) away. This "stony desert"
appearance is typical of about 40 percent
of Mars' surface. Some Martian landforms,
however, are more dramatic. Olympus
Mons towers 13 miles (21 km) high.

*Olympus Mons, a giant
shield volcano, is the tallest
mountain in the
solar system.*

*Earth's Mauna Kea volcano is
dwarfed by comparison.*

Hawaiian Islands   *Ocean floor*   *Sea level*

ORBITS OF MARS' MOONS

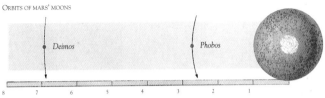

Deimos   *Phobos*

SCALE IN RADIUSES OF MARS

8   7   6   5   4   3   2   1

SMALL MOONS

Mars has two tiny moons, Phobos and Deimos, neither of them more than 18.5 miles (30 km) in length. Both are irregularly shaped and have every appearance of being asteroids that were captured by Mars' gravity. Phobos orbits Mars at a distance of 5,827 miles (9,378 km) every 7 hours and 40 minutes. Deimos orbits three times farther away, at a distance of 14,577 miles (23,459 km), and takes about 30 hours to circle the planet.

Smaller and darker than its companion

DEIMOS

PHOBOS

The crater Stickney is nearly 6.2 miles (10 km) across.

MARS: SELECTED EXPLORATION EVENTS		
Vehicle	Date	Result
Mariner 4	14/7/65	First flyby images
Mariner 9	13/11/71	First Mars orbiter
Mars 3	2/12/71	Orbit achieved, lander failed after 20 seconds
Viking 1 & Viking 2	20/7/76 3/9/76	Provided images and soil analysis
Mars Pathfinder	4/7/97	Lander carrying Sojourner micro-rover
Mars Global Surveyor	11/9/97	Orbiter, mapped and measured surface detail

MORE FACTS

• Phobos means "fear," and Deimos means "terror" – suitable companions for the planet named after a god of war.

• Viewed from the surface of Mars, Phobos crosses the sky three times each day.

JUPITER

THE LARGEST of the planets, Jupiter has two and a half times more mass than all the other planets together. Jupiter has a small rock core, but consists mainly of gas in various physical states. The mantle of cold liquefied gas merges into a dense atmosphere. Giant wind systems give Jupiter a banded appearance.

GAS GIANT
The Cassini probe took this image from a distance of 48.2 million miles (77.6 million km). The patterns are caused by rising and falling regions of gas in the atmosphere.

Earth   Jupiter

JUPITER: PLANETARY DATA	
Average distance from the Sun	483.7 million miles (778.4 million km)
Orbital period	11.86 Earth years
Orbital velocity	8.1 miles/sec (13.1 km/s)
Rotation period	9.84 hours
Diameter at equator	88,846 miles (142,984 km)
Cloud-top temperature	−238°F (−150°C)
Mass (Earth = 1)	318
Gravity (Earth = 1)	2.54
Number of moons	40

JUPITER FACTS

• The pressure in Jupiter's interior is so great that hydrogen gas exists naturally in a semisolid metallic form not yet made on Earth.

• Jupiter can be seen with the naked eye as a bright silver "star" in Earth's night sky.

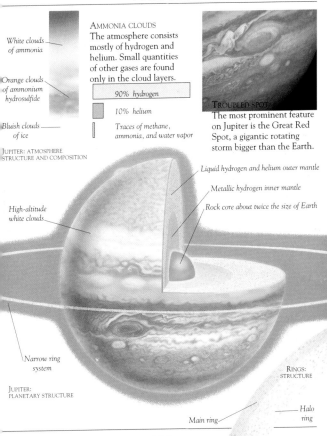

AMMONIA CLOUDS
The atmosphere consists mostly of hydrogen and helium. Small quantities of other gases are found only in the cloud layers.

White clouds of ammonia

Orange clouds of ammonium hydrosulfide

Bluish clouds of ice

JUPITER: ATMOSPHERE STRUCTURE AND COMPOSITION

| 90% hydrogen |

10% helium

Traces of methane, ammonia, and water vapor

TROUBLED SPOT
The most prominent feature on Jupiter is the Great Red Spot, a gigantic rotating storm bigger than the Earth.

Liquid hydrogen and helium outer mantle

Metallic hydrogen inner mantle

Rock core about twice the size of Earth

High-altitude white clouds

Narrow ring system

JUPITER: PLANETARY STRUCTURE

RINGS: STRUCTURE

Main ring

Halo ring

FASTEST SPINNER

Despite its enormous size, 11 times the diameter of Earth, Jupiter rotates on its axis faster than any other planet. This high-speed rotation causes the gas giant to bulge around the equator, giving it a slightly oval shape. The rapid rotation also produces the powerful wind systems which divide Jupiter's atmosphere into bands that lie parallel with the equator. The most powerful winds move at speeds of several hundred miles (kilometers) per hour.

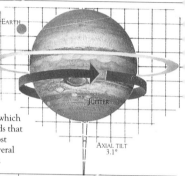

EARTH

JUPITER

AXIAL TILT
3.1°

THE GALILEAN MOONS:

EUROPA
Covered by a smooth layer of solid ice, Europa has sufficient internal heat to have seas of liquid water lying beneath its featureless surface.

CALLISTO
Covered with cracked and dirty ice around a rock core, Callisto is scarred by many craters. The largest is named Valhalla, with a diameter of 1,865 miles (3,000 km).

GANYMEDE
The largest moon in the solar system, Ganymede is larger than the planets Pluto and Mercury. Believed to consist mainly of ice and slush, Ganymede may have a silicate rock core.

IO
Debris from many volcanoes gives Io's surface an orange color. The interior is still molten, and Io has the first active volcanoes to be discovered outside the Earth.

MOONS OF JUPITER

The four largest moons were discovered by Galileo, hence their collective name. The others have been discovered subsequently, some of them by the Voyager I probe. Jupiter's 26 outer moons orbit from east to west, the opposite direction of the inner moons.

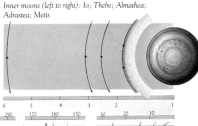

Inner moons (left to right): Io; Thebe; Almathea; Adrastea; Metis

Outer moons (left to right): Sinope; Pasiphae; Carme; Ananke; Elara; Lysithea; Himalia; Leda; Callisto; Ganymede; Europa; Io (also shown above)   SCALE IN RADIUSES OF JUPITER

JUPITER: SATELLITE DATA				
	Diameter		Distance from Jupiter	
	miles	km	miles	km
Metis	27	43	79,500	128,000
Adrastea	10	16	80,200	129,000
Amalthea	104	167	112,500	181,000
Thebe	62	99	138,000	222,000
Io	2,264	3,643	262,000	422,000
Europa	1,941	3,124	417,000	671,000
Ganymede	3,722	5,265	665,000	1,070,000
Callisto	2,994	4,819	1,170,000	1,883,000
Leda	6	10	6,914,000	11,127,000
Himalia	106	170	7,133,000	11,480,000
Lysithea	15	24	7,261,000	11,686,000
Elara	50	80	7,293,000	11,737,000
Ananke	12	20	13,220,000	21,276,000
Carme	19	30	14,543,000	23,404,000
Pasiphae	22	36	14,679,000	23,624,000
Sinope	17	28	14,875,000	23,939,000

MORE FACTS

• The orbital periods of planetary satellites increase according to their distance from the planet. Innermost Metis orbits Jupiter in 0.295 Earth days, while Sinope takes 758 days.

• The Voyager probes obtained 30,000 images of Jupiter and its moons.

• The volcanoes on Io eject material at speeds up to 3,285 ft per sec (1,000 m/s). This is about 20 times faster than material from volcanoes on Earth.

SATURN

FAMED FOR ITS magnificent ring system, Saturn is the second largest of the planets. Like its nearest neighbor Jupiter, Saturn is a gas giant. However, the mass is so spread out that on average the planet is less dense than water. Titan is the largest of Saturn's 30 moons. It has a very thick atmosphere and is bigger than the planet Mercury.

RINGED WORLD
Saturn is at the limit of easy telescopic viewing from Earth. This photograph was taken at a distance of 11 million miles (17.5 million km) by Voyager 2.

Earth   Saturn

SATURN: PLANETARY DATA	
Average distance from the Sun:	886.7 million miles (1,427 million km)
Orbital period	29.45 Earth years
Orbital velocity	6 miles/sec (9.7 km/s)
Rotation period	10.23 hours
Diameter at equator	74,897 miles (120,536 km)
Cloud-top temperature	−292°F (−180°C)
Mass (Earth = 1)	95
Gravity (Earth = 1)	0.92
Number of moons	30

SATURN FACTS

• Saturn's rings are less than 656 ft (200 m) thick, but over 167,800 miles (270,000 km) in diameter.

• The rings consist of billions of ice-covered rock fragments and dust particles.

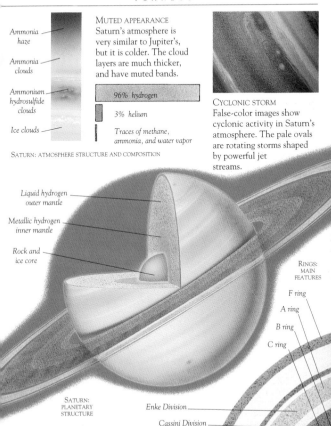

Ammonia haze

Ammonia clouds

Ammonium hydrosulfide clouds

Ice clouds

SATURN: ATMOSPHERE STRUCTURE AND COMPOSITION

MUTED APPEARANCE
Saturn's atmosphere is very similar to Jupiter's, but it is colder. The cloud layers are much thicker, and have muted bands.

96% hydrogen

3% helium

Traces of methane, ammonia, and water vapor

CYCLONIC STORM
False-color images show cyclonic activity in Saturn's atmosphere. The pale ovals are rotating storms shaped by powerful jet streams.

Liquid hydrogen outer mantle

Metallic hydrogen inner mantle

Rock and ice core

SATURN: PLANETARY STRUCTURE

RINGS: MAIN FEATURES

F ring

A ring

B ring

C ring

Enke Division

Cassini Division

TILTED SYSTEM

Saturn rotates very rapidly on an axis
that is tilted at 26.7° to the vertical.
The orbits of the rings and moons are
all aligned with this rotation, and lie
in the same plane as the planet's
equator, giving the whole system a
tilted appearance. Like the other
giant gas planets, Saturn bulges
noticeably at the equator where
the speed of rotation is faster than
at the poles. Inside the atmosphere,
winds sweep around the equator at
1,120 mph (1,800 km/h).

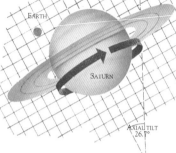

EARTH

SATURN

AXIAL TILT
26.7°

MANY MOONS

Saturn has 30 moons; one (Titan) is very
large, seven are of average size, and the
rest are small and irregularly shaped. Some
of the small moons are co-orbital: they
share an orbit with another moon. Mimas
(left), the closest of the larger moons, is
dominated by the huge crater Herschel,
perhaps the result of a co-orbital collision.

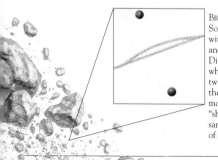

BRAIDED RINGS

Some of the inner moons orbit
within the rings, creating gaps
and braids. Pan sweeps the Enke
Division clear of ring material,
while Prometheus and Pandora
twist and braid the F ring with
their gravitational effect. These
moons are sometimes said to
"shepherd" the rings in the
same way that dogs keep a flock
of sheep together.

CROWDED SPACE
Saturn has both a pair and a triplet of co-orbital moons. In addition, two other moons, Janus and Epimetheus, have orbits that are extremely close to each other. Astronomers believe that these two were once a single moon that broke up.

Inner moons (left to right): Helene and Dione (co-orbital); Calypso, Telesto, and Tethys (co-orbital); Enceladus; Mimas; Janus; Epimetheus; Pandora; Prometheus; Atlas; Pan

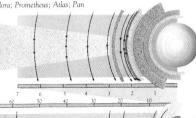

Outer moons (left to right): Phoebe; Iapetus; Hyperion; Titan; Rhea; Helene; and Dione (also shown above)

SCALE IN RADIUSES OF SATURN

SATURN: SATELLITE FACTS				
	Diameter		Distance from Saturn	
	miles	km	miles	km
Pan	12	20	83,000	133,580
Atlas	20	32	85,540	137,670
Prometheus	62	100	86,590	139,350
Pandora	52	84	88,050	141,700
Epimetheus	74	119	94,090	151,420
Janus	110	178	94,120	151,470
Mimas	247	397	115,280	185,520
Enceladus	310	499	147,900	238,020
Tethys	658	1,060	183,090	294,660
Telesto	14	22	183,090	294,660
Calypso	12	19	183,090	294,660
Dione	696	1,120	234,500	377,400
Helene	20	32	234,500	377,400
Rhea	949	1,528	327,490	527,040
Titan	3,200	5,150	759,210	1,221,830
Hyperion	165	266	920,310	1,481,100
Iapetus	892	1,436	2,212,900	3,561,300
Phoebe	137	220	8,048,000	12,952,000

MORE FACTS
• The rings of Saturn seem to be neatly graded, with the largest fragments found in the inner rings closest to the planet, while fine dust accumulates in the outer rings.

• Saturn is the only planet that has three moons sharing the same orbit – Tethys, Telesto, and Calypso.

• Mimas was to have been named "Arthur." Although this did not happen, many of its features are named after characters in the legend of King Arthur.

URANUS

A COLD GAS giant, Uranus is
the seventh planet from the
Sun. Little surface detail can
be seen, and even close-up
pictures show only a few
clouds of frozen methane
gas. Despite its featureless
appearance, Uranus has one
interesting peculiarity. The
planet, and its rings and
moons, are all tilted by more
than 90°, traveling around
the Sun on their side.

BLANK FACE
Faintly visible from Earth as a dim
"star" in the night sky, Uranus
was not identified as a planet
until 1781. The ring system was
not discovered until 1977 –
almost 200 years later.

Earth

Uranus

URANUS: PLANETARY DATA	
Average distance	1,784 million miles
from the Sun	(2,871 million km)
Orbital period	84 Earth years
Orbital velocity	4.2 miles/sec (6.8 km/s)
Rotation period	17.24 hours
Diameter at equator	31,763 miles (51,118 km)
Cloud-top temperature	–346°F (–210°C)
Mass (Earth = 1)	14.5
Gravity (Earth = 1)	0.89
Number of moons	21

URANUS FACTS

• Uranus is named after
Urania, the Greek muse
(patron goddess) of
astronomy.

• Light from the Sun,
which takes about eight
minutes to reach Earth,
takes more than 2 hours
30 minutes to travel as
far as Uranus.

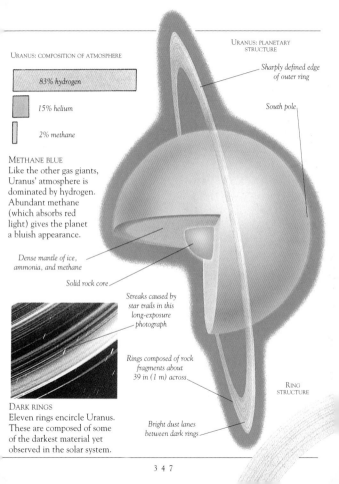

URANUS: COMPOSITION OF ATMOSPHERE

83% hydrogen

15% helium

2% methane

METHANE BLUE
Like the other gas giants, Uranus' atmosphere is dominated by hydrogen. Abundant methane (which absorbs red light) gives the planet a bluish appearance.

Sharply defined edge of outer ring

South pole

Dense mantle of ice, ammonia, and methane

Solid rock core

Streaks caused by star trails in this long-exposure photograph

Rings composed of rock fragments about 39 in (1 m) across

RING STRUCTURE

Bright dust lanes between dark rings

DARK RINGS
Eleven rings encircle Uranus. These are composed of some of the darkest material yet observed in the solar system.

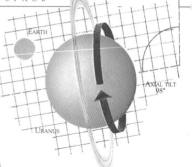

SIDEWAYS ORBIT

Uranus' axis of rotation is tilted at 98° to the vertical – the equator runs through the "top" and "bottom" of the planet. This extreme tilt also extends to the rings and moons. Uranus' sideways stance may have been the result of a collision with another celestial body at some time in the distant past.

EARTH

AXIAL TILT 98°

URANUS

LENGTHY SEASONS

Uranus' peculiar tilt creates extremely long seasons. As the planet travels around the Sun, each pole receives 42 Earth years of sunlight, followed by the same period of total darkness. However, the temperature does not vary with the seasons because Uranus is so far away from the Sun.

STRANGE MAGNETISM

Uranus generates a magnetic field which is tilted, but not the same way as the planet. The magnetic field is tilted at 60° to the axis of rotation, which means that the magnetosphere has a fairly normal shape. To make the situation even more extraordinary, Uranus' magnetic field is offset from the planet's center.

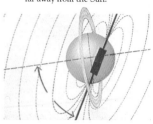

RINGS AND MOONS
Only the innermost moon, Cordelia, orbits within the ring system. Miranda is perhaps the most unusual moon in the solar system – it shows every sign of once having been blasted apart and then reassembled.

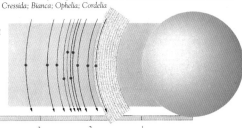

Inner moons (left to right): Puck; Belinda; Rosalind; Portia; Juliet; Desdemona; Cressida; Bianca; Ophelia; Cordelia

Outer moons (left to right): Oberon; Titania; Umbriel; Ariel; Miranda; Puck (also shown above)

URANUS: SATELLITE DATA				
	Diameter		Distance from Uranus	
	miles	km	miles	km
Bianca	26	42	36,770	59,170
Cressida	39	62	38,390	61,780
Desdemona	34	54	38,950	62,680
Juliet	52	84	39,990	64,350
Portia	67	108	41,070	66,090
Rosalind	34	54	43,460	69,940
Belinda	41	66	46,760	75,260
Puck	96	154	53,440	86,010
Miranda	293	472	80,400	129,390
Ariel	719	1,158	118,690	191,020
Umbriel	727	1,169	165,470	266,300
Titania	980	1,578	270,860	435,910
Oberon	946	1,523	362,580	583,520
Caliban	37	60	4,455,500	7,170,400
Sycorax	75	120	7,590,700	12,216,000

MORE FACTS
• Before Voyager 2, Uranus was believed to have five moons. The accepted total is now 21, with more awaiting confirmation.

• Many of the Uranian moons are named after characters in plays by William Shakespeare.

• In contrast to the planet Saturn, the outermost Uranian ring has no fragments less than about 8 in (20 cm) across.

NEPTUNE

THE OUTERMOST of the gas giants, Neptune is a near twin to Uranus. Too faint to be seen easily from Earth, its position was calculated mathematically. Neptune was first observed in 1846 exactly where it was predicted to be. Methane in the atmosphere gives Neptune a deep blue coloration. The rings and six of the moons were discovered by the Voyager 2 probe.

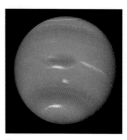

DARK STORMS
In this photograph, by the Voyager 2 probe in 1989, Neptune shows a huge cyclonic storm, called the Great Dark Spot (center right), overlain by bright, wispy methane clouds.

Earth

Neptune

NEPTUNE: PLANETARY DATA	
Average distance from the Sun	2,795 million miles (4,498 million km)
Orbital period	164.8 Earth years
Orbital velocity	3.4 miles/sec (5.4 km/s)
Rotation period	16.11 hours
Diameter at equator	30,775 miles (49,528 km)
Cloud-top temperature	−364°F (−220°C)
Mass (Earth = 1)	17.1
Gravity (Earth = 1)	1.1
Number of moons	11

NEPTUNE FACTS
• Neptune is named after the Roman god of the sea.
• Neptune radiates 2.6 times more heat than it receives from the Sun – a sign of an internal source of heat.

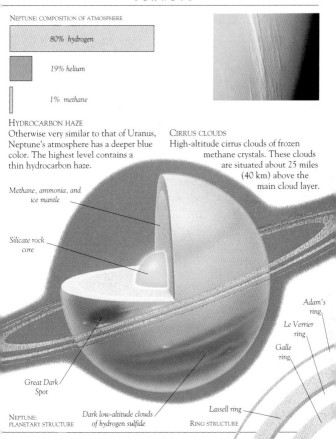

NEPTUNE: COMPOSITION OF ATMOSPHERE

80% hydrogen

19% helium

1% methane

HYDROCARBON HAZE
Otherwise very similar to that of Uranus, Neptune's atmosphere has a deeper blue color. The highest level contains a thin hydrocarbon haze.

CIRRUS CLOUDS
High-altitude cirrus clouds of frozen methane crystals. These clouds are situated about 25 miles (40 km) above the main cloud layer.

Methane, ammonia, and ice mantle

Silicate rock core

Adam's ring

Le Verrier ring

Galle ring

Great Dark Spot

NEPTUNE: PLANETARY STRUCTURE

Dark low-altitude clouds of hydrogen sulfide

Lassell ring

RING STRUCTURE

LACK OF SEASONS
Neptune rotates on its axis at approximately the same angle of tilt as Earth. However, Neptune is far too distant from the Sun for the tilt to result in a similar cycle of seasons. Conditions in the atmosphere are dominated by winds blowing at up to 1,250 mph (2,000 km/s) which carry the dark storms around the planet in a backward direction.

EARTH

NEPTUNE

AXIAL TILT
28.3°

GREAT DARK SPOT
Neptune's largest storm, the Great Dark Spot, is about the same size as Earth and rotates in a counter-clockwise direction. The bright spot below it is a cloud called the Scooter, which travels around the planet faster than the Great Dark Spot.

TRITON
The largest of Neptune's moons, Triton is the coldest place in the solar system at –391°F (–235°C). It has a thin atmosphere, mainly of nitrogen, and a large south polar ice cap composed of methane ice. Photographs show the ice to have a pink tinge, which is believed to be due to the presence of organic chemicals formed by the action of sunlight.

Inner moons (left to right): Larissa; Galatea; Despina; Thalassa; Naiad

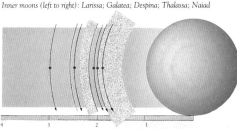

CIRCLING NEPTUNE
The four innermost
moons orbit within
the ring system.
Triton is the only
large moon in the
solar system that
orbits in a backward
direction compared to
the planet's rotation.

SCALE IN RADIUSES OF NEPTUNE

Outer moons (left to right): Nereid; Triton; Proteus; Larissa; and inner moons (also shown above)

DISTANT EXPLORER
Voyager 2 is the only probe that has so far visited
Uranus and Neptune. The journey to Neptune took 12
years, and information from Voyager 2 (transmitted at
the speed of light) took more than four hours to reach
Earth. Among Voyager 2's many discoveries were six of
Neptune's eight moons and ice volcanoes on Triton.

VOYAGER 2

NEPTUNE: SATELLITE DATA				
	Diameter		Distance from Neptune	
	miles	km	miles	km
Naiad	36	58	29,970	48,230
Thalassa	50	80	31,110	50,070
Despina	92	148	32,640	52,530
Galatea	98	158	38,490	61,950
Larissa	119	192	45,700	73,550
Proteus	258	416	73,100	117,650
Triton	1,681	2,705	220,440	354,760
Nereid	211	340	3,425,900	5,513,400

FACT
• The outermost moon,
Nereid, has the most
eccentric orbit of any
known satellite. During
a single orbit, Nereid's
distance from Neptune
varies between 800,000
miles (1,300,000 km)
and 6,000,000 miles
(9,700,000 km).

PLUTO

THE MOST DISTANT of all the planets, Pluto, is also the least understood. Pluto's orbit around the Sun is uniquely tilted at 17°, and is highly unusual in other ways. For about ten percent of its long orbital path, Pluto is closer to the Sun than Neptune. Pluto has a single large moon, Charon, and together they form a double planet.

BLURRED IMAGE
The clearest image of Pluto and Charon has been obtained by the Hubble Space Telescope orbiting Earth. Ground-based photographs show a single blur.

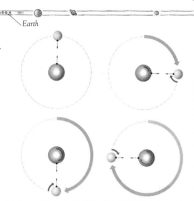

CLOSELY LINKED SYSTEM
Pluto and Charon exhibit a powerful effect on each other. Charon's orbit around Pluto has become synchronized with Pluto's own rotation, so that both have the same period – 6.4 Earth days. As a result, the same face of Charon is always turned to the same face of Pluto. From one side of Pluto, Charon is always visible in the sky. From the other side of the planet, the moon cannot be seen at all.

PLUTO: PLANETARY DATA	
Average distance from the Sun	3,670 million miles (5,906.4 million km)
Orbital period	247.9 Earth years
Orbital velocity	2.9 miles/sec (4.7 kms)
Rotation period	6.38 Earth days
Diameter at equator	1,485 miles (2,390 km)
Surface temperature	–382°F (–230°C)
Mass (Earth = 1)	0.06
Gravity (Earth = 1)	0.04 Moons: 1

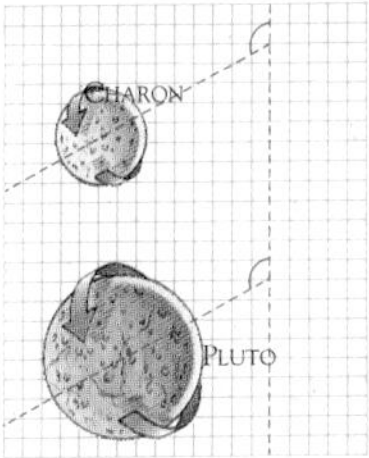

EXTREME TILT
Pluto and Charon both rotate on axes that are tilted at 122.6° to the vertical – the least upright of all the planets.

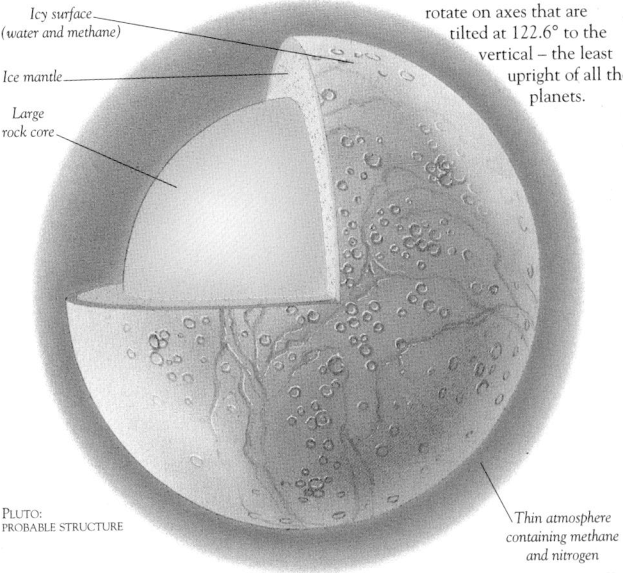

Icy surface
(water and methane)

Ice mantle

Large rock core

PLUTO:
PROBABLE STRUCTURE

Thin atmosphere containing methane and nitrogen

COMETS

A COMET IS a "dirty snowball" composed of snow and dust. Billions of comets orbit the Sun at a distance of about one light-year. A few comets have orbits that take them closer to the Sun. As they near the Sun and are heated, the snow turns to gas and forms a long bright tail.

COMET HALLEY
Most comets that approach the Sun are seen only once, but a few return periodically. Comet Halley returns every 76 years.

ORBITING THE SUN
A periodic comet has a regular orbit that brings it close to the Sun. For most of its orbit, the comet has no tail. The tail only develops as the comet nears the Sun and its surface is heated. The tail gets longer and longer, and then disappears as the comet moves away from the Sun.

Tail develops as the comet approaches the Sun

SUN

Tail is longest near the Sun

For most of its orbit, a comet is a tailless dirty snowball.

Tail shrinks as comet moves away

GLOWING GAS

The nucleus of a typical comet is about 0.62 miles (1 km) across. When heated by the Sun, jets of gas and dust erupt from the surface of the nucleus to form a glowing cloud called a coma, which surrounds the nucleus. The coma can be ten times larger than the Earth. The comet's tail may be millions of miles (kilometers) long.

Comets often have two distinct tails, one of gas and one of dust.

Coma

Nucleus made of dust and frozen gases

Dust reflects sunlight

HEART OF A COMET

This photograph of the nucleus of Comet Halley was taken by the Giotto probe from a distance of about 1,050 miles (1,700 km). Bright gas jets can be seen on the sunlit (upper) surface. Instruments aboard Giotto showed that the main constituent of the nucleus was water-ice.

COMET FACT

• The planet Jupiter is so massive that its gravity can affect the orbit of comets. In 1992, Comet Shoemaker-Levy passed close to Jupiter and was broken into several fragments by gravitational forces. During July 1994, these fragments crashed into Jupiter, causing a series of huge explosions in Jupiter's atmosphere.

METEORS

EVERY DAY, thousands of dust particles and rock fragments from space enter the Earth's atmosphere. Most burn up due to friction with the air. The streaks of light they produce are called meteors. Very rarely a larger fragment survives the atmosphere and hits Earth's surface. These "space-rocks" are called meteorites.

METEOR SHOWER
This is a a false-color photograph of a Leonid meteor shower (yellow streaks), which is associated with Comet Tempel-Tuttle.

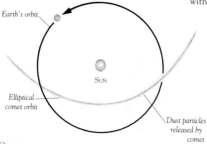

Earth's orbit

SUN

Elliptical comet orbit

Dust particles released by comet

CROSSING ORBITS
Most meteors are caused by dust and debris shed by comets as they pass close to the Sun. The debris stays in the path of the comet's orbit; and when the Earth's orbit crosses that of the comet, we experience a meteor shower. Some showers are regular annual events.

METEOR FACTS

• Each year 48,400 tons (44,000 tonnes) of extra-terrestrial material enters our atmosphere.

• Most meteors are vaporized at altitudes above 50 miles (80 km).

• Meteor showers are named after the constellation in which the radiant appears, e.g. the Perseids.

• In very heavy storms, thousands of meteors fall each hour.

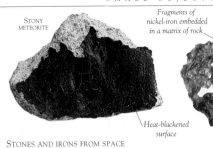

STONY METEORITE

Fragments of nickel-iron embedded in a matrix of rock

Heat-blackened surface

STONY-IRON METEORITE

STONES AND IRONS FROM SPACE

There are two main types of meteorite – those composed mainly of rock (called "stones") and those made mostly of metal (called "irons"). Rocky meteorites are far more common than "irons," but the rarest meteorites on Earth (less than one in every hundred found) are "stony-irons" that contain both metal and rock.

IMPACT CRATER

Barringer Crater in Arizona measures 0.8 miles (1.3 km) across. It was formed about 50,000 years ago when a meteorite about 150 ft (45 m) in diameter struck the surface at a speed of around 6.8 miles/sec (11 km/s). Meteorite hunters have found several "iron" fragments in the crater.

METEORITE FACTS

• More than 90% of identified meteorites that strike the Earth are "stones."

• The world's largest known meteorite still lies where it fell at Hoba West in southern Africa. Its weight is estimated at over 60 tons (tonnes).

• Last century, Czar Alexander of Russia had a sword made from an "iron" meteorite.

ASTEROIDS

MILLIONS OF CHUNKS of rock
orbit the Sun. These are the
asteroids, sometimes called
the minor planets. Asteroids
range in size from a few feet
(meters) across, to those that
are hundreds of miles
(kilometers) in diameter.
Most of the asteroids are
found in a wide belt between
the orbits of Mars and Jupiter.

SPACE ROCK
Ida is a typical asteroid – small
and irregular in shape with a
maximum length of 34 miles
(55 km). Its surface is heavily
cratered and covered by a thin
layer of dust.

Asteroid belt

Earth

Mars

Jupiter

*Trojan
asteroids*

ASTEROID GROUPS
About 50,000 of the millions of asteroids in the main belt
between Mars and Jupiter have so far been located and
identified. Other groups of asteroids follow different orbits.
Trojan asteroids are co-orbital with Jupiter, held in place
by the giant planet's powerful gravity.

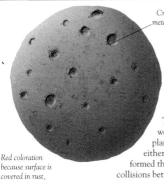

Craters due to meteorite impacts

Most asteroids are irregular in shape.

ASTEROID ORIGINS

The larger asteroids are spherical and were formed in the same way as the planets. The smaller irregular asteroids are either remnants of the original material that formed the solar system, or the result of collisions between two or more large asteroids.

Red coloration because surface is covered in rust

FAILED PLANET

The asteroid belt was probably formed at the same time as the rest of the solar system. Rock fragments and dust particles in this part of the system were prevented from clumping together to form a planet by Jupiter's gravity. But if all the asteroids were put together, their mass would be only a tiny fraction of the Earth's.

ASTEROID FACTS

• The first asteroid to be discovered was Ceres which has a diameter of 584 miles (940 km).

• Asteroids which have an average distance from the Sun less than Earth's are known as Aten asteroids.

• Earth has been struck by several asteroids in the past, and it is only a matter of time before another asteroid strikes our planet.

INFORMATION FROM SPACE

GATHERING AND STUDYING starlight is just
one way that we learn about the universe.
Visible light is only a small part of the
electromagnetic spectrum, which
covers all forms of radiation. By
studying different types of radiation,
we learn more about both the
visible and the invisible parts
of the universe.

*Ozone
layer*

*Gamma
rays
and
X-rays*

UV rays

*Most infrared
stopped here*

*Visible light and short-
wave radio reach surface*

ATMOSPHERIC SHIELD
The atmosphere shields Earth against
radiation from space. Gamma rays,
X-rays, and most ultraviolet (UV)
rays are stopped. Only visible
light, some infrared and UV
radiation, and some radio
signals reach the surface.

INFORMATION SPECTRUM
Electromagnetic radiation travels
through space as waves of
varying length (the distance
between wave crests). Gamma
rays have the shortest wavelength,
then X-rays, and so on through
the spectrum to the longest radio
waves. Visible light, which is all
that we can see naturally, occupies
a very narrow portion (less than
0.00001 percent) of the spectrum.

10^{-13} m
0.0000000000001 meters

X-RAYS

GAMMA RAYS

CRAB NEBULA AT DIFFERENT WAVELENGTHS

The Crab Nebula – the remnant of a supernova explosion seen in 1054 – emits a wide range of radiation wavelengths. When viewed in infrared light (right) the nebula looks like a huge cloud. The red areas represent the cooler parts of the nebula.

VISIBLE LIGHT

In visible light, vast filaments of hot gas can be seen spreading out into space after the explosion. The blue glow comes from fast-moving particles accelerated by the strong magnetic field of the inner nebula.

X-RAY

An X-ray image (right) reveals the source of the magnetism – a rapidly spinning pulsar at the heart of the nebula. The pulsar is surrounded by high-energy particles that spiral around the pulsar's magnetic field lines.

10^{-7} m
0.0000001 meters

10^5 m
100,000 meters

VISIBLE
LIGHT

MICROWAVES

.TRAVIOLET
LIGHT

INFRARED
LIGHT

RADIO
WAVES

OPTICAL TELESCOPES

THE OPTICAL TELESCOPE is one of the main tools of astronomy. But little time is spent looking through a telescope eyepiece – modern instruments collect and store visual information electronically. The optical telescope remains an important tool because it gathers basic information.

PALOMAR DOME
The protective dome of the Hale Telescope at the Mount Palomar Observatory, California, shields the telescope from the effects of weather.

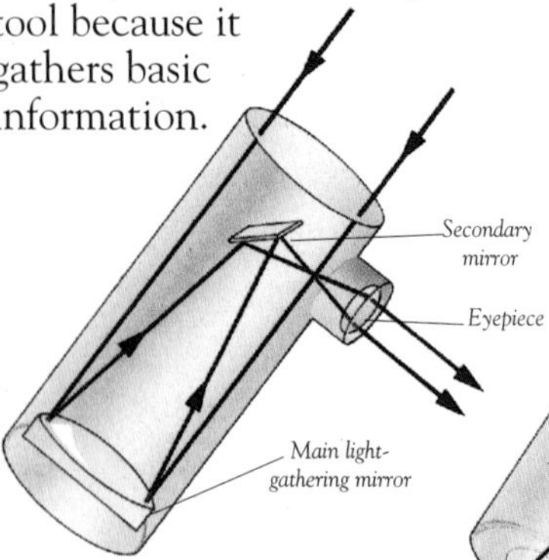

Secondary mirror

Eyepiece

Main light-gathering mirror

Main light-gathering lens

Eyepiece lens

REFLECTOR TELESCOPES
Telescopes use lenses and mirrors to gather light and produce an image. Reflector telescopes, which make use of curved mirrors, are the most useful type for astronomy.

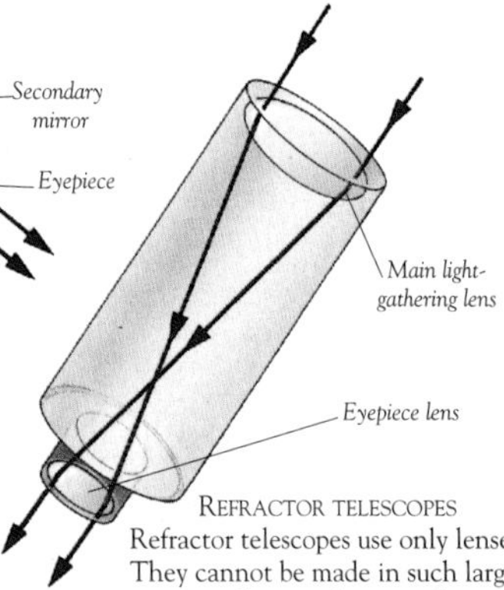

REFRACTOR TELESCOPES
Refractor telescopes use only lenses. They cannot be made in such large sizes as reflector telescopes, but they remain very popular with amateur astronomers.

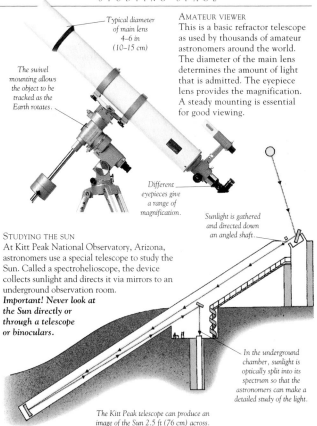

Typical diameter
of main lens
4–6 in
(10–15 cm)

The swivel
mounting allows
the object to be
tracked as the
Earth rotates.

Different
eyepieces give
a range of
magnification.

AMATEUR VIEWER
This is a basic refractor telescope
as used by thousands of amateur
astronomers around the world.
The diameter of the main lens
determines the amount of light
that is admitted. The eyepiece
lens provides the magnification.
A steady mounting is essential
for good viewing.

Sunlight is gathered
and directed down
an angled shaft.

STUDYING THE SUN
At Kitt Peak National Observatory, Arizona,
astronomers use a special telescope to study the
Sun. Called a spectrohelioscope, the device
collects sunlight and directs it via mirrors to an
underground observation room.
**Important! Never look at
the Sun directly or
through a telescope
or binoculars.**

In the underground
chamber, sunlight is
optically split into its
spectrum so that the
astronomers can make a
detailed study of the light.

The Kitt Peak telescope can produce an
image of the Sun 2.5 ft (76 cm) across.

RADIO ASTRONOMY

WE HAVE BEEN LISTENING in to the radio energy of the universe for more than 50 years. Radio astronomy can obtain additional information about familiar objects, as well as seek out new ones. Two major discoveries – quasars and pulsars – were made by radio astronomers.

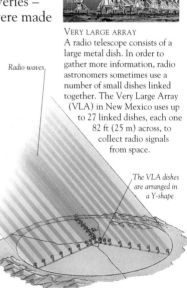

VERY LARGE ARRAY
A radio telescope consists of a large metal dish. In order to gather more information, radio astronomers sometimes use a number of small dishes linked together. The Very Large Array (VLA) in New Mexico uses up to 27 linked dishes, each one 82 ft (25 m) across, to collect radio signals from space.

Radio waves

The VLA dishes are arranged in a Y-shape

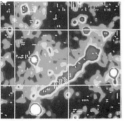

RADIO VISION
Radio telescopes, like ordinary radio sets, can be tuned to a particular wavelength, and the intensity of the radio energy can be measured. Computers are then used to produce "radio-maps" of the sky, such as this image of the bar-shaped radio source known as 1952+28.

LARGEST DISH

The world's largest radio telescope, the 1,000 ft (305 m) Arecibo dish, is built into a natural hollow in the hills of Puerto Rico. The dish is "steered" using the Earth's own rotation. Arecibo has also been used to send a radio message out into space.

Simple processing of the Arecibo message produces this visual image which contains a representation of a human being.

RADIO GALAXIES

Many galaxies that are quite faint visually are very "bright" at radio wavelengths. These are often called radio galaxies, or active galaxies. This optical image of radio galaxy 3C 33 has been color-coded according to the intensity of light in the visible part of the spectrum – ranging from white (most intense) to blue (the least).

IMAGES OF SPACE

MUCH OF THE information that astronomers obtain through their instruments is presented as visual images. Conventional and electronic cameras are used to record these images. The information is usually stored on computers that can process images to improve the picture and bring out details.

PIXELATED VIEW
Electronic cameras make images with a grid of tiny picture-elements (pixels). This view of a dim and distant star cluster was obtained with a ground-based telescope. The individual pixels are clearly visible, although it takes a trained eye to identify the image as a star cluster.

MARTIAN CHEMICAL PHOTOMAP
This image of the Martian surface was produced from data collected by a device called a neutron spectrometer aboard the Mars Odyssey probe. It is color-coded to show concentrations of hydrogen in the soil. Deep blue areas contain the most hydrogen, and red areas the least. In the deep blue regions near the poles, the hydrogen is mostly combined with oxygen in the form of water ice.

Soil near the poles may be up to 50 percent water ice.

FALSE COLOR GIVES A TRUER VIEW
Astronomers have several techniques for
analyzing the information contained in
images. One of the most important is
adding false color to the image.
Saturn has a fairly muted appearance
in ordinary photographs. This
image has been color-coded to
emphasize the banding of
the planet's upper
atmosphere.

COLORING THE SUN
This false-color ultraviolet image
from the TRACE spacecraft shows
plasma exploding off the Sun's
surface and traveling through the
solar atmosphere along loops of the
Sun's magnetic field. The colors
represent different temperatures.
The red regions are the hottest,
at 2.7 million°F (1.5 million°C).

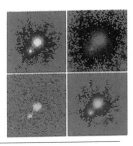

SEPARATE, THEN COMBINE
Images of space are often obtained through a series
of colored filters. The object is photographed
through each filter in turn, and the resulting
images are then combined to give a much fuller
picture than with any single ordinary photograph.
This series was taken with the Hubble Space
Telescope, and shows Pluto and its moon Charon.

OBSERVATORIES

OPTICAL TELESCOPES are usually installed in mountain-top observatories, where they suffer the least interference from Earth's atmosphere. Radio telescopes can be situated almost anywhere, and are usually located near universities. Observatories are often shared between countries because of the high cost of telescopes which use the latest technology.

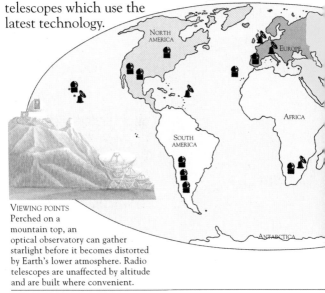

VIEWING POINTS
Perched on a mountain top, an optical observatory can gather starlight before it becomes distorted by Earth's lower atmosphere. Radio telescopes are unaffected by altitude and are built where convenient.

HIGH AND DRY

The European Southern Observatory is sited on Cerro Paranal, a 8,645-ft- (2,635-m-) high mountain in Chile's Atacama desert. A dry climate with cloud-free nights and a steady atmosphere makes this remote location ideal for clear viewing.

OBSERVATORY FACTS

• The oldest existing observatory was built in South Korea in AD 632.

• The flying observatory SOFIA will begin operation in 2005. It is a modified 747 jumbo jet fitted with a 100-in (2.5-m) telescope.

• The 36 elements of the Keck reflector make a mirror 396 in (1,000 cm) across.

• The world's highest observatory is on Mauna Kea island, Hawaii, 13,780 ft (4,200 m) above sea level.

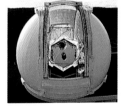

HIGH-TECH TELESCOPE

The Keck Telescope situated on Mauna Kea, Hawaii, is the world's largest optical telescope. The main mirror is made up of 36 computer-controlled hexagonal segments.

MAP KEY

OPTICAL TELESCOPE

RADIO TELESCOPE

ASIA

AUSTRALASIA

TELESCOPES IN SPACE

BY PLACING THEIR TELESCOPES in orbit above Earth's atmosphere, astronomers get a much better view. They can see farther and can collect information from wavelengths that are absorbed by the atmosphere. Information and images gathered in orbit are transmitted back to Earth for study and analysis.

ORBITING TELESCOPE
Two astronauts from the Space Shuttle *Columbia* make repairs to the Hubble Space Telescope in 2002.

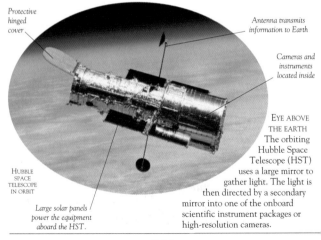

Protective hinged cover

Antenna transmits information to Earth

Cameras and instruments located inside

HUBBLE SPACE TELESCOPE IN ORBIT

Large solar panels power the equipment aboard the HST.

EYE ABOVE THE EARTH
The orbiting Hubble Space Telescope (HST) uses a large mirror to gather light. The light is then directed by a secondary mirror into one of the onboard scientific instrument packages or high-resolution cameras.

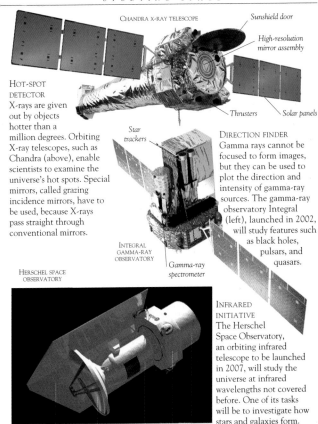

CHANDRA X-RAY TELESCOPE

Sunshield door

High-resolution mirror assembly

Thrusters

Solar panels

HOT-SPOT DETECTOR
X-rays are given out by objects hotter than a million degrees. Orbiting X-ray telescopes, such as Chandra (above), enable scientists to examine the universe's hot spots. Special mirrors, called grazing incidence mirrors, have to be used, because X-rays pass straight through conventional mirrors.

Star trackers

INTEGRAL GAMMA-RAY OBSERVATORY

Gamma-ray spectrometer

DIRECTION FINDER
Gamma rays cannot be focused to form images, but they can be used to plot the direction and intensity of gamma-ray sources. The gamma-ray observatory Integral (left), launched in 2002, will study features such as black holes, pulsars, and quasars.

HERSCHEL SPACE OBSERVATORY

INFRARED INITIATIVE
The Herschel Space Observatory, an orbiting infrared telescope to be launched in 2007, will study the universe at infrared wavelengths not covered before. One of its tasks will be to investigate how stars and galaxies form.

ROCKETS

SATELLITES, SPACE PROBES, and astronauts are lifted into space by rockets. There are two main types. The conventional tall, thin rocket is made from several stages stacked on top of each other. The newer Space Shuttle design lifts off with the aid of massive booster rockets. But when it returns from space, the Shuttle lands like an aircraft.

LIFTOFF
A Soyuz-Fregat rocket blasts off from the launchpad. Its engines burn fuel at a rate of thousands of gallons (liters) per second.

Nozzle shapes the stream of hot exhaust gases

Liquid fuel and oxygen are combined in the combustion chamber.

Fuel tank

Oxygen tank

Fuel and oxygen stored in reinforced pressurised tanks

Pumps control the flow of fuel and oxygen to the combustion chamber.

ROCKET POWER
A rocket is propelled upward by hot exhaust gases streaming from nozzles at the tail. These gases are the result of burning a mixture of liquid oxygen and fuel (such as liquid hydrogen) inside a combustion chamber. Carrying its own oxygen supply enables a rocket engine to function in the airless vacuum of space.

ESCAPE VELOCITY
A rocket, or any other object, is held on the Earth's surface by the force of gravity. To escape the effects of Earth's gravity and enter space, a rocket needs to achieve a speed of 24,840 mph (40,000 km/h) – this is the "escape velocity" of planet Earth. On the Moon, where the force of gravity is only one sixth as powerful as on Earth, the escape velocity is lower – only about 5,300 mph (8,500 km/h).

Payload – satellite or space probe

Third-stage rocket engines

ARIANE: A TYPICAL
THREE-STAGE LAUNCH VEHICLE

Second-stage rocket engines

First-stage rocket engines

External booster rockets assist first stage engines at liftoff

REUSABLE SPACE CRAFT
A streaming exhaust trail marks the beginning of another Space Shuttle mission. Unlike conventional rockets, which can be used only once, the Shuttle is reusable. The massive booster rockets are jettisoned two minutes after launch and recovered. The Shuttle's own engines carry it on into orbit, and small thruster rockets are used to maneuver it into position.

FLYBYS AND ORBITERS

LIFTED INTO SPACE by rockets, space probes are computer-controlled robots packed with scientific instruments. Probes are sent to fly by a planet, or even orbit around it, sending data and images back to Earth. After they have completed their planned missions, some probes continue on into space.

VOLCANIC DISCOVERY
The probe Voyager I obtained this image of Io which shows the first active volcano seen outside Earth.

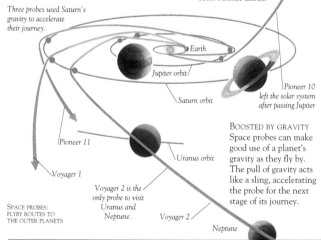

Three probes used Saturn's gravity to accelerate their journey.

Earth

Jupiter orbit

Saturn orbit

Pioneer 10 left the solar system after passing Jupiter

Pioneer 11

Voyager 1

Uranus orbit

BOOSTED BY GRAVITY
Space probes can make good use of a planet's gravity as they fly by. The pull of gravity acts like a sling, accelerating the probe for the next stage of its journey.

Voyager 2 is the only probe to visit Uranus and Neptune.

Voyager 2

SPACE PROBES:
FLYBY ROUTES TO
THE OUTER PLANETS

Neptune

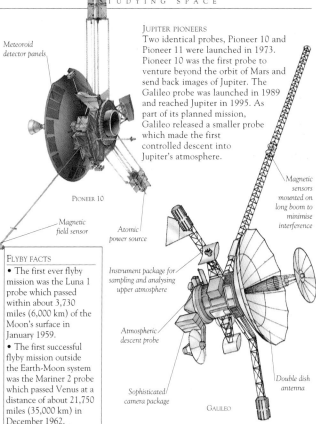

JUPITER PIONEERS
Two identical probes, Pioneer 10 and Pioneer 11 were launched in 1973. Pioneer 10 was the first probe to venture beyond the orbit of Mars and send back images of Jupiter. The Galileo probe was launched in 1989 and reached Jupiter in 1995. As part of its planned mission, Galileo released a smaller probe which made the first controlled descent into Jupiter's atmosphere.

Meteoroid detector panels

Magnetic field sensor

Atomic power source

PIONEER 10

Magnetic sensors mounted on long boom to minimise interference

Instrument package for sampling and analysing upper atmosphere

Atmospheric descent probe

Sophisticated camera package

Double dish antenna

GALILEO

FLYBY FACTS
• The first ever flyby mission was the Luna 1 probe which passed within about 3,730 miles (6,000 km) of the Moon's surface in January 1959.
• The first successful flyby mission outside the Earth-Moon system was the Mariner 2 probe which passed Venus at a distance of about 21,750 miles (35,000 km) in December 1962.

LANDERS

SPACE PROBES SENT to orbit a planet can release a second craft to land on the surface. The lander, a scientific robot, carries out its preprogrammed tasks and then relays the data it has obtained back to Earth. Only six piloted spacecraft have made landings, during the Apollo Moon program.

COMING IN TO LAND
This dramatic photograph of the Hadley Rille valley was taken from the piloted Apollo 15 lander during its low-altitude descent to the Moon's surface.

IS THERE LIFE ON MARS?
Two Viking orbiter craft each released a lander that descended safely to the Martian surface. In total about 3,000 photographic images were sent back to Earth. The landers also tested the Martian soil with four different experiments to check for any signs of life – none was found.

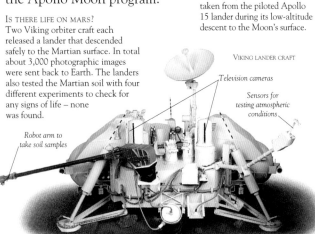

VIKING LANDER CRAFT

Television cameras

Sensors for testing atmospheric conditions

Robot arm to take soil samples

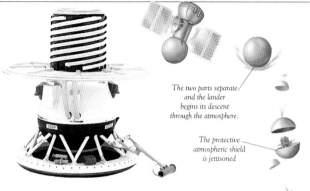

The two parts separate and the lander begins its descent through the atmosphere.

The protective atmospheric shield is jettisoned

VENERA 9 LANDER CRAFT

On-board braking engines begin to slow Venera 9

LANDER FACTS

• The first successful lander was Luna 9, which soft-landed on the Moon in 1966.

• Venera 7 became the first lander to transmit data from the surface of Venus in 1970.

• The Viking landers analysed Mars' soil and found that it contained the following chemical elements:

silica	14%
iron	18%
aluminum	2.7%
titanium	0.9%
potassium	0.3%

HOT LANDING

A series of Venera space probes was sent to Venus. Each consisted of two parts, one of which descended to the surface. Conditions on Venus – very high temperature and pressure – meant that the landers could function only for a few minutes.

Parachutes further slow the descent

Venera 9 obtains and transmits several images before failing

WORKING IN SPACE

ASTRONAUTS NOW WORK in
space on a regular basis. Many
experiments take place aboard
orbiting laboratories, while
satellites can be launched,
retrieved, and repaired while
circling Earth.

Antenna

Television
camera

Steering
control

Equipment
storage rack

Wire-mesh
wheels

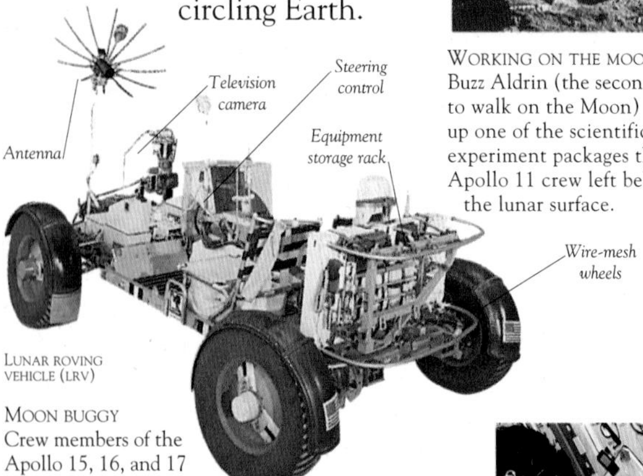

LUNAR ROVING
VEHICLE (LRV)

WORKING ON THE MOON
Buzz Aldrin (the second person
to walk on the Moon) sets
up one of the scientific
experiment packages that
the Apollo 11 crew left behind on
the lunar surface.

MOON BUGGY
Crew members of the
Apollo 15, 16, and 17
missions made effective
use of the LRV. This
"moon-buggy" enabled
them to travel dozens
of miles across the
lunar surface, collecting
samples over a
wide area.

SPACE SCIENCE
Orbiting laboratories
allow scientists to carry out
experiments in conditions
where gravity's influence is
negligible. This scientist is
testing how fuel burns in a
weightless enironment.

SPACE STATION
Assembled in space by astronauts aided by tools, cranes, and a robotic arm, the International Space Station (ISS) is a collaboration between 16 countries. Pressurized living modules for up to seven astronauts are linked to laboratories and work stations. Astronauts live and work on the ISS for up to six months at a time.

Some 43,000 sq ft (4,000 sq m) of solar panels provide power to the ISS.

RUNNING REPAIRS
Attached securely to the Space Shuttle's robotic arm – the Remote Manipulator System – astronauts can carry out repairs to satellites, telescopes, and the International Space Station in safety.

The Space Shuttle's robotic arm (at foot of picture) maneuvers the astronaut into the correct position to carry out a particular task.

MILESTONES IN ASTRONOMY

The astronomer's job is to observe, describe, and explain objects in space. The story of astronomy is marked by a series of milestone achievements. Advances in technology have led to better descriptions and more comprehensive explanations.

EUDOXUS OF CNIDUS (408-355 B.C.) was a Greek thinker who studied at Athens under the philosopher Plato. In later life he developed the theory of crystal spheres – the first scientific attempt to explain the observed motion of the planets, and stars.

MILESTONE
According to Eudoxus, the Earth was at the center of the universe. The stars and planets were set into a series of transparent crystal spheres that surrounded the Earth in space.

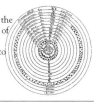

PTOLEMY (c.A.D. 120-180) lived in Alexandria, Egypt, at the height of the Roman Empire. Although little is known about him, he has become famous as the "father of astronomy." The idea that the Earth is at the center of the universe is often referred to as the "Ptolemaic System."

MILESTONE
He compiled a compendium, known as the "Almagest," of ancient Greek astronomical knowledge. Handed down over the centuries, Ptolemy's book continued to provide the basis of scientific astronomy for more than 1,000 years.

AL-SUFI (903-86) was a Persian nobleman, and one of the leading astronomers of his time. His "Book of Fixed Stars" listed the position and brightness of more than 1,000 stars, and beautifully illustrated the main constellations.

MILESTONE
During the Dark Ages, scientific astronomy was kept alive in the Islamic empire. Our knowledge of the works of Ptolemy is entirely due to Arab translators.

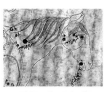

NICOLAUS COPERNICUS (1473-1543) worked as a church lawyer in Poland. Near the end of his life he published an exciting new view of the universe which replaced Ptolemy's.

MILESTONE

Copernicus removed the Earth from its traditional place at the center of the universe, and replaced it with the Sun. This was considered to be revolutionary view, and the "Copernican Revolution" was strongly opposed by the Christian Church.

GALILEO GALILEI (1564-1642) was an Italian scientist and astronomer who supported Copernicus' new theory. As a result, he was put on trial by the Church, and he remained a virtual prisoner for the rest of his life.

MILESTONE

Galileo pioneered the use of the refractor telescope for astronomy. He made several major discoveries, including mountains on the Moon, the phases of Venus, and the four largest moons of Jupiter.

ISAAC NEWTON (1643-1727) was a professor of mathematics and a great scientist. He is supposed to have had the idea for his theory of gravity after seeing an apple fall from a tree.

MILESTONE

The theory of gravity explained why apples fall, and why planets orbit around the Sun. Newton was able to establish the scientific laws that apply to the motion of objects in space. He also experimented with optics – splitting sunlight into its spectrum – and designed a reflecting telescope.

EDMOND HALLEY (1656-1742) became Britain's Astronomer Royal – one of the first official government scientists. As a young man he voyaged to the remote island of St. Helena, and charted the stars of the Southern Hemisphere.

MILESTONE

Halley is famous for predicting the return of the periodic comet that now bears his name. His work reinforced the idea that astronomy is a very precise science that can make accurate predictions.

WILLIAM HERSCHEL (1738-1822) was born in Hanover, Germany, but moved to England where he at first worked as a professional musician. His interest in astronomy led him to design and build his own telescopes.

MILESTONE
Herschel became famous for his discovery of the planet Uranus in 1781. Today he is remembered as one of the greatest astronomical observers. By studying the Milky Way over many years, he was able to make the first reasonably accurate estimate of its size and shape.

JOSEPH VON FRAUNHOFER (1787-1826) was an orphan who eventually became the director of a scientific institute in Germany. He was a trained optical worker who made some of the world's highest-quality telescope lenses.

MILESTONE
Fraunhofer identified and studied the dark absorption lines (now called Fraunhofer lines) in the solar spectrum. These lines enable scientists to tell which chemical elements are present in a source of light.

NEPTUNE (FIRST LOCATED IN 1846) The position of a new planet in the solar system was predicted mathematically. But its existence could not be confirmed until it had been observed.

MILESTONE
The "discovery" of Neptune was made possible by astronomers' increased understanding of the universe. Following the work of Newton and Halley, they were able to make increasingly accurate predictions about the behavior of objects in space.

WILLIAM HUGGINS (1824-1910) was an English astronomer who had his own private observatory in London. He was a pioneer of the technique of stellar spectroscopy (analysing the spectra produced by starlight).

MILESTONE
Huggins studied the light from many different stars. As a result of his work, he was able to show that stars are made of the same chemical elements that are found on Earth. He also showed that some nebulae are composed of gas.

GIOVANNI SCHIAPARELLI (1835-1910) was an Italian astronomer who became director of the Brera Observatory at Turin. He made headlines in 1877, when he claimed to be able to see a network of canals on Mars.

MILESTONE
Schiaparelli's most famous discovery was mistaken, but it did focus popular interest and attention on astronomy. He also established the link between comets and meteor showers.

EJNAR HERTZSPRUNG (1873-1967) and HENRY RUSSELL (1877-1957) were two scientists who, working independently, came to the same conclusions about the color and temperature of stars.

MILESTONE
The Hertzsprung-Russell (HR) diagram shows the relationship between surface temperature and color. Astronomers can identify the so-called "main sequence" of stellar development. Giant, supergiant, and dwarf stars are also located on the diagram.

ARTHUR EDDINGTON (1882-1945) was born in the north of England and became Professor of Astronomy at Cambridge. He was interested in the origin of stars, and he wrote science books for a general audience.

MILESTONE
Eddington was able to describe the structure of a star. He also explained how a star stays in one piece – balanced by the forces of gravity (pulling in), and gas pressure and radiation pressure (pushing out).

HARLOW SHAPLEY (1885-1972) was an American astronomer who became director of Harvard College Observatory. He used various stars as markers to study the distance and distribution of star clusters.

MILESTONE
Shapley was able to give the first accurate estimate of the size and shape of the Milky Way galaxy. He also showed that the Sun is located a very long way from the center of the galaxy.

CECILIA PAYNE-GAPOSCHKIN (1900-79) was born in England, but spent most of her working life at Harvard Observatory in the US. She is thought by many people to have been the greatest ever woman astronomer.

MILESTONE
By analysing the spectra of many different stars, Payne-Gaposchkin was able to show that all stars in the main sequence of development (the Sun for example) are composed almost entirely of the chemical elements hydrogen and helium.

EDWIN HUBBLE (1889-1953) was an American who began his working life as a lawyer before becoming a professional astronomer. He showed that the Andromeda spiral was definitely not part of the Milky Way galaxy.

MILESTONE
By showing that some objects are located outside the Milky Way, Hubble proved the existence of other galaxies. He also discovered that the universe appears to be constantly expanding.

GEORGES LEMAITRE (1894-1966) was a Belgian mathematician who worked in Britain and the US. His work had an important influence on the way that astronomers think about the universe.

MILESTONE
Lemaître proposed and developed the Big Bang theory about the origin of the universe. According to this theory, all matter and energy were created simultaneously by a huge explosion. This theory explains why many galaxies appear to be speeding away from us.

KARL JANSKY (1905-49) was an American radio engineer. While trying to solve the problem of static and interference with radio broadcasts, he discovered radio waves coming from the Milky Way.

MILESTONE
Without realizing it, Jansky discovered the basic techniques of radio astronomy. As a result of his work, astronomers have been able to to gather information from other parts of the electromagnetic spectrum, and not just from visible light.

FRED HOYLE (1915-2001) was a British astronomer who began his career as a mathematician. He became famous for his theory that life on Earth was the result of infection by bacteria from space carried by comets.

MILESTONE Hoyle's most important work concerned the basic nuclear reactions at work deep inside stars. He explained the processes by which stars convert hydrogen into helium and other heavier elements.

FRED WHIPPLE (b. 1906) was appointed professor of astronomy at Harvard in 1945, and became director of the Smithsonian Astrophysical Observatory in 1955. He is best known for his studies of comets and the solar system.

MILESTONE His theory that comets are "dirty snowballs" has recently been proved correct by space probes such as Giotto. It now seems likely that comets are "leftovers" from the formation of the solar system.

ARNO PENZIAS (b. 1933) AND ROBERT WILSON (b. 1936) are American scientists. In 1978 they received the Nobel prize for physics for discovering the background radio energy of the universe – energy that is left over from the Big Bang.

MILESTONE This radio energy ("the microwave background") gives the universe an average temperature about 5°F (3°C) above absolute zero. Many people believe that its discovery confirmed the Big Bang theory.

SUPERNOVA 1987A The observation of a bright supernova during 1987 gave astronomers their first opportunity to study a supernova event with modern telescopes and other equipment.

MILESTONE Analysis of the energy and particles produced by the event confirmed the theory that all chemical elements heavier than iron are made by very high-temperature nuclear reactions during supernova explosions.

SPACE MISSIONS I

THE SPACE AGE began in 1957
with the launch of the
first satellite. Four years later
Yuri Gagarin became the
world's first astronaut. The
next 20 years saw a surge of
interest in space exploration.

FIRST SPACE VEHICLE
A model of Vostok I, the
craft in which Yuri Gagarin
made his historic first orbit of
the Earth on April 12, 1961.

CONTROLLED LANDING
The probe Luna 9 was the first to make a
successful soft landing on the Moon in
February 1966. Luna 9 sent back the
first panoramic images taken from
the surface of the Moon.

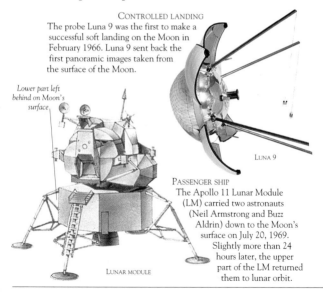

*Lower part left
behind on Moon's
surface*

LUNA 9

PASSENGER SHIP
The Apollo 11 Lunar Module
(LM) carried two astronauts
(Neil Armstrong and Buzz
Aldrin) down to the Moon's
surface on July 20, 1969.
Slightly more than 24
hours later, the upper
part of the LM returned
them to lunar orbit.

LUNAR MODULE

ROBOT MOON ROVER
Two Lunokhod robot vehicles were sent to the Moon in the early 1970s. Equipped with television cameras that enabled them to be driven from a control room on Earth, the two vehicles traveled a total of 29.5 miles (47.5 km) across the Moon.

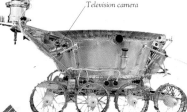

Television camera

LUNOKHOD I

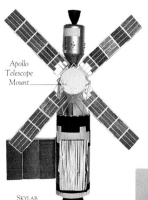

Apollo Telescope Mount

SKYLAB

SCIENTIFIC PLATFORM
Launched in 1973, the Skylab orbiting laboratory and observatory gave astronauts the opportunity to work in space for weeks at a time. Skylab also enabled scientists to study the workings of Earth's atmosphere and climate systems from the viewpoint of space.

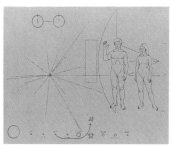

MESSAGE TO THE STARS
The two Pioneer probes each carry a gold-covered plaque that shows a visual representation of human beings, as well as simple directions for locating the solar system and planet Earth.

SPACE MISSIONS II

WORKING IN ORBIT became much easier with the introduction of the Space Shuttle in 1981. Probes have now visited all but one of the outer planets, and further exploration is underway.

The Shuttle has a mechanical arm which can be used to launch or retrieve satellites.

The external fuel tank breaks away at a height of 70 miles (110 km)

The booster rockets operate for about two minutes and are jettisoned at a height of 28 miles (45 km).

The Shuttle can lift off with eight crew and up to 32 tons (29 tonnes) of cargo.

INCREASING COMMUNICATIONS
The communications satellite Intelsat was launched by astronauts on the 49th Space Shuttle mission in May 1992. Improved communications is just one of the benefits of space technology now enjoyed by the general public.

ENDURANCE RECORD
Russian astronauts (cosmonauts) have spent increasingly long periods of time in space. The present record of 437 consecutive days was achieved aboard the space station Mir during 1994-95. The picture shows a cosmonaut on the rigorous exercise program devised to keep the crew in shape during long periods of weightlessness. Mir burned up when it reentered Earth's atmosphere in 2001, after 18 years in orbit.

ROSETTA PROBE

COMET-CHASER
The Rosetta orbiter/lander (right) will attempt to rendezvous with a comet. The lander will detach from the orbiter and descend to the comet's nucleus. Having anchored itself to the surface, it will transmit data to the orbiter, for relaying back to Earth. Scientists hope that Rosetta will shed light on how comets form.

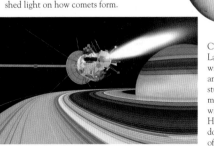

CASSINI-HUYGENS PROBE
Launched in 1997, Cassini will reach Saturn in 2004 and then spend four years studying the planet and its moons. On arrival, Cassini will release the mini-probe Huygens, which will touch down on Titan, the largest of Saturn's many moons.

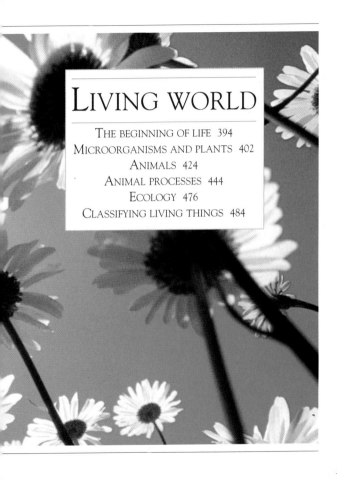

LIVING WORLD

WHAT IS NATURE?

Humans are the most intelligent of all animals

MOST SCIENTISTS divide nature into five kingdoms: animals, plants, fungi, and two kingdoms called Monera and Protista. Monerans and protists include single-celled forms of life, such as bacteria and algae. Animals, plants, and most fungi are multicellular.

HUMANS

Humans are mammals, and more specifically primates, along with apes and monkeys. Like most mammals, humans give birth to live young.

Some fungi absorb nutrients from dead matter

FUNGI AND LICHENS

Fungi and lichens were considered plants. Now, more is known about how they live, and they are thought of as a separate kingdom.

FUNGI

LARKSPUR

Flowering plants are very successful

CHARACTERISTICS OF LIVING THINGS

- Able to use energy
- Able to take in raw materials
- Able to get rid of waste
- Able to respond to the outside world
- Able to reproduce
- Able to grow and develop

PLANTS

Early plants lived in water and then adapted to conditions on land. Nearly all plants are able to use sunlight to turn simple materials into food.

GIRAFFE
WEEVIL

*Flying insects
can travel
to find food*

MONERANS AND PROTISTS
The Monera kingdom includes
the simplest forms of life, such as
bacteria. It has over 5,000 species.
The Protista kingdom is more varied.
It includes simple-form algae
and protozoa, and at least
60,000 other species.

COCCI
BACTERIA

SPIRAL
BACTERIA

AMOEBA

INSECTS
The most successful
animals on Earth are
insects. There are more
species of insects than any
other group of animals on
Earth. Insects are able to
survive in almost all
habitats except the sea.

*Mammals, like
the lion, are
warm-blooded*

ANIMALS
The animal kingdom includes
simple creatures such as sponges
and complex mammals such as lions
and humans. Animals cannot make
their own food as plants do; they must
find it and eat it. They are able to
survive in many different habitats.

LION

HOW LIFE BEGAN

THROUGHOUT HISTORY, people have wondered how life on Earth began. Some people believe it was created by God. Scientists think that the first simple life forms were the result of chemical reactions four billion years ago.

EARTH'S STEAMING SURFACE

THE BEGINNING OF THE EARTH

In the early days of the Earth, the planet was a fiery mass of molten rock. Earth's surface cracked and hot lava poured out, filling the atmosphere with steam and gases. The lava hardened and the steam cooled to rain, creating steaming, muddy pools.

Surface covered with sizzling lava

MIXTURE OF GASES

Scientists have filled this flask with a mixture of gases like those that existed in the early days of the Earth. To simulate lightning, electric sparks are added. The gases combine and produce compounds that are found in all living things.

Steam rises to condense and fall again as rain

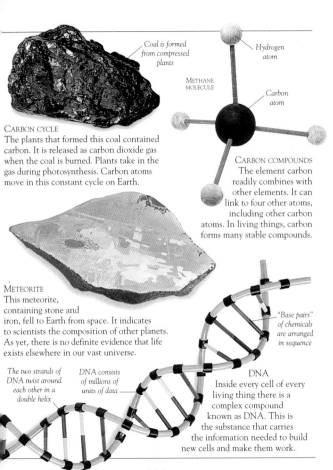

Coal is formed from compressed plants

METHANE MOLECULE

Hydrogen atom

Carbon atom

CARBON CYCLE
The plants that formed this coal contained carbon. It is released as carbon dioxide gas when the coal is burned. Plants take in the gas during photosynthesis. Carbon atoms move in this constant cycle on Earth.

CARBON COMPOUNDS
The element carbon readily combines with other elements. It can link to four other atoms, including other carbon atoms. In living things, carbon forms many stable compounds.

METEORITE
This meteorite, containing stone and iron, fell to Earth from space. It indicates to scientists the composition of other planets. As yet, there is no definite evidence that life exists elsewhere in our vast universe.

The two strands of DNA twist around each other in a double helix

DNA consists of millions of units of data

"Base pairs" of chemicals are arranged in sequence

DNA
Inside every cell of every living thing there is a complex compound known as DNA. This is the substance that carries the information needed to build new cells and make them work.

EVOLUTION

FOSSILS SHOW THAT certain life forms have altered
or "evolved" over time and that others have died out.
British naturalists Charles Darwin and
Alfred Russel Wallace formed
the theory of evolution.
It is based on "natural
selection," a process that
supports the best adapted
members of a species.

AN EVOLUTIONARY LINK
This fossil is *Archaeopteryx* – a birdlike
dinosaur with wings. It may show a link
between reptiles and birds. This kind of link is
important to scientists because it is evidence of how
one species may have evolved from another.

GALÁPAGOS FINCHES

GATHERING EVIDENCE
When Charles Darwin visited
the Galápagos Islands in 1832,
he found 13 species of
finches. He noticed that the
birds had different beak shapes
suited to their eating habits. Darwin
believed that the finches had gradually
evolved from a single species long ago.

WARBLER
FINCH

*The sharp
point of this
beak catches
small insects*

*Strong,
heavy beak
for crushing
big seeds*

LARGE
GROUND
FINCH

*Insect and seed eater
has a small beak*

SMALL TREE FINCH

*This finch
uses a cactus
spine to pick
up insects*

WOODPECKER
FINCH

Hyracotherium lived 50 million years ago. It had four toes on its front feet

Mesohippus, which lived 30 million years ago, had three toes on its front feet

Merychippus existed 20 million years ago. One of its three toes formed a large hoof

Equus is the modern horse

EVOLUTION OF THE HORSE

The earliest fossils of a horselike animal, called *Hyracotherium*, show a small mammal, about the size of a dog, that ate leaves. Over time, descendants became larger with longer legs and a different diet. Modern horses are larger still and eat grass.

Equus evolved about two million years ago. It has a single toe or hoof on each foot

NATURAL SELECTION

Darwin believed evolution supported individuals that were best suited to their environment. Less successful individuals of the same species would naturally die out. In 19th-century England, dark peppered moths became more common than pale peppered moths. Pollution meant that dark moths were better camouflaged from birds on the blackened trees.

PEPPERED MOTHS ON LIGHT BARK

ARTIFICIAL SELECTION

The size, color, and shape of animals such as horses, dogs, and cats can be modified artificially through selective breeding. Breeders choose individuals with the desired qualities and reject the rest.

Sphynx is bred to be hairless

SPHYNX CAT

Human evolution

Apes are humans' closest relatives. Apes and humans together are known as hominoids. Humans and their direct ancestors are called hominids. The earliest hominid fossils are from about 4 million years ago. One such fossil, found in Ethiopia, is called "Lucy." She had a small brain but walked upright. The most recent hominids belong to the group *Homo* and appeared about two million years ago. These include *Homo habilis*, who used tools.

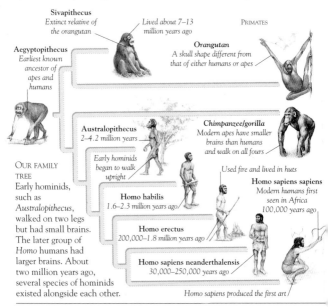

Sivapithecus
Extinct relative of the orangutan

Lived about 7–13 million years ago

Primates

Aegyptopithecus
Earliest known ancestor of apes and humans

Orangutan
A skull shape different from that of either humans or apes

Australopithecus
2–4.2 million years

Early hominids began to walk upright

Chimpanzee/gorilla
Modern apes have smaller brains than humans and walk on all fours

Our family tree
Early hominids, such as *Australopithecus*, walked on two legs but had small brains. The later group of *Homo* humans had larger brains. About two million years ago, several species of hominids existed alongside each other.

Used fire and lived in huts

Homo habilis
1.6–2.3 million years ago

Homo erectus
200,000–1.8 million years ago

Homo sapiens neanderthalensis
30,000–250,000 years ago

Homo sapiens sapiens
Modern humans first seen in Africa 100,000 years ago

Homo sapiens produced the first art

SKELETON SHAPES
Gorillas walk on their feet and hands. The human skeleton is adapted for upright walking. It has a forward-pointing big toe, whereas the gorilla's toe is angled for grasping. Human hip bones are smaller to make striding easier.

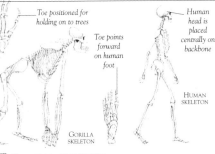

Toe positioned for holding on to trees

Toe points forward on human foot

Human head is placed centrally on backbone

HUMAN SKELETON

GORILLA SKELETON

FIRST HUMAN FOOTPRINTS
Mary Leakey, a British fossil expert, unearthed these fossilized footprints in Africa in 1977. They were left by three hominids in volcanic ash nearly 4 million years ago.

Apes evolved 30 million years ago

Hominids appeared only around 4 million years ago

Earth was formed 4.6 billion years ago

Dinosaurs lived 200 million years ago

Reptiles appear

Land plants emerge

If you imagine Earth's history in one hour, then humans appear just before the hour strikes

Plant life in the oceans began 1.5 billion years ago

Bacteria appeared 3.8 billion years ago

ARRIVAL TIMES OF HUMANS

Humans originated in Africa, but spread to many other regions much more recently.

REGION	APPROXIMATE ARRIVAL TIME
Australia	At least 50,000 years ago
North America	At least 15,000 years ago
Madagascar	2,000 years ago
New Zealand	1,000 years ago
Antarctica	150 years ago

EVOLUTIONARY CLOCK
Scientists believe simple life forms first appeared on Earth 3.8 billion years ago. It was not until about 4 million years ago that the first hominids appeared.

MICROSCOPIC LIFE

THERE ARE MANY kinds of life that are so tiny they are invisible except through a microscope. These include billions of bacteria and viruses, some of which live in the human body. Another group of small organisms, called protists, also consist of just a single cell.

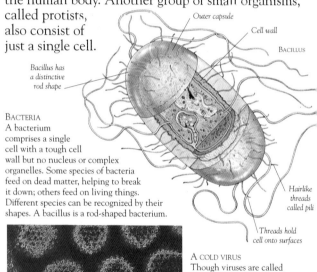

Outer capsule

Cell wall

BACILLUS

Bacillus has a distinctive rod shape

BACTERIA
A bacterium comprises a single cell with a tough cell wall but no nucleus or complex organelles. Some species of bacteria feed on dead matter, helping to break it down; others feed on living things. Different species can be recognized by their shapes. A bacillus is a rod-shaped bacterium.

Hairlike threads called pili

Threads hold cell onto surfaces

A COLD VIRUS
Though viruses are called microorganisms, they are not strictly living things because they cannot reproduce without the help of living cells. In animals, viruses can cause colds and flu or diseases such as AIDS.

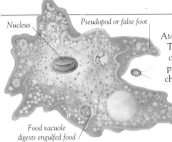

Nucleus

Pseudopod or false foot

Food vacuole digests engulfed food

AMOEBA

The jellylike amoeba belongs to a group of single-celled organisms known as protists. Amoebas move by constantly changing shape. They take in food by surrounding and engulfing it. Food is stored and digested in a structure called a food vacuole.

CELLS

ANIMAL CELL

The flexible skin around an animal cell allows some chemicals into the cell but not others. The cell is controlled by the nucleus. In the fluid around the nucleus, called cytoplasm, lie tiny organelles that perform specific tasks.

Plasma membrane

Cytoplasm

Nucleus – the cell's command center

Energy-producing organelle

Chloroplasts trap the energy in sunlight

Plasma membrane

Cell wall

Vacuole used to store cell sap

Nucleus

PLANT CELL

A plant cell differs from an animal cell in two important ways. It has an additional rigid cell wall as well as a plasma membrane around it and it contains green organelles called chloroplasts.

Slug forms into fruiting body

Fruiting body releases spores

Spores germinate

Amoeba grows from spore

Amoebas come together into slug

Slug migrates

LIFE OF A SLIME MOLD

A slime mold reproduces in an unusual way. First, slime mold amoebas gather together to form a mass called a slug. The slug moves toward the light. Eventually, it forms a tall, fruiting body that releases spores. The spores produce new amoebas.

FUNGI AND LICHENS

FUNGI ARE NEITHER plants nor animals but members of a separate kingdom that includes mushrooms, molds, and yeasts. Many fungi exist as tiny threads that form large fruiting bodies. Lichens are living partnerships between fungi and algae.

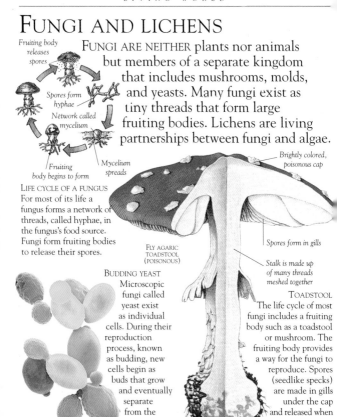

Fruiting body releases spores

Spores form hyphae

Network called mycelium

Fruiting body begins to form

Mycelium spreads

LIFE CYCLE OF A FUNGUS
For most of its life a fungus forms a network of threads, called hyphae, in the fungus's food source. Fungi form fruiting bodies to release their spores.

FLY AGARIC TOADSTOOL (POISONOUS)

Brightly colored, poisonous cap

Spores form in gills

Stalk is made up of many threads meshed together

BUDDING YEAST
Microscopic fungi called yeast exist as individual cells. During their reproduction process, known as budding, new cells begin as buds that grow and eventually separate from the parent cell.

TOADSTOOL
The life cycle of most fungi includes a fruiting body such as a toadstool or mushroom. The fruiting body provides a way for the fungi to reproduce. Spores (seedlike specks) are made in gills under the cap and released when conditions are right.

PUFFBALL

A puffball fungus starts out as a solid head of cells. Gradually, the cells dry out and form a papery bag. When drops of rain or an animal brush the bag, a cloud of spores is released into the air. The spores are very light and can be carried long distances.

The fruiting body of the puffball puffs out spores

FUNGI FACTS

• The fungus *Penicillium notatum* produces the well-known antibiotic drug, penicillin.

• A giant puffball can release seven trillion spores in its life.

• The seeds of many orchids will not germinate without the presence of a fungus.

TYPES OF LICHENS

A lichen is not a plant, but a partnership between a fungus and an alga that exists as one organism. Lichens grow on rocks and tree trunks. The fungus dissolves substances that the alga uses; and the alga supplies the fungus with food made by photosynthesis. Lichens grow in five forms, of which three – leafy (foliose), crusty and flat (crustose), and mixed (squamulose) are shown here.

Leafy type of lichen

Tree bark

Lichens will eventually dissolve minerals from the rock

Spore-producing body

CLADONIA FLOERKEANA

HYPOGYMNIA PHYSODES

Flat and crusty lichens

CALOPLACA HEPPIANA

Mixture of shrubby and leafy lichen

ALGAE AND SIMPLE PLANTS

PLANTS EVOLVED FROM GREEN ALGAE, which consist of either one cell or many cells. Algae do not have true roots or leaves, and also lack flowers. Liverworts and mosses were some of the earliest plants on Earth. They grow in damp, shady places. Ferns and horsetails were among the first plants to develop water-carrying systems. They are known as vascular plants.

EXAMPLES OF ALGAE

New colonies growing

Adult colony

VOLVOX
Volvox is a freshwater alga. It consists of many cells and is often found in ponds.

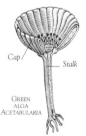

Cap

Stalk

GREEN ALGA ACETABULARIA

ACETABULARIA
This is a single-celled, cup-shaped alga found in shallow seawater.

SEAWEEDS
A seaweed is a plant-like marine alga made of many cells. It usually anchors itself to the seabed near the shore, and its leaflike fronds trap the energy in sunlight.

Kelp is a brown seaweed

Bladder wrack has air bladders to make it float on the surface

Sugar kelp has fronds – long, leaflike flaps

Carrageenan

Dulse is a red seaweed

Liverworts grow close to the ground

LIVERWORT

Liverworts usually grow in damp areas where there is shade. Like mosses, liverworts are bryophytes, a group of simple plants that have no real stems, leaves, or roots. Liverworts are flat, ribbonlike plants. Their life cycle, like that of ferns, has two stages.

Moss grows on rotting wood

MOSSY LOG

Other simple plants, mosses, live mostly in damp places. Mosses do not have true roots but only threadlike rhizoids. Mosses are also nonvascular, meaning that they lack a system for carrying water.

LIFE CYCLE OF A FERN

The life cycle of a fern has two different stages. During the first stage, a leafy plant (the sporophyte) creates spores. These produce the small, heart-shaped second stage (the gametophyte). This makes male and female cells that fuse, forming a new sporophyte.

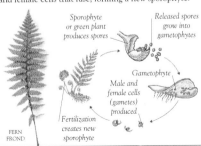

Sporophyte or green plant produces spores

Released spores grow into gametophytes

Gametophyte

Male and female cells (gametes) produced

Fertilization creates new sporophyte

FERN FROND

Side branches in circles from the stem

HORSETAIL

Common in damp places, horsetails are an ancient, brushlike plant. They spread by spores and have creeping underground stems.

407

CONIFERS

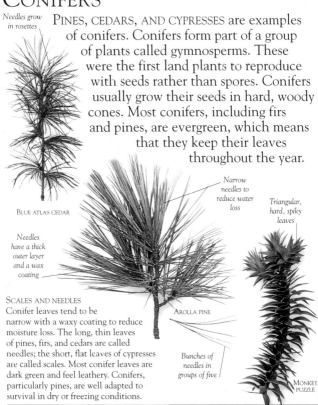

Needles grow in rosettes

PINES, CEDARS, AND CYPRESSES are examples of conifers. Conifers form part of a group of plants called gymnosperms. These were the first land plants to reproduce with seeds rather than spores. Conifers usually grow their seeds in hard, woody cones. Most conifers, including firs and pines, are evergreen, which means that they keep their leaves throughout the year.

BLUE ATLAS CEDAR

Narrow needles to reduce water loss

Triangular, hard, spiky leaves

Needles have a thick outer layer and a wax coating

AROLLA PINE

SCALES AND NEEDLES
Conifer leaves tend to be narrow with a waxy coating to reduce moisture loss. The long, thin leaves of pines, firs, and cedars are called needles; the short, flat leaves of cypresses are called scales. Most conifer leaves are dark green and feel leathery. Conifers, particularly pines, are well adapted to survival in dry or freezing conditions.

Bunches of needles in groups of five

MONKEY PUZZLE

LIFE CYCLE OF A CONIFER
A conifer grows male and female cones. Pollen from male cones fertilizes female cones that later form seeds.

Mature cones release seeds

Female and male cones grow separately

Male cone releases pollen to fertilize female

Seeds in cone

Mature female cone sits upright on tree

CEDAR CONES

Cones break up over a few months

TALLEST AND HEAVIEST TREES

TALLEST TREE
Coast redwoods are the world's tallest trees, reaching 364 ft (111 m).

HEAVIEST TREE
Another redwood, the giant sequoia, is the world's heaviest tree.

CEDAR CONE
The seed scales inside the mature cedar cone peel away and the cone disintegrates while still on the tree.

SCOTS PINE CONE
The mature female cone of the Scots pine opens; and the seeds flutter away into the air.

AMBER
Some conifers produce resin to protect themselves from insects, which get trapped in the sticky sap. Prehistoric insects have been preserved in fossilized resin, called amber.

FLOWERING PLANTS

THE MOST SUCCESSFUL PLANTS on Earth are the flowering plants. They can survive in many kinds of habitats, from mountainsides to deserts. There are more than 250,000 species of flowering plants and nearly all produce food by a process called photosynthesis. Most of these plants have green leaves and live in soil.

Leaves reduced to spines

Flowers form distinctive, five-petal shape

CACTUS FAMILY
Cactus family (Cactaceae) plants live in dry places. They have no leaves and store water in their stems.

PEA FAMILY
The pea family (Leguminosae) includes the food plants, beans and peas. The flowers have five petals and produce a fruit known as a legume. The legume holds one or more seeds.

FLOWERING PLANT FACTS
• The Tallipot palm *Corypha umbraculifera* takes about 100 years to flower and then dies.

• Potatoes, peppers, and tomatoes are members of the nightshade family, which includes many poisonous plants.

GRASS FAMILY
The most widespread flowering plants are grasses (Gramineae). Many are grown for their seeds (grain), such as wheat, rice, corn, and oats.

Flowers have five petals

Thorns grow on stems

ROSE FAMILY
In the rose family, (Rosaceae) many plants, such as roses, apples, cherries, and strawberries, are cultivated. Some rose family species are trees or shrubs. The flowers usually have four or five petals and many stamens at the center.

BEECH FAMILY
The beech family (Fagaceae) includes trees such as sweet chestnuts, oaks, and beeches. Their fruits are nuts and their flowers are frequently catkins. In the northern hemisphere beech trees are used as a source of timber.

Many pollen-producing stamens

Adapted flowers attract animals

ORCHID FAMILY
The second-largest family of flowering plants is the orchid family (Orchidaceae). Their specialized flowers attract animal pollinators. Orchids rely on a special relationship with fungi to grow.

LARGEST FAMILIES OF FLOWERING PLANTS		
SCIENTIFIC NAME	COMMON NAME	NUMBER OF SPECIES
Compositae	Daisy family	25,000
Orchidaceae	Orchid family	18,000
Leguminosae	Pea family	17,000
Gramineae	Grass family	9,000
Rubiaceae	Coffee family	7,000
Euphorbiaceae	Spurge family	5,000
Cyperaceae	Rush family	4,000

Plants and leaves

A plant's stem supports its buds, leaves, and flowers. Inside the stem are cells that carry water, minerals, and food to different parts of the plant. Roots anchor the plant and absorb water and minerals from the soil. Leaves use the Sun's energy to make food.

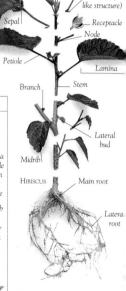

Stigma · Petal · Flower bud
Stamen
Bract (leaf-like structure)
Sepal · Receptacle
Node
Petiole
Lamina
Branch · Stem
Lateral bud
Midrib
HIBISCUS · Main root
Lateral root

LEAVES

LEAF SHAPES

A simple leaf has a single blade (lamina), but a compound leaf is divided into separate leaflets. In a bipinnate compound leaf, the leaflets are divided.

SIMPLE LEAF · Apex
Leaf vein
Lamina or blade – from apex to base
Midrib
Base
Petiole or leaf stalk

BIPINNATE

PINNATE

LINEAR

PALMATE

BITERNATE

PLANT ANATOMY

The visible part of the plant is the shoot. It consists of a stem supporting buds (undeveloped shoots), leaves, and flowers. The shoot grows toward the light. Roots fix the plant to the ground and collect water.

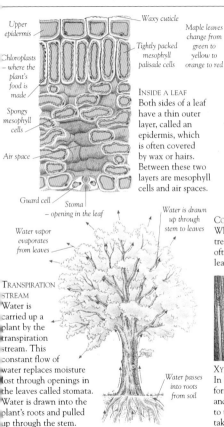

Upper epidermis

Waxy cuticle

Tightly packed mesophyll palisade cells

Chloroplasts – where the plant's food is made

Spongy mesophyll cells

Air space

Guard cell

Stoma – opening in the leaf

INSIDE A LEAF
Both sides of a leaf have a thin outer layer, called an epidermis, which is often covered by wax or hairs. Between these two layers are mesophyll cells and air spaces.

Maple leaves change from green to yellow to orange to red

COLORFUL LEAVES
When leaves of deciduous trees die, chemical changes often occur, turning the leaves bright colors.

Water is drawn up through stem to leaves

Water vapor evaporates from leaves

TRANSPIRATION STREAM
Water is carried up a plant by the transpiration stream. This constant flow of water replaces moisture lost through openings in the leaves called stomata. Water is drawn into the plant's roots and pulled up through the stem.

Water passes into roots from soil

XYLEM AND PHLOEM
In the stem, xylem cells form tubes that carry water and minerals from the roots to the leaves. Phloem cells take food to all parts.

PHOTOSYNTHESIS

PLANTS MAKE THEIR FOOD by a process known as photosynthesis. It requires sunlight, water, and carbon dioxide. Photosynthesis is carried out mostly in the leaves, where the pigment that gives leaves their green color, called chlorophyll, is stored. Oxygen is released during this process.

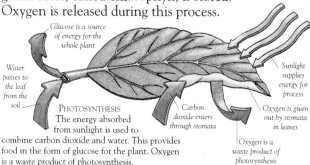

Glucose is a source of energy for the whole plant

Water passes to the leaf from the soil

PHOTOSYNTHESIS
The energy absorbed from sunlight is used to combine carbon dioxide and water. This provides food in the form of glucose for the plant. Oxygen is a waste product of photosynthesis.

Carbon dioxide enters through stomata

Sunlight supplies energy for process

Oxygen is given out by stomata in leaves

Oxygen is a waste product of photosynthesis

PHOTOSYNTHESIS FACTS

• If photosynthesis stopped, almost all life on Earth would cease.

• Each year, plants make about 110 billion tons of glucose by harnessing the light of the Sun.

• Earth's atmosphere would contain no oxygen without photosynthesis.

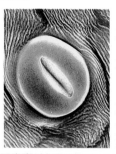

STOMATA
On the underside of leaves are microscopic pores called stomata. These openings allow the gases carbon dioxide and oxygen to pass into and out of the leaf. Guard cells are situated on either side of each pore and control its opening and closing.

INSIDE A CHLOROPLAST
Photosynthesis takes
place in structures
called chloroplasts.
These are inside
plant cells, mostly
in the leaves.
They contain
chlorophyll, a green
pigment that absorbs
energy from sunlight.

CHLOROPLAST

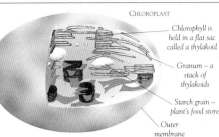

*Chlorophyll is
held in a flat sac
called a thylakoid*

*Granum – a
stack of
thylakoids*

*Starch grain –
plant's food store*

*Outer
membrane*

*Daytime: plant
gives out more
oxygen than it uses*

*Twilight: plant
releases equal
amounts of gases*

*Nighttime: plant
releases more
carbon dioxide*

CHLOROPHYLL
When sunlight reaches a
plant, red and blue light is
absorbed and green light is
reflected, making the plant
appear green. The pigment
chlorophyll, in chloroplasts,
reflects the green color.

PHOTOSYNTHESIS AND RESPIRATION
During the day, plants make food by
photosynthesis. They take in carbon dioxide
and release oxygen. At night, photosynthesis
stops and plants respire. They break
down food, taking in oxygen and
releasing carbon dioxide.

*Enzymes inside
leaf digest insects*

VENUS FLY
TRAP

*Trap sealed with
interlocking
spines*

*Lobes of trap formed
from modified leaves*

VENUS FLY TRAP
Some plants living in acid, boggy
soils make food by photosynthesis
but get some nutrients from animals.
The Venus fly trap has a spring-trap
mechanism that allows it to catch insects.

*Insects nudge
trigger hairs on the
edge of the trap*

PLANT GROWTH

WHEN A PLANT BEGINS TO GROW, its shoot reaches up so its leaves can absorb sunlight, and its roots grow down to absorb water and nutrients from the soil. Once a plant is mature, it reproduces by flowering or in other ways. Many plants store food for the next growing season.

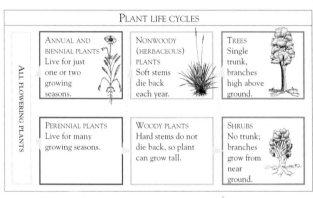

PLANT LIFE CYCLES

ALL FLOWERING PLANTS

ANNUAL AND BIENNIAL PLANTS Live for just one or two growing seasons.

NONWOODY (HERBACEOUS) PLANTS Soft stems die back each year.

TREES Single trunk, branches high above ground.

PERENNIAL PLANTS Live for many growing seasons.

WOODY PLANTS Hard stems do not die back, so plant can grow tall.

SHRUBS No trunk; branches grow from near ground.

Seed provides food for young plant

Roots

Leaves begin to photosynthesize

Shoot

Seedling's leaves now make food to fuel growth

1 GERMINATION
Once the seed coat (testa) has split and the roots have begun to grow down, the first shoot reaches up toward the light.

2 GROWING
Growth takes place at the tips of the seedling's roots and shoot. The shoot reaches upward.

3 SEEDLING
Leaves provide the plant with fuel by photosynthesis. Roots take in nutrients and water from the soil.

REPRODUCING WITHOUT SEEDS

Many plants, including this strawberry, can reproduce without making seeds. To do this, they grow parts that can take root and grow. This is asexual reproduction, because only one parent is involved.

Parent plant reproduces in two ways – it also makes seeds

New plant begins to grow in different place

Parent plant sends out runners over the ground

STORAGE SYSTEMS

SWEET POTATO

Plants such as the sweet potato store food from one growing season to the next. The food is held in a swollen underground root called a tuber.

GRAPE HYACINTH

The bulb produced by plants such as the grape hyacinth is another type of storage system. Food is stored in layers of fleshy scales packed into the bulb.

A bulb is a type of short underground stem

HOW TREES GROW

TREE RINGS

Wood is a strong material that supports trees and shrubs. It consists of layers of xylem cells toughened with a substance called lignin. Each growing season a new ring of xylem is added.

Young tree has smooth bark

Cracked bark of mature tree

BARK

The layer on the outside of a woody plant's stem is known as bark. The outer layer of bark is dead, but under this there are living phloem cells. Tiny pores in the bark, called lenticels, allow gases to pass through.

FLOWERS

FLOWERS ALLOW A PLANT to be pollinated and then to
form seeds. Flowers consist of male and female organs
surrounded by petals that may be colored and scented
to attract visiting animals.
The male parts of a flower
(stamens) make pollen;
the female parts (carpels)
make cells that form seeds.

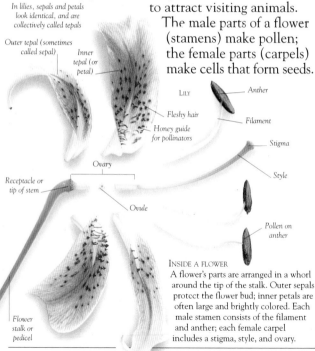

*In lilies, sepals and petals
look identical, and are
collectively called tepals*

*Outer tepal (sometimes
called sepal)*

*Inner
tepal (or
petal)*

LILY

Anther

Fleshy hair

*Honey guide
for pollinators*

Filament

Stigma

Style

Ovary

*Receptacle or
tip of stem*

Ovule

Pollen on
anther

*Flower
stalk or
pedicel*

INSIDE A FLOWER

A flower's parts are arranged in a whorl
around the tip of the stalk. Outer sepals
protect the flower bud; inner petals are
often large and brightly colored. Each
male stamen consists of the filament
and anther; each female carpel
includes a stigma, style, and ovary.

GIANT FLOWER
The giant rafflesia (*Rafflesia arnoldii*) is the world's largest flower. It can grow up to 3.5 ft (105 cm) across and weigh up to 15.4 lb (7 kg). It is at risk from the destruction of its habitat in the rain forests of Sumatra.

CAPITULUM

UMBEL

SPIKE

RACEME

INFLORESCENCE
Inflorescences are groups of flowers arranged on a single stem. Sunflowers and their relatives form a capitulum, which contains many flowers but looks like one flower. A spike consists of stalkless flowers on a straight stem; a raceme has flowers with stalks. An umbel is umbrella-shaped.

ENDANGERED FLOWERING PLANTS		
Of the 250,000 or so species identified, about six percent are endangered. Plants are at risk from overcollection or destruction of their habitat. This is a selection of key endangered species.		
CONTINENT	SPECIES	THREATENED BY
North America	Saguaro cactus (*Carnegia gigantea*)	Overcollection
South America	Chilean wine palm (*Juba chilensis*)	Land clearance
Africa	African violet (*Saintpaulia ionantha*)	Forest clearance
Asia	Orchid (*Paphiopedilum rothschildianum*)	Overcollection
Europe	Madonna lily (*Lilium candidum*)	Overcollection
Australia	Lobster claw (*Clianthus puniceus*)	Grazing by livestock

POLLINATION

POLLINATION INSURES that a plant
can develop seeds and reproduce.
The process can be carried out
by animals, usually insects, or
by the wind or water. Pollen is
transferred from the male part
of one flower to the female
part of another. Both flowers
must be of the same species.

SUNFLOWER UNDER
ULTRAVIOLET LIGHT

*Outer petals
look pale*

ANIMAL POLLINATION

When an insect, such as a bee, visits a flower,
pollen from the flower's anthers is brushed onto it.
The bee collects nectar and pollen to take to the
hive, and may visit other flowers of the same species,
transferring
pollen grains
between
flowers as
it feeds.

ATTRACTING INSECTS

Seen under ultraviolet light, the
center of this sunflower looks
dark and the petals look pale.
Honeybees see this contrast,
and are attracted to the nectar-
rich, dark center of the flower.

BUMBLEBEE ON
A DOG ROSE

*Pollen is
stored in
sacs on the
bee's legs*

*Bee collects
nectar from inside
the flower*

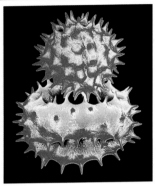

WIND POLLINATION
The flowers of wind-pollinated plants are often small and dull. When the flowers are mature, their dry, dusty pollen is scattered by the wind to other flowers. Many grasses, in particular, are wind-pollinated.

SWEET CHESTNUT (MALE)

Filament

Anther

Hanging flowers are called catkins

POLLEN GRAINS
The pollen grains above are enlarged many times. Unmagnified, they look like particles of yellow dust. Pollen is produced by the anthers of a flower. It contains the male sex cells.

Sticky pollen grains attach themselves to feathers

HUMMINGBIRD FROM THE AMAZON RAINFOREST

HUMMINGBIRD
Some flowers are pollinated by birds or bats. A hummingbird drinks nectar from inside a flower and picks up pollen grains on its feathers. It then carries this pollen to other flowers.

POLLINATION FACTS
• The smallest pollen grains are only 0.0008 in (0.02 mm) across.

• Ribbonweed, a water plant, has pollen that floats in "boats" to female flowers.

• A species of orchid in Madagascar is pollinated by a moth with a tongue 1 ft (30 cm) long.

FERTILIZATION AND FRUITS

Pollen grain

Pollen tube

AFTER A FLOWER IS POLLINATED, male and female cells join to produce seeds. To do this, nuclei from pollen grains travel down special tubes to the female ovules, and fertilization takes place. The plant's ovaries then expand around the developing seeds, forming fruits.

Ovule

Ovum (female sex cell)

FERTILIZATION
Fertilization occurs after a pollen grain containing male cells reaches a flower's stigma. A tube grows down from the grain to the ovule. Male nuclei travel along the tube to join a female cell.

SEED FACTS

• The coco-de-mer palm *Laodicea maldivica* has the largest seeds. Each fruit weighs up to 44 lb (20 kg) and has one seed.

• Orchids have the smallest seeds. A billion can weigh 0.035 oz (1 g).

DEVELOPMENT OF A SUCCULENT FRUIT

FLOWER BLOOMS
A flower in full bloom attracts pollinators by its fragrance and color.

Stamen

Ovary

OVARY SWELLING
Stamens wither and the ovaries enlarge as ovules develop into seeds.

Ovary

MATURING FRUIT
Ovaries grow and their walls become fleshy. They begin to change color.

Drupelet

RIPE FRUIT
The ovaries darken as they become ripe. Each contains a single seed.

LEMON
A lemon is a succulent fruit. It is brightly colored to attract animals to eat it and disperse its seeds.

FIG
The fig is a false fruit. Its flesh surrounds tiny internal flowers that form seeds.

SEED DISPLAY

SEED DISPERSAL

LESSER BURDOCK
This fruit of the lesser burdock has a coat covered in hooked burrs. The hooks fasten onto the fur of passing animals and are dispersed in this way.

SYCAMORE
The dry fruit of the sycamore has become flat and elongated. It forms a double wing shape that allows the seed to be carried by the wind.

Seed

Fruit flattened into wings

Remains of the flower

PEA
A pea pod is a type of dry fruit called a legume. It splits along two sides to release its seeds.

CHESTNUT
Nuts, a dry fruit with a hard wall around the seed, are "indehiscent." This means they do not split open to release the seeds.

STRAWBERRY
A strawberry is a swollen flower base studded with achenes (hard, one-seeded fruits).

HONESTY
This "dehiscent" dry fruit has a fruit wall that splits so that the seeds can be carried by the wind.

SIMPLE INVERTEBRATES

AN ANIMAL WITHOUT a backbone is known as an invertebrate. Invertebrates make up over 95 percent of all animal species. Some are simple, microscopic creatures; others larger and more complex.

Digestive cavity in the middle of the bell

Plankton trapped in mucus

JELLYFISH

A jellyfish moves by contracting its bell-shaped body. It has trailing tentacles that pull food into the digestive cavity, which is in the middle of the jellyfish.

Adult jellyfish

Fleshy arms collect food

The ephyrae break free

Polyp splits into eight-armed buds called ephyrae

Small polyps form

LIFE CYCLE OF A JELLYFISH

Adult jellyfish release fertilized larvae that rest on the seabed. The larvae grow into small polyps that divide into buds and swim away as tiny adults.

MUSHROOM CORAL
FUNGIA

CORAL

A coral is a polyp with a cylindrical shape. Most corals live together in colonies. Corals may build hard cases of calcium carbonate which form coral reefs when they die.

TYPES OF SIMPLE INVERTEBRATES

There are more than a million known species of invertebrates divided into 30 phyla (types). These are two of the simplest.

INVERTEBRATE	NAME OF PHYLUM	FEATURES	NUMBER OF SPECIES
	Poriferans (sponges)	Simple animals that filter food from water	9,000
	Cnidarians (sea anemones, corals, jellyfish)	Simple animals with stinging threads	9,500

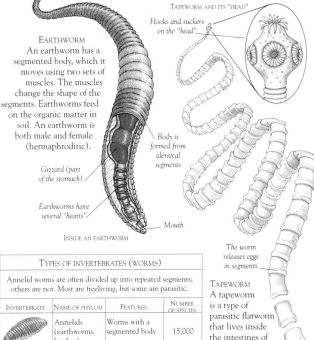

EARTHWORM

An earthworm has a segmented body, which it moves using two sets of muscles. The muscles change the shape of the segments. Earthworms feed on the organic matter in soil. An earthworm is both male and female (hermaphroditic).

Gizzard (part of the stomach)

Earthworms have several "hearts"

Body is formed from identical segments

Mouth

INSIDE AN EARTHWORM

TAPEWORM AND ITS "HEAD"

Hooks and suckers on the "head"

The worm releases eggs in segments

TAPEWORM

A tapeworm is a type of parasitic flatworm that lives inside the intestines of animals such as pigs, cats, or even humans. The worm's "head" has hooks and suckers that grasp the intestines. Food is absorbed from the host animal's gut.

TYPES OF INVERTEBRATES (WORMS)

Annelid worms are often divided up into repeated segments; others are not. Most are freeliving, but some are parasitic.

INVERTEBRATE	NAME OF PHYLUM	FEATURES	NUMBER OF SPECIES
	Annelids (earthworms, leeches)	Worms with a segmented body	15,000
	Platyhelminthes (flatworms, flukes, tapeworms)	Worms with a simple, flattened body	20,000
	Nematodes (roundworms)	Worms with an unsegmented, cylindrical body	20,000

MOLLUSKS AND ECHINODERMS

THE SOFT BODY of a mollusk is usually covered by a hard shell. Mollusks include gastropods (such as snails), bivalves (such as oysters), and cephalopods (such as squids). Echinoderms have a five-part body and live in the sea.

Reproductive organ

Mantle

Mucus gland

Eye

INSIDE A SNAIL
A snail's body has three parts: the head, the muscular foot, and the body, which is covered by a mantle of skin and contains the main organs.

Muscular foot

Lung

Sensory tentacle

Mollusk sinks to a suitable spot on the seabed

Egg hatches into freeswimming larvae

Sperm cells fertilize egg cells outside the adult's body

This is the veliger larvae stage

Shell forms

LIFE CYCLE OF AN OYSTER
Mollusks usually lay eggs that hatch into larvae. As a larva grows, its shell develops. The young adult then settles on the seabed. Some snails hatch out as miniature adults.

TYPES OF MOLLUSKS			
There are more than 50,000 species of mollusk. These are divided into seven classes. Five are listed below.			
MOLLUSK	NAME OF CLASS	FEATURES	NUMBER OF SPECIES
	Bivalves (clams and relatives)	Shells in two parts, which hinge together	8,000
	Polyplacophorans (chitons)	Shell made of several plates	600
	Gastropods (slugs, snails, and relatives)	Mollusks with a muscular sucker-like foot	40,000
	Scaphopods (tusk shells)	Mollusks with tapering tubular shells	350
	Cephalopods (octopus, squid, cuttlefish)	Mollusks with a head and ring of tentacles	650

CUBAN LAND SNAILS

MOLLUSK SHELLS
Mollusk shells have a huge variety of colors and shapes. They are formed from calcium carbonate, which is secreted by the mantle. Bivalves have a two-part shell with a hinge.

SCALLOP

TRITON

PACIFIC THORNY OYSTER

A sea star can grow a new arm to replace a damaged limb

SCARLET SEA STAR

SEA STARS
A sea star is a typical echinoderm. It has a spiny-skinned body with five equal parts, tiny sucker feet, and an internal skeleton made from hard plates called ossicles. It lives in the sea. Sea stars pry open the shells of bivalves to eat the soft meat inside.

TYPES OF ECHINODERMS

Echinoderms are a distinctive group of invertebrates that live in the sea. There are 7,000 species in six classes (four listed here).

ECHINODERM	NAME OF CLASS	FEATURES	NUMBER OF SPECIES
	Asteroids (sea stars)	Central mouth surrounded by arms	1,500
	Echinoids (sea urchins)	Body surrounded by a case bearing spines	1,000
	Crinoids (feather stars)	Mouth surrounded by feathery arms	625
	Holothuroidea (sea cucumbers)	Wormlike body with feeding tentacles	1,150

MOLLUSK FACTS
• The world's most venomous gastropod is the geographer cone in the Pacific Ocean. Its venom can kill a human.

• The largest land snail is the giant African land snail *Achatina achatina*. It can grow up to 15.4 in (39 cm) from head to tail.

ARTHROPODS

ARACHNIDS, CRUSTACEANS, and insects are part of the arthropod group of invertebrates. Insects are by far the largest of these three groups. All arthropods have a jointed body with a tough body case. The case is shed as the animal grows.

The egg is laid in a silk sac to protect it

Spiderlings resemble the adult spider

Spiderling molts

LIFE CYCLE OF A SPIDER
Arachnids such as spiders lay eggs that hatch into tiny versions of adults. They molt several times before they are mature.

IMPERIAL SCORPION

Poison gland
Sting
Heart
Cephalothorax
Pedipalps – a pair of pincers for feeding
Intestine
Abdomen
Spiracle – air hole

INSIDE AN ARACHNID
The body of an arachnid is divided into a front and middle part (cephalothorax) and a rear part (abdomen). Arachnids have four pairs of walking legs.

TYPES OF ARACHNIDS

The class Arachnida includes spiders, mites, and scorpions. It contains 73,000 species, which are grouped into 12 orders. Six orders are listed below.

ARACHNID	NAME OF ORDER	NUMBER OF SPECIES	ARACHNID	NAME OF ORDER	NUMBER OF SPECIES
	Scorpiones (scorpions)	1,200		Uropygi (whip scorpions)	100
	Solifugae (camel spiders)	900		Opiliones (harvestmen)	5,000
	Acari (mites and ticks)	30,000		Araneae (spiders)	35,000

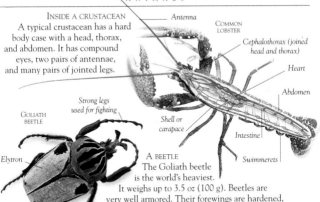

INSIDE A CRUSTACEAN
A typical crustacean has a hard body case with a head, thorax, and abdomen. It has compound eyes, two pairs of antennae, and many pairs of jointed legs.

Antenna

COMMON LOBSTER

Cephalothorax (joined head and thorax)

Heart

Abdomen

GOLIATH BEETLE

Strong legs used for fighting

Shell or carapace

Intestine

Swimmerets

Elytron

A BEETLE
The Goliath beetle is the world's heaviest. It weighs up to 3.5 oz (100 g). Beetles are very well armored. Their forewings are hardened, curved plates called elytra. The elytra protect the fragile hind wings that are used for flying.

TYPES OF CRUSTACEANS

There are more than 50,000 species of crustaceans divided into eight classes. These include the four classes below.

CRUSTACEAN	NAME OF CLASS	FEATURES	NUMBER OF SPECIES
	Branchiopods (fairy shrimp, water fleas)	Small animals of freshwater and salty lakes	1,000
	Cirripedia (barnacles)	Immobile animals with a boxlike case	1,000
	Copepods (cyclopoids and relatives)	Small animals often found in plankton	9,000
	Malacostracans (shrimp, crabs, lobsters)	Many-legged animals, often with pincers	20,000

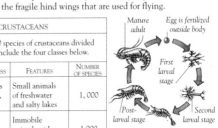

Mature adult

Egg is fertilized outside body

First larval stage

Post-larval stage

Second larval stage

LIFE CYCLE OF A SHRIMP
Crustaceans usually lay their eggs in water. Once hatched, the egg begins its first larval stage. After two more larval stages, there is a final post-larval stage before adulthood.

INSECTS

INSECTS MAKE UP over two-thirds of all the animal
species on Earth. About 1,000,000 species are known,
and many thousands more are discovered each year.
Insects live in almost every habitat on land,
from rain forest to desert. Many live in
fresh water, but hardly any live in the
sea. Most insects can fly, and many
change shape as they mature.

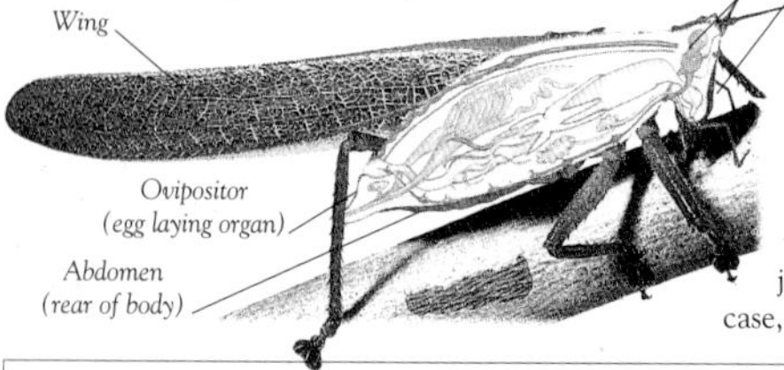

Antenna

KATYDID (FEMALE)

Brain

Mandibles (mouthparts)

Wing

*Ovipositor
(egg laying organ)*

*Abdomen
(rear of body)*

INSIDE
AN INSECT
An insect's body is split
into three parts: the
head, the thorax, and
the abdomen. It has six
jointed legs, a hard body
case, and it usually has wings.

TYPES OF INSECTS

Insects are part of the phylum Arthropoda. There are 1,000,000 known species of insects in the
class Insecta. They are grouped into about 30 orders, six of which are shown below.

INSECT	NAME OF ORDER	NUMBER OF SPECIES	INSECT	NAME OF ORDER	NUMBER OF SPECIES
	Odonata (dragonflies)	5,500	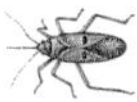	Hemiptera (bugs)	35,000
	Orthoptera (grasshoppers and crickets)	20,000		Coleoptera (beetles)	300,000
	Lepidoptera (butterflies and moths)	120,000		Hymenoptera (ants, bees, and wasps)	125,000

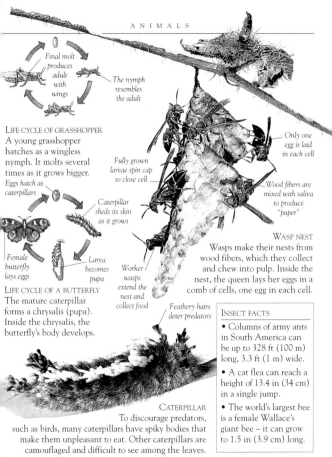

Final molt produces adult with wings

The nymph resembles the adult

LIFE CYCLE OF GRASSHOPPER
A young grasshopper hatches as a wingless nymph. It molts several times as it grows bigger.

Fully grown larvae spin cap to close cell

Only one egg is laid in each cell

Wood fibers are mixed with saliva to produce "paper"

Eggs hatch as caterpillars

Caterpillar sheds its skin as it grows

Female butterfly lays eggs

Larva becomes pupa

Worker wasps extend the nest and collect food

WASP NEST
Wasps make their nests from wood fibers, which they collect and chew into pulp. Inside the nest, the queen lays her eggs in a comb of cells, one egg in each cell.

LIFE CYCLE OF A BUTTERFLY
The mature caterpillar forms a chrysalis (pupa). Inside the chrysalis, the butterfly's body develops.

Feathery hairs deter predators

CATERPILLAR
To discourage predators, such as birds, many caterpillars have spiky bodies that make them unpleasant to eat. Other caterpillars are camouflaged and difficult to see among the leaves.

INSECT FACTS

• Columns of army ants in South America can be up to 328 ft (100 m) long, 3.3 ft (1 m) wide.

• A cat flea can reach a height of 13.4 in (34 cm) in a single jump.

• The world's largest bee is a female Wallace's giant bee – it can grow to 1.5 in (3.9 cm) long.

FISH

WITH MORE THAN 25,000 species, fish are more numerous than all other vertebrates (animals with backbones). Fish are very well suited to life in the water. They have streamlined bodies, and most have slippery scales and a special organ that helps them float. There are three distinct types of fish; bony fish are the most widespread.

INSIDE A FISH
Bony fish have a skeleton made of bone. They swim using their tail and are covered by slimy scales. Fish have gills to absorb oxygen and a gas-filled swim bladder to keep them buoyant.

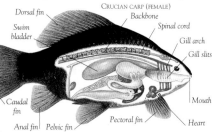

CRUCIAN CARP (FEMALE)

Dorsal fin
Backbone
Swim bladder
Spinal cord
Gill arch
Gill slits
Mouth
Caudal fin
Heart
Pectoral fin
Anal fin
Pelvic fin

Very few eggs survive

Young fish resemble the adult

Trout may take from 8 months to 3 years to mature

LIFE CYCLE OF A TROUT
Some fish give birth to fully formed young but most release eggs, often thousands at a time. The young fish are called fry.

TYPES OF FISH			
There are more than 25,000 species of fish. These are divided into three groups. The largest group is made up of bony fish.			
FISH	NAME OF CLASS	FEATURES	NUMBER OF SPECIES
	Agnatha (jawless fish)	Fish with suckerlike mouths	75
	Chondrichthyes (cartilaginous fish)	Fish with skeletons of cartilage	800
	Osteichthyes (bony fish)	Fish with skeletons of bone	24,000

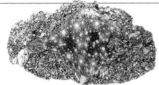

CAMOUFLAGE
Flatfish such as flounder or sole gradually alter their skin color and pattern to blend in with their seabed background.

SEAHORSES
The seahorse is an unusual fish. It swims upright and holds onto weeds with its grasping tail. Females lay their eggs in a pouch on the male's abdomen.

LOACH

UPSIDE-DOWN CATFISH

Mountain lakes and streams
Fish such as loach and salmon can live at altitudes of up to 16,000 ft (4,900 m).

Lakes and rivers
In freshwater lakes and rivers live carp, characins, and catfish.

FISH HABITATS
Fish can live almost anywhere there is water. They have adapted to life in the deepest oceans as well as along the shore and even in underwater caves.

Shoreline
Along the shoreline are fish, such as the mudskipper, that spend some time out of water.

MUDSKIPPER

Coastal waters
Coral reefs in tropical coastal waters are home to many brightly colored fish.

MANDARIN FISH

PACIFIC MANTA RAY

Open ocean
In the open ocean, fish such as rays and skates can grow to a large size. Sharks hunt in this environment.

Caves
Some cave-dwelling fish have no eyes because they spend their lives in darkness.

Deep ocean
The large mouths and expanding stomachs of deep-sea fish trap more of the food available.

BLIND CAVE CHARACIN

GULPER EEL

Middle-ocean depths
With little sunlight reaching these depths and the water cooler, few fish live here.

OARFISH

AMPHIBIANS

AMPHIBIANS WERE THE FIRST GROUP of vertebrates to
move from water to live on land. Most amphibians
spend the early part of their
lives in water. Later,
they grow legs, lose
their gills, and can
live both on land
and in water.

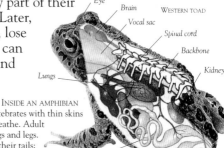

WESTERN TOAD

Eye
Brain
Vocal sac
Spinal cord
Backbone
Kidney
Lungs
Intestine

INSIDE AN AMPHIBIAN

Amphibians are vertebrates with thin skins
through which they breathe. Adult
amphibians have lungs and legs.
Frogs and toads lose their tails;
newts and salamanders do not.

Adult has lungs
and lives on land
and in water

After
three weeks
front legs appear

Back
legs grow

LIFE CYCLE OF A NEWT
Larvae, called tadpoles,
hatch out in water. They
breathe through gills.
After about eight weeks,
the tadpoles develop legs
and their gills disappear.

TYPES OF AMPHIBIANS

There are over 4,000 species of amphibians that make up
the class Amphibia. They are divided into three orders.

AMPHIBIANS	NAME OF ORDER	NUMBER OF SPECIES
	Apoda (caecilians)	200
	Anura (frogs and toads)	3,500
	Urodela (newts and salamanders)	360

AMPHIBIAN FACTS

• Female marine or cane toads lay 30,000 – 35,000 eggs during each spawning.

• A golden poison-arrow frog from Colombia is the most poisonous frog. An adult frog has enough poison to kill 1,000 humans.

AXOLOTL
This unusual Mexican salamander does not mature. It stays in its tadpole stage, breathing through gills and living in water. Axolotls can reproduce in their immature state.

Axolotls keep their feathery red gills

Yellow and black coloration warns predators

SALAMANDER
A tiger salamander, like many salamanders, has brightly patterned skin. This warns predators that it is poisonous. Adult salamanders breathe through their skin.

Skin can ooze poisons

Salamanders have long, slim bodies

Thin skin absorbs oxygen

Mottled colors hide frog

Strong back legs help the frog leap away from danger

ASIAN LEAF FROG
Amphibians have developed many ways to avoid being eaten. The Asian leaf frog has the color and shape of a dead leaf. It blends in perfectly with the debris on the forest floor.

Rough, dry skin

Male wraps eggs around his back legs

MALE MIDWIFE TOAD
Midwife toads mate on land, which is unusual for amphibians. When the female has laid her eggs and they have been fertilized, the male carries the eggs on his back legs for at least a month.

REPTILES

MILLIONS OF YEARS AGO, reptiles dominated the Earth. Some of these reptiles – including dinosaurs – died out, but others are still alive today. Unlike amphibians, reptiles may live entirely on dry land, but they are also cold-blooded, and so need warmth to become active. Most reptiles lay eggs.

Nostril

Brain

INSIDE A REPTILE
Reptiles are vertebrates with scaly skins. Except for snakes and some lizards, most reptiles have four legs. A reptile's skin is tough and waterproof, which helps it to retain water in hot, dry conditions.

Heart

Stomach

Bladder

Kidney

Backbone

EYED LIZARD
(FEMALE)

TYPES OF REPTILES		
There are about 6,500 species of reptiles in the class Reptilia. These are divided into four orders.		
REPTILE	NAME OF ORDER	NUMBER OF SPECIES
	Squamata (lizards and snakes)	6,200
	Crocodilia (crocodilians)	22
	Rhynochocephalia (tuataras)	2
	Chelonia (turtles, tortoises, and terrapins)	270

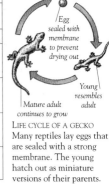

Egg sealed with membrane to prevent drying out

Young resembles adult

Mature adult continues to grow

LIFE CYCLE OF A GECKO
Many reptiles lay eggs that are sealed with a strong membrane. The young hatch out as miniature versions of their parents.

CROCODILES

The ancient Crocodilia order includes crocodiles, alligators, and gavials, which have narrower jaws. Crocodiles spend a lot of time in water and can shut their nostrils when they dive. Despite a vicious appearance (sharp teeth, strong jaws, and a powerful tail), they are careful parents.

Crocodiles carry their young in their mouth

FEMALE
NILE CROCODILE

BOA CONSTRICTOR

Pythons, boa constrictors, and anacondas are snakes that feed mainly on mammals that they kill by constriction. The snake coils around its prey, and as the animal struggles, it squeezes tighter until the animal suffocates. Then the snake swallows it.

The snake opens its special hinged jaws to swallow its victim

KOMODO
DRAGON

Wrinkly, loose-fitting skin

LARGEST LIZARD

The world's largest lizard is a monitor lizard called the Komodo dragon. It can grow up to 10 ft (3 m) long and weigh up to 365 lb (166 kg). There are fewer than 5,000 Komodo dragons left. They live on a few islands in Indonesia, including Komodo Island.

BIRDS

BIRDS ARE THE LARGEST ANIMALS capable of powered flight. Their streamlined bodies are covered with feathers, and many bones are hollow to save weight. Birds live in different habitats, and reproduce by laying hard-shelled eggs. Some species have lost the ability to fly.

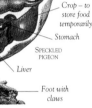

Brain

Backbone

Beak

Crop – to store food temporarily

Stomach

SPECKLED PIGEON

Liver

Foot with claws

Rectum

Tail feathers

INSIDE A BIRD
Birds are warm-blooded vertebrates. Their feathers give them a lightweight, warm covering. They have beaks (or bills) and lay eggs that have hard shells.

TYPES OF BIRDS

About 9,600 species of birds have been discovered. These divide into 27 orders. Perching birds (Passeriformes) make up the largest order (5,712 species). Six other orders are listed here.

BIRD	NAME OF ORDER	NUMBER OF SPECIES	BIRD	NAME OF ORDER	NUMBER OF SPECIES
	Rheiformes (rheas)	2		Anseriformes (waterfowl)	151
	Piciformes (woodpeckers, toucans, barbets)	378		Falconiformes (birds of prey)	292
	Psittaciformes (parrots, lories, cockatoos)	330		Strigiformes (owls)	162

Eggs have hard shells

Chick uses special tooth to escape egg

Bird has adult plumage after six weeks and can then fly

Chick has soft down feathers

LIFE CYCLE OF A MOORHEN

A moorhen's eggs are incubated by both parents. After 21 days, the chicks hatch, using a special tooth to chip their way out. The young can swim and feed a few hours after hatching.

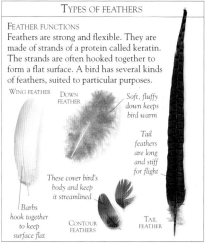

TYPES OF FEATHERS

FEATHER FUNCTIONS

Feathers are strong and flexible. They are made of strands of a protein called keratin. The strands are often hooked together to form a flat surface. A bird has several kinds of feathers, suited to particular purposes.

WING FEATHER

DOWN FEATHER

Soft, fluffy down keeps bird warm

Tail feathers are long and stiff for flight

These cover bird's body and keep it streamlined

Barbs hook together to keep surface flat

CONTOUR FEATHERS

TAIL FEATHER

TYPES OF BEAKS

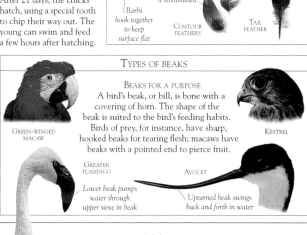

BEAKS FOR A PURPOSE

A bird's beak, or bill, is bone with a covering of horn. The shape of the beak is suited to the bird's feeding habits. Birds of prey, for instance, have sharp, hooked beaks for tearing flesh; macaws have beaks with a pointed end to pierce fruit.

GREEN-WINGED MACAW

KESTREL

GREATER FLAMINGO

AVOCET

Lower beak pumps water through upper sieve in beak

Upturned beak swings back and forth in water

MAMMALS

MAMMALS ARE A VERY DIVERSE GROUP of animals.
They range from tiny shrews to huge rhinos and from
whales that spend their lives in the oceans to bats that
spend time in the air. Mammals can live in nearly all
habitats – jungles, rivers,
and deserts. Humans
belong to this group
of animals.

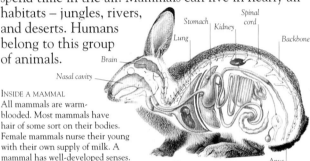

Stomach

Spinal cord

Kidney

Lung

Backbone

Brain

Nasal cavity

INSIDE A MAMMAL
All mammals are warm-
blooded. Most mammals have
hair of some sort on their bodies.
Female mammals nurse their young
with their own supply of milk. A
mammal has well-developed senses.

MALE RABBIT

Anus

TYPES OF MAMMALS					
There are about 4,000 species in the class Mammalia. They are divided into 21 orders. The largest order is the Rodentia, which includes 2,021 species of rodents. Six orders are listed here.					
MAMMAL	NAME OF ORDER	NUMBER OF SPECIES	MAMMAL	NAME OF ORDER	NUMBER OF SPECIES
	Monotremes (egg-laying mammals)	3		Artiodactyla (even-toed, hoofed mammals)	220
	Marsupials (mammals that grow in a pouch)	272		Carnivora (meat-eaters)	237
	Insectivora (insect-eaters)	428		Cetacea (whales and dolphins)	78

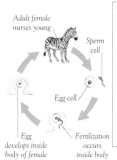

Adult female nurses young

Sperm cell

Egg cell

Egg develops inside body of female

Fertilization occurs inside body

LIFE CYCLE OF A ZEBRA

Sperm cells from the male must join an egg cell in the female for fertilization to take place. This occurs inside the female mammal. Most mammals develop in the womb of their mother and all are fed on her milk.

MARSUPIALS

Wallabies, kangaroos, and koalas are marsupials. Their young are born in a very immature state after a short gestation time. They crawl into the mother's pouch and spend time nursing there while they develop.

INDIAN FRUIT BAT

FLYING MAMMALS

Bats are the only mammals capable of powered flight. A bat flies by flapping a thin membrane of skin stretched between each of its front and back legs. The largest bat may have a wingspan of 6.5 ft (2 m).

Mother squirrel nurses young for first few weeks

SQUIRREL WITH YOUNG

A mammal whose baby develops inside the mother's womb (uterus) is known as a placental mammal. Inside the womb, the babies are protected while they develop and are fed with oxygen and food via the placenta.

Young are well developed at birth and grow rapidly

Baby squirrels can soon find their own food

PRIMATES

THIS GROUP OF MAMMALS includes monkeys, apes, and humans. The primates form the most intelligent group of animals. With forward-facing eyes for judging distances, grasping fingers, and long limbs, primates are ideally suited to life in the trees. Some primates also have prehensile tails that grip onto branches.

PATAS MONKEY

Closely set nostrils of Old World monkey

OLD WORLD MONKEY

Monkeys from the Old World, which includes Europe, Africa, and Asia, have long noses and closely set nostrils. The Patas monkey lives in groups of up to 20 females and one male on the plains, where it eats grass and seeds.

SQUIRREL MONKEY

NEW WORLD MONKEY

New World monkeys live in scrub and forest in Central and South America. Most of these monkeys have flat faces and nostrils set wide apart, and many also have prehensile tails that can wrap around branches like an extra limb. Howler and squirrel monkeys are both New World monkeys.

LORIS

Animals such as lemurs, lorises, and bushbabies are known as prosimians, or primitive primates. They are almost all nocturnal (active at night) and they have excellent eyesight. Most eat leaves, insects, and birds.

Large eyes provide good night vision

Grasping hands cling to branches

GORILLA

The fearsome-looking gorilla is actually a vegetarian. Gorillas walk on their feet and front knuckles and spend most of their time on the ground. Some gorillas live in lowland rainforests and others in the mountains.

ORANGUTAN
Like gorillas, chimpanzees, and gibbons, orangutans are not monkeys but apes. These shy and solitary primates live in the rainforests of Borneo and Sumatra, and spend all their life in the trees.

AVERAGE PRIMATE WEIGHTS		
The 256 species of primate vary in size from the tiny pygmy marmoset to the mighty gorilla and between males and females.		
SPECIES	AVERAGE WEIGHT (FEMALE)	AVERAGE WEIGHT (MALE)
Gorilla	231 lb (105 kg)	452 lb (205 kg)
Human	115 lb (52 kg)	165 lb (75 kg)
Proboscis monkey	20 lb (9 kg)	42 lb (19 kg)
Patas monkey	12 lb (5.5 kg)	22 lb (10 kg)
Pygmy marmoset	4.2 oz (120 g)	5 oz (140 g)

NUTRITION AND DIGESTION

ANIMALS LIVE BY TAKING IN FOOD and breaking it down into simple substances. It fuels their muscles and body processes and provides the raw materials for growth. Herbivores are animals that feed only on plants. Carnivores eat meat, while omnivores eat a variety of foods.

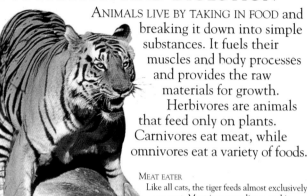

MEAT EATER

Like all cats, the tiger feeds almost exclusively on meat. Meat is easy to digest, and it contains a lot of useful nutrients, so a single meal will last a tiger for several days. However, meat has to be caught and a tiger uses a large amount of energy tracking its prey.

CHEWING THE CUD

Cows feed on grass, which is easy to find but difficult to digest. They break it down with the help of microorganisms in a digestive chamber called the rumen. When the grass is partially broken down, a cow regurgitates it and chews it again – "chewing the cud."

Cows belong to a group of animals called ruminants

Omasum (third stomach chamber)

Rumen (first stomach chamber)

Intestines absorb nutrients and water from digested food

Digestion is completed in abomasum (fourth stomach chamber)

Reticulum (second stomach chamber)

FLUID FEEDERS

Many adult insects survive entirely on liquid food. They include mosquitoes that feed on blood, and aphids and cicadas that feed on plant sap. Butterflies feed mainly on nectar from flowers, using a long drinking tube that coils up when not used.

Sugary nectar is a good source of energy

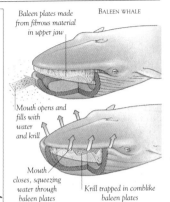

BALEEN WHALE

Baleen plates made from fibrous material in upper jaw

Mouth opens and fills with water and krill

Mouth closes, squeezing water through baleen plates

Krill trapped in comblike baleen plates

FILTER FEEDING

Small animals called krill are abundant in the sea but are difficult to collect in any quantity. Whales filter them from the water using rows of baleen plates.

EGG-EATING SNAKE

Some snakes specialize in a diet of eggs. An African egg-eating snake works its jaws around its food, and swallows it. As the egg travels down the snake's throat, bony spines break it open. It spits out the broken shell.

FEEDING FACTS

• Insects eat unusual foods. Certain moths in Southeast Asia feed on the tears of wild cattle.

• Parasitic tapeworms lack a digestive system. They absorb digested food from their hosts.

• Cold-blooded animals, such as spiders, may live for weeks without food.

TEETH AND JAWS

ANIMALS USE THEIR TEETH to grip their food and to cut or chew it so that it is easier to digest. Teeth, brought together by powerful jaw muscles, are tough enough to withstand pressure without breaking. Human teeth stop growing when they are fully formed, but some animals' teeth – such as those of rodents – grow all their life.

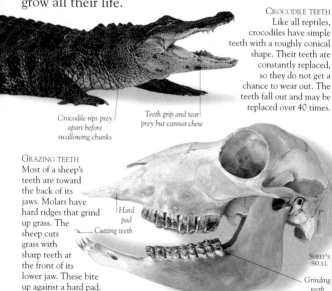

CROCODILE TEETH
Like all reptiles, crocodiles have simple teeth with a roughly conical shape. Their teeth are constantly replaced, so they do not get a chance to wear out. The teeth fall out and may be replaced over 40 times.

Crocodile rips prey apart before swallowing chunks

Teeth grip and tear prey but cannot chew

GRAZING TEETH
Most of a sheep's teeth are toward the back of its jaws. Molars have hard ridges that grind up grass. The sheep cuts grass with sharp teeth at the front of its lower jaw. These bite up against a hard pad.

Hard pad

Cutting teeth

SHEEP'S SKULL

Grinding teeth

THE DENTAL TOOLKIT

A VARIETY OF TEETH
Unlike other animals, mammals have several kinds of teeth that work together. In a dog, incisors and canines grab hold of food. Carnassials slice through it, and molars and premolars chew the food.

DOG'S TEETH

MOLAR CARNASSIAL PREMOLAR INCISOR CANINE

BITING AND CUTTING TEETH
A dog usually has a total of 42 teeth (10 more than an adult human). For dogs, biting is more important than chewing, and most of their teeth have sharp points or edges.

Bony ridge anchors jaw muscles DOG'S SKULL *Molars in angle of jaw*

SPECIALIZED TEETH
Tusks are unusually long teeth that protrude beyond a mammal's jaws. Elephant tusks are specialized incisors, teeth that other mammals use for biting. Elephants use them mainly to dig up food, to strip bark from trees, and for fighting.

Upper part of tusk is solid

Lower part of tusk has a soft pulpy center

ELEPHANT'S TUSKS

TEETH FACTS

• Shark's teeth constantly move to the edge of its jaw. Each one falls out after about two weeks to be replaced by one behind it.

• An adult elephant chews with four huge teeth. The teeth are replaced slowly. This stops when 24 teeth have been replaced.

• Turtles and tortoises are completely toothless.

BREATHING

ALL ANIMALS NEED TO TAKE IN OXYGEN, and at the same time they have to get rid of the waste gas carbon dioxide. Very small animals breathe through the surface of their bodies, but most larger animals breathe with the help of specialized organs, such as gills or lungs.

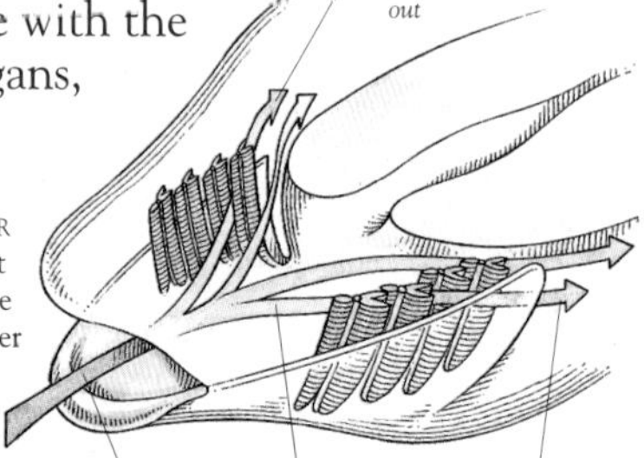

Water flows out

BREATHING IN WATER

A fish's gills are arches that support stacks of thin flaps, which are supplied with blood. When water flows past the flaps, oxygen travels into the blood and carbon dioxide flows into the water.

Water enters through mouth

Water flows past gill flaps

Water leaves through gill flaps

Mudskippers are careful to stay damp

FISH OUT OF WATER

Mudskippers are small fish that live in mangrove swamps. They can survive underwater as well as in air. In the air, they breathe by taking gulps of water to keep some water in their gills. They probably absorb some oxygen through their gills and some through the lining of their mouths.

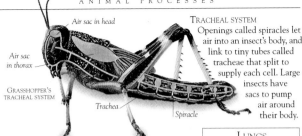

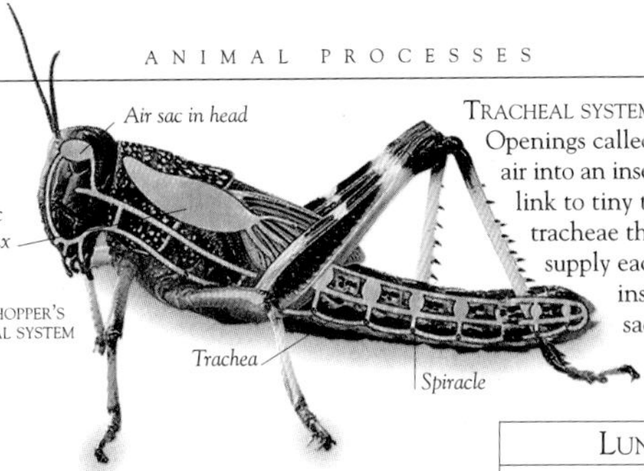
Air sac in head
Air sac in thorax
Trachea
Spiracle

GRASSHOPPER'S TRACHEAL SYSTEM

TRACHEAL SYSTEM

Openings called spiracles let air into an insect's body, and link to tiny tubes called tracheae that split to supply each cell. Large insects have sacs to pump air around their body.

BIRD'S ONE-WAY LUNGS

Birds need a lot of oxygen to fly. They are very efficient at extracting it from the air they breathe. Special air sacs allow air to move straight through their lungs, which ensures they get as much oxygen as possible from the air.

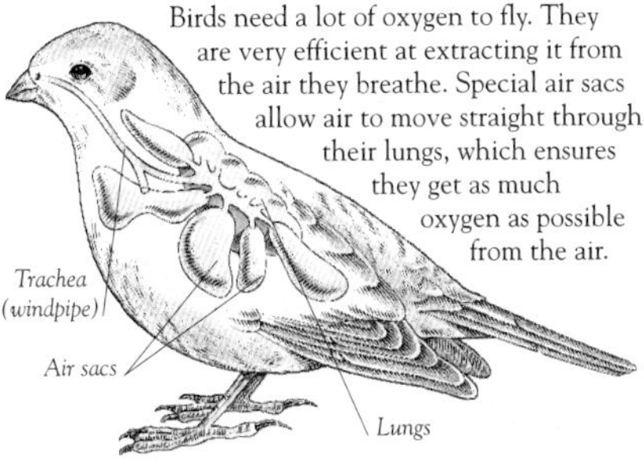
Trachea (windpipe)
Air sacs
Lungs

BIRD'S RESPIRATORY SYSTEM

COMING UP FOR AIR

Like all mammals, whales have lungs and they breathe air. They have a "blowhole" on the top of their head rather than nostrils. Some whales can hold their breath for over an hour when they dive.

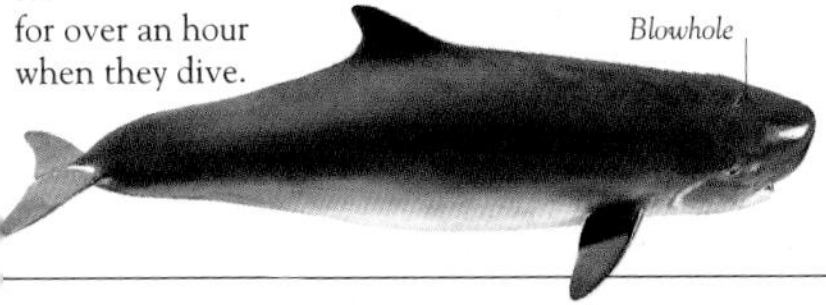
Blowhole

LUNGS

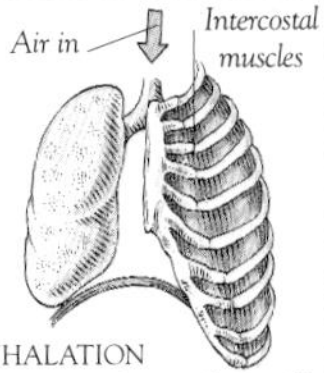
Air in
Intercostal muscles

INHALATION

Intercostal muscles pull ribs up while diaphragm moves down; rib cage expands and air flows in.

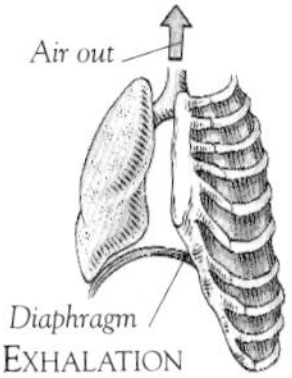
Air out
Diaphragm

EXHALATION

Intercostal muscles and diaphragm relax, lungs and rib cage deflate. Air is forced out of lungs.

BLOOD AND CIRCULATION

BLOOD DELIVERS SUBSTANCES that cells need, and
takes away their waste. In simple animals, like
mollusks and insects, it flows mainly through open
spaces inside the body, but in vertebrates, including
mammals, it flows through a system of tubes called
blood vessels. Blood is pumped around by the heart.

EUROPEAN LOBSTER

BLUE-BLOODED CRUSTACEAN
In many animals, blood is colored red because it
contains a red substance called hemoglobin
that carries oxygen. In lobsters and
other crustaceans, the
oxygen-carrier
is blue.

Lobster's
blood contains a blue
pigment – hemocyanin

MOVING HEAT
As well as moving dissolved
chemicals, blood also moves
heat. When a lizard basks in the
sunshine, the blood beneath its
skin warms up. The blood
carries this heat to its
internal organs.

Blood absorbs
heat from skin

Body begins to warm
up, enabling lizard
to become active

OCELLATED LIZARD
BASKING IN SUN

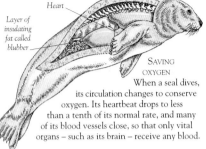

Heart

Layer of insulating fat called blubber

CIRCULATION FACTS

• Earthworms have five pairs of hearts, close to the front of their bodies.

• During hibernation, many animals' blood temperature drops close to 32° F (0° C).

• In a lifetime, a human heart pumps enough blood to fill 100 full-sized swimming pools.

SAVING OXYGEN

When a seal dives, its circulation changes to conserve oxygen. Its heartbeat drops to less than a tenth of its normal rate, and many of its blood vessels close, so that only vital organs – such as its brain – receive any blood.

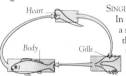

Heart

Body

Gills

SINGLE CIRCULATION

In fish, blood flows in a single circuit. From the heart, it flows through the gills, collects oxygen, and flows on to the body.

Lungs

CIRCULATION THROUGH LUNGS

Heart pumps blood around two circuits

Blood returns to other side of heart

CIRCULATION AROUND BODY

Body

ANIMAL HEART RATES

Animals with small bodies have much faster heartbeats than larger ones.

ANIMAL	BEATS PER MINUTE
Gray whale	9
Harbor seal (diving)	10
Elephant	25
Human	70
Harbor seal (at surface)	140
Sparrow	500
Shrew	600
Hummingbird (hovering)	1,200

DOUBLE CIRCULATION

In humans and other mammals, blood makes two circuits, and the heart is a double pump. In the first circuit, it flows from the heart to the lungs and back. In the second, it flows around the rest of the body.

SKELETONS

ANIMALS SUCH AS JELLYFISH have completely soft bodies that work well in water, but create problems on land. Other animals have a solid framework, or skeleton. This gives them their shape, and provides something for their muscles to pull against. Skeletons can be inside the body or surround it from the outside.

Armored thorax

Tubular legs

AN OUTSIDE SKELETON
An insect's body is covered by an exoskeleton made of separate plates that hinge together at flexible joints. The advantage of this skeleton is that it is very tough, and helps to stop insects from drying out. To grow, an insect sheds its exoskeleton from time to time and grows a larger one in its place.

All organs are inside the skeleton

Hard forewing (elytron)

Separate plates on abdomen

JEWEL BEETLE'S EXOSKELETON

NAUTILUS SHELL

INSIDE A SHELL
A shell is a hard case that protects a soft-bodied animal. Unlike an insect's exoskeleton, it can grow, so the animal inside never has to shed it. This nautilus shell has gas-filled compartments to help the mollusk control its depth in water.

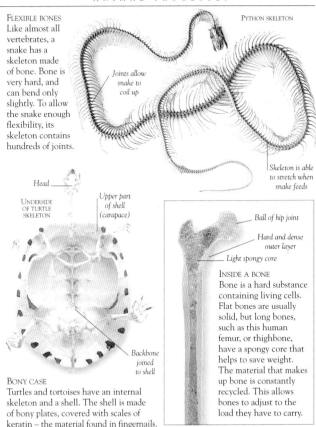

FLEXIBLE BONES
Like almost all
vertebrates, a
snake has a
skeleton made
of bone. Bone is
very hard, and
can bend only
slightly. To allow
the snake enough
flexibility, its
skeleton contains
hundreds of joints.

PYTHON SKELETON

*Joints allow
snake to
coil up*

*Skeleton is able
to stretch when
snake feeds*

Head

UNDERSIDE
OF TURTLE
SKELETON

*Upper part
of shell
(carapace)*

*Backbone
joined
to shell*

BONY CASE
Turtles and tortoises have an internal
skeleton and a shell. The shell is made
of bony plates, covered with scales of
keratin – the material found in fingernails.

Ball of hip joint

*Hard and dense
outer layer*

Light spongy core

INSIDE A BONE
Bone is a hard substance
containing living cells.
Flat bones are usually
solid, but long bones,
such as this human
femur, or thighbone,
have a spongy core that
helps to save weight.
The material that makes
up bone is constantly
recycled. This allows
bones to adjust to the
load they have to carry.

More skeletons

The skeletons of vertebrates,
or animals with backbones,
all follow the same underlying plan, but
over millions of years they have become
modified for many different ways of life.
For some animals – particularly birds –
lightness is important; for others, such as
elephants, the emphasis is on strength; and
for others, such as fish, flexibility is vital.

Paper-thin skull

Highly flexible neck

CROW SKELETON

Ribs anchor muscles used in swimming

COD SKELETON

Backbone

Keel anchors wing muscles

SUPPORTED IN WATER
A fish's body is buoyed up by water, so its skeleton
does not have to be as strong as that of an animal that
lives on land. Fish have a large number of vertebrae,
and many pairs of thin and flexible ribs.

Slender leg bones

LIGHT BONES
Compared to other land
animals, birds have
lightweight skeletons with
few bones. Many of the
bones are honeycombed with
air spaces (reducing bones'
weight), and some of these
spaces connect to the air sacs
that a bird uses to breathe.

FOUR-LEGGED SKELETON
A salamander's
skeleton shows
the typical, four-
legged plan that
evolved long ago, when
vertebrates first took up life on
land. The salamander's legs are
small and weak and splay outward.

Large skull

JAPANESE SALAMANDER SKELETON

Long backbone

Small legs

Salamander often rests with its body on ground

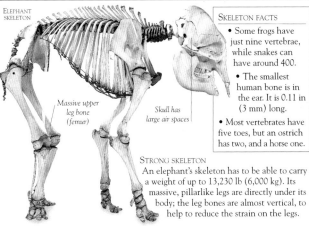

ELEPHANT
SKELETON

Massive upper
leg bone
(femur)

Skull has
large air spaces

SKELETON FACTS

• Some frogs have
just nine vertebrae,
while snakes can
have around 400.

• The smallest
human bone is in
the ear. It is 0.11 in
(3 mm) long.

• Most vertebrates have
five toes, but an ostrich
has two, and a horse one.

STRONG SKELETON

An elephant's skeleton has to be able to carry
a weight of up to 13,230 lb (6,000 kg). Its
massive, pillarlike legs are directly under its
body; the leg bones are almost vertical, to
help to reduce the strain on the legs.

COMPARING LIMBS

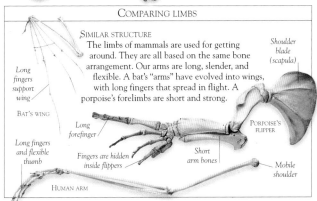

SIMILAR STRUCTURE

The limbs of mammals are used for getting
around. They are all based on the same bone
arrangement. Our arms are long, slender, and
flexible. A bat's "arms" have evolved into wings,
with long fingers that spread in flight. A
porpoise's forelimbs are short and strong.

Shoulder
blade
(scapula)

Long
fingers
support
wing

BAT'S WING

Long
forefinger

Long fingers
and flexible
thumb

Fingers are hidden
inside flippers

Short
arm bones

PORPOISE'S
FLIPPER

Mobile
shoulder

HUMAN ARM

MUSCLES AND MOVEMENT

THE ABILITY TO MOVE is a sign of life in the animal world. Animals move by using muscles. These contain special cells that can contract or relax, making parts of the body change their position or shape. Muscles need energy to work, and animals get this from food.

Frog is propelled forward

Powerful muscles extend back legs

Body is streamlined in flight

JUMPING FROG
Frogs, fleas, and kangaroos move by jumping. A frog has strong muscles in its back legs that contract to produce enough leverage to push the animal through the air.

MOTION FACTS
• A flea can jump 100 times its own height using energy stored in pads in its leg joints. A cat flea can leap 13.4 in (34 cm).
• A sea gooseberry moves through water by beating clusters of tiny hairs called cilia.

HUMAN MUSCLES

A pair of muscles raises the forearm

Triceps relaxes

RELAXED
Muscles pull but they do not push. They are often found in pairs where they work against each other. When the arm is at rest, the muscles are relaxed.

Biceps contracts

CONTRACTED
To raise the forearm, the biceps muscle contracts and the triceps relaxes. To lower the arm again, the triceps contracts and the biceps relaxes.

FASTEST MAMMALS

The cheetah is the fastest animal on land over short distances.
Over long distances, the pronghorn antelope is faster.

COMMON NAME	SCIENTIFIC NAME	MAXIMUM SPEED MPH	KM/H
Cheetah	*Acinonyx jubatus*	65	105
Pronghorn antelope	*Antilocapra americana*	53	86
Mongolian gazelle	*Procapra gutturosa*	50	80
Springbok	*Antidorcas marsupialis*	50	80
Grant's gazelle	*Gazella granti*	47	76
Thomson's gazelle	*Gazella thomsoni*	47	76
European hare	*Lepus europaeus*	45	72

Limpet is held fast by its muscular foot

STUCK FAST
A mollusk such as a limpet
has special muscles that stay
contracted for hours and
use up very little energy.
The muscles are used to
close the mollusk's shell,
or to clamp it to a rock.

SIDEWINDER MOVEMENT
Most snakes curve from
side to side as they push
against the ground. This
is known as serpentine
movement. The
sidewinder is different.
It throws itself forward,
leaving a distinctive trail.

ROUGH LIMPET

FOUR-LEGGED MOVEMENT
Animals with four legs
move in a coordinated way.
To walk, a cheetah moves its
front right leg and its rear left
leg forward and then the opposite
pair. However, when it runs, its
front legs move together and then
its back legs move together.

A cheetah can reach 60 mph (96 km/h) in three seconds

CHEETAH RUNNING

Animal movement

All animals are able to move parts of their bodies, even though some spend all their adult lives fixed in one place. The way animals move depends on their size and shape, and also on their surroundings. Land animals are able to push against solid ground, but animals that fly or swim push against moving air or water. To do this, most of these animals use wings or fins – but a few, such as octopuses and squid, use jet propulsion.

INSECT TAKEOFF
A locust launches itself into the air using strong muscles in its legs, and with its wings flat against its body. Once in the air, the locust opens wide both of its pairs of wings and flaps them vigorously.

Hind legs push out strongly

Surface area of wings increased by feathers

During upstroke, broad wings sweep upward

Bird has strong pectoral muscles to pull wings up

MOVING THROUGH WATER
A dogfish, like a shark, is a cartilaginous fish. It swims by curving its body into an S-shape. This motion propels the fish through the water, as its body and fins push the water aside. A bony fish swims in a different way. It keeps its body straight and beats its tail to move forward.

Movement begins at the head and follows through body

Tail pushes against water at the end of each wave

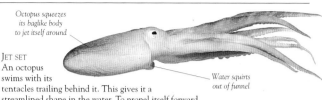

Octopus squeezes
its baglike body
to jet itself around

Water squirts
out of funnel

JET SET
An octopus
swims with its
tentacles trailing behind it. This gives it a
streamlined shape in the water. To propel itself forward,
it contracts a water-filled cavity, known as the mantle,
and squirts a stream of water out of its body via a funnel.

A BIRD IN FLIGHT

MOVING THROUGH AIR
Birds, insects, and bats are the only animals capable of powered flight. They
use energy to flap their wings and push against gravity, so that they stay
airborne. A bird's wings are specially curved in a shape called an
aerofoil that helps to produce an upward lift. If the bird stops
flapping, it slows, lift decreases, and the bird starts to drop.

BLUE PIGEON

Muscles now
push wings
downward

Downstroke pushes
bird up and forward

Wings move
up for a new
upstroke

Wing
movement
produces lift to
counteract gravity

Dogfish body
bends in S-shape

Flat fins
maintain fish
at same level
in water

Head swings
around and
new curve starts

NERVOUS SYSTEM AND BRAIN

NERVE CELLS, OR NEURONS, carry signals from one part of an animal's body to another, so that it can work in a coordinated way. Together, neurons form a network called the nervous system. In many animals, this is controlled by the brain, which receives and processes information from the nerve cells.

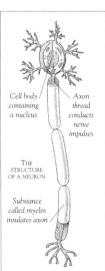

Cell body containing a nucleus

Axon thread conducts nerve impulses

THE STRUCTURE OF A NEURON

Substance called myelin insulates axon

CARRYING SIGNALS
A typical nerve cell has a cell body, with a nucleus, and an axon that carries signals. In vertebrates, the insulated axon helps signals travel quickly.

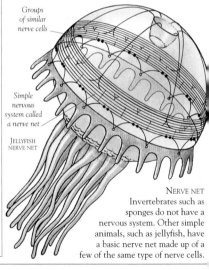

Groups of similar nerve cells

Simple nervous system called a nerve net

JELLYFISH NERVE NET

NERVE NET
Invertebrates such as sponges do not have a nervous system. Other simple animals, such as jellyfish, have a basic nerve net made up of a few of the same type of nerve cells.

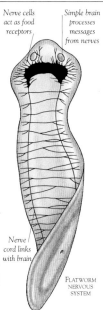

Nerve cells act as food receptors

Simple brain processes messages from nerves

Nerve cord links with brain

FLATWORM NERVOUS SYSTEM

BRAIN AND NERVE NET
A flatworm has a simple brain, which is connected to two nerve cords that run the length of its body. The nerve cords carry sensory signals to the brain. Once the brain has processed the signal, it makes the body respond.

BRAIN STRUCTURE

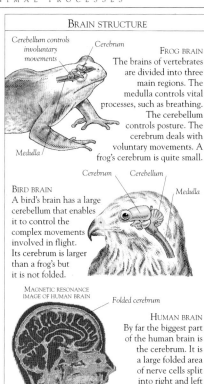

Cerebellum controls involuntary movements

Cerebrum

Medulla

FROG BRAIN
The brains of vertebrates are divided into three main regions. The medulla controls vital processes, such as breathing. The cerebellum controls posture. The cerebrum deals with voluntary movements. A frog's cerebrum is quite small.

Cerebrum   *Cerebellum*

Medulla

BIRD BRAIN
A bird's brain has a large cerebellum that enables it to control the complex movements involved in flight. Its cerebrum is larger than a frog's but it is not folded.

MAGNETIC RESONANCE IMAGE OF HUMAN BRAIN

Folded cerebrum

HUMAN BRAIN
By far the biggest part of the human brain is the cerebrum. It is a large folded area of nerve cells split into right and left cerebral hemispheres. It governs memory, learning, and senses.

Medulla

SENSES

ANIMALS USE THEIR SENSES to gather information about the world around them. Many animals rely on their eyesight, but others depend on different senses. Some insects and mammals have highly developed hearing, and use sounds to build up an "image" of their surroundings.

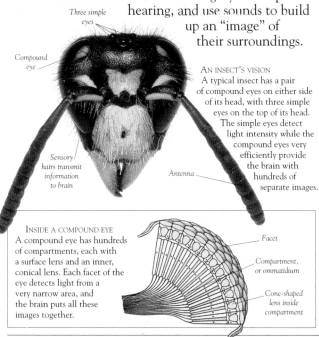

Three simple eyes

Compound eye

Sensory hairs transmit information to brain

Antenna

AN INSECT'S VISION
A typical insect has a pair of compound eyes on either side of its head, with three simple eyes on the top of its head. The simple eyes detect light intensity while the compound eyes very efficiently provide the brain with hundreds of separate images.

INSIDE A COMPOUND EYE
A compound eye has hundreds of compartments, each with a surface lens and an inner, conical lens. Each facet of the eye detects light from a very narrow area, and the brain puts all these images together.

Facet

Compartment, or ommatidium

Cone-shaped lens inside compartment

CHAMELEON

Eye is able to swivel independently

DOUBLE VISION

When a chameleon spots its prey, it can keep one eye on it and still check all around for predators. This is because it is able to move its eyes independently. The chameleon's brain receives two separate images and must make sense of them. As it nears its prey, the chameleon focuses both eyes on it and takes careful aim.

WHITEFIN DOLPHIN

Chameleon has wide field of vision

ECHO-LOCATION

Some animals send out high-frequency sounds to put together a picture of the world. Dolphins and bats emit squeaks that bounce off surrounding objects – including prey – and return to the animal as echoes. They are interpreted by the animal's brain.

Cricket's ears are near the knee joint on its front legs

SENSING SOUNDS

Insects such as crickets and grasshoppers learn about the world mostly through their ability to detect vibrations. Crickets have "ears" on their knees made from a taut membrane that is sensitive to sound vibrations.

CENTRAL AMERICAN CRICKET

HEARING RANGE OF SELECTED ANIMALS

Sound is measured by its pitch in units called Hertz (Hz). A higher Hertz number means a higher pitch – a lower number, a lower pitch.

SPECIES	HEARING RANGES IN Hz
Elephant	1 – 20,000 Hz
Dog	10 – 35,000 Hz
Human	20 – 20,000 Hz
Bat	100 – 100,000 Hz
Frog	100 – 2,500 Hz

More senses

In addition to using their eyes
and ears, animals have special organs
to give them extra information about
their environment. Taste and smell are
similar senses that detect chemicals
and help animals find food. In the
water and in the dark, animals need
special senses to survive.

*Gundogs have
an excellent
sense of smell*

BRAQUE DU
BOURBONNAIS

DOG SCENTS

A dog's most advanced sense is its sense of smell.
Moisture on a dog's nose helps to dissolve scent
particles. Inside its muzzle is a large folded
area that traps scents and passes sensory
information to the brain. A large part of a
dog's brain is concerned with interpreting scents.

TASTING THE AIR

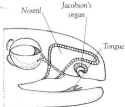

*Snake uses Jacobson's organ
to sense the presence of food,
enemies, or a mate*

INDIAN
PYTHON

*Snake
uses its
tongue to
"sniff"
the air*

Nostril   Jacobson's
organ

Tongue

JACOBSON'S ORGAN

A snake has a special sense organ in the roof of
its mouth called the Jacobson's organ. It flicks out
its tongue and collects chemical particles from the
air. These are transferred to sensory cells in the Jacobson's
organ so that the snake can taste the chemicals.

NIGERIAN
CAVE
CRICKET

USING ANTENNAE

In a dark cave, a cave cricket relies on its very long, sensitive antennae to find its way. Antennae are sensory feelers that pick up air movements, smells, and vibrations.

Antenna helps cricket feel its way in the dark

SENSE FACTS

• A dog's nose has 200 million scent receptors. A human nose has five million.

• A dragonfly can spot an insect moving 33 ft (10 m) away.

• Some bats can detect a tiny midge 65.5 ft (20 m) away.

LATERAL LINE

Most fish have a line of receptors on the sides of their bodies called a lateral line. This system detects changes in water pressure and signals to the fish that there is movement nearby.

MIRROR CARP

Large, shiny scales mark the lateral line

SENSING GRAVITY

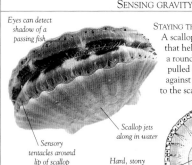

Eyes can detect shadow of a passing fish

STAYING THE RIGHT WAY UP

A scallop has organs called statocysts that help it to stay upright. Each is a round chamber with a ball that is pulled down by gravity so that it rests against sensory hairs. These indicate to the scallop which way up is.

Scallop jets along in water

Sensory tentacles around lip of scallop

Hard, stony ball pulled by gravity

Sensory hairs line chamber

DIAGRAM OF A STATOCYST

BEHAVIOR

THE THINGS THAT AN
ANIMAL DOES and the
way that it does them
make up its behavior.
This may include the
way an animal finds
food, looks after itself,
protects its territory,
finds a partner, or
cares for its young.

*A penguin must
keep its feathers
waterproof*

CARING FOR FEATHERS

To keep its feathers in good condition, a
bird must spend time each day caring for
them. It pushes its beak through ruffled feathers
to smooth them out and remove parasites such as
feather lice. Penguins and other water birds spread
oil from a special gland through their feathers to
keep them waterproof.

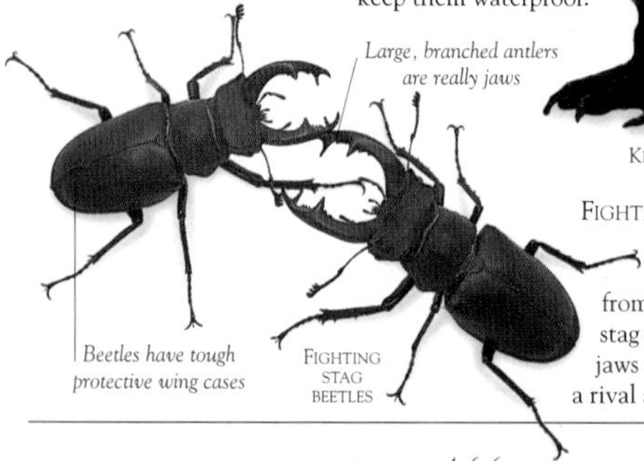

*Large, branched antlers
are really jaws*

*Special
gland near
the tail
contains
oil*

KING PENGUIN

FIGHTING FOR TERRITORY

Some animals fight to
defend their territory
from competitors. Male
stag beetles have powerful
jaws that they use to grasp
a rival and lift it out of the way.

*Beetles have tough
protective wing cases*

FIGHTING
STAG
BEETLES

USING TOOLS

Some animals have learned to use a tool to help them find food. Sea otters, for example, anchor themselves in a seaweed called kelp, and use a stone from the seabed to break open shellfish. They rest the stone on their chest and smash the shellfish against it. They can then eat the contents.

BIRD MIGRATION

ARCTIC TERN
Some birds fly long distances (migrate) to avoid bad weather or find food. Arctic terns fly from the Arctic to the Antarctic.

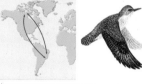

AMERICAN GOLDEN PLOVER
This bird makes the longest migration of any land bird. It breeds in Canada and flies south to Argentina for the winter.

SHORT-TAILED SHEARWATER
After breeding in the south of Australia, this shearwater flies around the North Pacific and back again.

GREATER WHITETHROAT
The greater whitethroat is a small warbler that breeds during spring and summer in Europe. It migrates to Africa for winter.

Communication and defense

To survive, animals have to communicate
with their own kind, and defend themselves
against predators. Animals communicate
in many ways. Some use sounds, while
others use visual signals or chemical
messages. Animal defenses include
camouflage, armor, and poisons.

CHEMICAL COMMUNICATION
Many insects communicate using
chemicals called pheromones that
they release onto the ground or
into the air. The female Indian
moon moth makes a pheromone
that attracts males from far away.

INDIAN
MOON
MOTH

*Moths are
able to respond
to scents*

*Bee performs
waggle dance
in the hive*

HONEYBEE DANCE
When a honeybee locates a good source
of nectar, it will return to the hive
and inform other bees of its find. The
bee performs a waggling dance that
surrounding bees are able to interpret.
It tells them the location, distance,
and quality of the food.

ROBIN IN
SONG

BIRDSONG
Animals such as birds and frogs
communicate with sounds. A bird has
a chamber called a syrinx that can
produce a range of sounds to warn
other birds to stay out of its territory.

CAMOUFLAGED INSECT

This spiny stick insect relies on camouflage to escape attack. It hides among foliage, where its body resembles a cluster of dead leaves. This disguise makes it very difficult to find, but works only if the insect remains still.

GIANT SPINY STICK INSECT

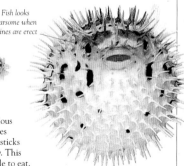

Brightly colored frog is easily seen in the forest

POISONOUS YELLOW MANTELLA

POISON FROG

Some frogs contain poisons in their skin that protect them from predators. They have brightly colored skin to warn predators that they are poisonous.

While stick insect stays still, it is hidden in the leaves

PORCUPINE FISH

When the fish relaxes, its spines lie flat against its body

Fish looks fearsome when spines are erect

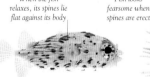

PUFFED UP

The porcupine fish has an ingenious method of defense. When it senses danger, it fills up with water and sticks out the spines that cover its body. This makes the fish virtually impossible to eat.

REPRODUCTION

ALL LIVING THINGS REPRODUCE. Animals do this in two ways. For most species, two parents come together, in a process called mating, to create a fertilized egg. In a few very simple animals, one individual reproduces itself.

Peacocks fan out their tail feathers in a display to the peahen

PEACOCK

COURTSHIP

Before an animal can reproduce, it must first find a partner of the opposite sex. To attract a mate, male animals put on a display and act out a ritual known as courtship. This complex behavior forms a bond between the pair.

ROD-SHAPED BACTERIA *ESCHERICHIA COLI*

Offspring are identical to the parents

ASEXUAL REPRODUCTION

Many simple forms of life, such as bacteria, reproduce by splitting in two. Animals such as aphids produce new individuals from an unfertilized egg.

MALE FROG FERTILIZES EGGS

The male frog sprays the eggs with his sperm

SEXUAL REPRODUCTION

Most reproduction requires that a male and a female parent come together so that the female's sex cells are fertilized. A frog's eggs are fertilized externally but in some animals the male's sperm enters the female to reach the egg cells inside her body.

REPRODUCTION RATES

Some animals can reproduce extremely rapidly, but only a few of their offspring survive to become adults.

SPECIES	BREEDING AGE	OFFSPRING PER YEAR
Northern gannet	5–6 years	1
Rabbit	8 months	10–30
Nile crocodile	15 years	50
Fruit fly	10–14 days	Up to 900

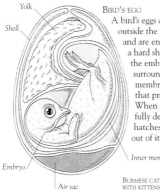

Yolk

Shell

BIRD'S EGG
A bird's eggs develop outside the mother and are encased in a hard shell. Inside, the embryo is surrounded by membrane layers that protect it. When a chick is fully developed it hatches (breaks out of its egg).

Inner membrane

Embryo

Air sac

DOGFISH
EGG CASES

Egg case hung by tendrils from seaweed

EGG CASES
The female dogfish releases rubbery egg cases, each containing an embryo. The embryo grows inside the case, living on yolk that acts as a food store. The fish emerges after 6 to 9 months.

Kittens born at the same time may look different

BURMESE CAT
WITH KITTENS

CARING FOR YOUNG
Mammals such as cats give birth to live young that are helpless for the first few weeks. The young rely on their mother's milk for food until they are strong enough to find their own food.

GROWTH AND DEVELOPMENT

AS LIVING THINGS GET OLDER they usually grow bigger. Parts of their bodies grow at different rates, so that their proportions gradually alter. Some animals grow all their lives; others develop rapidly when they are young, then stop when they are mature. Some animals can grow a new body part to replace a lost one.

GROWING A NEW TAIL

TREE SKINK
If a predator catches a tree skink by its tail, the tail breaks off at a fracture point, letting the skink escape. A new tail gradually grows, containing rubbery cartilage rather than bone. Eight months later, the tail has regrown to its original length.

Tail shed at fracture point

Growing new tail uses a lot of energy

1 STARTING LIFE
A hen's egg starts life as a single cell. Once it has been fertilized, the cell divides many times and these new cells form the chick's body.

Chick uses egg tooth to crack shell

2 BREAKING FREE
During hatching, the chick pecks through the shell, and kicks its way out. It now breathes fresh air for the first time.

Wet down feathers soon dry

GROWING A SHELL

Many mollusks grow hard shells by depositing crystals of calcium carbonate. As the mollusk grows, its shell grows too. Bands in the shell show each season's growth.

TRITON SHELL GROWTH

Whirls become larger and more pronounced

A fully developed shell has a thick lip

GROWING UP

Newborn cub is vulnerable

Eight-week-old cub is more independent

At 12 weeks, cub play-fights, preparing to catch its own prey

FOX CUB

A newborn fox cub is helpless for the first few weeks of life and its mother must take care of it. At eight weeks, it can walk and find its own food, though the mother still provides milk.

Chicks are able to find their own food

4 FOLLOWING THEIR MOTHER
The chicks now have dry down and can walk. They recognize their mother's call and soon recognize her by sight as well.

3 NEWBORN
The young chick has a well-developed head and feet but its wings are immature. It can run around and will peck at the ground looking for food.

METAMORPHOSIS

AS ANIMALS GROW, their bodies change shape. Some
animals change slightly, but the young of amphibians,
fish, and insects look very different from the adults.
This process of change is called metamorphosis.
Insects change shape in two ways – either by complete
metamorphosis (changing shape suddenly), or by
incomplete metamorphosis (changing by gradual stages).

COMPLETE METAMORPHOSIS: THE LADYBUG

*Eggs laid
on the
underside
of leaves*

*Soft, pale
larva
emerges*

*Mature larva
feeds on aphids*

1 THE EGG
A ladybug changes
shape completely. The
egg takes about four days
to hatch.

2 LARVA EMERGES
A soft-bodied larva
hatches from the egg.
Its first meal is its egg,
which contains nutrients.

3 MATURE LARVA
The mature larva
walks around slowly but
cannot fly. Its colors
warn off predators.

*Larval skin is
shed and pupal
skin forms*

*Wing cases
gradually
change
color*

*Adult ladybug feeds
on aphids*

4 FORMING A PUPA
After eating
enough aphids, the
larva attaches itself to
a leaf, ready to pupate.

5 YOUNG ADULT
A soft ladybug
hatches out of the pupa.
Its soft, yellow wing cases
start to harden.

6 MATURE ADULT
The adult looks
very different from its
larva. It has its adult
colors and is able to fly.

INCOMPLETE METAMORPHOSIS: THE DAMSELFLY

1 NYMPH
A damselfly nymph lives underwater, but carries out its final molt out of the water.

2 PULLING FREE
Blood pumped into the thorax makes it expand and burst out of its nymphal skin.

3 OLD SKIN
The adult head pulls out of the nymphal skin and leaves its mask behind.

4 SOFT WINGS
Free of its old skin, blood fills the damselfly's wings, making them longer.

5 GROWING
Thorax and abdomen are still growing. The wings are delicate.

6 ABLE TO FLY
The adult is ready to fly. Its abdomen is long and shiny and its wings are transparent.

INSECT METAMORPHOSIS

Insects have three or four stages in their life cycles, depending on whether they undergo complete or incomplete metamorphosis. The stages are often very different in length. The first section of this chart shows the length of time needed for the four stages of complete metamorphosis.

SPECIES	EGG	LARVA	PUPA	ADULT
Bluebottle fly	1 day	8 days	9 days	35 days
Ladybug	4 days	18 days	15 days	9 months
Large white butterfly	14 days	1 month	6 months	2 months

INCOMPLETE METAMORPHOSIS IN INSECTS

SPECIES	EGG	NYMPH		ADULT
Periodical cicada	1 month	17 years	–	2 months
Mayfly	1 month	3 years	–	1 day
Cockroach	1 month	3 months	–	9 months

ECOSYSTEMS

LIVING THINGS DO NOT EXIST IN ISOLATION; they constantly interact with each other and with their environment. The study of these interactions is called ecology. Groups of organisms and their surroundings make up separate ecosystems. An ecosystem can be a pond, a forest, a beach, or an entire mountainside.

UNIQUE PLANET
Earth is the only planet known to support life. Its atmosphere contains the elements that are essential to sustain life and to protect us from the harmful effects of the Sun's rays.

ECOLOGICAL SCALE
Individual plants or animals living together are known as a population. Several populations are called a community and several communities form an ecosystem. Ecosystems sharing the same climate make up a biome. All Earth's biomes form the biosphere.

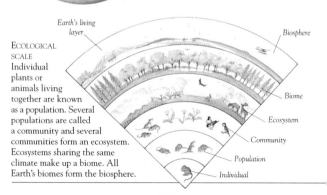

Earth's living layer

Biosphere

Biome

Ecosystem

Community

Population

Individual

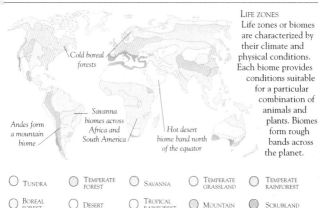

LIFE ZONES
Life zones or biomes are characterized by their climate and physical conditions. Each biome provides conditions suitable for a particular combination of animals and plants. Biomes form rough bands across the planet.

Cold boreal forests

Andes form a mountain biome

Savanna biomes across Africa and South America

Hot desert biome band north of the equator

○ TUNDRA

◐ TEMPERATE FOREST

○ SAVANNA

○ TEMPERATE GRASSLAND

○ TEMPERATE RAINFOREST

○ BOREAL FOREST

○ DESERT

○ TROPICAL RAINFOREST

◐ MOUNTAIN

◐ SCRUBLAND

EXAMPLES OF BIOMES

TUNDRA
Around the Arctic region are areas of tundra. Here the soil stays frozen for most of the year and only mosses and lichens grow. The climate is very dry.

TEMPERATE FOREST
Northern Europe and North America are known as temperate – their climates are neither very hot nor very cold. Deciduous trees flourish in these areas.

NUTRIENT CYCLES

ALL LIVING THINGS need chemical nutrients. These include carbon, oxygen, nitrogen, and water, and trace elements such as copper and zinc. Chemical nutrients are constantly recycled through Earth's biosphere – they pass between living and non-living things.

Carbon dioxide is given out by green plants during respiration

Animals breathe out carbon dioxide

Animals take in carbon from plants

Carbon dioxide absorbed by plants during photosynthesis

Bacteria break down or decompose dead matter and produce carbon dioxide

Dead plants and animals decay

NUTRIENT CYCLE FACTS

• At least 25 of Earth's 90 elements are used by living things.

• Plants absorb one-tenth of the atmosphere's carbon every year.

• Some parts of a nutrient cycle can take seconds, while others take thousands of years.

CARBON CYCLE

Carbon is a part of all living things. It moves around the living world in a constant cycle. Plants absorb carbon dioxide from the atmosphere during photosynthesis and animals take in carbon when they eat plants. Carbon is released when plants and animals decompose.

OXYGEN CYCLE
During photosynthesis, all plants release oxygen. Living things take in oxygen to break down energy in food.

NITROGEN CYCLE
Nitrogen is needed by living things to make proteins but it must be combined with other elements before it can be used. Some nitrogen is combined by lightning, but most is combined by bacteria that live in soil.

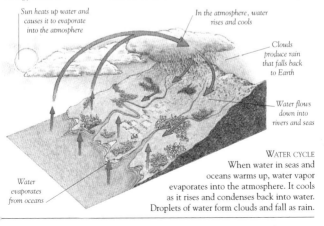

Sun heats up water and causes it to evaporate into the atmosphere

In the atmosphere, water rises and cools

Clouds produce rain that falls back to Earth

Water flows down into rivers and seas

Water evaporates from oceans

WATER CYCLE
When water in seas and oceans warms up, water vapor evaporates into the atmosphere. It cools as it rises and condenses back into water. Droplets of water form clouds and fall as rain.

FOOD WEBS AND CHAINS

IN ANY COMMUNITY, living things are linked together
in food chains or webs. Energy is passed along the
chain in the form of food. At the base of the chain
are the primary producers, usually plants, which make
their own food. When animals, or consumers, eat
plants, energy is passed on, though a great deal is lost
along the way.
Poisons can also
be passed through
the chain.

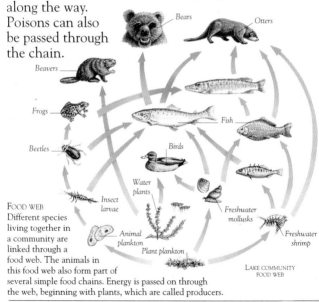

Bears

Otters

Beavers

Frogs

Fish

Beetles

Birds

*Water
plants*

*Insect
larvae*

*Freshwater
mollusks*

*Animal
plankton*

*Freshwater
shrimp*

Plant plankton

FOOD WEB
Different species
living together in
a community are
linked through a
food web. The animals in
this food web also form part of
several simple food chains. Energy is passed on through
the web, beginning with plants, which are called producers.

LAKE COMMUNITY
FOOD WEB

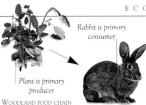

Rabbit is primary consumer

Plant is primary producer

WOODLAND FOOD CHAIN

FOOD CHAIN

A food chain contains living things that provide food for each other. The chain usually has only three or four links because energy is lost at each stage. The first stage of the chain is typically a plant.

Fox is secondary consumer

TROPHIC LEVELS

Ecologists call each stage of a food chain a trophic level. There is more living material and more energy available at the first trophic level, the primary producers. Energy is used up by organisms at each successive layer of consumption so that less can be stored and passed on.

TROPHIC LEVELS PYRAMID

At this trophic level, there are fewer consumers

Less energy available at this level

Energy is used up by living things

Primary producers

BELUGAS' POISON CHAIN

Belugas in North America are part of a river food chain. Toxins pumped into the river are absorbed by plankton, then passed to fish that eat plankton, and then to whales that eat fish. The toxins have become concentrated in the whales.

CONSERVATION

HUMAN ACTIVITY has a great impact on the environment. Humans use up Earth's resources and leave behind a great deal of waste and pollution. To protect the environment, we are learning to practice conservation and to manage our use of natural resources.

HABITAT CHANGE
Humans have drastically altered the natural world. Large amounts of land have been cleared to make way for the increased demand for houses and roads. As a result, the balance of the ecosystems in those areas is upset.

CLIMATE CHANGE
A rise of a few degrees in Earth's temperature has a significant effect on the environment. It can cause rivers, such as this one in Spain, to dry up, threatening freshwater fish and amphibians, and other animals that depend on the river.

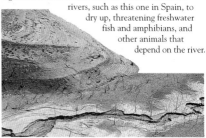

Trawlers locate and process huge amounts of fish

OVERFISHING
Technological advances in fishing have led to greater yields. Huge trawlers now catch such vast amounts of fish that the fish population in some areas has been severely reduced. Fishing bans have been enforced in an effort to help fish stocks recover.

REINTRODUCTION

In the 1970s, the red kite was on the verge of extinction and a program was set up to reintroduce the bird to Britain. In programs such as this one, young animals are raised in captivity and then set free. They are released in special areas where their progress can be carefully monitored.

CONSERVATION FACTS

• Since 1700, 200 species or subspecies of birds have become extinct.

• Over 1,000 of the world's bird species and 500 of its mammals are currently endangered.

• Conservation has saved species such as the gray whale and Hawaiian goose.

ALLIGATORS

Wild animals sometimes need to be protected by law. Alligators used to be hunted for their skins and became endangered. The alligators of the American South are now protected by a law that limits hunting.

NATURE PRESERVES

All over the world, nature preserves have been set up. This one in Kenya protects animals, such as rhinos, from poachers. The preserves conserve the environment and the animals, and attract tourists whose money helps maintain the preserves.

CLASSIFICATION 1

BIOLOGISTS USE CLASSIFICATION to identify types of living things, and show how they are related through evolution. Classification details and species totals alter as more is discovered about the living world. This scheme is based on five kingdoms. It includes the most important categories in each group.

CLASSIFYING A SPECIES

The key grouping in classification is a species. Each has a scientific name, and consists of living things that breed together. This shows how one species – the tiger – fits into the animal kingdom.

| Kingdom (Animalia) |
| Phylum (Chordata) |
| Class (Mammalia) |
| Order (Carnivora) |
| Family (Felidae) |
| Genus (Panthera) |
| Species (Panthera tigris) |

CLASSIFICATION GROUPS

A kingdom is subdivided into smaller and smaller groups. A division is the plant equivalent of a phylum.

- - - - - - KINGDOM
———— PHYLUM
———— SUBPHYLUM
———— CLASS
———— ORDER
———— DIVISION

ALGAE
(Several phyla)
20,000 species

MOSSES AND LIVERWORTS
(Bryophyta)
15,500 species

FERNS
(Pteridophyta)
11,000 species

LIVERWORT

MALE FERN

MONERANS
(Monera)

TYPICAL BACTERIUM

"PRIMITIVE" BACTERIA
(Archaebacteria)
500 species

TYPICAL BACTERIA
(Eubacteria)
5,000 species

PROTISTS
(Protista)

AMOEBAS
(Sarcodina)
20,000 species

FLAGELLATES
(Mastigophora)
8,500 species

CILIATES
(Ciliophora)
8,000 species

SPOROZOANS
(Sporozoa)
5,000 species

FUNGI
(Fungi)

CHYTRIDS
(Chytridiomycota)
575 species

MOLDS
(Zygomycota)
1,000 species

YEASTS AND TRUFFLES
(Ascomycota)
32,000 species

MUSHROOMS AND RUSTS
(Basidiomycota)
22,000 species

PLANTS
(Plantae)

FLOWERING PLANTS
(Angiospermophyta)

CLUBMOSSES
(Lycopodophyta)
1,000 species

HORSETAILS
(Sphenophyta)
15 species

GYMNOSPERMS
(Gymnospermophyta)

MONOCOTYLEDONS
80,000 species

CONIFERS
(Coniferopsida)
350 species

CYCADS
(Cycadopsida)
140 species

JOINT PINES
(Gnetopsida)
70 species

DICOTYLEDONS
170,000 species

Classification 2

Animals have been studied more closely than any other forms of life. Biologists have identified and classified nearly all the species of vertebrates (animals with backbones) although it is likely that new species of fish await discovery. By contrast, the world of invertebrates is not so well documented and there are many more species to be identified.

Springtails	Lice
Bristletails	Thrips
Diplurans	Booklice
Silverfish	Zorapterans
Mayflies	Bugs
Stoneflies	Beetles
Webspinners	Ants, bees, wasps
Dragonflies	Lacewings and antlions
Grasshoppers and crickets	Scorpionflies
Stick and leaf insects	Stylopids
Grylloblattids	Caddisflies
Earwigs	Butterflies and moths
Cockroaches	Flies
Praying mantids	Fleas
Termites	

INSECTS
(Insecta)
1,000,000 species

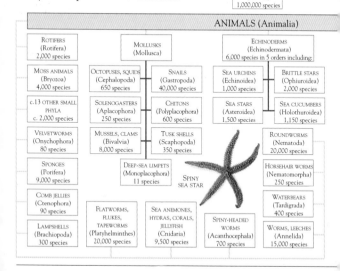

ANIMALS (Animalia)

ROTIFERS
(Rotifera)
2,000 species

MOSS ANIMALS
(Bryozoa)
4,000 species

c.13 OTHER SMALL PHYLA
c. 2,000 species

VELVETWORMS
(Onychophora)
80 species

SPONGES
(Porifera)
9,000 species

COMB JELLIES
(Ctenophora)
90 species

LAMPSHELLS
(Brachiopoda)
300 species

MOLLUSKS
(Mollusca)

OCTOPUSES, SQUIDS
(Cephalopoda)
650 species

SOLENOGASTERS
(Aplacophora)
250 species

MUSSELS, CLAMS
(Bivalvia)
8,000 species

SNAILS
(Gastropoda)
40,000 species

CHITONS
(Polyplacophora)
600 species

TUSK SHELLS
(Scaphopoda)
350 species

DEEP-SEA LIMPETS
(Monoplacophora)
11 species

SPINY
SEA STAR

FLATWORMS, FLUKES, TAPEWORMS
(Platyhelminthes)
20,000 species

SEA ANEMONES, HYDRAS, CORALS, JELLYFISH
(Cnidaria)
9,500 species

SPINY-HEADED WORMS
(Acanthocephala)
700 species

ECHINODERMS
(Echinodermata)
6,000 species in 5 orders including:

SEA URCHINS
(Echinoidea)
1,000 species

SEA STARS
(Asteroidea)
1,500 species

BRITTLE STARS
(Ophiuroidea)
2,000 species

SEA CUCUMBERS
(Holothuroidea)
1,150 species

ROUNDWORMS
(Nematoda)
20,000 species

HORSEHAIR WORMS
(Nematomorpha)
250 species

WATERBEARS
(Tardigrada)
400 species

WORMS, LEECHES
(Annelida)
15,000 species

TARANTULA

PARROT

| HORSESHOE CRABS (Merostomata) 4 species | SAND SHRIMP (Cephalocarida) 9 species | MYSTACOCARIDEANS (Mystacocarida) 10 species |

Scorpions
Tick spiders
Microwhip scorpions
Tail-less whip scorpions
Whipscorpions
Camel spiders
Pseudoscorpions
Harvestmen
Mites and ticks
Spiders

| SEA SPIDERS (Pycnogonida) 1,000 species | SPINY SAND SHRIMP (Branchiura) 125 species | CRABS, LOBSTERS, AND SHRIMP (Malacostraca) 20,000 species |

| CENTIPEDES (Chilopoda) 2,500 species | BARNACLES (Cirripedia) 1,000 species | MUSSEL SHRIMP (Ostracoda) 2,000 species |

| MILLIPEDES (Diplopoda) 10,000 species | BRANCHIOPODS (Branchiopoda) 1,000 species | COPEPODS (Copepoda) 9,000 species |

| ARACHNIDS (Arachnida) 73,000 species | ARTHROPODS (Arthropoda) | CRUSTACEANS (Crustacea) 50,000 species |

CHORDATES
(Chordata)

BIRDS
(Aves)
9,600 species

MAMMALS
(Mammalia)
4,600 species

Ostriches
Rheas
Cassowaries, emus
Kiwis
Albatrosses, petrels, shearwaters, fulmars
Pelicans, gannets, cormorants, frigatebirds, darters
Penguins
Grebes
Divers or loons
Tinamous
Herons, storks, ibises, flamingos
Ducks, geese, swans
Eagles, hawks, vultures, falcons, kites, buzzards
Pheasants, partridges, grouse, turkeys
Cranes, rails, coots, bustards
Wading birds, gulls, terns, auks
Sandgrouse
Pigeons, doves
Parrots
Cuckoos, roadrunners, turacos
Owls
Nightjars, frogmouths
Swifts, hummingbirds
Trogons
Mousebirds
Kingfishers, bee-eaters, rollers, hoopoes
Woodpeckers, toucans, barbets, honeyguides, puffbirds, jacamars
Passerines

| AMPHIBIANS (Amphibia) 4,000 species | Frogs and toads Newts and salamanders Caecilians |

| REPTILES (Reptilia) 6,500 species | Lizards and snakes Turtles, tortoises, and terrapins Crocodilians Tuataras |

| JAWLESS FISH (Agnatha) 75 species | |

| SHARKS AND RAYS (Chondrichthyes) 800 species | Sharks, dogfish Skates, rays |

| BONY FISH (Osteichthyes) 24,000 species | More than 20 orders including: Eels Herrings, anchovies Salmon, trout Carp Catfish Perch, marlin, swordfish, tunas Flying fish |

| SEA SQUIRTS (Urochordata) 2,500 species | |

Monotremes (egg-laying mammals)
Marsupials (pouched mammals)
Insectivores
Elephant shrews
Flying lemurs
Bats
Tree shrews
Primates
Edentates (anteaters, sloths, armadillos)
Pangolins
Aardvarks
Hares, rabbits, pikas
Rodents
Whales and dolphins
Carnivores
Seals, sea lions, walrus
Elephants
Hyraxes
Sea cows
Odd-toed hoofed mammals
Even-toed hoofed mammals

WEIGHTS AND MEASURES

TWO MAJOR SYSTEMS OF MEASUREMENT exist: metric and imperial. Although some countries still use the older imperial system, scientists worldwide use metric.

THE SEVEN BASE SI UNITS

SI (Système Internationale d'Unités) is the standard system of units for scientists worldwide. There are seven base units, from which the other units are derived.

Quantity	Symbol	Unit
Mass	kg	Kilogram
Length	m	Meter
Time	s	Second
Electric current	A	Ampere
Temperature	K	Kelvin
Luminous intensity	cd	Candela
Amount of substance	mol	Mole

IMPERIAL & USCS UNIT

Imperial units include the pound, mile, and gallon. With no scientific basis, it is a complex system. In the US, this system is called USCS (US Customary Systems).

STANDARD KILOGRAM

STANDARDS

Several units have precisely defined standards. This ensures that everyone means the same thing when stating measurements.

THE STANDARD SECOND

One second is defined as "the duration of 9,192,631,770 periods of the radiation corresponding to the transition between the hyperfine levels of the ground state of the cesium-133 atom."

THE STANDARD KILOGRAM

A standard kilogram is kept in carefully controlled conditions at the Bureau of Weights and measures at Sèvres, France.

THE STANDARD METER

One meter is defined as "the length equal to the 1,650,763.73 wavelengths, in a vacuum, of the radiation corresponding to the transition between the levels 2p10 and 5d5 of the krypton-86 atom."

NUMBER TERMS GREAT AND SMALL*

Prefix	Symbol	Meaning	Prefix	Symbol	Meaning
tera	T	One trillion	deci	d	One-tenth
giga	G	One billion	denti	c	One-hundredth
mega	M	One million	milli	m	One-thousandth
kilo	k	One thousand	micro	μ	One-millionth
hecto	h	One hundred	nano	n	One-billionth

*Prefixes inserted before a unit signify multiples or fractions of that unit.

Adjustable jaw

MEASURING SOLIDS
Calipers are used to find the width of solid objects.

LENGTH

METRIC	
1 millimeter (mm)	
1 centimeter (cm)	10 mm
1 meter (m)	100 cm
1 kilometer (km)	1,000 m
IMPERIAL	
1 inch (in)	
1 foot (ft)	12 in
1 yard (yd)	3 ft
1 mile	1,760 yd

LIQUID MEASURES
Measuring jugs are used to find the volumes of liquids.

MEASUREMENT FACTS

• France was the first country to adopt the metric system. King Louis XVI approved it in 1791, the day before he tried to flee the Revolution.

• China was the first country to use a decimal system. Wooden rulers divided into units of ten have been found and dated to the 6th century BC.

• In England, the length of a human top thumb-joint was a widely used measure that became the precursor of the inch.

MASS AND WEIGHT

METRIC	
1 gram (g)	
1 kilogram (kg)	1,000 g
1 tonne (t)	1,000 kg
IMPERIAL	
1 ounce (oz)	
1 pound (lb)	16 oz
1 stone	14 lb
1 hundredweight (cwt)	8 stones
1 ton	20 cwt

AREA

METRIC	
1 square millimeter (sq mm)	
1 square centimeter (sq cm)	100 sq mm
1 square meter (sq m)	10,000 sq cm
1 hectare (ha)	10,000 sq m
1 square kilometer (sq km)	1,000,000 sq m
IMPERIAL	
1 square inch (sq in)	
1 square foot (sq ft)	144 sq in
1 square yard (sq yd)	9 sq ft
1 acre	4,840 sq yd
1 square mile	640 acres

VOLUME

METRIC	
1 cubic millimeter (cu mm)	
1 cubic centimeter (cu cm)	1,000 cu mm
1 cubic meter (cu m)	1,000,000 cu cm
1 liter	1,000 cu cm
IMPERIAL	
1 cubic inch (cu in)	
1 cubic foot (cu ft)	1,728 cu in
1 cubic yard (cu yd)	27 cu ft
1 fluid ounce (fl oz)	
1 pint (pt)	20 fl oz
1 gallon (gal)	8 pt

CONVERSION TABLES

FOOT RULE

LENGTH CONVERSION

TO CONVERT:	INTO:	MULTIPLY BY:
IMPERIAL	METRIC	
Inches	Centimeters	2.54
Feet	Meters	0.3048
Yards	Meters	0.9144
Miles	Kilometers	1.6093
METRIC	IMPERIAL	
Centimeters	Inches	0.3937
Meters	Feet	3.2808
Meters	Yards	1.0936
Kilometers	Miles	0.6214
Meters	Furlongs	0.005
Meters	Fathoms	0.547
Kilometers	Nautical miles	0.54
Meters	Chains	0.0497

VOLUME CONVERSION

TO CONVERT:	INTO:	MULTIPLY BY:
IMPERIAL	METRIC	
Cubic inches	Cubic cm (ml)	16.3871
Cubic feet	Litres	28.3169
Cubic yards	Cubic meters	0.7646
Fluid ounces	Cubic cm (ml)	28.413
Pints	Liters	0.5683
Gallons	Liters	4.5461
METRIC	IMPERIAL	
Cubic cm	Cubic inches	0.061
(milliliters)	Fluid ounces	0.0352
Liters	Cubic feet	0.0353
Cubic meters	Cubic yards	1.308
Liters	Pints	1.7598
	Gallons	0.22

AREA CONVERSION

TO CONVERT:	INTO:	MULTIPLY BY:
IMPERIAL	METRIC	
Sq inches	Sq centimeters	6.4516
Sq feet	Sq meters	0.0929
Sq yards	Sq meters	0.8361
Acres	Hectares	0.4047
Sq miles	Sq kilometers	2.59
METRIC	IMPERIAL	
Sq centimeters	Sq inches	0.155
Sq meters	Sq feet	10.7639
Sq meters	Sq yards	1.196
Hectares	Acres	2.4711
Sq kilometers	Sq miles	0.3861

MASS AND WEIGHT CONVERSIONS

TO CONVERT:	INTO:	MULTIPLY BY:
IMPERIAL	METRIC	
Ounces	Grams	28.3495
Pounds	Kilograms	0.4536
Stones	Kilograms	6.3503
Hundredweights	Kilograms	50.802
Tons	Tonnes	0.9072
METRIC	IMPERIAL	
Grams	Ounces	0.0352
Kilograms	Pounds	2.2046
	Stones	0.1575
	Hundredweights	0.0197
Tonnes	Tons	1.1023

COOKING MEASURES

Object	Metric	Imperial
1 thimble	2.5 ml	30 drops
60 drops	5 ml	1 teaspoon
1 teaspoon	5 ml	1 dram
1 desert spoon	10 ml	2 drams
1 tablespoon	20 ml	4 drams
2 tablespoons	40 ml	1 fl oz
1 wine glass	100 ml	2 fl oz
1 tea cup	200 ml	5 fl oz (1 gill)
1 mug	400 ml	10 fl oz

OVEN TEMPERATURES

Gas mark*	Electricity		Rating
(* not US)	°C	°F	
1/2	120	250	Slow
1	140	275	-
2	150	300	-
3	170	325	-
4	180	350	Moderate
5	190	375	-
6	200	400	Hot
7	220	425	-
8	230	450	Very hot
9	260	500	

2.5 ML (1/2 TEASPOON)

FAHRENHEIT TO CELSIUS TO KELVIN

°F	°C	K	°F	°C	K	°F	°C	K
-4.0	-20	253	32.0	0	273	68.0	20	293
-2.2	-19	254	33.8	1	274	69.8	21	294
-0.4	-18	255	35.6	2	275	71.6	22	295
1.4	-17	256	37.4	3	276	73.4	23	296
3.2	-16	257	39.2	4	277	75.2	24	297
5.0	-15	258	41.0	5	278	77.0	25	298
6.8	-14	259	42.8	6	279	78.8	26	299
8.6	-13	260	44.6	7	280	80.6	27	300
10.4	-12	261	46.4	8	281	82.4	28	301
12.2	-11	262	48.2	9	282	84.2	29	302
14.0	-10	263	50.0	10	283	86.0	30	303
15.8	-9	264	51.8	11	284	87.8	31	304
17.6	-8	265	53.6	12	285	89.6	32	305
19.4	-7	266	55.4	13	286	91.4	33	306
21.2	-6	267	57.2	14	287	93.2	34	307
23.0	-5	268	59.0	15	288	95.0	35	308
24.8	-4	269	60.8	16	289	96.8	36	309
26.6	-3	270	62.6	17	290	98.6	37	310
28.4	-2	271	64.4	18	291	100.4	38	311
30.2	-1	272	66.2	19	292	102.2	39	312

TEMPERATURES

• To convert Fahrenheit (°F) into Celsius (°C), use the following formula:
$$°C = (°F - 32) \div 1.8$$
• To convert Celsius (°C) into Fahrenheit (°F), use the following formula:
$$°F = (°C \times 1.8) + 32$$
• To convert Celsius (°C) into Kelvin (K), use the following formula:
$$K = °C + 273.16$$

Thermometers measure temperature on Celsius and Fahrenheit scales

Index

asteroids, 360–1
asthenosphere, 150, 152, 154
astronauts, 380–1, 388
  Moon landings, 331, 380, 388
  rockets, 374
  Space Shuttle, 381, 390
  space stations, 381, 391
astronomy: galaxies, 276–83
  milestones, 382–7
  solar system, 310–61
  stars, 284–97, 300–9
  studying space, 362–83
  universe, 270–5
Aten asteroids, 361
atmosphere, Earth's, 146–7, 326, 327
  air masses, 252–3, 267
  formation, 141
  oxygen content, 147, 326
  as a radiation shield, 362
  temperature and pressure, 250–1
atmospheres, planetary:
  Jupiter, 339
  Mars, 334, 335
  Mercury, 319
  Neptune, 350, 351
  Pluto, 355
  Saturn, 343
  Uranus, 347
  Venus, 322–3, 324
atolls, coral, 222, 223
atoms, 22–3

bonds, 26–7
  chemical reactions, 48–51
  elements, 34–9
  matter, 14, 15
  nuclear energy, 88–9
aurora australis, 299
aurora borealis, 298, 299
Australia, 149
avalanches, 171, 212
axles, 76
axolotls, 435

B

bacteria, 395, 402
balance, 69
bark, 417
barkhan dunes, 177
Barnard's Star, 305
barometers, 267
basalt, 163, 178, 179, 333
bases, 56–7
bathyscapes, 219
bats, 441, 455, 463
batteries, 116, 117
bayhead beaches, 225
beaches, 224–5
beaks, 439
Beaufort scale, winds, 262
becquerels, 24
beech trees, 411
bees, 56, 420, 468
beetles, 429, 466
behavior, 466–9
belugas, 481
benzene, 59
beta rays, 24
Betelgeuse, 303

biennial plants, 416
Big Bang, 273, 274–5
Big Dipper constellation, 301
binary code, 126
binoculars, 103
bioluminescence, 92
biomes, ecology, 476, 477
biosphere, 476, 478
birds, 438–9
  brains, 461
  breathing, 449
  conservation, 483
  evolution, 398
  flight, 459
  migration, 467
  pollination, 421
  preening, 466
  reproduction, 471, 472–3
  skeletons, 454
  songs, 468
bitumen, 194
bivalves, 426, 427
black holes, 291
black smokers, 220
blizzards, 264–5
blood, 450–1
boa constrictors, 437
boiling points, 39, 85
Bombay, 237
bombs, volcanoes, 161
bonds, 26–7, 49, 51
bones, 453–5
Boyle's law, 19
brain, 460–1
breathing, 448–9
breccia, 181, 333

Acknowledgments

Contributors to this title include:
Editors: Tim Hetherington, Esther Labi, Scarlett O'Hara, Clint Twist.
Designers: Janet Allis, Alexandra Brown, Jacqui Burton, Susan Downing, Carlton Hibbert, Clair Watson.
PAGEOne: Chris Clark, Matthew Cook, Thomas Keenes, Neil Kelly, Sarah Watson.

Dorling Kindersley would like to thank:
Hilary Bird for the index; DK Cartography for the maps; Michael Dukes for assistance; Robert Graham for editorial assistance; Peter Griffiths and Stephen Oliver for model making; Dr. David W. Hughes of Sheffield University for professional advice; Robin Hunter for artwork; Stephen Johnson of International Computers Ltd, Manchester; Kodak; Dr. M. Matson and Dr. A. Roberts for reference material; Alison McKittrick for additional picture research; National Meteorological Office, London; Natural History Museum; Old Royal Observatory, Greenwich; Caroline Potts for picture library services; Science Museum; Scientific American; University of Archeology and Anthropology, Cambridge; and Martin Wilson and Steve Wong for design assistance.

Photographs by:
Peter Anderson, Geoff Brightling, Jane Burton, Peter Chadwick, Andy Crawford, Geoff Dann, Philip Dowell, Andreas von Einsiedel, Neil Fletcher, Frank Greenaway, Colin Keates, G. Kevin, Dave King, Cyril Laubscher, Mike Linley, Andrew McRobb, Tracy Morgan, Roger Phillips, Tim Ridley, Karl Shone, S. Shott, J. Stevenson, Clive Streeter, Harry Taylor, Kim Taylor, Jerry Young.

Illustrations by:
Zirrinia Austin, Julian Baum, Rick Blakely, Richard Bonson, Bill Botten, Peter Bull, Kyokan G. Chen, Julia Cobbold, Richard Coombes, Luciano Corbella, Brian Delf, Bill Donohoe, Richard Draper, Mike Dunning, Angelica Elsebach, Simone End (Linden Artists), Eugene Fleury, Roy Flookes, Mark Franklin, Mike Grey, Robert Garwood, Will Giles, Mick Gillah, Jeremy Gower, Andrew Green, Mike Grey, Nick Hall, Nick Hewetson, John Hutchinson, Stanley Johnson, Norman Lacey, Richard Lewis, Kenneth Lilly, R. Lindsay, N. Loates, Chris Lyon, Andrew Macdonald, Stuart Mackay, Kevin Maddison, Janos Marfy, Sergio Momo, Richard Orr, Sandra Pond, Daniel J. Pyne, S. Quigley, Jim Robins, Colin Rose, Colin Salmon, Mike Saunders, Pete Serjeant, Rodney Shackell, Guy Smith, Roger Stewart, Taurus Graphics,

J. Temperton, John Templeton, G. Tomlin, Raymond Turvey, François Vincent, P. Visscher, Richard Ward, Alistair Wardle, Brian Watson, P. Williams, John Woodcock, D. Woodward, Martin Woodward, Dan Wright.

University: 318tr; NASA/JPL/University of Arizona: 338tr; NASA/JPL/University of Arizona/Los Alamos National Laboratories: 368b; NASA/Palomar Obs 363cl; NASA/W. M. Keck Obs: 363tr; National Maritime Museum: 2tr; Natural History Museum: 6tr, 183bc, 184cl, 185bl, Peter Chadwick 413tr, Philip Dowell 439tr, 447tr, Colin Keates 409cr, 429cl, Dave King 427cr, Karl Shone 472cl, 472cr; N.C.A.R.: 265br; NOAA: 253cr; NOAO/AURA/NSF: Bill Schoening, Vanessa Harvey/REU Program 276tr; Novosti: 391tl; Scarlett O'Hara: 443cl, 479tl; Oxford Scientific Films/London Scientific Films: 18br, 413br; Pictor International: 44r; Planet Earth: J.B. Duncan 482bl, J. Fawcett 164tl, R. Hessler 165tr, Robert A. Jureit 409tc, J. Lithgoe 210tr, Mike Potts 483bl, W. M. Smithey 207bl, N. Tapp 204bl; Rex Features: A. Fernandez 161t; Royal Greenwich Observatory: 367cl; John Sanford: 300tr, 359br; Dr. Seth Shostak: 367tl; Starland Picture Library/ESO: 289tl; UPI/Bettman: 386cr; Science Photo Library: D. Allan 206t, Alex Bartel 33tl, 43tr, 364tr, Dr Jeremy Burgess 382tl, 414bc, 421tl, Colin Cuthbert 128bl, European Southern Observatory 271tr; European Space agency 357br, 357bl, Fred Espenak 297t, Dan Farber 262br, S. Fraser 261bl, François Gohier 366tr, P. Hawtin, University of Southampton 402bl, J. Heseltine 174tl, Manfred Kage 404bl, James King-Holmes 129br, Mehau Kelyk 461br, Patrice Loiez/CERN 12–13, 23cl, David Mclean 358tr, Lawrence Migdale 129cl, NASA 35tr, 222, 360tr, 369cl, 381bl; NOAO 363c, David Parker 65çr, 129tr, 133br, Pekka Parviainen 299tl, D. Pellegrini 212tr, Max Planck Institute of Radioastronomy 366bl, 386b, John Reader 401cl, Roger Ressmeyer, Royal Observatory Edinburgh/Anglo-Australian Telescope Board 268–269, 278tr, 282bl, 302tr, F. Sauze 216tr, Starlight 296tl, Statism 374tr, Simon Terrey 15c, U.S. Navy 89b; SIPA Press: 168tl; Solarfilma 162tr; Frank Spooner Pictures: Barr/Liaison 160br, Garties/LN 163tl, Vitti/Gamma Liaison; Sporting Pictures (UK) Ltd: 71t; Telegraph Colour Library: 138–139; Tony Stone Images: 178t, 180br, 196tr, 198tr, Peter Lambreti 483br, John Lund 40tl; US Space and Rocket Center, Alabama: 2cc; Tony Waltham: 156cl, 158tl; Weymouth Sea Life Centre: Frank Greenaway 459tr; L.White: 226t; Jerry Young: 433tr, 435cl, 441c, 456c; Zefa: 63cl, 87cl, 170bc, 202cl, 260t, 392–393.

Every effort has been made to trace the copyright holders and we apologize in advance for any unintentional omissions. We would be pleased to insert the appropriate acknowledgment in any subsequent edition of this publication.

All other images © Dorling Kindersley For further information see: **www.dkimages.com**